Quantum Computing Fundamentals

Quantum Computing Fundamentals

Dr. Chuck Easttom

✦Addison-Wesley

Boston • Columbus • New York • San Francisco • Amsterdam • Cape Town
Dubai • London • Madrid • Milan • Munich • Paris • Montreal • Toronto • Delhi • Mexico City
São Paulo • Sydney • Hong Kong • Seoul • Singapore • Taipei • Tokyo

Library of Congress Control Number: 2021903471

ISBN-13: 978-0-13-679381-6
ISBN-10: 0-13-679381-9

1 2021

Editor-in-Chief
Mark Taub

Director, ITP Product Manager
Brett Bartow

Executive Editor
James Manly

Development Editor
Christopher A. Cleveland

Managing Editor
Sandra Schroeder

Project Editor
Mandie Frank

Copy Editor
Bart Reed

Indexer
Cheryl Ann Lenser

Proofreader
Donna Mulder

Technical Reviewers
Izzat Alsmadi,
Renita Murimi

Editorial Assistant
Cindy Teeters

Designer
Chuti Prasertsith

Compositor
codeMantra

Credits

Cover   ZinetroN/Shutterstock

Figure Number	Credit Attribution
Figure 12-1A	Screenshot © Microsoft Corporation
Figure 16-1	Screenshot of Microsoft QDK for Visual Studio Code © Microsoft 2021
Figure 16-2	Screenshot of New Q# Program in Visual Studio Code © Microsoft 2021
Figure 16-3	Screenshot of Save Program in Visual Studio Code © Microsoft 2021
Figure 16-4	Screenshot of QDK Samples © Microsoft 2021
Figure 16-5	Screenshot of Q# Random Number Generator © Microsoft 2021
Figure 16-6	Screenshot of Q# Open Statements © Microsoft 2021
Figure 16-7	Screenshot of Operation QuantumPseudoRandomNumberGenerator © Microsoft 2021
Figure 16-8	Screenshot of Operation RandomNumberInRange © Microsoft 2021
Figure 16-9	Screenshot of Operation SampleRandomNumber © Microsoft 2021
Figure 16-10	Screenshot of Open Statements in Grover's Algorithm Code © Microsoft 2021
Figure 16-11	Screenshot of ReflectMarked © Microsoft 2021
Figure 16-12	Screenshot of ReflectUniform © Microsoft 2021
Figure 16-13	Screenshot of Additional Functions for Grover's algorithm © Microsoft 2021
Figure 16-14	Screenshot of Entry Point for Grover's Algorithm © Microsoft 2021
Figure 16-15	Screenshot of NumberofIterations Function © Microsoft 2021
Figure 16-16	Screenshot of Beginning of Deutsch-Jozsa © Microsoft 2021
Figure 16-17	Screenshot of Deutsch-Jozsa Entry Point © Microsoft 2021
Figure 16-18	Screenshot of IsConstant Function © Microsoft 2021
Figure 16-19	Screenshot of Remaining Functions for Deutsch-Jozsa © Microsoft 2021
Figure 16-20	Screenshot of Entanglement © Microsoft 2021
Figure 17-1	Screenshot of Quantum Inspire Editor © 2021 Quantum Inspire
Figure 17-2	Screenshot of Two Qubits © 2021 Quantum Inspire
Figure 17-3	Screenshot of CNOT Gate © 2021 Quantum Inspire
Figure 17-4	Screenshot of Hadamard Gate © 2021 Quantum Inspire
Figure 17-5	Screenshot of Multiple Gates © 2021 Quantum Inspire
Figure 17-6	Screenshot of Start a New Project © 2021 Quantum Inspire
Figure 17-7	Screenshot of New Project Editor © 2021 Quantum Inspire
Figure 17-8	Screenshot of Error Correction © 2021 Quantum Inspire
Figure 17-9	Screenshot of Grover's Algorithm © 2021 Quantum Inspire
Figure 17-10	Screenshot of Grover's Algorithm Results © 2021 Quantum Inspire
Figure 17-11	Screenshot of Deutsch-Jozsa Algorithm © 2021 Quantum Inspire
Unnumbered Figure 17-1	Screenshot of CNOT Gate Symbol © 2021 Quantum Inspire

Dedication

As always, I dedicate my work to my wonderful wife Teresa. A quote from my favorite movie is how I usually thank her: "What truly is logic? Who decides reason? My quest has taken me to the physical, the metaphysical, the delusional, and back. I have made the most important discovery of my career—the most important discovery of my life. It is only in the mysterious equations of love that any logic or reasons can be found. I am only here tonight because of you. You are the only reason I am. You are all my reasons."

Table of Contents

Chapter 10: Quantum Algorithms   194

Part III   Quantum Computing and Cryptography

Chapter 11: Current Asymmetric Algorithms   212

Part IV   Quantum Programming

Chapter 16: Working with Q#   292

Chapter 17: Working with QASM   314

Preface

Writing a book is always a challenging project. But with a topic like quantum computing, it is much more so. If you cover too much, the reader will be overwhelmed and will not gain much from the book. If you cover too little, you will gloss over critical details. With quantum computing, particularly a book written for the novice, it is important to provide enough information without overwhelming. It is my sincere hope that I have accomplished this.

Clearly some readers will have a more robust mathematical background than others. Some of you will probably have some experience in quantum computing; however, for those of you lacking some element in your background, don't be concerned. The book is designed to give you enough information to proceed forward. Now this means that every single chapter could be much larger and go much deeper. In fact, I cannot really think of a single chapter that could not be a separate book!

When you are reading a section that is a new concept to you, particularly one you struggle with, don't be concerned. This is common with difficult topics. And if you are not familiar with linear algebra, Chapter 1, "Introduction to Essential Linear Algebra," will start right off with new concepts for you— concepts that some find challenging. I often tell students to not be too hard on themselves. When you are struggling with a concept and you see someone else (perhaps the professor, or in this case the author) seem to have an easy mastery of the topic, it is easy to get discouraged. You might think you are not suited for this field. If you were, would you not understand it as readily as others? The secret that no one tells you is that all of those "others," the ones who are now experts, struggled in the beginning, too. Your struggle is entirely natural. Don't be concerned. You might have to read some sections more than once. You might even finish the book with a solid general understanding, but with some "fuzziness" on specific details. That is not something to be concerned about. This is a difficult topic.

For those readers with a robust mathematical and/or physics background, you are likely to find some point where you feel I covered something too deeply, or not deeply enough. And you might be correct. It is quite difficult when writing a book on a topic such as this, for a novice audience, to find the proper level at which to cover a given topic. I trust you won't be too harsh in your judgment should you disagree with the level at which I cover a topic.

Most importantly, this book should be the beginning of an exciting journey for you. This is the cutting edge of computer science. Whether you have a strong background and easily master the topics in this book (and perhaps knew some already) or you struggle with every page, the end result is the same. You will be open to a bold, new world. You will see the essentials of quantum mechanics, understand the quantum computing revolution, and perhaps even be introduced to some new mathematics. So please don't get too bogged down in the struggle to master concepts. Remember to relish the journey!

Register your copy of *Quantum Computing Fundamentals* on the InformIT site for convenient access to updates and/or corrections as they become available. To start the registration process, go to informit. com/register and log in or create an account. Enter the product ISBN (9780136793816) and click Submit. Look on the Registered Products tab for an Access Bonus Content link next to this product, and follow that link to access any available bonus materials. If you would like to be notified of exclusive offers on new editions and updates, please check the box to receive email from us.

Acknowledgments

There are so many people who made this book possible. Let me start with Professor Izzat Alsmadi (Texas A&M–San Antonio) and Professor Renita Murimi (University of Dallas) who were gracious enough to provide technical review of each and every chapter. Chris Cleveland was the lead editor, and I must confess, I am not the easiest person to edit. His patience and careful eye for detail were essential to this book. I also want to thank Bart Reed for his work in copy editing. All the people working on this book have done an extremely good job helping me create a book that can be clear and accurate for the reader to learn this challenging topic.

About the Author

Dr. Chuck Easttom is the author of 31 books, including several on computer security, forensics, and cryptography. His books are used at more than 60 universities. He has also authored scientific papers (more than 70 so far) on digital forensics, cyber warfare, cryptography, and applied mathematics. He is an inventor with 22 computer science patents. He holds a Doctor of Science in cyber security (dissertation topic: a study of lattice-based cryptographic algorithms for post-quantum computing). He also has a Ph.D. in Technology, focusing on nanotechnology (dissertation title: "The Effects of Complexity on Carbon Nanotube Failures") and a Ph.D. in Computer Science (dissertation title: "On the Application of Graph Theory to Digital Forensics"). He also has three master's degrees (one in applied computer science, one in education, and one in systems engineering). He is a senior member of the IEEE and a senior member of the ACM (Association of Computing Machinery) as well as a member of IACR (International Association of Cryptological Research) and INCOSE (International Council on Systems Engineering). He is also a distinguished speaker of the ACM and a distinguished visitor of the IEEE Computer Society. He currently is an adjunct lecturer for Georgetown University.

Chapter 1

Introduction to Essential Linear Algebra

Chapter Objectives

After reading this chapter and completing the review questions you will be able to do the following:

- Understand basic algebraic concepts
- Calculate dot products and vector norms
- Be able to use vectors and vector spaces
- Be able to work with essential linear algebra
- Perform basic mathematical operations on matrices and vectors

One cannot really have even a fundamental understanding of quantum physics and quantum computing without at least a working knowledge of linear algebra. Clearly, a single chapter of a book cannot make you a master of any topic, including linear algebra. That is not the goal of this book or this chapter. Rather, the purpose of this chapter is to provide you with a working knowledge of linear algebra sufficient to facilitate understanding quantum computing. With that goal in mind, this chapter will endeavor to fully explain concepts, without assuming any prior knowledge at all. That is a departure from many books on mathematics, which always seem to assume some level of prior knowledge. Furthermore, this chapter will not explore mathematical proofs. These are, of course, quite important to mathematicians, but you can certainly proceed with your exploration of quantum computing without the proofs. It also happens that such proofs tend to be daunting for the mathematical novice.

Linear algebra is so important to quantum computing and quantum physics because this is how quantum states are represented. Quantum states of a particle such as a photon are represented by vectors. Quantum logic gates are represented by matrices. Both vectors and matrices will be explored in this chapter. This is not to say that no other math is required. Certainly, fields such as calculus and number theory are related to quantum physics and quantum computing. However, linear algebra is the most critical mathematical skill for you to have.

It should also be noted that if you have a background in linear algebra, this chapter will be a review—and frankly, it might seem a bit pedantic at times. The purpose is to aid the reader with no prior knowledge in gaining an adequate baseline to proceed through this book. If instead you are that reader with no prior knowledge of linear algebra, it is quite important that you fully grasp the topics in this chapter before you proceed. You may wish to read portions of the chapter more than once, and there are exercises at the end of the chapter you should probably do. Particularly if you are new to linear algebra, it is highly recommended that you do those exercises.

First, let us define what a linear equation is. A linear equation is just an equation with all factors having exponents of 1, which is usually represented as no exponent at all. So, you will not see any x^2 or y^3 in this chapter. This might seem like an inauspicious beginning for a topic that seems so promising. I assure you that linear algebra is critical for many topics. In addition to quantum computing, it is also important to machine learning. In this chapter you will gain a working knowledge of the basics of linear algebra. Our focus in this chapter and in this book will be the application of linear algebra to quantum computing, but the skills you gain (or review) in this chapter can be applied to other areas.

1.1 What Is Linear Algebra?

It seems like a rather elementary question, but it is a good place to start our examination of linear algebra. Again, this chapter does not assume any prior knowledge on the part of the reader. While linear algebra has applications in many fields, including quantum physics, it began as a way to solve systems of linear equations (thus the name). Linear equations are those for which all elements are of the first power. Thus, the following three equations are linear equations:

$a + b = 20$

$2x + 4 = 54$

$2x + 3y - z = 21$

However, the following are not linear equations:

$2x^2 + 3 = 10$

$4y^2 + 2x + 3 = 8$

The first three equations have all elements to the first power (often with a number such as x^1, the 1 is simply assumed and not written). However, in the second set of equations, at least one element is raised to some higher power. Thus, they are not linear.

One of the earliest books on the topic of linear algebra was *Theory of Extension*, written in 1844 by Hermann Grassman. The book included other topics, but also had some fundamental concepts of linear algebra. In 1856, Arthur Cayley introduced matrix multiplication, which we will explore later in this chapter. In 1888, Giuseppe Peano gave a precise definition of a vector space, which is another topic that will be prominent in this chapter and throughout this book. We will explore vectors and vector spaces later in this chapter. As you can see, the modern subject of linear algebra evolved over time.

Basically, matrices are the focus. If you consider this for just a moment, a matrix can be thought of as a special type of number. Now this might sound a bit odd, but it might help to start with some basic algebra. After all, linear algebra is a type of algebra.

1.2   Some Basic Algebra

It is quite likely that at least some of this section will be a review for many readers. If you find most or all is a review for you, then that is excellent! However, if any of this is new to you, do not be concerned. This book does not assume previous mathematical sophistication, and all that you need will be explained to you.

It is a certainty that you have encountered at least basic algebra in school as a youth; however, a brief perusal of any university math department will show a number of different courses with algebra in the name. Obviously, linear algebra is one. There are also courses in abstract algebra, algebraic graph theory, and several others. This might make you question if the understanding you gained as a youth might be inadequate, and you would be correct.

There are actually quite a few definitions provided for algebra, and most of them are correct. One simple definition is that algebra is the study of manipulating mathematical symbols according to a set of rules. That is correct, but a bit limited. A definition from the *Encyclopedia Britannica* is "Algebra, branch of mathematics in which arithmetical operations and formal manipulations are applied to abstract symbols rather than specific numbers."[1] MathWorks states, "Algebra encompasses relationships, the use of symbols, modeling, and the study of mathematical change."[2]

One of my favorite books for the person with a weak background in math who would like to learn more, *Mathematics for the Nonmathematician* by Morris Kline, says this: "Reasoning about numbers—if one is to go beyond the simplest procedures of arithmetic—requires the mastery of two facilities, vocabulary and technique, or one might say, vocabulary and grammar. In addition, the entire language of mathematics is characterized by the extensive use of symbolism. In fact, it is the use of symbols and of reasoning in terms of symbols which is generally regarded as marking the transition from arithmetic to algebra, though there is no sharp dividing line."

Let us attempt to bring these seemingly diverse definitions into a coherent working definition you can use in this chapter. Algebra is a study of symbols and the rules for how they relate. Those symbols are

---

1. https://www.britannica.com/science/algebra
2. https://www.mathworksheetscenter.com/mathtips/whatisalgebra.html

sometimes actual numbers (integers, real numbers, etc.) and sometimes abstract symbols that represent a broad concept. Consider this simple equation:

$$a^2 = a * a$$

This use of abstract symbols allows us to contemplate the concept of what it means to square a number, without troubling ourselves with any actual numbers. While this is a terribly simple equation, it illustrates the usefulness of studying concepts apart from concrete applications. That is one use of algebra. Of course, it can be used for concrete problems and frequently is.

You can derive a number system based on different properties. Elementary algebra taught to youth is only one possible algebra. Table 1.1 outlines some basic properties that might or might not exist in a given number system.

TABLE 1.1   Basic Properties of a Number System

Axiom	Signification
Associativity of addition	$u + (v + w) = (u + v) + w$
Commutativity of addition	$u + v = v + u$
Associativity of multiplication	$u (v * w) = (u * v) w$
Commutativity of multiplication	$u * w = w * u$
Distributivity of scalar multiplication with respect to vector addition	$a(u + v) = au + av$
Distributivity of scalar multiplication with respect to field addition	$(a + b)v = av + bv$

While Table 1.1 summarizes some basic properties, a bit more explanation might be in order. What we are saying with the associativity property of addition is that it really does not matter how you group the numbers, the sum or the product will be the same. Commutativity is saying that changing the order does not change the sum or product. An interesting point is that when dealing with matrices, this does not hold. We will explore that later in this chapter. Distributivity means that the value outside the parentheses is distributed throughout the parentheses.

You are undoubtably accustomed to various types of numbers, such as integers, rational numbers, real numbers, etc. These are all infinite; however, these are not the only possible groupings of numbers. Your understanding of algebra will be enhanced by examining some elementary concepts from abstract algebra.

Before we continue forward, we should ensure that you are indeed comfortable with integers, rational numbers, etc. A good starting point is with the natural numbers. These are so called because they come naturally. That is to say that this is how children first learn to think of numbers. These are often also called counting numbers. Various sources count only the positive integers (1, 2, 3, 4, ...) without including zero. Other sources include zero. In either case, these are the numbers that correspond to counting. If you count how many pages are in this book, you can use natural numbers to accomplish this task.

The next step is the integers. While negative numbers may seem perfectly normal to you, they were unheard of in ancient times. Negative numbers first appeared in a book from the Han Dynasty in China.

Then in India, negative numbers first appeared in the fourth century C.E. and were routinely used to represent debts in financial matters by the seventh century C.E. Now we know the integers as all whole numbers, positive or negative, along with zero: $-3, -2, -1, 0, 1, 2, 3, \ldots$.

After the integers, the next type of number is the rational numbers. Rational numbers were first noticed as the result of division. A mathematical definition of rational numbers is "any number that can be expressed as the quotient of two integers." However, one will quickly find that division of numbers leads to results that cannot be expressed as the quotient of two integers. The classic example comes from geometry. If you try to express the ratio of a circle's circumference to its radius, the result is an infinite number. It is often approximated as 3.14159, but the decimals continue on with no repeating pattern. Irrational numbers are sometimes repeating, but they need not be. As long as a number is a real number that cannot be expressed as the quotient of two integers, it is classified as an irrational number.

Real numbers are the superset of all rational numbers and all irrational numbers. It is likely that all the numbers you encounter on a regular basis are real numbers, unless of course you work in certain fields of mathematics or physics. For example, $-1, 0, \sqrt{5}, \left(\dfrac{3}{17}\right)^5$, and π are all real numbers.

Imaginary numbers developed as a response to a rather specific problem. The problem begins with the essential rules of multiplications. If you multiple a negative with a negative, you get a positive number. For example, $-2 * -2 = 4$. This becomes a problem if you contemplate the square root of a negative number. Clearly the square root of a positive number is also positive: $\sqrt{4} = 2$, $\sqrt{1} = 1$, etc. But what is the $\sqrt{-1}$? If you answer that it is -1, that won't work, because $-1 * -1$ yields positive 1. This problem led to the development of imaginary numbers. Imaginary numbers are defined as follows: $i^2 = -1$ (or, conversely, $\sqrt{-1} = i$). Thus, the square root of any negative number can be expressed as some integer multiplied by i. A real number combined with an imaginary number is referred to as a complex number. Chapter 2, "Complex Numbers," addresses this concept in more detail.

1.2.1   Groups, Rings, and Fields

The very first algebraic concept we will explore in this chapter is one that might not seem like algebra at all to some readers. Readers with a less rigorous mathematical background might think of algebra as solving linear and quadratic equations as they probably did in secondary school. However, that is only an application of algebra. This section expands on that concept to examine more abstract concepts. In this section we will explore algebraic structures, specifically groups, rings, and fields.

One of the major concepts studied in abstract algebra is that of special sets of numbers and the operations that can be done on those numbers. Mathematics students frequently struggle with these concepts, so I will endeavor to make them as simple as I can without leaving out any important details. The concepts of groups, rings, and fields are just sets of numbers with associated operations.

First, think about a set of numbers. Let us begin with thinking about the set of real numbers. This is an infinite set, as I am sure you are aware. Now ask what operations can you do on numbers that are members of this set wherein the result will still be in the set? You can certainly add two real numbers, and the answer will always be a real number. You can multiply two real numbers, and the answer will always be a real number. What about the inverse of those two operations? You can subtract two real numbers, and the answer will always be a real number. You can divide two real numbers, and the answer will always be a real number. Now at this point, you might think all of this is absurdly obvious; you might even think it odd I would spend a paragraph discussing it. However, there are operations wherein the answer won't always be a real number. Consider the square root operation. The square root of any positive number is a real number, but what about the square root of -1? That is an imaginary number (which we will be exploring in some detail in Chapter 2). The answer to the problem $\sqrt{-1}$ is not a real number. Your answer is outside the set of numbers you were contemplating. This is one example of operations that might lead to numbers that are not in your set.

Think about the set of all integers. That is certainly an infinite set, just like the set of real numbers. You can certainly add any two integers, and the sum will be another integer. You can multiply any two integers, and the product will still be an integer. So far this sounds just like the set of real numbers. Now consider the inverse operations. You can certainly subtract any integer from another integer and the answer is still an integer, but what about division? There are infinitely many scenarios where you cannot divide one integer by another and still have the answer be an integer. Certainly dividing 6 by 2 gives you an integer, as would dividing 10 by 5, and 21 by 3, and infinitely more examples. However, what if I divide 5 by 2? The answer is not an integer; it is instead a rational number. Also, if I divide 20 by 3, the answer is not an integer, and there are infinitely many other examples wherein I cannot divide and still get an integer. Therefore, if I wish to limit myself only to integers, I cannot use division as an operation.

Imagine for a moment that you wish to limit your mathematics to an artificial world in which only integers exists. Set aside, for now, any considerations of why you might do this and just focus on this thought experiment for just a moment. As we have already demonstrated, in this artificial world you have created, the addition operation exists and functions as it always has. So does the inverse of addition, subtraction. The multiplication operation behaves in the same fashion you have always seen it. However, in this imaginary world, the division operation simply does not exist because it has the very real possibility of producing non-integer answers—and such answers do not exist in your imaginary world of "only integers."

Before continuing on with more specific examples from the world of abstract algebra, consider one more hypothetical situation that should help clarify these basic points. What if you have limited yourself to only natural numbers, or counting numbers. Certainly, you can add any two counting numbers and the answer will always be a natural number. You can also multiply any two natural numbers and you can rest assured that the product will indeed be another natural number. But what of the inverse of these operations? You can certainly subtract some natural numbers and have an answer that is still a natural number, but there are infinitely many cases where this is not true. For example, if you attempt to subtract 7 from 5, the answer is a negative number, which is not a natural number. In fact, any time you attempt to subtract a larger natural number from a smaller natural number, the result will not be a natural number. Furthermore, division is just as tricky with natural numbers as it is with integers. There are infinitely many cases where the answer will not be a natural number. So, in this imaginary world of only natural numbers, addition and multiplication work exactly as you would expect them to; however, their inverse operations, subtraction and division, simply do not exist.

Abstract algebra concerns itself with structures just like this. These structures (groups, rings, fields, etc.) have a set of numbers and certain operations that can be performed on those numbers. The only allowed operations in a given structure are those whose result would still be within the prescribed set of numbers. This discussion of algebraic groups will be applied in the discussion of vector spaces in section 1.4 later in the chapter.

Don't be overly concerned with the term *abstract algebra*. There are certainly practical applications of abstract algebra. In fact, some sources prefer to call this *modern algebra*; however, because it dates back a few centuries, even that might be a misnomer. So, let us now examine some of these structures.

1.2.1.1 Groups

A *group* is an algebraic system consisting of a set, an identity element, one operation, and its inverse operation. Let us begin with explaining what an identity element is. An identity element is simply some number within a set that you can use to apply some operation to any other number in the set, and the other number will still be the same. Put more mathematically,

$a * I = a$

where * is any operation that we might specify, not necessarily multiplication. An example would be with respect to the addition operation, zero is the identity element. You can add zero to any member of any given group, and you will still have that same number. With respect to multiplication, 1 is the identity element. Any number multiplied by 1 is still the same number.

There are four properties any group must satisfy:

- **Closure:** Closure is the simplest of these properties. It simply means that an operation performed on a member of the set will result in a member of the set. This is what was discussed a bit earlier in this section. It is important that any operations allowed on a particular set will result in an answer that is also a member of the set.

- **Associativity:** The associative property just means that you can rearrange the elements of a particular set of values in an operation without changing the outcome. For example, $(2 + 2) + 3 = 7$. Even if I change the order and instead write $2 + (2 + 3)$, the answer is still 7. This is an example of the associative property.

- **Identity:** The identity element was already discussed.

- **Invertibility:** The invertibility property simply means that a given operation on a set can be inverted. As we previously discussed, subtraction is the inversion of addition; division is the inversion of multiplication.

Think back to the example of the set of integers. Integers constitute a group. First, there is an identity element, zero. There is also one operation (addition) and its inverse (subtraction). Furthermore, you have closure. Any element of the group (any integer) added to any other element of the group (any other integer) still produces a member of the group (the answer is still an integer).

1.2.1.2 Abelian Group

Now that you have the general idea of a group down, it's time to move on to discuss specific types of groups. The first and easiest to understand is an *abelian group* or commutative group has an additional property. That property being the commutative property: a + b = b + a if the operation is addition. Commutativity means ab = ba if the operation is multiplication.

This commutative requirement simply means that applying the group operation (whatever that operation might be) does not depend on the order of the group elements. In other words, whatever the group operation is, you can apply it to members of the group in any order you wish. To use a trivial example, consider the group of integers with the addition operation. Order does not matter:

$$4 + 2 = 2 + 4$$

Therefore, the set of integers with the operation of addition is an abelian group. As you can see, abelian groups are a subset of groups. They are groups with an additional restriction: the commutative property.

1.2.1.3 Cyclic Group

A *cyclic group* is a group that has elements that are all powers of one of its elements. So, for example, if you start with element x, then the members of a cyclic group would be

$$x^{-2}, x^{-1}, x^0, x^1, x^2, x^3, \ldots$$

Of course, the other requirements for a group, discussed previously, would still apply to a cyclic group. It must be a set of numbers, with an operation, and its inverse. The basic element x is considered to be the generator of the group, because all other members of the group are derived from it. It is also referred to as a *primitive element* of the group. Integers could be considered a cyclic group with 1 being the primitive element (i.e., generator). All integers can be expressed as a power of 1. This might seem like a rather trivial example, but it is also one that is easy to understand.

1.2.1.4 Rings

A *ring* is an algebraic system consisting of a set, an identity element, two operations, and the inverse operation of the first operation. That is the formal definition of a ring, but it might seem a bit awkward to you at first read and therefore warrants a bit more explanation.

A ring is essentially just an abelian group that has a second operation. Previously, you learned that the set of integers with the addition operation form a group, and furthermore they form an abelian group. If you add the multiplication operation, then the set of integers with both the addition and the multiplication operations form a ring.

Note that you only have to have the inverse of the first operation. Therefore, if we consider the set of integers with addition as the first operation and multiplication as the second operation, we do have a ring. As an example, 4 + 5 = 9, which is still an integer (still in the ring). However, so is 4 − 5 = −1. The answer is still an integer, thus still in the ring. With multiplication, we don't need the inverse (division) to always yield an integer, but any two integers multiplied together, such as 4 * 5 = 20, will always yield an integer.

1.2.1.5 Fields

A *field* is an algebraic system consisting of a set, an identity element for each operation, two operations, and their respective inverse operations. You can think of a field as a group that has two operations rather than one, and it has an inverse for both of those operations. It is also the case that every field is a ring, but not every ring will necessarily be a field. For example, the set of integers is a ring, but not a field, if you consider the operations of addition and multiplication. The inverse of multiplication, division, won't always yield an integer.

A classic example of a field is the field of rational numbers. Each number can be written as a ratio (i.e., a fraction), such as x/y (x and y could be any integers you like), and the additive inverse is simply −x/y. The multiplicative inverse is just y/x. Fields are often used in cryptography, and you will see them again in Chapter 11, "Current Asymmetric Algorithms," Chapter 13, "Lattice-Based Cryptography," and Chapter 15, "Other Approaches to Post-Quantum Cryptography."

1.3 Matrix Math

Before delving into matrix math, you need to understand what a matrix is. A *matrix* is a rectangular arrangement of numbers in rows and columns. Rows run horizontally, and columns run vertically. The dimensions of a matrix are stated as $m \times n$, where m is the number of rows and n is the number of columns. Here is an example:

$$\begin{bmatrix} 1 & 2 \\ 2 & 0 \\ 3 & 1 \end{bmatrix}$$

A matrix is just an array that is arranged in columns and rows. Vectors are simply matrices that have one column or one row. The examples in this section focus on 2×2 matrices, but a matrix can be of any number of rows and columns; it need not be a square. A vector can be considered a $1 \times m$ matrix. A vector that is vertical is called a column vector, and one that is horizontal is called a row vector. Matrices are usually labeled based on column and row:

$$\begin{bmatrix} a_{ij} & a_{ij} \\ a_{ij} & a_{ij} \end{bmatrix}$$

The letter i represents the row, and the letter j represents the column. A more concrete example is shown here:

$$\begin{bmatrix} a_{11} & a_{12} \\ a_{21} & a_{22} \end{bmatrix}$$

This notation is commonly used for matrices including row and column vectors.

There are different types of matrices, the most common of which are as follows:

- **Column matrix:** A matrix with only one column.

- **Row matrix:** A matrix with only one row.

- **Square matrix:** A matrix that has the same number of rows and columns.

- **Equal matrices:** Two matrices are considered equal if they have the same number of rows and columns (the same dimensions) and all their corresponding elements are exactly the same.

- **Zero matrix:** Contains all zeros.

Each of these has a role in linear algebra, which you will see as you proceed through the chapter.

1.3.1 Matrix Addition and Multiplication

If two matrices are of the same size, then they can be added to each other by simply adding each element together. You start with the first row and first column in the first matrix and add that to the first row and first column of the second matrix thus in the sum matrix. This is shown here:

$$\begin{bmatrix} a_{11} & a_{12} \\ a_{21} & a_{22} \end{bmatrix} + \begin{bmatrix} b_{11} & b_{12} \\ b_{21} & b_{22} \end{bmatrix} = \begin{bmatrix} A_{11} + b_{11} & a_{12} + b_{12} \\ A_{21} + b_{21} & a_{22} + b_{22} \end{bmatrix}$$

Consider the following more concrete example:

$$\begin{bmatrix} 3 & 2 \\ 1 & 4 \end{bmatrix} + \begin{bmatrix} 2 & 3 \\ 2 & 1 \end{bmatrix} = \begin{bmatrix} 3+2 & 2+3 \\ 1+4 & 2+1 \end{bmatrix} = \begin{bmatrix} 5 & 5 \\ 5 & 3 \end{bmatrix}$$

Multiplication, however, is a bit more complicated. You can multiply two matrices only if the number of columns in the first matrix is equal to the number of rows in the second matrix. First, let us take a look at multiplying a matrix by a scalar (i.e., a single number). The previous section demonstrated a scalar multiplied by a vector; it works much the same way to multiply a scalar by a vector with more columns. You simply multiply the scalar value by each element in the matrix:

$$c \begin{bmatrix} a_{ij} & a_{ij} \\ a_{ij} & a_{ij} \end{bmatrix} = \begin{bmatrix} ca_{ij} & ca_{ij} \\ ca_{ij} & ca_{ij} \end{bmatrix}$$

For a more concrete example, consider the following:

$$2 \begin{bmatrix} 1 & 3 \\ 2 & 2 \end{bmatrix} = \begin{bmatrix} 2*1 & 2*3 \\ 2*2 & 2*2 \end{bmatrix} = \begin{bmatrix} 2 & 6 \\ 4 & 4 \end{bmatrix}$$

Multiplication of two matrices is a bit more complex. The two matrices need not be of the same size. The requirement is that the number of columns in the first matrix is equal to the number of rows in the second matrix. If that is the case, then you multiply each element in the first row of the first matrix by each element in the second matrix's first column. Then you multiply each element of the second row of the first matrix by each element of the second matrix's second column. Let's first examine this using variables rather than actual numbers. The example also uses square matrices to make the situation even simpler.

$$\begin{bmatrix} a & b \\ c & d \end{bmatrix} + \begin{bmatrix} e & f \\ g & h \end{bmatrix}$$

This is multiplied in the following manner:

a * e + b * g $(a_{11} * b_{11} + a_{12} * b_{21})$

a * f + b * h $(a_{11} * b_{12} + a_{12} * b_{22})$

c * e + d * g $(a_{11} * b_{11} + a_{12} * b_{21})$

c * f + d * h $(a_{11} * b_{11} + a_{12} * b_{21})$

Thus, the product will be

$$\begin{matrix} (a*e+b*g) & (a*f+b*h) \\ (c*e+d*g) & (c*f+d*h) \end{matrix}$$

It is worthwhile to memorize this process. Now, consider this implemented with a concrete example:

$$\begin{bmatrix} 1 & 2 \\ 3 & 1 \end{bmatrix} \begin{bmatrix} 2 & 2 \\ 1 & 3 \end{bmatrix}$$

We begin with

1 * 2 + 2 * 1 = 6

1 * 2 + 2 * 3 = 8

3 * 2 + 1 * 1 = 7

3 * 2 + 1 * 3 = 9

The final answer is

$$\begin{bmatrix} 6 & 8 \\ 7 & 9 \end{bmatrix}$$

Now you can see why, as previously stated, you can multiply two matrices only if the number of columns in the first matrix is equal to the number of rows in the second matrix.

It is important to remember that matrix multiplication, unlike traditional multiplication (with scalar values), is not commutative. Recall that the commutative property states the following: $a * b = b * a$. If a and b are scalar values, then this is true; however, if they are matrices, this is not the case. For example, consider the matrix multiplication shown in Equation 1.1.

$$\begin{bmatrix} 2 & 3 \\ 1 & 4 \end{bmatrix} \begin{bmatrix} 1 & 1 \\ 2 & 3 \end{bmatrix} = \begin{bmatrix} 8 & 11 \\ 9 & 13 \end{bmatrix}$$

EQUATION 1.1   Matrix Multiplication

Now if you simply reverse the order, you can see that an entirely different answer is produced, as shown in Equation 1.2.

$$\begin{bmatrix} 1 & 1 \\ 2 & 3 \end{bmatrix} \begin{bmatrix} 2 & 3 \\ 1 & 4 \end{bmatrix} = \begin{bmatrix} 3 & 7 \\ 7 & 15 \end{bmatrix}$$

EQUATION 1.2   Matrix Multiplication Is Not Commutative

This example illustrates the rather important fact that matrix multiplication is not commutative.

1.3.2   Matrix Transposition

Matrix transposition simply reverses the order of rows and columns. While the focus so far has been on 2×2 matrices, the transposition operation is most easily seen with a matrix that has a different number of rows and columns. Consider the matrix shown in Equation 1.3.

$$\begin{bmatrix} 2 & 3 & 2 \\ 1 & 4 & 3 \end{bmatrix}$$

EQUATION 1.3 3×2 Matrix

To transpose it, the rows and columns are switched, creating a 2×3 matrix. The first row is now the first column. You can see this in Equation 1.4.

$$\begin{bmatrix} 2 & 1 \\ 3 & 4 \\ 2 & 3 \end{bmatrix}$$

EQUATION 1.4   Matrix Transposed

If you label the first matrix A, then the transposition of that matrix is labeled A^T. Continuing with the original matrix being labeled A, a few properties of matrices need to be described, as outlined in Table 1.2.

TABLE 1.2   Basic Properties of a Matrix

Property	Explanation
$(A^T)^T = A$	If you transpose the transposition of A, you get back to A.
$(cA)^T = cA^T$	The transposition of a constant, c, multiplied by an array, A, is equal to multiplying the constant c by the transposition of A.
$(AB)^T = B^T A^T$	Multiplying A by B and then transposing the product is equal to B transposed multiplied by A transposed.
$(A + B)^T = A^T + B^T$	Adding the matrix A and the matrix B and then transposing the sum is equal to first transposing A and B and then adding those transpositions.
$A^T = A$	If a square matrix is equal to its transpose, it is called a symmetric matrix.

Table 1.2 is not exhaustive; rather, it is a list of some of the most common properties regarding matrices. These properties are not generally particularly difficult to understand; however, there is an issue with why you would apply them. What do they mean? All too often, introductory linear algebra texts focus so intensely on helping a student to learn how to do linear algebra that the meaning behind operations is lost. Let us take just a moment to explore what transpositions are. A transposition is rotating about the diagonal. Remember that matrices can be viewed graphically. Consider a simple row matrix:

[1 2 4]

Transposing that row matrix creates a column matrix:

$$\begin{bmatrix} 1 \\ 2 \\ 4 \end{bmatrix}$$

Think of a vector as a line in some space. For now, we will limit ourselves to 2D and 3D space. You can then think of a matrix as a transformation on a line or set of lines.

1.3.3 Submatrix

A *submatrix* is any portion of a matrix that remains after deleting any number of rows or columns. Consider the 5×5 matrix shown in Equation 1.5.

$$\begin{bmatrix} 2 & 2 & 4 & 5 & 3 \\ 3 & 8 & 0 & 2 & 1 \\ 2 & 3 & 2 & 2 & 1 \\ 4 & 3 & 1 & 2 & 4 \\ 1 & 2 & 2 & 0 & 3 \end{bmatrix}$$

EQUATION 1.5 5×5 Matrix

Suppose you remove the second column and second row, as shown in Equation 1.6.

$$\begin{bmatrix} 2 & 2 & 4 & 5 & 3 \\ 3 & 0 & 0 & 2 & 1 \\ 2 & 3 & 2 & 2 & 1 \\ 4 & 3 & 1 & 2 & 4 \\ 1 & 2 & 2 & 0 & 3 \end{bmatrix}$$

EQUATION 1.6   Removing Rows and Columns

You are now left with the matrix shown in Equation 1.7.

$$\begin{bmatrix} 2 & 4 & 5 & 3 \\ 2 & 2 & 2 & 1 \\ 4 & 1 & 2 & 4 \\ 1 & 2 & 0 & 3 \end{bmatrix}$$

EQUATION 1.7   Submatrix

The matrix shown in Equation 1.7 is a submatrix of the original matrix.

1.3.4   Identity Matrix

An identity matrix is actually rather simple. Think back to the identity property of groups. An identity matrix accomplishes the same goal: multiplying a matrix by its identity matrix leaves it unchanged. To create an identity matrix, just have all the elements along the main diagonal set to 1 and the rest to 0. Consider the following matrix:

$$\begin{bmatrix} 3 & 2 & 1 \\ 1 & 1 & 2 \\ 3 & 0 & 3 \end{bmatrix}$$

Now consider the identity matrix. It must have the same number of columns and rows, with its main diagonal set to all 1s and the rest of the elements all 0s. The identity matrix looks like this:

$$\begin{bmatrix} 1 & 0 & 0 \\ 0 & 1 & 0 \\ 0 & 0 & 1 \end{bmatrix}$$

If you multiply the original matrix by the identity matrix, the product will be the original matrix. You can see this in Equation 1.8.

$$\begin{bmatrix} 3 & 2 & 1 \\ 1 & 1 & 2 \\ 3 & 0 & 3 \end{bmatrix} \times \begin{bmatrix} 1 & 0 & 0 \\ 0 & 1 & 0 \\ 0 & 0 & 1 \end{bmatrix} = \begin{bmatrix} 3 & 2 & 1 \\ 1 & 1 & 2 \\ 3 & 0 & 3 \end{bmatrix}$$

EQUATION 1.8   Matrix Multiplication

The examples so far have focused not only on square, 2×2 or 3×3, matrices, but also on matrices that only consist of integers. A matrix can consist of rational numbers, real numbers, and even complex numbers; however, because the goal was just to give you an introduction to the concepts of matrix algebra, those nuances have been omitted.

One application of matrix algebra is with linear transformations. A linear transformation is sometimes called a *linear mapping* or even just a *linear function*. It is essentially just some mapping between two vector spaces that has the operations of addition and scalar multiplication.

> **Note**
>
> Wolfram MathWorld defines a vector space as follows: "A vector space V is a set that is closed under finite vector addition and scalar multiplication." Another way of putting this is, a vector space is a collection of objects (in our case, integers) called vectors, which may be added together and multiplied ("scaled") by numbers, called scalars.

1.3.5   Deeper Into the Matrix

After the preceding section, you should be basically comfortable with the fundamental concepts and operations on matrices. If you are not, then please review before continuing into this section. Now we will explore a few more concepts that you will need later in this book.

We will start with something easy—the length of a vector, which is computed using the Pythagorean theorem:

$$\|vector\| = \sqrt{x2 + y2}$$

Consider the vector:

[2, 3, 4]

Its length is

$$\sqrt{2^2 + 3^2 + 4^2} = 5.38$$

This is simple but will be quite important as we move forward. Now we will add just a bit more detail to this concept. The nonnegative length is called the *norm* of the vector. Given a vector v, this is written as $\|v\|$. This will be important later on in this book. One more concept to remember on lengths/norms: if the length is 1, then this is called a *unit vector*.

Next, we will turn our attention to another relatively easy computation—the determinant of a matrix.

The determinant of a matrix A is denoted by |A|. An example of a determinant in a generic form follows:

$$|A| \begin{bmatrix} a & b \\ c & d \end{bmatrix} = ad - bc$$

A more concrete example might help elucidate this concept:

$$|A| \begin{bmatrix} 2 & 3 \\ 1 & 2 \end{bmatrix} = (2)(2) - (3)(1) = 1$$

A determinant is a value that is computed from the individual elements of a square matrix. It provides a single number, also known as a scalar value. Only a square matrix can have a determinant. The calculation for a 2×2 matrix is simple enough; we will explore more complex matrices in just a moment. However, what does this single scalar value mean? There are many things one can do with a determinant, most of which we won't use in this text. It can be useful in solving linear equations (i.e., changing variables in integrals—yes, linear algebra and calculus go hand in hand); however, what is immediately useable for us is that if the determinant is nonzero, then the matrix is invertible. This will be important later in this book when we discuss various quantum algorithms.

What about a 3×3 matrix, such as that shown in Equation 1.9?

$$\begin{bmatrix} a_1 & b_1 & c_1 \\ a_2 & b_2 & c_2 \\ a_3 & b_3 & c_3 \end{bmatrix}$$

EQUATION 1.9 3×3 Matrix

This calculation is substantially more complex. There are a few methods to do this. We will use one called "expansion by minors." This method depends on breaking the 3×3 matrix into 2×2 matrices. The 2×2 matrix formed by b_2, c_2, b_3, c_3, shown in Equation 1.10, is the first.

$$\begin{bmatrix} a_1 & b_1 & c_1 \\ a_2 & \boxed{\begin{matrix} b_2 & c_2 \\ b_3 & c_3 \end{matrix}} \\ a_3 \end{bmatrix}$$

EQUATION 1.10 3×3 Matrix Determinant, Part 1

This one was rather simple, as it fits neatly into a contiguous 2×2 matrix. However, to find the next one, we have a bit different selection, as shown in Equation 1.11.

$$\begin{bmatrix} a_1 & b_1 & c_1 \\ a_2 & b_2 & c_2 \\ a_3 & b_3 & c_3 \end{bmatrix}$$

EQUATION 1.11 3×3 Matrix Determinant, Part 2

The next step is to get the lower-left corner square matrix, as shown in Equation 1.12.

$$\begin{bmatrix} a_1 & b_1 & c_1 \\ a_2 & b_2 & c_2 \\ a_3 & b_3 & c_3 \end{bmatrix}$$

EQUATION 1.12 3×3 Matrix Determinant, Part 3

As with the first one, this one forms a very nice 2×2 matrix. Now what shall we do with these 2×2 matrices? The formula is actually quite simple and is shown in the Equation 1.13. Note that "det" is simply shorthand for determinant.

$$\det \begin{bmatrix} a_1 & b_1 & c_1 \\ a_2 & b_2 & c_2 \\ a_3 & b_3 & c_3 \end{bmatrix} = a_1 \det \begin{bmatrix} b_2 & c_2 \\ b_3 & c_3 \end{bmatrix} - a_2 \det \begin{bmatrix} a_2 & c_2 \\ a_3 & c_3 \end{bmatrix} + a_3 \det \begin{bmatrix} a_2 & b_2 \\ a_3 & b_3 \end{bmatrix}$$

EQUATION 1.13 3×3 Matrix Determinant, Part 4

We take the first column and multiply it by its cofactors, and with a bit of simple addition and subtraction, we arrive at the determinant for a 3×3 matrix. A more concrete example might be useful. Let us calculate the determinant for this matrix:

$$\begin{bmatrix} 3 & 2 & 1 \\ 1 & 1 & 2 \\ 3 & 0 & 3 \end{bmatrix}$$

This leads to

$$3 * \det \begin{bmatrix} 1 & 2 \\ 0 & 3 \end{bmatrix} = 3 * ((1*3) - (2*0)) = 3(3) = 9$$

$$2 * \det \begin{bmatrix} 1 & 2 \\ 3 & 3 \end{bmatrix} = 2 * ((1*3) - (2*3)) = 2(-3) = -6$$

$$1 * \det \begin{bmatrix} 1 & 1 \\ 3 & 0 \end{bmatrix} - 1 * (((1 * 0) - (1 * 3)) = 1(-3) = -3$$

And that leads us to $9 - (-6) + (-3) = 12$.

Yes, that might seem a bit cumbersome, but the calculations are not overly difficult. We will end our exploration of determinants at 3×3 matrices, but, yes, one can take the determinant of larger square matrices. One can calculate determinants for matrices that are 4×4, 5×5, and as large as you like. However, the goal in this chapter is to give you a general foundation in linear algebra, not to explore every nuance of linear algebra.

As you move forward in this book, a great deal of the focus will be on vectors. A *vector* is simply a matrix that is either a single column or a single row. This brings us to some interesting properties of vectors. Like the determinant for square matrices, these properties give us information. Let's begin with the dot product. The dot product of two vectors is simply the two vectors multiplied. Consider vectors X and Y. Equation 1.14 shows what the dot product would be.

$$\sum_{i=1}^{n} X_i Y_i$$

EQUATION 1.14   Dot Product

Examining a concrete example to see how this works should be helpful. Consider two column vectors:

$$\begin{bmatrix} 1 \\ 2 \\ 1 \end{bmatrix} \begin{bmatrix} 3 \\ 2 \\ 1 \end{bmatrix}$$

The dot product is found as follows: $(1 * 3) + (2 * 2) + (1 * 1) = 8$.

That is certainly an easy calculation to perform, but what does it mean? Put more frankly, why should you care what the dot product is? Recall that vectors can also be described graphically. You can use the dot product, along with the length of the vectors, to find the angle between the two vectors. We already know the dot product is 8. Recall that length:

$$\|\text{vector}\| = \sqrt{x2 + y2}$$

Thus, the length of vector X is $\sqrt{1^2 + 2^2 + 1^2} = 2.45$.

The length of vector Y is $\sqrt{3^2 + 2^2 + 1^2} = 3.74$.

Now we can easily calculate the angle. It turns out that the $\cos \theta$ = dot product / length of X * length of Y, or the following:

$$\cos \theta = \frac{8}{(2.45)(3.74)} = 8.7307$$

Finding the angle from the cosine is straightforward; you probably did this in secondary school trigonometry. However, even with just the dot product, we have some information. If the dot product is 0, then the vectors are perpendicular. This is because the cos θ of a 90° angle is 0. The two vectors are referred to as *orthogonal*.

Recall that the length of a vector is also called the vector's *norm*. If that length/norm is 1, it is the *unit vector*. This leads us to another term we will see frequently later in this book. If two vectors are both orthogonal (i.e., perpendicular to each other) and have unit length (length 1), the vectors are said to be *orthonormal*.

Essentially, the dot product is used to produce a single number, a scalar, from two vertices or two matrices. This is contrasted with the tensor product. In math, a *tensor* is an object with multiple indices, such as a vertex or array. The tensor product of two vector spaces V and W, $V \otimes W$, is also a vector space.

Another special type of matrix is a unimodular matrix. Unimodular matrices are also used in some lattice-based algorithms. A unimodular matrix is a square matrix of integers with a determinant of +1 or −1. Recall that a determinant is a value computed from the elements of a square matrix. The determinant of a matrix A is denoted by |A|.

Cyclic lattices are also used in some cryptographic applications. A cyclic lattice is a lattice that is closed under a rotational shift operator. A more rigorous definition follows:

A Lattice $L \subseteq Z^n$ is cyclic if $\forall x \in L$: rot(x) $\in$ L.

The symbols here might be a bit confusing to some readers. The symbol $\subseteq$ means "a subset of." So, we are saying this lattice is a subset of the integers (Z). It is cyclic if there exists ($\forall$) some x in the lattice that when rotated is still in the lattice.

Eigenvalues are a special set of scalars associated with a linear system of equations (i.e., a matrix equation), sometimes also known as characteristic roots, characteristic values, proper values, or latent roots. To clarify, consider a column vector we will call v. Then also consider an $n \times n$ matrix we will call A. Then consider some scalar, λ. If it is true that

$Av = \lambda v$

then we say that v is an eigenvector of the matrix A and that λ is an eigenvalue of the matrix A.

Let us look a bit closer at this. The prefix *eigen* is actually a German word that can be translated as "specific," "proper," "particular," etc. Put in its most basic form, an eigenvector of some linear transformation, T, is a vector that when T is applied to it does not change direction; it only changes scale. It changes scale by the scalar value λ, the eigenvalue. Now we can revisit the former equation just a bit and expand our knowledge of linear algebra:

$T(v) = \lambda v$

This appears precisely like the former equation, but with one small difference: the matrix A is now replaced with the transformation T. Not only does this tell us about eigenvectors and eigenvalues, it tells us a bit more about matrices. A matrix, when applied to a vector, transforms that vector. The matrix itself is an operation on the vector! Later in this book, you will see these transformations used quite frequently, particularly in reference to logic gates for quantum computers. So make certain you are quite familiar with them before proceeding.

Let us add something to this. How do you find the eigenvalues and eigenvectors for a given matrix? Surely it is not just a matter of trial and error with random numbers. Fortunately, there is a very straightforward method—one that is actually quite easy, at least for 2×2 matrices. Consider the following matrix:

$$\begin{bmatrix} 5 & 2 \\ 9 & 2 \end{bmatrix}$$

How do we find its eigenvalues?

Well, the Cayley-Hamilton Theorem provides insight on this issue. The theorem essentially states that a linear operator A is a zero of its characteristic polynomial. For our purposes, it means that

$$\det|A - \lambda I| = 0$$

We know what a determinant is, and we also know that I is the identity matrix. The λ is the eigenvalue we are trying to find, and the A is the matrix we are examining. Remember that in linear algebra you can apply a matrix to another matrix or vector, so a matrix is, at least potentially, an operator. So we can fill in this equation:

$$\det \left| \begin{bmatrix} 5 & 2 \\ 9 & 2 \end{bmatrix} - \lambda \begin{bmatrix} 1 & 0 \\ 0 & 1 \end{bmatrix} \right| = 0$$

Now, we just have to do a bit of algebra, beginning with multiplying λ by our identity matrix, which will give us

$$\det \left| \begin{bmatrix} 5 & 2 \\ 9 & 9 \end{bmatrix} - \begin{bmatrix} \lambda & 0 \\ 0 & \lambda \end{bmatrix} \right| = 0$$

which in turn leads to

$$\det \left| \begin{bmatrix} 5-\lambda & 2 \\ 9 & 2-\lambda \end{bmatrix} \right| = 0$$

$$= (5 - \lambda)(5 - \lambda) - 18$$

$$= 10 - 7\lambda + \lambda^2 - 18 = 0$$

$$\lambda^2 - 7\lambda - 8 = 0$$

This can be factored (note that if the result here cannot be factored, things do get a bit more difficult, but that is beyond our scope here):

$$(\lambda - 8)(\lambda + 1) = 0$$

This means we have two eigenvalues:

$$\lambda_1 = 8$$

$$\lambda_2 = -1$$

For a 2 × 2 matrix, you will always get two eigenvalues. In fact, for any n × n matrix, you will get n eigenvalues, but they may not be unique.

Now that you have the eigenvalues, how do you calculate the eigenvectors?

We know the following:

$$A = \begin{bmatrix} 5 & 2 \\ 9 & 2 \end{bmatrix}$$

$$\lambda_1 = 8$$

$$\lambda_2 = -1$$

We are seeking unknown vectors, so let us label the vector $\begin{bmatrix} X \\ Y \end{bmatrix}$.

Now recall the equation that gives us eigenvectors and eigenvalues:

$$Av = \lambda v$$

Let us take one of our eigenvalues and plug it in:

$$\begin{bmatrix} 5 & 2 \\ 9 & 2 \end{bmatrix} \begin{bmatrix} X \\ Y \end{bmatrix} = 8 \begin{bmatrix} X \\ Y \end{bmatrix}$$

$$\begin{bmatrix} 5x & + & 2y \\ 9x & + & 2y \end{bmatrix} = \begin{bmatrix} 8X \\ 8Y \end{bmatrix}$$

This gives us two equations:

$$5x + 2y = 8x$$

$$9x + 2y = 8y$$

Now we take the first equation and do a bit of algebra to isolate the y value. Subtract the 5x from each side to get

$$2y = 3x$$

Then divide both sides by 2 to get

$$y = 3/2 \ x$$

It should be easy to see that to solve this with integers (which is what we want), then $x = 2$ and $y = 3$ solves it. Thus, our first eigenvector is

$$\begin{bmatrix} 2 \\ 3 \end{bmatrix} \text{ with } \lambda_1 = 8$$

You can work out the other eigenvector for the second eigenvalue on your own using this method.

1.4 Vectors and Vector Spaces

Vectors are an essential part of linear algebra. We normally represent data in the form of vectors. In linear algebra, these vectors are treated like numbers. They can be added and multiplied. A vector will look like what is shown here:

$$\begin{bmatrix} 1 \\ 3 \\ 2 \end{bmatrix}$$

This vector has only integers; however, a vector can have rational numbers, real numbers, and even complex numbers (which will be discussed later in this chapter). Vectors can also be horizontal, as shown here:

$$[1\ 3\ 2]$$

Often you will see variables in place of vector numbers, such as

$$\begin{bmatrix} a \\ b \\ c \end{bmatrix}$$

The main point that you saw in the previous section is that one can do math with these vectors as if they were numbers. You can multiple two vectors together; you can also multiply a vector by a scalar. Scalars are individual numbers, and their name derives from the fact that they change the scale of the vector. Consider the scalar 3 multiplied by the first vector shown in this section:

$$3 \begin{bmatrix} 1 \\ 3 \\ 2 \end{bmatrix} = \begin{bmatrix} 3 \\ 9 \\ 6 \end{bmatrix}$$

You simply multiply the scalar by each of the elements in the vector. We will be exploring this and other mathematical permutations in more detail in the next section, but let us address the issue of why it is called a scalar now. We are viewing the data as a vector; another way to view it would be as a graph. Consider the previous vector [1,3,2] on a graph, as shown in Figure 1.1.

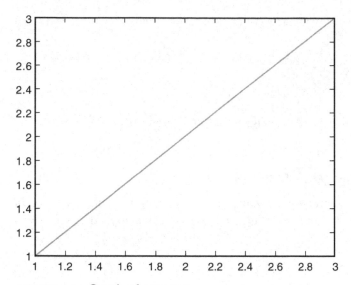

FIGURE 1.1   Graph of a vector

Now what happens when we perform the scalar operation of 3 multiplied by that vector? We literally change the scale of the vector, as shown in Figure 1.2.

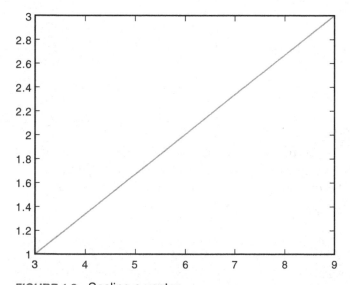

FIGURE 1.2   Scaling a vector

Figures 1.1 and 1.2 might appear identical, but look closer. In Figure 1.2 the x value goes to 9, whereas in Figure 1.1 the x value only goes to 3. We have *scaled* the vector. The term *scalar* is used because it literally changes the scale of the vector. Formally, a *vector space* is a set of vectors that is closed under addition and multiplication by real numbers. Think back to the earlier discussion of abstract algebra with groups, rings, and fields. A vector space is a group. In fact, it is an abelian group. You can do addition of vectors, and the inverse. You also have a second operation scalar, multiplication, without the inverse. Note that the first operation (addition) is commutative, whereas the second operation (multiplication) is not.

So, what are basis vectors? If you have a set of elements E (i.e., vectors) in some vector space V, the set of vectors E is considered a basis if every vector in the vector space V can be written as a linear combination of the elements of E. Put another way, you could begin with the set E, the basis, and through a linear combinations of the vectors in E, create all the vectors in the vector space V. As the astute reader will have surmised, a vector space can have more than one basis set of vectors.

What is linear dependence and independence? You will see these terms a great deal later in this book as we discuss quantum computing. In the theory of vector spaces, a set of vectors is said to be linearly dependent if one of the vectors in the set can be defined as a linear combination of the others; if no vector in the set can be written in this way, then the vectors are said to be linearly independent.

A *subspace* is a subset of a vector space that is a vector space itself; for example, the plane z=0 is a subspace of R^3 (it is essentially R^2). We'll be looking at R^n and subspaces of R^n.

1.5   Set Theory

Set theory is an important part of discrete mathematics. A *set* is a collection of objects, which are called the members or elements of that set. If we have a set, we say that some objects belong (or do not belong) to this set, or are (or are not) in the set. We also say that sets consist of their elements.

As with much of mathematics, terminology and notation are critical. So let us begin our study in a similar fashion, building from simple concepts to more complex ones. The simplest way to define an element of a set is that we say x is a member of set A. This can be denoted as

$x \in A$

Sets are often listed in brackets. For example, the set of all odd integers < 10 would be shown as follows:

$A = \{1, 3, 5, 7, 9\}$

Also, a member of that set would be denoted as follows:

$3 \in A$

Negation can be symbolized by a line through a symbol. For example, in

$2 \notin A$

2 is not an element of set A.

If a set is not ending, you can denote that with ellipses. For example, the set of all odd numbers (not just those less than 10) can be denoted as follows:

$A = \{1, 3, 5, 7, 9, 11, \ldots\}$

You can also denote a set using an equation or formula that defines membership in that set.

Sets can be related to each other; the most common relationships are briefly described here:

- **Union:** If you have two sets, A and B, elements that are members of A, B, or both represent the union of A and B, symbolized as A $\cup$ B. This is shown in Figure 1.3, with the shaded area being the area in common between A and B.

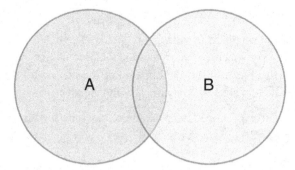

FIGURE 1.3   Union of A and B

- **Intersection:** If you have two sets, A and B, elements that are in both A and B are the intersection of sets A and B, symbolized as A $\cap$ B. If the intersection of set A and B is empty (i.e., the two sets have no elements in common), then the two sets are said to be disjoint, as illustrated in Figure 1.4.

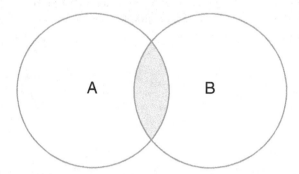

FIGURE 1.4   Intersection of A and B

- **Difference:** If you have two sets, A and B, elements that are in one set but not both are the difference between A and B. This is denoted as A \ B. This is shown in Figure 1.5.

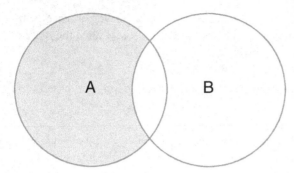

FIGURE 1.5   A \ B

- **Complement:** Set B is the complement of set A if B has no elements that are also in A. This is symbolized as $B = A^c$ and is shown in Figure 1.6.

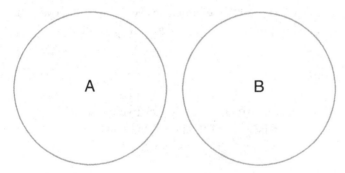

FIGURE 1.6 $B = A^c$

- **Double complement:** The complement of a set's complement is that set. In other words, the complement of A^c is A. That may seem odd at first read, but reflect on the definition of the complement of a set for just a moment. The complement of a set has no elements in that set. Therefore, it stands to reason that to be the complement of the complement of a set, it would have to have all elements within the set.

These are basic set relationships. Now a few facts about sets:

- **Order is irrelevant:** {1, 2, 3} is the same as {3, 2, 1} or {3, 1, 2} or {2, 1, 3}.

- **Subsets:** Set A could be a subset of set B. For example, if set A is the set of all odd numbers < 10, and set B is the set of all odd numbers < 100, then set A is a subset of set B. This is symbolized as $A \subseteq B$.

- **Power set:** As you have seen, sets can have subsets. Consider set A as all integers < 10. Set B is a subset; it is all prime numbers < 10. Set C is a subset of A; it is all odd numbers < 10. Set D is a subset of A; it is all even numbers < 10. We could continue this exercise making arbitrary sub-sets such as E = {4, 7}, F {1, 2, 3}, etc. The set of all subsets for a given set is called the *power set* for that set.

Sets also have properties that govern the interaction between sets. The most important of these properties are as follows:

- **Commutative law:** The intersection of set A with set B is equal to the intersection of set B with set A. The same is true for unions. Put another way, when one is considering the intersections and unions of sets, the order in which the sets are presented is irrelevant. That is symbolized as follows:

  (*a*) $A \cap B = B \cap A$

  (*b*) $A \cup B = B \cup A$

- **Associative law:** Basically, if you have three sets and the relationships between all three are all unions or all intersections, then the order does not matter. This is symbolized as follows:

  (*a*) $(A \cap B) \cap C = A \cap (B \cap C)$

  (*b*) $(A \cup B) \cup C = A \cup (B \cup C)$

- **Distributive law:** The distributive law is a bit different from the associative law, and order does not matter. The union of set A with the intersection of B and C is the same as taking the union of A and B intersected with the union of A and C. This is symbolized as follows:

  (*a*) $A \cup (B \cap C) = (A \cup B) \cap (A \cup C)$

  (*b*) $A \cap (B \cup C) = (A \cap B) \cup (A \cap C)$

- **De Morgan's laws:** These laws govern issues with unions and intersections and the complements thereof. These are more complex than the previously discussed properties. Essentially, the complement of the intersection of set A and set B is the union of the complement of A and the complement of B. The symbolism of De Morgan's laws are shown here:

  (*a*) $(A \cap B)^c = A^c \cup B^c$

  (*b*) $(A \cup B)^c = A^c \cap B^c$

These are the basic elements of set theory. You should be familiar with them before proceeding.

1.6 Summary

In this chapter you have learned the basic principles of linear algebra—just enough to enable you to understand the rest of this book. A few other mathematical details of linear algebra will be introduced as needed, but provided you fully understand this chapter, you can proceed. This chapter covered basic algebra, matrix mathematics, dot products, vector length, orthogonality, vector norms, and vector spaces. While this provides only an elementary introduction to linear algebra, it is important that you fully understand these concepts before proceeding.

Test Your Skills

REVIEW QUESTIONS

1. You have a set of numbers that has two operations, with the inverse of only one of those operations. The set is not necessarily commutative. What is the best description for this set?

   a. Group

   b. Abelian group

   c. Ring

   d. Field

2. Solve this equation:

$$3\begin{bmatrix} 2 \\ 1 \\ 3 \end{bmatrix}$$

   a. $\begin{bmatrix} 6 \\ 3 \\ 9 \end{bmatrix}$

   b. $\begin{bmatrix} 5 \\ 4 \\ 6 \end{bmatrix}$

   c. 18

   d. 15

3. What is the dot product of these two vectors?

$$\begin{bmatrix} 3 \\ 2 \\ 0 \end{bmatrix} \begin{bmatrix} 1 \\ 3 \\ 2 \end{bmatrix}$$

   a. 11

   b. 10

   c. 28

   d. 0

4. Solve this determinant:

$$|A| \begin{bmatrix} 2 & 1 \\ 1 & 3 \end{bmatrix}$$

   a. 8

   b. 6

   c. 0

   d. 5

5. Solve this determinant:

$$|A| \begin{bmatrix} 1 & 2 & 3 \\ 2 & 1 & 4 \\ 3 & 1 & 2 \end{bmatrix}$$

   a. 11

   b. 12

   c. 15

   d. 10

6. What is the dot product of these two vectors?

$$\begin{bmatrix} 1 \\ 2 \\ 2 \end{bmatrix} \begin{bmatrix} 3 \\ 3 \\ 4 \end{bmatrix}$$

   a. 65

   b. 17

   c. 40

   d. 15

7. What is the length of this vector?

$$\begin{bmatrix} 2 \\ 2 \\ 3 \end{bmatrix}$$

    a. 4.12

    b. 2.64

    c. 3.46

    d. 4.56

8. What is the product of these two matrices?

$$\begin{bmatrix} 2 & 3 \\ 1 & 4 \end{bmatrix}\begin{bmatrix} 3 & 2 \\ 3 & 7 \end{bmatrix}$$

    a. $\begin{bmatrix} 15 & 25 \\ 15 & 10 \end{bmatrix}$

    b. $\begin{bmatrix} 15 & 10 \\ 15 & 30 \end{bmatrix}$

    c. $\begin{bmatrix} 10 & 15 \\ 15 & 30 \end{bmatrix}$

    d. $\begin{bmatrix} 15 & 25 \\ 15 & 30 \end{bmatrix}$

9. Are these two vectors orthogonal?

$$\begin{bmatrix} 1 \\ 0 \end{bmatrix}\begin{bmatrix} 0 \\ 1 \end{bmatrix}$$

    a. Yes

    b. No

10. Write the identity matrix for this matrix:

$$\begin{bmatrix} 3 & 2 & 1 \\ 3 & 5 & 6 \\ 3 & 4 & 3 \end{bmatrix}$$

Chapter | **2**

Complex Numbers

Chapter Objectives

After reading this chapter and completing the quiz, you will be able to do the following:

- Understand complex numbers
- Calculate complex conjugates
- Represent complex numbers graphically
- Work with vector representations of complex numbers
- Understand Pauli matrices

Just as linear algebra is central to understanding quantum physics and quantum computing, so are complex numbers. There are some sources that attempt to explain quantum physics and quantum computing without complex numbers. To some extent they succeed, at least in conveying a generalized understanding of quantum phenomena; however, quantum physicists and those working with quantum computing use complex numbers. If you are to proceed past a general layman's understanding, then you must have an understanding of complex numbers.

2.1   What Are Complex Numbers?

It might seem to some that mathematicians simply invent number systems to amuse themselves. Fortunately, this is not generally the case. Number systems are developed for particular reasons. It is useful to examine the history of numbers to bring us to how complex numbers develop. We begin, naturally enough, with what are called the *counting numbers*. These are positive integers (1, 2, 3, ...). Even small children naturally come to grasp these numbers. Various archeological discoveries have shown numbers used in ancient times. The earliest use of base 10 (which you are most familiar with) dates to 3100 B.C.E. in ancient Egypt. In parts of Mesopotamia, a base 60 system was used as early as 3400 B.C.E.

However, the use of zero did not occur for some time. This might seem rather odd to our modern way of thinking. It is most likely that zero seems quite ordinary and natural to you; however, the first documented use of zero was by the Indian mathematician Brahmagupta in 628 C.E. He used zero in various operations, treating it as a number. Given he was using it widely at this time, it is likely it had been used for some time; however, this was the first documented case of it being used as a number. It is important to note there were earlier uses of zero, but only as a placeholder. In ancient Egypt there was the ability to note a zero balance, but it was not used in any calculations.

This brings us to negative numbers. These seem perfectly natural to us today. For example, $3 - 5 = -2$ is a trivial equation. However, like zero, negative numbers were not always recognized. There were some uses of negative numbers as an abstract concept for some time. The famous Greek mathematician Diophantus referred to a particular equation that had a negative solution as having an "absurd result." Around 600 C.E. in India, negative numbers were used in relation to debts. By the twelfth century C.E., negative roots were given as solutions for quadratic equations. Now we view negative numbers as completely natural.

As our understanding of numbers has grown, so has the need for new number systems. Another step in our evolution of understanding numbers was the advent of rational numbers. It might seem odd, but rational numbers or fractions actually date back further than the use of negative numbers. Even Euclid used rational numbers. Rational numbers are, of course, any number that can be represented as a fraction. A sample of rational numbers is shown here:

$$\frac{1}{4} \qquad \frac{3}{7} \qquad \frac{2}{3}$$

These are all rational numbers. Now what about numbers that cannot be represented in this form? There is an interesting story regarding irrational numbers that might or might not be true. Supposedly, Hippasus discovered that the square root of 2 cannot be presented as a fraction. Pythagoras believed numbers to be absolute and would not accept irrational numbers. There are various different versions of the story, but all end in Hippasus being thrown into the sea to drown by his fellow Pythagoreans for suggesting irrational numbers. While mathematicians today might still engage in vigorous debate over mathematics, it rarely raises to the level of homicide.

The whole body of irrational numbers and rational numbers includes the previous sets of integers, zero, and negative numbers—and all of this together forms the set we call real numbers. This brings us to the advent of imaginary numbers. I am sure you are aware that a negative number when squared gives a positive product, such that $-2^2 = 4$, $-3^2 = 9$, and $-4^2 = 16$. This leads to a bit of a conundrum if one wants to know the square root of a negative number. The classic example is to inquire as to the square root of -1. We know it is not 1, because $1^2 = 1$. We know it is not -1, because $-1^2 = 1$. This led to the creation of a new set of numbers, termed *imaginary numbers*. The number i is defined as the $\sqrt{-1}$. This is shown in the following equation:

$$i = \sqrt{-1}$$

Imaginary numbers work just as real numbers do. If you see the expression 2i, that denotes $2 * \sqrt{-1}$. It should also be noted that the name imaginary number is unfortunate. It makes it seem as if these are just made up and have no use. As you will see later in this book, they do have uses, particularly in quantum physics. These numbers do indeed exist, and you will see them used later in this book. They are often used in quantum physics and quantum computing.

Complex numbers are simply real and imaginary numbers together in an expression. The following is an example of a complex number:

$$3 + 4i$$

There is the real number 3, combined with the imaginary number 4i, or $4 * \sqrt{-1}$. Let us put this a bit more formally. A complex number is a polynomial with real coefficients and i for which $i^2 + 1 = 0$ is true. You can perform all the usual arithmetic operations with complex numbers that you have performed with real numbers (i.e., rational numbers, irrational numbers, integers, etc.).

While any symbol can be used to denote number groups, certain symbols have become common. Table 2.1 summarizes those symbols.

TABLE 2.1   Symbols Denoting Number Groups

Symbol	Description
N	N denotes the natural numbers. These are also sometimes called the counting numbers. They are 1, 2, 3, etc.
Z	Z denotes the integers. These are whole numbers (–1, 0, 1, 2, etc.). Integers are the natural numbers combined with zero and the negative numbers.
Q	Q denotes the rational numbers (ratios of integers). Rational numbers are any number that can be expressed as a ratio of two integers. Examples are 3/2, 17/4, and 1/5.
P	P denotes the irrational numbers. An example is $\sqrt{2}$.
R	R denotes the real numbers. This includes the rational numbers as well as the irrational numbers.
i	i denotes the imaginary numbers. These are numbers whose square is a negative. An example is $\sqrt{-1} = 1i$.

2.2 Algebra of Complex Numbers

Chapter 1, "Introduction to Essential Linear Algebra," provided some discussion of basic algebra, including the concept of properties, such as the commutative and associative properties of both addition and multiplication. Chapter 1 also discussed topics such as groups, rings, and similar algebraic structures. In this section, we will explore basic algebra with complex numbers.

Let us begin with some basic complex number algebra:

$(a + bi) \pm (c + di) := (a \pm c) + (b \pm d)i$

In this case, the symbol $:=$ means "is defined to be." Thus, when we say $(a + bi) \pm (c + di) := (a \pm c) + (b \pm d)i$, we mean that $(a + bi) \pm (c + di)$ *is defined to be* $(a \pm c) + (b \pm d)i$. Let us look at a few examples:

$(2 + 4i) + (3 + 2i)$

$= (2 + 3) + (4 + 2)i$

$= 5 + 6i$

Here is another example, this time subtracting:

$(1 + 2i) - (3 + 4i)$

$= (1 - 3) - (2i - 4i)$

$= 2 - 2i$

As you can see, basic addition and subtraction with complex numbers is very easy. Multiplying complex numbers is also quite straightforward. We use the same method you probably learned in elementary algebra as a youth: FOIL, or First – Outer – Inner – Last, as illustrated in Figure 2.1.

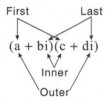

FIGURE 2.1 The FOIL method

Therefore:

$(a + bi)(c + di)$

$= ac + adi + cbi + bdi^2$

It is beneficial to examine a few concrete examples to ensure this concept is thoroughly understood. Let's begin with this:

$(2 + 2i)(3 + 2i)$

$= (2 * 3) + (2 * 2i) + (2i * 3) + (2i * 2i)$

$= 6 + 4i + 6i + 4i^2$

$= 6 + 10i + 4i^2$

$= 6 + 10i + -4$ (remember that $i^2 = -1$)

$= 2 + 10i$

Let's examine one more example before moving on:

(3 + 2i)(2 − 2i)

= (3 * 2) + (3 * −2i) + (2i * 2) + (2i * −2i)

= 6 + −6i + 4i + −4i^2

= 6 − 2i − 4i^2

= 6 − 2i + 4

= 10 − 2i

The next step would naturally seem to be to move on to division. However, before we do that, we must first explore another concept: the complex conjugate. This is something you will use frequently later in this book. Fortunately, it is very simple. The complex conjugate has the same real and imaginary parts, but with an opposite sign for the imaginary portion. Table 2.2 provides several examples to ensure you understand this concept.

TABLE 2.2 Complex Conjugates

Complex Number	Complex Conjugate
2 + 3i	2 − 3i
3 − 4i	3 + 4i
5 + 4i	5 − 4i

If we have a complex number, z, then the complex conjugate is usually denoted by either $\overline{z}$ or z*. So, if you have

z = 3 + 2i

then

$\overline{z}$ = 3 − 2i

Now we can divide complex numbers. The first step is to multiply the numerator and denominator by the complex conjugate of the denominator. In general, this looks like what you see in Equation 2.1.

$$\frac{a+bi}{c+di} \times \frac{c-di}{c-di}$$

EQUATION 2.1 Multiplying by the Complex Conjugate

Now recall that when we multiply, we use the FOIL method, so this becomes what is shown in Equation 2.2.

$$\frac{a+bi}{c+di} \times \frac{c-di}{c-di} = \frac{ac-adi+bci-bdi}{c^2-cdi+cdi-di^2} = \frac{ac-adi+bci-bdi}{c^2-d^2}$$

EQUATION 2.2 Complex Multiplication

Let's look at a concrete example to understand the process. We wish to divide 2 + 3i by 5 + 2i. That gives us what is shown in Equation 2.3.

$$\frac{2+3i}{5+2i} \times \frac{5-2i}{5-2i} = \frac{5(2)+2(-2i)+5(3i)+3i(-2i)}{(5)(5)+5(-2i)+5(2i)+2i(-2i)}$$

EQUATION 2.3 Complex Division

Of course, that can be further simplified, as shown in Equation 2.4.

$$= \frac{10-4i+15i-6i^2}{25-10i+10i-4i^2}$$

EQUATION 2.4 Simplification, Step 1

This is further simplified to what is shown in Equation 2.5.

$$= \frac{10-19i+(-6)}{25-(-4)}$$

(remember $i^2 = -1$)

EQUATION 2.5 Simplification, Step 2

And that finally brings us to what is shown in Equation 2.6.

$$= \frac{4-19i}{29}$$

EQUATION 2.6 The Answer to the Division Example

The first thing you should note is that by multiplying by the complex conjugate, we have removed the imaginary factor from the denominator. There is only one thing left to do, and that is put this into the form a + bi. Thus, we now have

$$\frac{4}{29} - \frac{19}{29}i$$

So, at this point you should be able to add, subtract, multiply, divide, and find the complex conjugate of complex numbers. You have the basic algebraic skills for complex numbers.

2.3 Complex Numbers Graphically

It is often helpful to view complex numbers graphically. The way this is generally done is to use a typical Cartesian coordinate system, as you see in Figure 2.2.

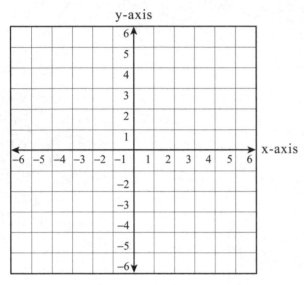

FIGURE 2.2   Cartesian coordinate system

The x-axis is used for real numbers, and the y-axis for imaginary numbers. This is fairly easy to use. A pure real number such as 3 would simply appear on the x-axis as shown in Figure 2.3.

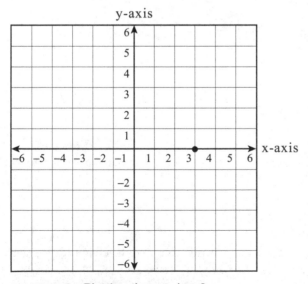

FIGURE 2.3   Plotting the number 3

As you can probably surmise, a pure imaginary number will be on the y-axis. For example, 2i would be plotted as shown in Figure 2.4.

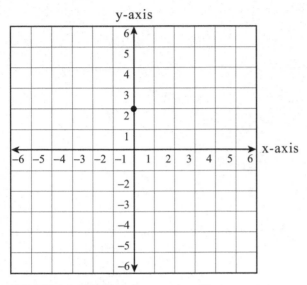

FIGURE 2.4   Plotting the number 2i

For complex numbers, one simply combines the x- and y-coordinates. Thus, something like 3 + 2i would be represented as shown in Figure 2.5.

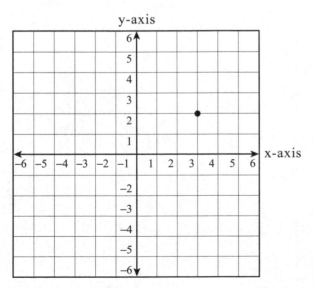

FIGURE 2.5   Plotting the number 3 + 2i

Now we turn to something that should remind you of Chapter 1. Let us determine precisely how far our point 3 + 2i is from the origin (0, 0). Just as when working with vectors, we will use the Pythagorean theorem. Given a complex number z, the length of z from the origin is the absolute value of z, or $|z|$. This is typically $\sqrt{a^2 + b^2}$. In this case it is

$$\sqrt{(3)^2 + (2i)^2}$$

$$3^2 = 9$$

$$i^2 = -1$$

Thus, $2i^2 = -2$

So, $|z| = \sqrt{9 - 4}$

$$|z| = \sqrt{5}$$

$$|z| = 2.2361$$

If you look at the graph, this actually seems intuitively correct. That appears to be about the length of the vector. It must also be noted that $|z|$ is always a nonnegative number. Thus, if the formula leads to a negative answer, then the positive should be used. Consider this example:

4 + 4i

This is shown in a graph in Figure 2.6.

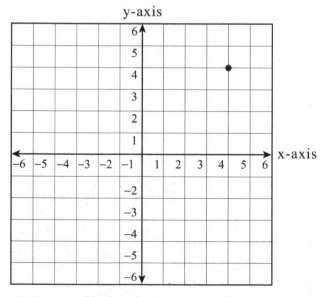

FIGURE 2.6 Plotting the number 4 + 4i

Now, to calculate $|z|$, we would use

$$\sqrt{(4)^2 + (4i)^2}$$
$$4^2 = 16$$
$$4i^2 = -4$$

This leads to

$$\sqrt{8 - 4}$$
$$\sqrt{2}$$

which is 2.

Because $|z|$ is always positive and always a real number, we say that

$$|z| = 2$$

Again, if you look at the graph, this makes intuitive sense. It seems like it would be a little less than 3, and indeed it is.

It should be noted that when we use this plane for describing complex numbers, it is referred to as either the *complex plane* or the *z-plane*. Some sources will refer to this plane as an Argand diagram because this method of representing complex numbers was proposed independently by Caspar Wessel in 1797 then by Jean Pierre Argand in 1806. Wessel's use of this representation was not widely known until much later, which is why the name Argand diagram is used and not Wessel diagram.

Now that we can get the absolute value of z, or to use proper notation, $|z|$, we are ready to discuss plotting the distance between points. Consider a point defined by the complex number $3 + 1i$ and a point defined by the complex number $1 + 4i$, as shown in Figure 2.7.

What is the distance between these two points? In general, the form of these numbers is $z_1 = a_1 + b_1 i$ and $z_2 = a_2 + b_2 i$. In this case, $z_1 = 3 + 1i$ and $z_2 = 1 + 4i$. The distance is merely the absolute value $|(a1 - a2) + (b1 - b2)i|$. This is expressed similarly to what we did previously, as follows:

$$\sqrt{(a_1 - a_2) + (b_1 - b_2)^2}$$

Thus, in our specific example, this would be the following (notice we are not worried about the i itself, just the real coefficient):

$$\sqrt{(3-1)^2 + (1-4)^2}$$
$$= \sqrt{(2)^2 + (-3)^2}$$
$$= \sqrt{4 + 9}$$
$$= \sqrt{13}$$
$$= 3.873$$

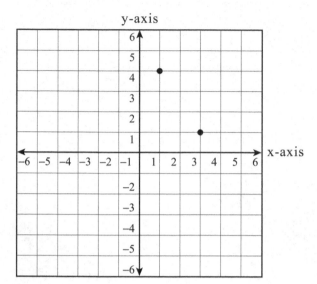

FIGURE 2.7   Plotting two points

The first thing to address is why we dropped the actual i and just dealt with the coefficient. That is because we are simply plotting coordinates on an x, y or Cartesian coordinate system. You can label −4 as −4i or anything you wish (−4m, −4d, etc.) and it does not alter the coordinates. The next thing is to contemplate why we are doing this. Well, let's add just a little bit to our diagram by drawing a line from the origin (0, 0) to each of our points, as illustrated in Figure 2.8.

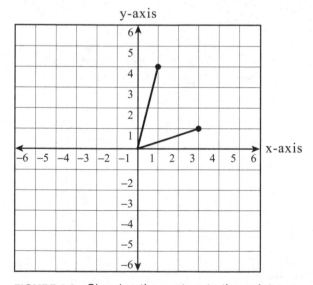

FIGURE 2.8   Showing the vectors to the points

This is almost a triangle—just one side is missing. We can fill that in with a dashed red line, as you see in Figure 2.9.

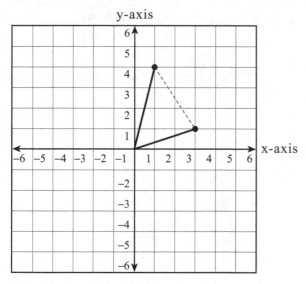

FIGURE 2.9   Completing the triangle

This should now remind you of the Pythagorean theorem: $a^2 + b^2 = c^2$.

Let us try this with another example that should help clarify this situation for you:

$z_1 = 7 + 3i$

$z_2 = 2 - 2i$

Recall from earlier in this chapter the basic form:

$$\sqrt{(a_1 - a_2) + (b_1 - b_2)^2}$$

Thus, in our specific example, this would be the following (notice we are not worried about the i itself, just the real coefficient):

$$\sqrt{(2-7)^2 + (-2-3)^2}$$

$$= \sqrt{(-5)^2 + (-5)^2}$$

$$= \sqrt{25 + 25}$$

$$= \sqrt{50}$$

$$= 7.07$$

These two examples should provide with you a general idea of how this process works. If you need them, there are practice problems at the end of this chapter. At this point, as we are exploring graphical representations, it is appropriate to return to a previous concept—that of complex conjugates. Consider the complex number 4 + 1i. Graphically represented, it appears as shown in Figure 2.10.

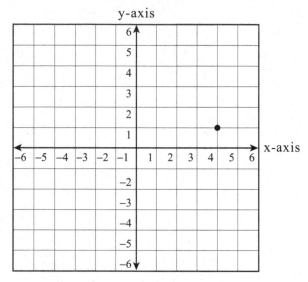

FIGURE 2.10   Plotting the number 4 + 1i

The complex conjugate of 4 + 1i is 4 − 1i. As you can see in Figure 2.11, this simply rotates the number around the real axis (x). Hopefully, this provides a bit more insight into complex conjugates and how they alter the number. They leave the real portion unchanged and reverse the imaginary portion, as demonstrated in the Figure 2.11.

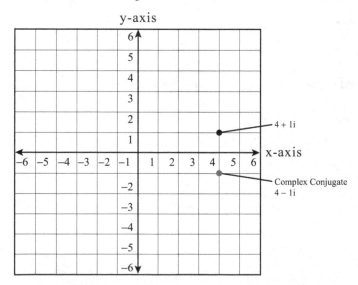

FIGURE 2.11   The complex conjugate

2.4   Vector Representations of Complex Numbers

At this point you should be comfortable with complex numbers. You should also be familiar with representing them graphically as coordinates. It is a very minor step now to represent complex numbers as vectors. This is important, as it will play a big role in future chapters. In fact, you have already used vectors; we just did not represent them as you are accustomed to seeing them from Chapter 1. Consider the complex number 4 + 1i. That can be represented as a vector:

$$\begin{bmatrix} 4 \\ 1 \end{bmatrix}$$

This is actually quite simple. The real portion is on the top, with the coefficient of i on the bottom. Put in general terms:

$$z = a + bi$$

$$= \begin{bmatrix} a \\ b \end{bmatrix}$$

Now recall previously we computed the distance between two complex numbers:

$$z_1 = 7 + 3i$$

$$z_2 = 2 - 2i$$

Let us think about these each as vectors stemming from the origin O, like so:

$$OZ_1 = \begin{bmatrix} 7 \\ 3 \end{bmatrix}$$

$$OZ_2 = \begin{bmatrix} 2 \\ -2 \end{bmatrix}$$

Now our goal is to find a vector that connects the point at OZ_1 to OZ_2. In general terms that will be

$$OZ_1 - OZ_2$$

Using our specific vectors, we have

$$\begin{bmatrix} 7 \\ 3 \end{bmatrix} - \begin{bmatrix} 2 \\ -2 \end{bmatrix}$$

Recall matrix and vector addition and subtraction from Chapter 1; this is really rather easy:

$$\begin{bmatrix} 7 \\ 3 \end{bmatrix} - \begin{bmatrix} 2 \\ -2 \end{bmatrix} = \begin{bmatrix} 5 \\ 5 \end{bmatrix}$$

Now we need to take the magnitude of that vector. Recall that when we did this before, we considered

$$\sqrt{\left(a_1 - a_2\right) + \left(b_1 - b_2\right)^2}$$

This time it is virtually the same, but our vector already is $a_1 - a_2$ over $b_1 - b_2$. So, what we need is simpler:

$$\sqrt{(a)^2 + (b)^2}$$

In our case, that is

$$\sqrt{(5)^2 + (5)^2}$$

$$= \sqrt{50}$$

$$= 7.07$$

That is the same answer when we calculated this in the previous method! This is, of course, quite important. The two methods can both work only if they provide the same answer. Quantum physics and quantum computing deal quite a bit with vector representations, so this is a critical technique to understand.

Vector form also works quite well when integrated with a graphical representation. Consider two complex numbers, which we will call z1 and z2. These form a vector from the origin to the point. We can call those vectors v1 and v2. Now let us be a bit more concrete. We will define z1 as 4 + 1i and z2 as 2 + 3i. The line going from the origin to each of these points defines a vector, as seen in Figure 2.12.

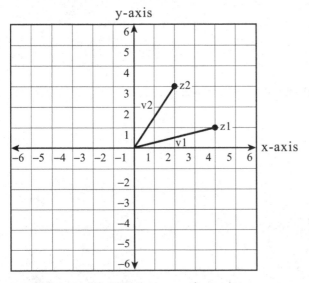

FIGURE 2.12 Plotting two complex points

The vector sum can be calculated using the parallelogram law. The parallelogram law states that the sum of the squares of the lengths of the four sides of a parallelogram equals the sum of the squares of the lengths of the two diagonals. You might comment that we don't have the two diagonals. However, we do have the two sides, which will also give us the other two sides, as shown in Figure 2.13.

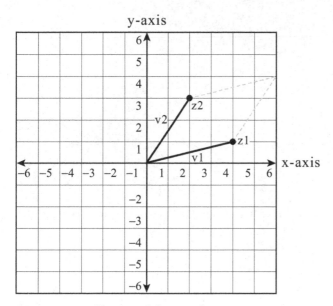

FIGURE 2.13   The parallelogram law

If instead you simply add the vectors, $z1 = 4 + 1i$ and $z2 = 2 + 3i$, you get

$$x = (4 + 2)\ y = (1i + 3i)$$

for a point of $z3 = 6 + 4i$. Even a casual examination of the parallelogram in Figure 2.13 shows that this is precisely the point we find.

There are two other parameters that describe the vector from the origin to any number z. These are r and θ of the point z and are called the polar coordinates. The r is the distance from the origin to z and the θ is the angle of inclination. That angle is always measured counterclockwise from the positive real axis. This gives us more information regarding the coordinates of a complex number via the following equations:

$$x = r \cos \theta \qquad y = \sin \theta$$

From the Pythagorean theorem, it should also be clear that

$$r = |z| = \sqrt{(x)^2 + (y)^2}$$

Therefore, given a point defined by the complex number 2 + 3i, we know that

$$r = \sqrt{(2)^2 + (3)^2}$$

$$r = \sqrt{4 + 9}$$

$$r = \sqrt{13}$$

$$r = 3.605$$

And a little basic trigonometry shows us that

$$\cos\theta = \frac{x}{|z|} \qquad \sin\theta = \frac{y}{|z|}$$

Then a little algebra applied to the Pythagorean theorem gives us the following:

$$r\cos\theta = x \quad \text{and} \quad r\sin\theta = y \quad \text{and} \quad \tan\theta = \frac{y}{x}$$

Now remember that we represent our point z as a + bi (or more commonly x + yi), which gives us this:

$$z = a + bi$$
$$= r\cos\theta + (r\sin\theta)i$$
$$= r(\cos\theta + i\sin\theta)$$

You will most frequently see angles measured in radians. As a brief refresher from basic trigonometry, 1 radian equals 57.3 degrees, and the full 360 degrees of a circle is equal to 2π rad.

2.5   Pauli Matrices

The basics of Pauli matrices is not difficult. The "why" of Pauli matrices might be just a bit more complicated. These are a set of three 2×2 matrices. This might seem like a return to Chapter 1; however, in Chapter 1 we had not yet discussed complex numbers, which is why Pauli matrices are covered here. The three matrices are

$$\begin{bmatrix} 0 & 1 \\ 1 & 0 \end{bmatrix}$$

$$\begin{bmatrix} 0 & -i \\ i & 0 \end{bmatrix}$$

$$\begin{bmatrix} 1 & 0 \\ 0 & -1 \end{bmatrix}$$

These are usually represented with the σ notation, like so:

$$\sigma 1 = \begin{bmatrix} 0 & 1 \\ 1 & 0 \end{bmatrix}$$

$$\sigma 2 = \begin{bmatrix} 0 & -i \\ i & 0 \end{bmatrix}$$

$$\sigma 3 = \begin{bmatrix} 1 & 0 \\ 0 & -1 \end{bmatrix}$$

The representation of these three matrices is certainly not complicated, but they have two properties. These matrices are both Hermitian and unitary. Hermitian refers to a square matrix that is equal to its own conjugate transpose. Conjugate transpose means first taking the transpose of the matrix and then taking the complex conjugate of the matrix. In Chapter 1 we saw transposition using 3×2 matrices. It works the same way for square matrices. Recall the symbol for transpose is T:

$$\begin{bmatrix} a & b \\ c & d \end{bmatrix}^T = \begin{bmatrix} a & c \\ b & d \end{bmatrix}$$

Let's look at one of the Pauli matrices to see this in a more concrete form:

$$\sigma 1 = \begin{bmatrix} 0 & 1 \\ 1 & 0 \end{bmatrix}^T = \begin{bmatrix} 0 & 1 \\ 1 & 0 \end{bmatrix}$$

That demonstrates the transposition, but where does the conjugate come in? Recall earlier in this chapter we explored complex conjugates.

A square matrix is unitary if its conjugate transpose is also its inverse. Put in another way, a unitary matrix is a complex generalization of an orthogonal matrix. Unitary matrices are characterized by the following property for a matrix A:

$$AA^T = A^TA = I$$

Consider the following Pauli matrix:

$$\sigma 2 = \begin{bmatrix} 0 & -i \\ i & 0 \end{bmatrix}$$

This could be represented as follows:

$$\sigma 2 = \begin{bmatrix} 0 + 0i & 0 - i \\ 0 + i & 0 + 0i \end{bmatrix}$$

Well, if you take the complex conjugate (simply changing the sign for the imaginary portion), you get the following:

$$\sigma 2 = \begin{bmatrix} 0 - 0i & 0 + i \\ 0 - i & 0 + 0i \end{bmatrix}$$

Now take the transpose of that, like so:

$$\begin{bmatrix} 0 - 0i & 0 + i \\ 0 - i & 0 + 0i \end{bmatrix} T = \begin{bmatrix} 0 - 0i & 0 - i \\ 0 + i & 0 + 0i \end{bmatrix}$$

This simplifies to

$$\begin{bmatrix} 0 & -i \\ i & 0 \end{bmatrix}$$

The matrix is unchanged.

Okay, the basic mechanics of these matrices don't seem too difficult. Now let us look a bit more into the why. These three matrices are named after the physicist Wolfgang Pauli, and they occur in the Pauli equation, which takes into account the spin of a particle with an external electromagnetic field. The actual Pauli equation we won't be exploring just yet, but for those readers who are curious, Equation 2.7 demonstrates it.

$$\hat{H}|\psi\rangle = \left[\frac{1}{2m} \left[(\mathrm{p} - q\mathrm{A})^2 - q\hbar\sigma \cdot \mathrm{B} \right] + q\phi \right] |\psi\rangle = i\hbar \frac{\partial}{\partial t} |\psi\rangle$$

EQUATION 2.7 The Pauli Equation

Don't panic—you won't need to understand this now. A few chapters from now, much of it will actually make sense to you.

One of the interesting facts about Pauli matrices is that they form a basis for the vector space of 2×2 Hermitian matrices. Recall from Chapter 1 that a basis vector means that this means that all the 2×2 Hermitian matrices can be written as some linear combination of the Pauli matrices.

Allow me to introduce you to a new mathematical symbol, in connection with Pauli matrices. It is possible to write all three Pauli matrices in a compacted expression, shown in Equation 2.8.

$$\begin{pmatrix} \delta_{a3} & \delta_{ia1} - i\delta_{a2} \\ \delta_{a1} + i\delta_{a2} & -i\delta_{a3} \end{pmatrix}$$

EQUATION 2.8 Compact Form of Pauli Matrices

You already know what the symbol i represents, the $\sqrt{-1}$, but you might not be familiar with the symbol δ, which represents the Kronecker delta. The Kronecker delta is a fascinating function. It is named after the mathematician Leopold Kronecker. It is a function of two variables. If the variables are equal, then the function returns 1. If the functions are not equal, then the function returns 0. This is expressed a bit more formally in Equation 2.9.

$$\delta_{ij} = \begin{cases} 0 & \text{if } i \neq j, \\ 1 & \text{if } i = j. \end{cases}$$

EQUATION 2.9 Kronecker Delta

Note that the Kronecker delta must always have two arguments. That is how it determines what to return. In Equation 2.8, you saw the Pauli matrices expressed as a single expression. Recall there are three Pauli matrices. Substitute either 1, 2, or 3 for the a in Equation 2.8 and you will have one of the Pauli matrices. Let's do this by substituting $a = 2$. That gives us what you see in Equation 2.10.

$$\begin{pmatrix} \delta_{33} & \delta_{31} - i\delta_{32} \\ \delta_{31} + i\delta_{32} & -i\delta_{33} \end{pmatrix}$$

EQUATION 2.10 Kronecker Delta with Pauli Matrices

Then, using the Kronecker delta with the inputs shown, you then get what is shown in Equation 2.11.

$$\begin{pmatrix} 1 & 0 - i0 \\ 0 & 1 \end{pmatrix}$$

EQUATION 2.11 Applying the Kronecker Delta to a Pauli Matrix

This can, of course, be simplified to what is shown in Equation 2.12.

$$\begin{pmatrix} 1 & 0 \\ 0 & 1 \end{pmatrix}$$

EQUATION 2.12 The Resulting Pauli Matrix

This is obviously one of the Pauli matrices. Specifically, it is the σ1 Pauli matrix. Now that you have seen how to represent all the Pauli matrices in a single expression and have learned a new symbol and function, Kronecker delta δ, it is time to learn another term related to matrices. The Pauli matrices have a property that is called *involutory* (not to be confused with involuntary). An involutory matrix is one that is its own inverse.

Let us go just a bit further. If we include the identity matrix I with the Pauli matrices, that forms an orthogonal basis of the real Hilbert space of 2×2 complex Hermitian matrices. Recall from Chapter 1 that orthogonal means perpendicular to each other.

A Hilbert space is a vector space, like you were introduced to in Chapter 1; however, it extends the two-dimensional Euclidean plane and three-dimensional Euclidean space you are familiar with to any number of dimensions, including infinite dimension spaces. The German mathematician David Hilbert first described the eponymously named Hilbert spaces in his work on integral equations and Fourier series.

A Hilbert space is essentially a vector space that is generalized to potentially infinite dimensions.

The inner product is basically a dot product that has three properties:

1. The dot product is symmetric, which means the order of the dot product does not matter.

2. It is linear in its first argument, which means that given any scalars a and b and any vectors x1, x2, and y, then (ax1 + bx2) * y = ax1 * y + bx2 * y.

3. For any x that is an element of the vector space (the Hilbert vector space), the inner product of x with itself is positive definite (i.e., the inner product is > 0).

All this is a bit simplified, but it is sufficient for you to understand the essentials of both Hilbert spaces and inner products. Let us expand a bit on point 1. The inner product satisfies specific conditions. The inner product must have conjugate symmetry. The inner product of two elements in the Hilbert space is the complex conjugate of the two elements in the opposite order.

An inner product is a generalization of the dot product. It allows you to multiply two vectors together and produce a scalar. In practice, there is not really any difference between dot product and inner product, at least insofar as calculating either is concerned. Dot products are usually used in reference to only real numbers. If complex numbers are used or you are dealing with non-Euclidean spaces, then the term *inner product* is normally used.

2.5.1 Algebraic Properties of Pauli Matrices

There are some interesting algebraic properties of Pauli matrices. The first is that the determinant of all of these matrices is −1. Recall from Chapter 1 that the determinant of a square matrix is calculated as follows:

$$|A| \begin{bmatrix} a & b \\ c & d \end{bmatrix} = ad - bc$$

Now consider the Pauli matrices:

$$\sigma 1 = \begin{bmatrix} 0 & 1 \\ 1 & 0 \end{bmatrix}$$

$\det = (0 * 0) - (1 * 1) = -1$

$\sigma2 = \begin{bmatrix} 0 & -i \\ i & 0 \end{bmatrix}$

$\det = (0 * 0) - (-i * i) = -1$

$\det = 0 - (-i^2)$

$\det = 0 - (1)$

$\det = -1$

$\sigma3 = \begin{bmatrix} 1 & 0 \\ 0 & -1 \end{bmatrix}$

$\det = (1 * -1) - (0 *))$

$\det = -1$

This is an interesting property of Pauli matrices. What about the eigenvalues and eigenvectors of the Pauli matrices? Recall from Chapter 1 that eigenvalues are a special set of scalars associated with a linear system of equations. Given a matrix A and some scalar λ, if it is true that

$Av = \lambda v$

then we say that v is an eigenvector of the matrix A and that λ is an eigenvalue of the matrix A. So, consider one of the Pauli matrices:

$\begin{bmatrix} 0 & 1 \\ 1 & 0 \end{bmatrix}$

We are looking for some value such that

$\begin{bmatrix} 0 & 1 \\ 1 & 0 \end{bmatrix} v = \lambda v$

We start with finding the eigenvalue λ, which will be a value that satisfies the formula

$\det (A - \lambda I) = 0$

where A is the matrix in question.
Let us begin by taking our original matrix and subtracting λ from the diagonal:

$\begin{bmatrix} 0 & 1 \\ 1 & 0 \end{bmatrix} \rightarrow \begin{bmatrix} 0-\lambda & 1 \\ 1 & 0-\lambda \end{bmatrix}$

Now we want to know the determinant of that matrix:

$$\det \begin{bmatrix} 0-\lambda & 1 \\ 1 & 0-\lambda \end{bmatrix}$$

Recall from Chapter 1 that a determinant is calculated as follows:

$$|A| \begin{bmatrix} a & b \\ c & d \end{bmatrix} = ad - bc$$

So, we have $(0-\lambda)(0-\lambda)-(1*1)$

$$= \lambda^2 - 1$$

This can be easily solved:

$$\lambda^2 = 1$$

Thus, $\lambda = 1$ or -1.

It turns out that the eigenvalues of all the Pauli matrices are 1, and -1. You can try this yourself with any of the Pauli matrices. We are now ready to find eigenvectors. Recall that we are looking for a vector that satisfies the following:

$$Av = \lambda v$$

A is our initial matrix, and we now know that λ can be $+1$ or -1. Put another, more formal way, we have two eigenvalues: $\lambda_1 = 1$; $\lambda_2 = -1$. Let us begin with the second eigenvalue. This brings us to the following:

$$\begin{bmatrix} 0 & 1 \\ 1 & 0 \end{bmatrix} \begin{pmatrix} x \\ y \end{pmatrix} = -1 \begin{pmatrix} x \\ y \end{pmatrix}$$

The vector $\begin{pmatrix} x \\ y \end{pmatrix}$ is what we are trying to find. We can start by taking either the upper or lower row, so let's use the lower:

$$1x + 0y = -y$$

$$x = -y$$

Thus, $\begin{pmatrix} 1 \\ -1 \end{pmatrix}$ is an eigenvector of this Pauli matrix. Let us plug that back in to check it:

$$\begin{bmatrix} 0 & 1 \\ 1 & 0 \end{bmatrix} \begin{pmatrix} 1 \\ -1 \end{pmatrix} = -1 \begin{pmatrix} 1 \\ -1 \end{pmatrix}$$

Let us begin with the left side. We multiple row 1 by the vector:

$$[0 \; 1]\begin{pmatrix} 1 \\ -1 \end{pmatrix} = (0*1) + (1*-1)$$

$$= -1$$

Now the same for row 2:

$$[1 \; 0]\begin{pmatrix} 1 \\ -1 \end{pmatrix} = (1*1) + (0*-1)$$

$$= 1$$

This gives us $\begin{pmatrix} -1 \\ 1 \end{pmatrix}$.

Let us check to see if that matches the right side:

$$-1\begin{pmatrix} 1 \\ -1 \end{pmatrix} = \begin{pmatrix} -1 \\ 1 \end{pmatrix}$$

So, we have found the eigenvalues and one of the eigenvectors of one of the Pauli matrices. Now let's work out the other eigenvector for this particular Pauli matrix:

$$\begin{bmatrix} 0 & 1 \\ 1 & 0 \end{bmatrix}\begin{pmatrix} x \\ y \end{pmatrix} = 1\begin{pmatrix} x \\ y \end{pmatrix}$$

We again start by taking either the upper or lower row; let's use the lower. This gives us

$1x + 0y = y$

which is simplified to

$x = y$

This suggests that $\begin{pmatrix} 1 \\ 1 \end{pmatrix}$ is another eigenvector of this Pauli matrix. So now we have the following:

$$\begin{bmatrix} 0 & 1 \\ 1 & 0 \end{bmatrix}\begin{pmatrix} 1 \\ 1 \end{pmatrix} = 1\begin{pmatrix} 1 \\ 1 \end{pmatrix}$$

Again, we start with the left side:

$$\begin{bmatrix} 0 & 1 \\ 1 & 0 \end{bmatrix}\begin{pmatrix} 1 \\ 1 \end{pmatrix}$$

The first row gives us this:

$$[0 \; 1]\begin{pmatrix} \frac{1}{1} \end{pmatrix} = (0*1) + (1*1)$$

$$= 1$$

Now the second row:

$$[1 \; 0]\begin{pmatrix} \frac{1}{-11} \end{pmatrix} = (1*1) + (0*1)$$

$$= 1$$

That gives us $\begin{pmatrix} \frac{1}{1} \end{pmatrix}$.

Now the right side:

$$1\begin{pmatrix} \frac{1}{1} \end{pmatrix}$$

It should be obvious this equals $\begin{pmatrix} \frac{1}{1} \end{pmatrix}$ and we have found a second eigenvector of this Pauli matrix. If this is not completely clear to you, it is suggested that you continue and calculate the eigenvalues and eigenvectors for the other Pauli matrices. You will often see this in another form, one which will be introduced in Chapter 3, "Basic Physics for Quantum Computing."

2.6 Transcendental Numbers

Not directly part of the issue of complex numbers, but related, is the topic of transcendental numbers. Transcendental numbers are numbers other than algebraic numbers. This, of course, begs the question, what is an algebraic number? An algebraic number is a root of a nonzero polynomial. Algebraic numbers include both real numbers and complex numbers.

Two examples of transcendental numbers are π and e; however, there are actually infinitely many transcendentals. One fact regarding real transcendental numbers is that they are irrational; however, the reverse is not true. Certainly not all irrational numbers are transcendental. A good example is $\sqrt{2}$, because that is actually a root of the polynomial equation $x^2 - 2 = 0$.

Euler's number is not only one of the more common examples of a transcendental number, but Leonhard Euler was one of the first to provide a definition of transcendental numbers. He did so in the eighteenth century. It was Joseph Liouville in 1844 who first provided the existence of transcendental numbers. In 1873 Charles Hermite proved that (e) was indeed a transcendental number. The famous mathematician David Hilbert proposed a number of problems. Hilbert's seventh problem is stated as follows:

If a is an algebraic number that is not zero or one, and b is an irrational algebraic number, is a^b necessarily transcendental?

In case you thought transcendental numbers are simply mathematical curiosities, without practical purpose, let us examine one that clearly has practical applications. *Chaitin's constant*, sometimes called *Chaitin's construction*, is essentially the probability that a randomly constructed program will halt. There are actually an infinite number of halting probabilities, given the infinite possibilities for encoding a program. Oftentimes this is simply represented by the single symbol, Ω. Gregory Chaitin described this eponymously named constant. Each halting probability is a transcendental real number. The details of Chaitin's constant are beyond our current scope, but the interested reader is encouraged to delve deeper into the topic.

2.7 Summary

This chapter began with the basics of complex numbers, including how complex numbers originated. You learned how to do basic algebraic functions with complex numbers. Then working with graphical representations of complex numbers was covered. The next topic was vector representation. Both graphical and vector representations are very common in quantum physics and quantum computing, so it is quite important that you understand these concepts.

A section of this chapter was devoted to Pauli matrices. This topic is central to understanding quantum computing. You must absolutely ensure you are comfortable with the material on Pauli matrices before moving on. There was also a brief discussion of transcendental numbers.

Test Your Skills

REVIEW QUESTIONS

1. Add the following two complex numbers:

   (3 + 2i) (2 + 3i)

2. What is the product of $(4 + 2i)(2 + 2i)$?

3. What is the product of $(2 + 2i)(-2 + 3i)$?

4. Divide $(6 + 4i)$ by $(2 + 2i)$.

5. Given the two complex numbers $(3 + 2i)$ and $(4 + 4i)$, what is the distance between them?

6. Which of the following statements accurately describes the Kronecker delta?

   a. It returns a 1 if the two inputs are equal, and a zero otherwise.

   b. It returns a 0 if the two inputs are equal, and a 1 otherwise.

   c. It calculates the distance between two complex numbers.

   d. It calculates the distance between two points on a graph.

7. Calculate the determinant of the following Pauli matrix: $\sigma 2 = \begin{bmatrix} 0 & -i \\ i & 0 \end{bmatrix}$

8. What is the primary difference between a dot product and an inner product from a practice viewpoint?

9. What is an involutory matrix?

   a. One that has a complex inverse

   b. One that has a determinant of −1

   c. One that is its own inverse

   d. One that has no inverse

10. What are the eigenvalues of the following Pauli matrix?

$$\begin{bmatrix} 1 & 0 \\ 0 & -1 \end{bmatrix}$$

Chapter | **3**

Basic Physics for Quantum Computing

Chapter Objectives

After reading this chapter and completing the quiz, you will be able to do the following:

- Have a basic understanding of quantum physics
- Be able to explain quantum states
- Comprehend the uncertainty principle
- Describe quantum entanglement

Our ultimate goal in this book is to explore quantum computing; however, quantum computing is (quite obviously) based on quantum physics. In order to understand quantum computing, you must have some generalized idea of quantum physics. This chapter begins with a general overview of physics and then discusses the discoveries that led to quantum physics. This will provide us with a foundation to discuss the fundamentals of quantum physics. Obviously, one can fill several books and several courses on the topic of quantum physics. The goal of this chapter is to provide you with just enough working knowledge to proceed with the rest of the book.

It must also be noted that many concepts in this chapter can be quite difficult for the novice. Do not be surprised if you struggle with some concepts, or even need to re-read sections. This is quite normal for those who are new to quantum physics. For those who already have a background in physics, understand the goal of this chapter is to provide the novice just enough knowledge to pursue quantum computing at a working level. Clearly, there is much more that could be written on quantum physics than appears in this chapter, and the topics in this chapter could all be given more detail. However, the goal of this chapter is not to be a textbook on quantum physics. It is to provide just enough knowledge for the reader to proceed with concepts presented later in this book.

3.1   The Journey to Quantum

To best understand quantum physics, it is advantageous to learn the history of what led to quantum physics. There were a number of important discoveries in the latter days of the nineteenth century and the beginning of the twentieth century. Each of these discoveries added to a body of evidence that would ultimately require the revision of classical physics.

The real issue in quantum physics, however, begins with understanding the nature of light. Is light a wave or a particle? The debate goes back to the 1600s. Isaac Newton had proposed that light was a particle or corpuscle. Christian Huygens had advocated that light was a wave, much like a sound wave or water wave. Huygens was not alone in his view of light as a wave, but the prominence of Isaac Newton certainly gave weight to the corpuscular view of light. This began what would become the birth of quantum mechanics. Classical physics could not explain several things, including the nature of light.

These two competing concepts would continue to fuel debate in physics for quite some time, until experiments could be conducted to help settle the matter. Waves generally propagate through some medium. Sound waves, as an example, propagate through the air. Proponents of the wave view of light proposed an ether that light propagated through. In fact, it was believed that all electromagnetic radiation propagated through this ether (also spelled *aether*). The concept of aether would hold sway in physics until the very early twentieth century. This aether was thought to be a space-filling substance or medium that was the transmission medium for not just light, but gravity and other forces. In fact, physicists attempted to understand planetary motion in the context of aether.

In 1801, Thomas Young performed an experiment that demonstrated the wave behavior of light. Young shined a light through two slits in a barrier and had a photosensitive plate on the other side. When the light went through two apertures, it appeared to have interference on the receiving side, much like a water wave or sound wave. Figure 3.1 demonstrates these results.

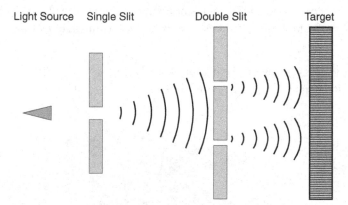

FIGURE 3.1   Double-slit experiment

Light is shown through the single slit, then on to the double slit. When the target is reached, the two light sources (one from each of the slits in the double slit) exhibit an interference pattern. The target will show stripes that become wider as the target is moved further from the two slits. At the time, this seemed to settle the question of whether light was a particle or a wave. The light appeared to be clearly a wave, and not a particle (or corpuscle, as it was then called). Essentially, the thought was that if light was a particle, then one would expect the pattern on the opposite side to match the shape and size of the slit. The appearance of an interference pattern seemed to demonstrate light was a wave.

Further variations of the double-slit experiment began to shed some light on the situation. First, it was noted that when waves/particles were sent through the double slit one at a time, they certainly appeared as dots, or particles, on the target. This can be done by simply closing one of the slits. However, as more were sent through the slits, a wave pattern emerged. This type of experiment has been done with photons, electrons, and other particles. Essentially, it led to the idea that light is both a particle and a wave. This is also true for other subatomic particles. The concept is often referred to as *wave-particle duality*. We will return to this concept a bit later in this chapter.

The history of quantum mechanics also includes some questions that may seem a bit obscure today. One of those issues was the study of black body radiation. This topic was very important in the 1800s. A *black body* is an opaque, nonreflective object. The radiation is the thermal radiation (heat) in and around such a black body. A perfect absorber absorbs all electromagnetic radiation incident to it; such an object is called a black body. Obviously, such an object is hypothetical, as no object can perfectly absorb energy.

When any object is heated, that heat has specific wavelengths. Those are inversely related to the intensity. As a body is heated and the temperature rises, the wavelength shortens; thus, the light changes colors. Measuring black body radiation led to results that did not seem to match existing theories. This was particularly true at higher frequencies.

Balfour Stewart performed experiments comparing the radiation emitted from polished plates versus lamp-black surfaces, using the same temperature for both. He used a galvanometer and a microscope to read the radiated energy. In his paper he did not mention wavelengths or thermodynamics. He claimed that the heat radiated did so regardless of the surface being lamp black or reflective. Ultimately he was in error.

In 1859, Gustav Kirchoff proved that the energy emitted from a black body depends only on the temperature of the black body and the frequency of the energy absorbed. He developed the rather simple formula shown in Equation 3.1.

$$E = J\,(T, v)$$

EQUATION 3.1 Kirchoff's Black Body Energy

In this formula, E is energy, T is temperature, and v is frequency. However, Kirchoff did not know what the function J was, and he challenged other physicists to find it.

The late 1800s and early 1900s were a time of numerous discoveries. In 1887, Heinrich Hertz discovered the photoelectric effect, which we will discuss in more detail in just a bit. Max Planck posited in 1900 that energy radiating from an atomic system did so in discrete elements. These discrete elements are called *quanta* and are the root of the term *quantum physics*. This led to his rather famous formula, shown in Equation 3.2.

$$\varepsilon = h\nu$$

EQUATION 3.2 Quantum Energy

This formula states that the energy elements (ε) are proportional to the frequency (ν) multiplied by Planck's constant (h). Planck's constant is a very small number, and we will explore it in more detail later in this chapter. Planck's constant, and the subsequent formula, was created from his attempt to derive a mathematical formula that accurately predicted the observed spectral distribution of the radiation from a black body.

Furthermore, Planck defined Planck's law of black body radiation. The formula is shown in Equation 3.3.

$$B_\nu(\nu, T) = \frac{2h\nu^3}{c^2} \frac{1}{e^{h\nu/kT} - 1}$$

EQUATION 3.3 Planck Law

This formula has the following values:

- h is the Planck constant.

- c is the speed of light in a vacuum.

- k is the Boltzmann constant.

- ν is the frequency of the electromagnetic radiation.

- T is the absolute temperature of the body.

Another issue that was difficult to explain with classical physics is the photoelectric effect. Essentially, when some electromagnetic radiation, such as light, hits the material, electrons (or other particles) are emitted. This seems simple enough to understand. Classical (i.e., pre-quantum or relativity) electromagnetic theory held that the intensity of light would be proportional to the kinetic energy of the electrons emitted. This should mean that a dim light will produce lower-energy electrons than a bright light. However, experiments did not show this. Rather, experiments showed a correlation between frequency and the electrons dislodged. In fact, below a certain frequency, no electrons are emitted at all.

Einstein proposed this photoelectric effect was due to light being a collection of discrete wave packets, termed *photons*, rather than a wave propagating through space. Work by Einstein, Planck, and others would eventually establish what is now known as wave-particle duality. This seems to counter the previous experiments by Young and others that clearly showed light was a wave.

Note

For the reader who has a strong mathematical background and wants a more rigorous discussion of relativity and quantum physics, Randy Harris's *Modern Physics, Second Edition*, published by Pearson, is a good choice.

Classical physics had always considered energy, in any form, to be a wave. However, Max Planck demonstrated experimentally that in certain situations, energy could behave like an object or particle. For this work, he was awarded the Nobel Prize in Physics in 1918.

In 1923, Louis de Broglie made the assertion in his doctoral dissertation that one could determine the wavelength of any particle via the formula

$$\lambda = h/p$$

where

- λ, or lambda, is the wavelength.

- h is Planck's constant, which is $6.62607015 \times 10^{-34}$ J·s (joules per second). A joule can be defined as the work required to produce one watt of power for one second.

- p is the momentum. Momentum can, in turn, be defined as mass (m) times velocity (v).

As you can probably surmise by seeing the very small number for Planck's constant, the wavelength is going to be quite small in most cases. The work of de Broglie is essentially parallel to the wave-particle duality of light. What de Broglie posited was that matter (i.e., particles) can also behave as waves; however, given the small wavelengths involved, we do not normally see this behavior in the macro world. This is why when you throw a baseball, it behaves entirely like a particle.

There have been various experiments that demonstrated the wave behavior of matter. Among the most famous was the Davisson-Germer experiment. Without getting bogged down in all the details of that experiment, essentially in the 1920s, Clinton Davisson and Lester Germer showed that electrons scattered by the surface of a nickel metal displayed a diffraction pattern, like a wave.

The concept of wave-particle duality is central to quantum physics. It basically states that a particle can be described as a particle or a wave, and that considering it as simply either a particle or wave is simply inaccurate. The term *particle* refers to photons, electrons, and other subatomic particles. We will explore this in more depth later in this chapter, but for now, a basic description will suffice. This brief history lesson should give you some context for our further discussions of quantum physics.

3.2 Quantum Physics Essentials

With the brief history of quantum physics from the last section, you should now be aware that in the subatomic world, things are both particles and waves, and you should be aware that the energy of these *particles* is in discrete levels, or quanta. Let us begin by exploring this fact a bit more.

3.2.1 Basic Atomic Structure

When taking introductory chemistry, one is often taught a model of the atom that has protons and neutrons in the nucleus, with electrons orbiting it, much like planets around a star. This is not actually the way that electrons behave, but it does provide a general starting point for students to study the atomic structure. This model is often called the Bohr model, after its creator, Neils Bohr. Figure 3.2 illustrates the Bohr model for helium.

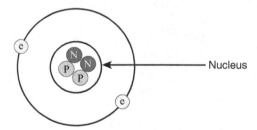

FIGURE 3.2 Bohr model

As was discussed earlier, this is not quite accurate. First, it must be noted that the electrons don't orbit like planets around a star. What we call an *atomic orbital* is really a mathematical function that calculates the probability of finding an electron in a particular region around the nucleus. This brings us to a very important fact about quantum physics. Much of what we find in the subatomic world is probabilistic, not deterministic. We will return to this concept later in this chapter; in fact, it will come up throughout this book. The probability of finding an electron depends on the orbital and the energy levels. The orbitals themselves are regions of the probability of finding an electron. The energy levels are given integer values 1, 2, 3, and 4.

Each electron is described by four numbers. The first is n, which is the principal quantum number. Next is l, which is the orbital quantum number (sometimes called the orbital angular momentum quantum number). Then comes m, which is the magnetic quantum number, and m_s, which is the electron spin quantum number. The letter n, the principal quantum number, is sometimes referred to as the *shell*. The l is sometimes also called the *azimuthal quantum number*. The value of l can be any number from 1 to $n-1$. So, if $n=2$, then $l=1$. This number will tell you the shape of the orbital. Remember, this shape determines an area of probability for finding an electron, not a path, such as a planet orbiting a star.

The orbitals (the l value) have letters to define them. They are the s, p, d, and f orbitals. The s orbital is drawn as a sphere, but bear in mind this is just the area of the probability of finding an electron. Figure 3.3 shows the s orbital.

FIGURE 3.3   The *s* orbital

This is $l = 0$. Now there can be *s* subshells or orbitals in any shell. So, there can be an $n = 1$ *s* subshell, an $n = 2$ *s* subshell, etc.

For $l = 1$ (which happens if *n* is at least 2), the orbital begins to look a bit strange. It has a dumbbell-like shape, as illustrated in Figure 3.4.

FIGURE 3.4   The *p* orbital

Put more technically, *p* orbitals are wave functions with $l = 1$. Their distribution is angular, but not uniformly so, thus the shape of their distribution. There are three different *p* orbitals for three different m_l values (−1, 0, and 1). Essentially, these orbitals have different orientations.

If the wave function has $l = 2$, then it is a *d* orbital. This has an even more odd distribution. The *d* orbital is often described as a cloverleaf, but it's essentially like two dumbbells in a plane for most *d* orbitals, as illustrated in Figure 3.5. There are five different *d* orbitals for the m_l values −2, −1, 0, 1, and 2.

FIGURE 3.5   The *d* orbital

The *d* orbital can also appear as two lobes going through a torus—or put more colloquially, a dumbbell going through a donut. There are variations of this based on the m_l values. Figure 3.6 shows the "donut" shape.

FIGURE 3.6   The *d* orbital alternate form

If the *l* is 3, then it is an *f* orbital. The *f* orbitals take on a range of possible shapes. The shapes depend on the m_l values. There are seven m_l values: −3, −2, −1, 0, 1, 2, and 3. Figure 3.7 shows their respective shapes.

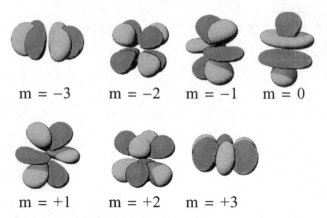

FIGURE 3.7   The *f* orbitals

The spin is represented by +1/2 or −1/2. This brings us to the Pauli exclusion principle. Wolfgang Pauli formulated the eponymously named Pauli exclusion principle in 1925. It states that no two fermions can occupy the same state within a quantum system at the same time. Fermions are those subatomic particles that have 1/2 integer spins. This includes electrons, which are our focus here.

The Pauli exclusion principle has some practical implications for electron distribution. An *s* suborbital can contain at most two electrons, and then only if they have different spins. So, in helium, there are two electrons, and both are in the *s* suborbital but have different spins; one is +1/2 and the other −1/2. The *p* subshells have at most six electrons in pairs, with each member of the pair having an opposite spin. The *d* subshells have at most ten electrons, again in pairs, with each member of the pair having an opposite spin.

This general overview of the structure of atoms should give you a general working knowledge sufficient to follow the rest of this book. We have just scratched the surface in this section; however, the goal here is not to teach a chemistry course but to ensure that you have a general overview of atomic structure.

3.2.2   Hilbert Spaces

Now we can tie in some of the mathematics covered in the first chapter. Think back to vectors, particularly unit vectors. A unit vector has a length of 1. Recall that the length of a vector is computed as follows:

$$\|vector\| = \sqrt{x2 + y2}$$

The possible state of a given quantum system or wave particle is represented by a unit vector. When applied to quantum states, they are called *state vectors*.

The various state vectors are part of a vector space called the *state space*. This state space is a complex Hilbert space. Now to describe Hilbert spaces, we will use the information we covered in both Chapter 1, "Introduction to Essential Linear Algebra," and Chapter 2, "Complex Numbers."

You can complete this book and understand it with only a general understanding of Hilbert spaces; however, if you intend to go further with quantum physics or quantum computing, you will need to have a stronger understanding of Hilbert spaces. A Hilbert space is a generalization of Euclidean space. This, of course, necessitates some explanation of Euclidean space.

Euclidean space is the space of classical geometry. It was initially three-dimensional space. This is the space you probably studied in primary or secondary school. The Cartesian coordinates, invented by Rene Descartes in the seventeenth century, are used in Euclidean space. For quite a long time, Euclidean space was limited to just three dimensions, and that comports well with our daily experiences.

In the nineteenth century, Ludwig Schlafi extended Euclidean space to include n dimensions. In conjunction with this, Schlafi did a lot of work with polytopes, which are analogues of the traditional Platonic solids with more dimensions.

Euclidean space is a space over the real number system. A Euclidean vector space is a finite-dimensional inner product space over the real numbers. Recall from Chapter 2 that an inner product is a dot product with the properties of being symmetric: its first argument is linear and is greater than zero. Also recall from Chapter 1 that the dot product of two vectors is simply the two vectors multiplied.

A Hilbert space is any dimension; it can be finite or infinite. A Hilbert space also can be real or complex (recall complex numbers from Chapter 2). Every inner product gives rise to a norm. Remember from Chapter 1 that the nonnegative length is called the norm of the vector.

If the space is complete with respect to that norm, then it is a Hilbert space. This part might be a bit difficult for readers without a rigorous mathematical background, so allow me to devote a bit of space to explain this in some detail (feel free to skip this explanation if this is all old news to you).

In this case, the term *completeness* simply means that every Cauchy sequence of elements in that space converges to an element in this space. This, at least for some readers, begs the question as to what a Cauchy sequence is and why it is so important. Cauchy sequences are named after Augustin-Louis Cauchy. Incidentally, Cauchy is pronounced *koh-shee*. A Cauchy sequence is a sequence whose elements become arbitrarily close to each other as the sequence progresses. There are actually quite a few rather simple examples of this. Here is an example of a Cauchy sequence:

$$a_n = \frac{1}{2^N}$$

Why is this a Cauchy sequence? Well, let us examine it a bit closer. First, select any $i > 0$. Now choose an N, such that $2^{-N} < i$. Next, consider n and m that are $>$ than N. Then

$$|a_n - a_m| = \left| \frac{1}{2^n} - \frac{1}{2^m} \right| \leq \frac{1}{2^n} + \frac{1}{a^m} \leq \frac{1}{2^N} + \frac{1}{2^N} = i$$

This might still not be completely clear to some readers. Consider a visual representation of a Cauchy sequence, as shown in Figure 3.8.

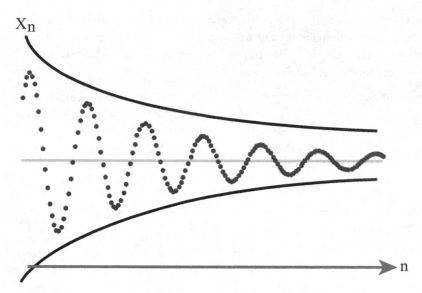

FIGURE 3.8   Graphical representation of a Cauchy sequence

Basically, as the function progresses, it is progressing to a particular point. For those just trying to get the basic gist of quantum computing, you need not be overly concerned with the details of Cauchy sequences, but this explanation should help you to understand them and how they relate to Hilbert spaces.

3.2.3   Uncertainty

Now we come to a very conceptually difficult part of quantum mechanics: the Heisenberg uncertainty principle. Essentially, this principle states that the more you know about one property of a subatomic particle, the less you know about a related property. This principle was introduced in 1927 by Werner Heisenberg. While the principle applies to any property of a protocol, it is most often stated as 'the more precisely you know the position of a given particle, the less precisely you can know its momentum'. The reverse is also true: the more precisely you know the momentum, the less precisely you can know the position. The practical effect of this is that you can never know with certainty the precise position and momentum of a given particle at a specific point in time.

This concept does not fit well into our understanding of the world. As I sit at my desk, I can take any object in my office and know precisely its position and momentum. You might think that those objects are all stationary, and unless something has gone very wrong, they are. However, I can apply that to moving objects. As I watch my dog walk across the floor, I can quite easily measure precisely his position and momentum at any given instant. This is simply how our everyday world works, but in the subatomic world, things operate in a quite counterintuitive manner. In fact, if you will forgive me for being so informal in my writing, the quantum world is frankly bizarre. Although there are many things we know about it, for some things we "don't know why." We just know that countless experiments have verified them.

Now that you have a generalized idea of the Heisenberg uncertainty principle, let's explore a bit more rigorous treatment of the concept. Consider this formula:

$$\sigma_p \, \sigma_x \geq \frac{h}{2}$$

In this equation, σ_p is the momentum, and σ_x is the position. If you think h is the Planck constant, you are almost correct. It is actually what is commonly called the *reduced Planck constant*, which is the Planck constant h (6.626×10^{-34} J·s) / 2π. Why is this modification used? In angular applications (frequency, momentum, etc.), 360 degrees is a complete circle. In fact, a Hertz, the standard unit of frequency, represents one complete 360-degree cycle in one second. For those readers who don't recall their trigonometry, 360 degrees expressed in radians is 2π radians.

> **Note**
>
> For those readers wanting just enough quantum physics to understand the basics of quantum computing, you now have sufficient information on the Heisenberg uncertainty principle. For those who want more information, you can continue with the rest of this section.

To explain a bit more of the "why" of the Heisenberg uncertainty principle, we first need to discuss Fourier transforms. These are functions widely used with anything that can be described as a waveform. This includes electromagnetic fields, stock prices, and a number of other things. A Fourier transform essentially takes a function (one that can be expressed as a waveform) and decomposes it into its constituent frequencies.

What does the Fourier transform do? Given some wave function, it essentially extracts the frequencies present in that function. That might be an oversimplification, but it is a good place to start. Put a bit more precisely, a Fourier transform takes a function of time and transforms it into a function of frequency. Now let us take a look at the actual math. There are various forms of the Fourier transform, but one common form is shown in Equation 3.4.

$$\hat{f}(\varepsilon) = \int_{-\infty}^{\infty} f(x) e^{-2\pi i \times \xi} dx$$

EQUATION 3.4 Fourier Transform

If this is new to you, don't be overwhelmed by the apparent complexity. We will walk through each of the symbols, and even without a background in calculus, you should be able to grasp the essence of this formula.

First, the odd-looking f is a symbol for the Fourier transform itself. The symbol over the f is called a circumflex. The ε represents some real numbers. This symbol is called the epsilon. Moving to the right side of the equation we encounter

For those readers without a background in calculus, this represents integration. An integral might be difficult to master, but the essence is quite easy. An integral basically takes small pieces of something and sums them up for a total. The classic example is the area under a curve. Imagine you have a curve, as shown in Figure 3.9, and want to know its area.

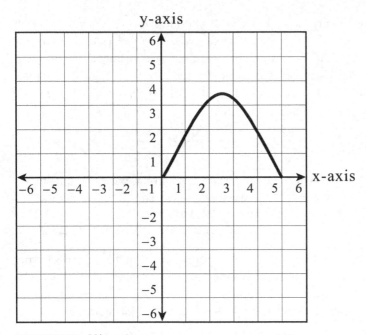

FIGURE 3.9   X/y-axis

One way to compute this is to use smaller and smaller rectangular slices of it, summing up the areas of those slices, as shown in Figure 3.10.

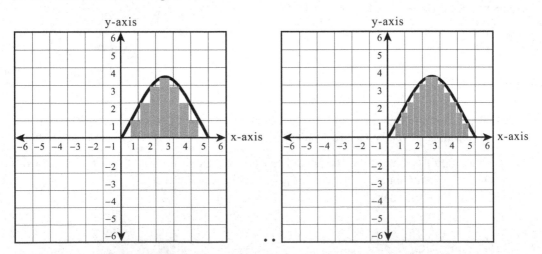

FIGURE 3.10   Approximating the area of a curve

As you get progressively narrower rectangles and sum their areas, your total area of the curve becomes more accurate. Now computing an integral does not actually involve adding up progressively narrower rectangles. In fact, it is because of integrals that one does not have to do that. However, that is the concept. The integral symbol is followed by the function one wishes to compute the integral of. This takes us back to what is remaining in the Fourier transform, shown in Equation 3.5.

$$f(x)e^{-2\pi i \times \xi}$$

EQUATION 3.5 Fourier Transform, Partial

The function, $f(x)$, is e (remember Euler's number from Chapter 2) raised to the power of $-2\pi ix \varepsilon$. The precise reasons those particular numbers work is well beyond the scope of this chapter. However, do keep in mind that 2π radians is 360 degrees. The final symbol, dx, is the symbol of differentiation. All integration is the integral of some differential. Differentiation deals with change. The process of differentiation is about finding the rate of change at a particular point. It is not inaccurate to think of integration and differentiation as opposite operations.

The relation between position and momentum arises because the wave functions that describe two corresponding orthonormal bases in the Hilbert space are actually Fourier transforms of each other. This should provide you with a bit more insight into the "why" of the Heisenberg uncertainty principle.

3.2.4 Quantum States

Recall from Chapter 1 the discussion of eigenvectors and eigenvalues. In Chapter 1 you were asked to consider an n × n matrix we will call A. Then consider some scalar, λ. If it is true that

$$Av = \lambda v$$

then we say that v is an eigenvector of the matrix A and λ is an eigenvalue of the matrix A. In the study of quantum mechanics, the quantum states correspond to vectors in Hilbert space. Various properties, such as the momentum of a particle, are associated with some operator. Also, recall that vectors are matrices. This means those vectors have eigenvalues and eigenvectors. In quantum mechanics, the eigenvalues of the operator correspond to the values of the property, such as momentum. The eigenvector corresponding to that eigenvalue is a quantum state. Physicists call this an eigenstate.

Before we delve deeper into quantum states, we need to address another question. Why are vectors and linear algebra even used for quantum physics? This relates to results that did not make sense without linear algebra. Returning to the position and momentum we discussed in relation to the Heisenberg uncertainty principle, Equation 3.6 expresses that relationship.

$$QP - PQ = \frac{ih}{2\pi}$$

EQUATION 3.6 Position and Momentum

Recall that h is Planck's constant, and the 2π is 360 degrees expressed in radians. The i is the imaginary number, such that $i^2 = -1$. Recall that h is a very small number ($6.62607004 \times 10^{-34}$ m^2 kg / s). But shouldn't QP – PQ = 0? If one considers the numbers we normally encounter, this is true. For example, $4e^3 - e^34 = 0$. This is because multiplication is commutative; however, with matrices and vectors, it is not necessarily commutative. Matrix multiplication, unlike traditional multiplication (with scalar values), is not commutative. In Chapter 1, that point was illustrated with two images, shown again here in Equation 3.7.

$$\begin{bmatrix} 2 & 3 \\ 1 & 4 \end{bmatrix} \begin{bmatrix} 1 & 1 \\ 2 & 3 \end{bmatrix} = \begin{bmatrix} 8 & 11 \\ 9 & 13 \end{bmatrix}$$

$$\begin{bmatrix} 1 & 1 \\ 2 & 3 \end{bmatrix} \begin{bmatrix} 2 & 3 \\ 1 & 4 \end{bmatrix} = \begin{bmatrix} 3 & 7 \\ 9 & 15 \end{bmatrix}$$

EQUATION 3.7 Noncommutative Matrices

Therefore, the facts of quantum mechanics make sense only when states (such as momentum and position) are represented as vectors. It is not that physicists chose to use linear algebra to describe quantum states; it is rather that such states are naturally best described by linear algebra.

The values could be represented as vectors (1,0) or (0,1). However, in the field of quantum physics, it is typical to use a notation known as bra-ket notation. The right part is the ket; this is a vector usually shown as $| \psi \rangle$. The left half is termed the bra, denoted as $\langle \phi |$. Yes, this means bracket.

The term bra on one side and ket on the other were deliberately chosen to make the word *braket*, or *bracket*. This notation was introduced by Paul Dirac and is often known as Dirac notation. It is also common to see representations such as $\alpha | \psi \rangle$.

Quantum states have coefficients. These coefficients are complex numbers (recall the discussion on complex numbers in Chapter 2). These coefficients are time-dependent, meaning they change with time. Now, taking this a bit further and bringing our attention back to both Heisenberg and the wave-particle duality, quantum objects (for want of a better term) are in a state of superposition of different states. The possible different states are denoted by Φ_n. A number P_n represents the probability of a randomly selected system being in the state Φ_n.

This should provide you a bit better understanding of quantum states. This will be important for later chapters discussing quantum bits, or qubits. Another fact, which will also have significance for quantum computing, is that measuring or observing a state changes the state. This is completely contrary to what you find in your everyday world. Certainly, measuring one's weight does not change it, regardless of however much one might wish it were so.

This section provided you with a general understanding of quantum states. This will be sufficient for you to understand our discussions in later chapters regarding qubits. Bear in mind that much of quantum physics is counterintuitive. So, if some of this seems just a bit odd to you, that is actually a good sign that you indeed understand it.

3.2.5 Entanglement

This particular facet of quantum physics may be the oddest yet. In fact, Albert Einstein famously called it "spooky action at a distance." In this section, I will not be able to provide you with the "why" of entanglement. That is because we simply do not know the "why." Whoever can fully explain this is certainly a candidate for a Nobel Prize; however, countless experiments have confirmed it is true.

Entanglement begins with two particles being generated in such a way that the quantum state of each particle is inextricably linked to the other. Before we continue this description, it is very important that you realize that this is not some theoretical concept. Entanglement has been rigorously verified in countless independent experiments.

If one particle in an entangled pair has a spin that is clockwise, the other particle in the pair will have a counterclockwise spin. A 1935 paper by Albert Einstein, Boris Podolsky, and Nathan Rosen described this process as what would become known as the EPR paradox. Einstein insisted that this meant there must be some issue with our understanding of quantum physics. The EPR paradox involves a thought experiment. In the experiment, one considers a pair of entangled particles. The issue in the paper was that if these particles are so entangled that their states are complementary, then altering the state of the first particle could instantaneously change the state of the other particle. This would, essentially, mean information regarding the state of the first particle was transmitted instantly to the second particle. The theory of relativity tells us that nothing can travel faster than the speed of light. In the alternative, the state of the second particle must be set before any measurement of either particle is taken. This was counter to both theory and experiment, which demonstrates that particles are in a state of superposition until measured, and then the wave function collapses into a single state. Thus, a paradox exists.

The EPR paradox was the subject of much debate in physics and numerous papers. In 1951, David Bohm published a paper proposing a variation of the EPR thought experiment. Bohm's ideas can be expressed mathematically, as shown in Equation 3.8, using math you have already explored previously in this book.

$$S_x = \frac{\hbar}{-2}\begin{bmatrix} 0 & 1 \\ 1 & 0 \end{bmatrix}, \quad S_y = \frac{\hbar}{-2}\begin{bmatrix} 0 & -i \\ i & 0 \end{bmatrix}, \quad S_z = \frac{\hbar}{-2}\begin{bmatrix} 1 & 0 \\ 0 & -1 \end{bmatrix}$$

EQUATION 3.8 Spin Matrices

The h with a bar is the reduced Planck constant discussed earlier. The matrices given are the Pauli matrices discussed in previous chapters. The S_x, S_y, and S_z are the spins in the x-, y- and z-axes. Bohm went on to use this basic math to explore the states of two entangled particles. However, despite the apparent paradox, numerous experiments have confirmed entanglement.

In 2013, researchers created two pairs of entangled photons and proved that their polarization was correlated regardless of distance in space or time. This is yet another experiment demonstrating that entanglement is true, even if we don't know why. As late as 2015, experiments were still being conducted that confirmed entanglement.

Essentially, entangled particles are treated not as individual particles but rather as a whole. The state of this composite system is the sum or superposition of the product states of each local constituent. There are various ways particles become entangled. Subatomic particle decay is one such way. What we find consistently is that if we separate two entangled particles, then measure a property of one particle, such as spin, and then measure the other particle's property, the two will be complementary. They are inextricably entangled.

There have been several different proposed explanations for entanglement. None have been verified. It is beyond the scope of this chapter or this book to more fully explore entanglement, but keep in mind that the fact of entanglement has been experimentally verified numerous times. However, we can briefly review some of the proposed explanations, even those that may have fallen out of favor in the physics community.

The hidden variables hypothesis contends that the particles actually have some hidden variables that, right at the moment the particles are separated, determine the outcome of properties such as spin. This would mean that there really is no nonlocality, simply variables we don't know about. Einstein was a proponent of this idea. However, no experiments have given any evidence to support this.

It is also known that entanglement occurs naturally. For example, in multi-electron atoms, the electron shells always consist of entangled electrons. So entanglement is not just the result of physicists experimenting with nature; it is how nature actually works.

3.3 Summary

In this chapter, we have covered some difficult topics; however, these are the bare minimum you need to understand quantum computing. Therefore, it is important that you fully understand the material in this chapter before proceeding. Some readers, particularly those without a mathematical or physics background, might need to review this chapter more than once, and even return to the previous two chapters, before going forward.

The general history of quantum physics is important to provide context. The two most important concepts from that history are black body radiation and wave-particle duality. A general understanding of Hilbert spaces is also going to aid in understanding later material in this book. Understanding the Heisenberg uncertainty principle is also important. The most critical topic from this chapter is quantum states. Understanding quantum states, as well as the symbolism used, is critical to understanding quantum computing. Qubits are essentially data stored in quantum states.

Chapter 6, "Basic Quantum Theory," delves more deeply into quantum mechanics. It is important that you have a basic understanding of the material in this chapter before moving on to Chapter 6. This chapter provides a basis, along with Chapters 1 and 2, for forming a deeper understanding of quantum physics and thus quantum computing.

Test Your Skills

REVIEW QUESTIONS

1. Which of the following is the best description of light?

    a. It is a particle or corpuscle.

    b. It is a wave.

    c. It is neither particle nor wave.

    d. It is both a particle and a wave.

2. What is the reason for the term *quantum* in quantum physics?

    a. Particles have specific energy states rather than a continuum of states.

    b. The energy of a particle is quantifiable.

    c. The state of a particle can be quantified.

    d. The physics is highly mathematical (i.e., quantifiable).

3. Which of the following is the best description of the Pauli exclusion principle?

    a. No two fermions can occupy the same subshell at the same time.

    b. No two fermions can occupy the same state within a quantum system at the same time.

    c. No two fermions can occupy the same energy level at the same time.

    d. No two fermions can occupy the same shell at the same time.

4. Which of the following is the best description of electrons in the p subshell?

   a. There can be up to six electrons in any configuration.

   b. There must be up to six electrons, but they can be in any configuration.

   c. There can be up to six electrons, but they must all have the same spin.

   d. There can be up to six electrons, in pairs, and each pair has an opposite spin.

5. What is a Cauchy sequence?

   a. A sequence that converges to an element in the vector space

   b. A sequence of quantum states

   c. A sequence that shows quantum entanglement

   d. A sequence of vectors that define the vector space

6. What type of mathematical function extracts frequencies in a wave function?

   a. The Pauli exclusion principle

   b. Cauchy sequences

   c. Fourier transforms

   d. Integrals

7. Which of the following best describes an eigenstate?

   a. It is another name for an eigenvalue.

   b. It is the combination of an eigenvalue and eigenvector.

   c. It is the current state of the eigenvector.

   d. It is an eigenvector corresponding to an operation.

8. What does the symbol $\langle \phi \mid$ denote?

   a. The ket side of the notation

   b. The bra side of the notation

   c. The current state of the particle

   d. The wave function

9. What does the following equation describe?

   $$B_v(v,T) = \frac{2hv^3}{c^2} \frac{1}{e^{hv/kT} - 1}$$

   a. Planck's black body radiation

   b. Kirchoff's black body energy

   c. Cauchy sequence

   d. Fourier transform

Chapter **4**

Fundamental Computer Science for Quantum Computing

Chapter Objectives

After reading this chapter and completing the quiz, you will be able to do the following:

- Understand data structures
- Have a working knowledge of algorithms and algorithm analysis
- Be able to explain computational complexity
- Understand logic gates

I suspect that most readers of this book have some background related to computers. It would be rather surprising if you did not. You might think there is no need for a chapter on basic computer science, but first ask yourself a simple question: what is computer science? Is it programming? Perhaps network design? Maybe machine learning? All of those subjects, and many others, are related to computer science and can often be found in the curriculum of computer science degrees. However, computer science is more fundamental. It is more focused on how algorithms are designed than on how one codes algorithms in a particular language. The theory of computation dealing with how efficiently a given problem can be solved using a specific algorithm and model of computation is quite key to computer science. Computational complexity is yet another aspect of computer science. All of these topics are also covered in most computer science curriculum but might not be covered in other degree programs such as computer information systems, software engineering, business computing, or other computer-related degrees. So, there is a substantial likelihood that many readers won't have sufficient exposure to these topics, and those readers who have studied such topics might need a bit of a refresher.

Put more clearly, computer science is the study of computing and information. It has been said that the core of computer science can be summed up with the question, what can be efficiently automated?

Obviously, one chapter cannot replace a computer science degree or even a single computer science course. However, like the other chapters you have studied thus far, the goal of this chapter is just to ensure you have enough knowledge to continue with the rest of this book and develop a working knowledge of quantum computing.

You might think computer science begins in the mid-twentieth century, and that is certainly when it became such a major part of society. However, as early as 1672, Gottfried Leibniz demonstrated a mechanical calculator he named the Stepped Reckoner. However, most historians of science consider Charles Babbage to be the father of computer science. Babbage lived from 1791 to 1871. He invented the first mechanical computer. He began with a concept he called a difference engine, but that failed. He moved on to his analytical engine. By the 1940s, computers began to resemble something we might recognize today. For example, the ENIAC computer was the first electronic general-purpose digital computer. It was completed in 1945 for the U.S. Army Ballistic Research Laboratory. The power of computing was clearly demonstrated when ENIAC calculated a trajectory in only 30 seconds, which took human beings 20 hours to do.

Clearly, computers and computer science have grown a great deal since that time. There are many subfields, and one such subfield is theoretical computer science. Data structures, algorithms, and the theory of computation are more relevant to the goals of this book, and we will cover those topics in this chapter. Information theory is also relevant to quantum computing, and Chapter 5, "Basic Information Theory," will be devoted to that topic. We will also have some discussion about computer architecture.

4.1   Data Structures

A data structure is a formal way of storing data that also defines how the data is to be processed. This means that the definition of any given data structure must detail how the data is going to be stored as well as what methods are available for moving data into and out of that particular data structure. There are a number of well-defined data structures that are used in various situations. Different data structures are suited for different applications. In this section, we will examine several of the more commonly known data structures. Data structures are fundamental to computer science.

Quantum computers provide a very different way of accomplishing computer science, but they are still computer science. That means that fundamental things like data structures are still important. Therefore, an understanding of classical data structures will make it easier for you to understand quantum computing.

4.1.1   List

A list is one of the simplest of data structures. It is a structure consisting of an ordered set of elements, each of which may be a number, another list, etc. A list is usually denoted something like you see here:

```
(a, b, c, d, ...)
```

Many other data structures are some sort of extension of this basic concept. A list can be either homogenous or heterogeneous. That simply means that the elements in the list can all be the same type or not. If you have a background in set theory, this should look very familiar to you. A list is just a set.

The most common implementation of a list, in most programming languages, is the array, and in most programming languages, an array is usually homogenous (i.e., this means all elements of the array are of the same data type). It should be noted that several object-oriented programming languages offer a type of list known as a collection, which is heterogeneous (i.e., elements of that list may be of diverse data types).

To add data to a list, you simply append it to the end or insert it at a given point based on the index number. To remove data, you reference a specific index number and get that data. This just happens to be one major weakness with a list: it can quickly become disordered. The reason is that you can insert items anywhere in the list and remove them anywhere. Even if the list is perfectly sorted, adding items at random intervals can introduce informational entropy.

The ideal place to use a list is when you simply need to store data and the order of processing the data in or out of storage is not important. A list is an appropriate data structure to use, especially if your situation specifically requires that you be able to add and remove data at any point in the storage mechanism, rather than in a particular sequence.

The most common types of lists are linked lists. That simply means that each item is linked to the next item. There are also double-linked lists wherein each item is linked to the item before it and the item after it. Figure 4.1 displays the basic structure of a single linked list.

FIGURE 4.1 The list

Here is code for a simple linked list:

```
struct node {
   int data;
   int key;
   struct node *next;
};
/insert link at the first location
void insertFirst(int key, int data) {
   //create a link
   struct node *link = (struct node*) malloc(sizeof(struct node));

   link->key = key;
   link->data = data;
```

```
   //point it to old first node
   link->next = head;

   //point first to new first node
   head = link;
}
int length() {
   int length = 0;
   struct node *current;

   for(current = head; current != NULL; current = current->next) {
      length++;
   }

   return length;
}
```

4.1.1.1 Queue

A queue is simply a special case of a list, and it stores data in the same way that a list does. It is also often implemented as simply an array. The difference between a list and a queue is in the processing of the data contained in either data structure. A queue has a more formal process for adding and removing items than the list does. In a queue, data is processed on a first-in, first-out (FIFO) basis. Often there is some numerical pointer designating where the last data was input (often called a tail) and where the last data was extracted (often called a head). Putting data into the queue is referred to as enqueueing, and removing it is called dequeuing. Figure 4.2 shows the queue structure.

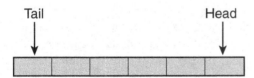

FIGURE 4.2 The queue

Clearly, the head and tail must also be moving in some direction. This is usually via a simple increment method (simply the ++ operator in C, C#, and Java). That would mean that in Figure 4.2, they are moving to the right. The queue is a relatively simple data structure to implement. Here is a C-like pseudo-code example of a queue implemented in a class:

```
class Q
{
     stringarray[20]; // this queue can hold up to 20 strings int head, tail;

            void enqueue(string item)
```

```
        {
            stringarray[head] = item; head++;
        }

        string dequeue()
        {
            return stringarray[tail]; tail++
        }

}
```

With a queue, data is added and removed in a sequential fashion. This is very different from a list, where data may be added at any point in the list. With the queue, data is always added at the next spot in the sequence and processed similarly; however, two problems immediately present themselves with the queue. The first problem is how to handle the condition of reaching the end of the queue. The usual answer to this is to create what is known as a circular queue. When the head (or tail) reaches the end of the queue, it simply starts over at the beginning. Referring to Figure 4.2, this would mean that if the head or tail reaches the end, it is simply repositioned back to the beginning. In code, you would add to the previous code sample something similar to this pseudo-code:

```
if (head==20) head = 0;
```

and

```
if (tail == 20 ) tail = 0
```

This still leaves us with the second problem: what happens if the head is adding new items faster than the tail is processing them? Without proper coding, the head will overtake the tail, and you will begin overwriting items in the queue that have not been processed; ergo, they are lost and will never be processed. This means you will be adding items to a space in the queue that already contains unprocessed data, and that unprocessed data will simply be lost. The answer to this problem is to stop allowing new items to be added whenever the head catches up to the tail. This should be communicated to the end user via a "queue is full" message.

Of course, there is another option, other than the circular queue, and that is the bounded queue. A bounded queue is simply one that can only contain a finite amount of data. When that limit is reached (i.e., when you reach the end of the queue), the queue is done. Clearly, this implementation of the queue is somewhat limited, and you will encounter it much less frequently than the unbounded queue (i.e., any queue that does not have an arbitrary, finite limit, such as the circular queue).

The queue is a very efficient data structure, and you will find it implemented in many diverse situations. The most common place to encounter a queue is with a printer. Printers usually have a queue in which print jobs are stored while awaiting processing. And, of course, they utilize circular queues. If you overload that queue, you will get a message telling you the print queue is full. If your programming problem requires orderly and sequential processing of data on a first-in, first-out basis, then the queue is an ideal data structure to use.

4.1.1.2   Stack

The stack is a data structure that is a special case of the list. With the stack, elements may be added to or removed from the top only. Adding an item to a stack is referred to as a push, and removing an item is referred to as a pop. In this scenario, the last item added must be the first one removed, which is also known as last in, first out (LIFO). A good analogy is to consider a stack of plates. Because the last item in is the first out, this data structure does not require a pointer. You can see the stack described in Figure 4.3.

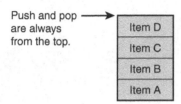

FIGURE 4.3   The stack

The problem with this particular data structure is the LIFO processing. If you have accumulated a number of data items and must get to one of the first you put on the stack, you will first need to process all of the subsequent items. For this reason, a stack is primarily used when a few items need to be stored for a short period of time. You will find stacks in temporary memory storage. It is probably worthwhile to compare LIFO with FIFO (first in, first out). The FIFO data structure requires that the first item put in also be the first one out. This is similar to the stack, but the popping and pushing take place on different ends. This is shown in Figure 4.4.

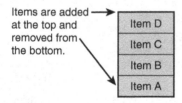

FIGURE 4.4   FIFO

As was mentioned, certain computer memory structures and the CPU registers will often use stacks. However, their method of LIFO makes them poor choices for many standard data-processing situations. For example, if a network printer utilized a stack rather than a queue, it would always attempt to process the last job first. Because new jobs are continually being added, it would be entirely possible for the first job sent to the printer to wait hours, if not days, to be printed. Clearly, that would be unacceptable.

Here is code for the stack with an entire class for all the operations of the stack:

```
class MyStack
{
  void push(int data) {
     if(!isFull()) {
        top = top + 1;
        stack[top] = data;
     } else {
        printf("Could not insert data, Stack is full.\n");
     }
  }
  int pop(int data) {

     if(!isempty()) {
        data = stack[top];
        top = top - 1;
        return data;
     } else {
        printf("Could not retrieve data, Stack is empty.\n");
     }
  }
  bool isfull() {
     if(top == MAXSIZE)
        return true;
     else
        return false;
  }
  int peek() {
     return stack[top];
  }
}
```

4.1.1.3   Linked List

A linked list is a data structure wherein each item has a pointer (or link) to the next item in the list or the item preceding it, but not both (a double-linked list, which will be discussed later in this chapter, does both). This can be quite useful because if an item is displaced for any reason, it is aware of the next item in the list. Each item knows what comes after it, or what comes before it, but not both.

There is a problem with the linked list. If you do not implement it in such a way that data is processed in an orderly, sequential fashion (such as FIFO), then items can be removed or added anywhere (as with a standard list). This means that when an item is inserted or deleted, you must adjust the pointer of the item it was inserted next to. For example, consider the diagram shown in Figure 4.5.

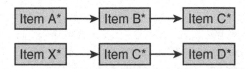

FIGURE 4.5   The linked list

Each of the items (B*, C*, etc.) in the boxes is a pointer to the next item in the linked list. The * notation is the same the C and C++ languages use to denote pointers. Note that when item X is inserted between item A and item B, item A's pointer must also be changed so that it now points to X rather than to B. The same situation occurs if an item is deleted. This problem is minimized, however, if items are always added or removed in a sequential fashion, such as FIFO.

4.1.1.4 Double-Linked List

A double-linked list is a data structure wherein each item has a pointer (or link) to the item in front of it and the item behind it. This data structure is the logical next step after the linked list. It is highly efficient in that any data point has links to the preceding and succeeding data points. The source code is virtually identical to that of a linked list. It simply has two pointers: one for the preceding item and one for the succeeding item. This sort of data structure is highly efficient.

Note there is also a special form of the double-linked list called a circularly linked list, where the first and last nodes are linked together. This can be done for both single- and double-linked lists. To traverse a circularly linked list, you begin at any node and follow the list in either direction until you return to the original node. Viewed another way, circularly linked lists can be seen as having no beginning or end. This type of list is very useful for managing buffers.

The circularly linked version of the double-linked list makes it ideal for the printer buffer. It allows the printer buffer to have every document aware of the documents on either side. This is because it has a double-linked list (each item has a pointer to the previous item and the next item) and its final item is linked back to the first item. This type of structure provides an unbroken chain of items.

Whatever method you use to implement the double-linked list (circular, etc.), it has the same complication as the linked list. When you insert or delete an item, you must update any other items that have pointers to the item you deleted or the space you are inserting the item into. The only difference between a double-linked list and a single-linked list is that when you insert or delete an item in a double-linked list, you must update the pointers on either side of that item, rather than only one pointer (either preceding or next). A double-linked list is shown in Figure 4.6.

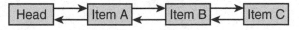

FIGURE 4.6   The double-linked list

4.1.2 Binary Tree

Yet another interesting data structure is the binary tree. A binary tree is an ordered data structure in which each node has at most two children. Typically, the child nodes are called left and right. For example, in Figure 4.7, the node *Science* has a left child node named *Physical* and a right child node named *Biological*.

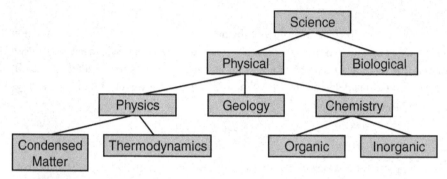

FIGURE 4.7 The binary tree

One common use of binary trees is binary search trees. You can see in Figure 4.7 that each item in the binary tree has child items that are related to the parent node. This is exactly the context in which binary trees are most useful (i.e., when there is a strong parent-child relationship between items).

The binary tree is the structure, and the binary search tree is a sorted binary tree that provides for searching. There are actually a wide range of different tree types. The binary tree is just a common example.

4.2 Algorithms

Before we can begin a study of algorithms, we must first define what one is. An *algorithm* is simply a systematic way of solving a problem. A recipe for an apple pie is an algorithm. If you follow the procedure, you get the desired results. Algorithms are a routine part of computer programming and an integral part of computer science. In fact, it was an algorithm that demonstrated that quantum computers would disrupt cybersecurity and cryptography. Peter Shor developed Shor's algorithm, which demonstrated that a quantum computer could factor an integer into its prime factors in polynomial time. We will discuss Shor's algorithm in some detail later in this book. We will also be discussing other quantum algorithms, and in Chapter 16, "Working with Q#," and Chapter 17 "Working with QASM," you will have the opportunity to program quantum algorithms. If you wish to go deeper into algorithms than this section does, there are some excellent books about algorithms available from Pearson (the publisher of this book), including the following:

- *Algorithms, Fourth Edition*, by Robert Sedgewick, Princeton University

- *An Introduction to the Analysis of Algorithms, Second Edition*, Robert Sedgewick, Princeton University

It is not enough to simply have some algorithm to accomplish a task. Computer science seeks to find the most efficient algorithm. Therefore, it is also important that we have a clear method for analyzing the efficacy of a given algorithm. When considering any algorithm, if the desired outcome is achieved, then clearly the algorithm worked. However, the real question is, how well did it work? If you are sorting a list of ten items, the time it takes to sort the list is not of particular concern. However, if your list has one million items, then the time it takes to sort the list, and hence the algorithm you choose, is of critical importance. Fortunately, there are well-defined methods for analyzing any algorithm.

When analyzing algorithms, we often consider the asymptotic upper and lower bounds. Asymptotic analysis is a process used to measure the performance of computer algorithms. This type of performance is based on the complexity of the algorithm. Usually this is a measure of either the time it takes for an algorithm to work or the resources (memory) needed. It should be noted that one usually can only optimize time or resources, but not both. The asymptotic upper bound is simply the worst-case scenario for the given algorithm, whereas the asymptotic lower bound is the best case.

Some analysts prefer to simply use an average case; however, knowing the best case and worst case can be useful in some situations. In simple terms, both the asymptotic upper bound and lower bound must be within the parameters of the problem you are attempting to solve. You must assume that the worst-case scenario will occur in some situations.

The reason for this disparity between the asymptotic upper and lower bounds has to do with the initial state of a set. If one is applying a sorting algorithm to a set that is at its maximum disorder, then the time taken for the sorting algorithm to function will be the asymptotic upper bound. If, on the other hand, the set is very nearly sorted, then one may approach or achieve the asymptotic lower bound.

Perhaps the most common way to formally evaluate the efficacy of a given algorithm is Big O notation. This method is a measure of the execution of an algorithm, usually the number of iterations required, given the problem size n. In sorting algorithms, n is the number of items to be sorted. Stating some algorithm $f(n) = O(g(n))$ means it is less than some constant multiple of $g(n)$. The notation is read, "f of n is big oh of g of n." This means that saying an algorithm is 2N means it will have to execute two times the number of items on the list. Big O notation essentially measures the asymptotic upper bound of a function. Big O is also the most often used analysis.

Big O notation was first introduced by the mathematician Paul Bachmann in his 1892 book *Analytische Zahlentheorie*. The notation was popularized in the work of another mathematician named Edmund Landau. Because Landau was responsible for popularizing this notation, it is sometimes referred to as a Landau symbol.

Omega notation (Ω) is the opposite of Big O notation. It is the asymptotic lower bound of an algorithm and gives the best-case scenario for that algorithm. It gives you the minimum running time for an algorithm.

Theta notation (Θ) combines Big O and Omega notation to give the average case (average being the arithmetic mean in this situation) for the algorithm. In our analysis, we will focus heavily on the Theta notation, also often referred to as the Big O running time. This average time gives a more realistic picture of how an algorithm executes.

Now that we have some idea of how to analyze the complexity and efficacy of a given algorithm, let's take a look at a few commonly studied sorting algorithms and apply these analytical tools. The algorithms selected in this section are among the most common. If you took a course in algorithm analysis, you would have encountered these.

4.2.1   Sorting Algorithms

Sorting algorithms are often used to introduce someone to the study of algorithms. This is because they are relatively easy to understand and are so common. There are many sorting algorithms, and we will examine some of the most commonly used; however, you can certainly examine others on your own. Here are a few sorting algorithms not covered in this section:

- Merge sort

- Comb sort

- Heap sort

- Shell sort

- Bucket sort

- Radix sort

4.2.1.1   Quick Sort

The quick sort is a very commonly used algorithm. This algorithm is recursive, meaning that it simply calls itself repeatedly until the list is sorted. Some books will even refer to the quick sort as a more effective version of the merge sort. The quick sort is the same as merge sort (n ln n); however, the difference is that this is also its best-case scenario. However, it has an $O(n^2)$, which indicates that its worst-case scenario is quite inefficient. So, for very large lists, the worst-case scenario may not be acceptable.

This recursive algorithm consists of three steps (which bear a strong resemblance to the merge sort):

Step 1.   Pick an element in the array to serve as a pivot point.

Step 2.   Split the array into two parts. The split will occur at the pivot point, so one array will have elements larger than the pivot and the other will have elements smaller than the pivot. Clearly, one or the other should also include the pivot point.

Step 3.   Recursively repeat the algorithm for both halves of the original array.

One very interesting aspect of this algorithm is that the efficiency of the algorithm is significantly impacted by which element is chosen as the pivot point. The worst-case scenario of the quick sort occurs when the list is sorted and the leftmost element is chosen; this gives a complexity of $O(n^2)$. Randomly choosing a pivot point rather than using the leftmost element is recommended if the data to be sorted isn't random. As long as the pivot point is chosen randomly, the quick sort has an algorithmic complexity of O(n log n). The following source code for a quick sort should help clarify this concept:

```
void quicksort(int number[25],int first,int last){
    int i, j, pivot, temp;

    if(first<last){
        pivot=first;
        i=first;
        j=last;

        while(i<j){
            while(number[i]<=number[pivot]&&i<last)
                i++;
            while(number[j]>number[pivot])
                j--;
            if(i<j){
                temp=number[i];
                number[i]=number[j];
                number[j]=temp;
            }
        }

        temp=number[pivot];
        number[pivot]=number[j];
        number[j]=temp;
        quicksort(number,first,j-1);
        quicksort(number,j+1,last);

    }
}
```

4.2.1.2   Bubble Sort

The bubble sort is the oldest and simplest sort in use. By simple I mean that from a programmatic point of view it is very easy to implement. Unfortunately, it's also one of the slowest. It has an O(n^2), which means that for very large lists, it is probably going to be too slow. As with most sort algorithms, its best case (lower asymptotic bound) is O(n).

The bubble sort works by comparing each item in the list with the item next to it and swapping them if required. The algorithm repeats this process until it makes a pass all the way through the list without swapping any items (in other words, all items are in the correct order). This causes larger values to "bubble" to the end of the list while smaller values "sink" toward the beginning of the list, thus the name of the algorithm.

The bubble sort is generally considered to be the most inefficient sorting algorithm in common usage. Under best-case conditions (the list is already sorted), the bubble sort can approach a constant O(n) level of complexity. The general case is an O(n^2).

Even though this is one of the slower algorithms available, it is seen more often simply because it is so easy to implement. Many programmers who lack a thorough enough understanding of algorithm efficiency and analysis will depend on the bubble sort.

Now that we have looked at two common sorting algorithms, you should have a basic understanding of both algorithms and algorithm analysis.

4.2.1.3   Euclidean Algorithm

The Euclidean algorithm is a method for finding the greatest common denominator of two integers. Now that might sound like a rather trivial task, but with larger numbers, it is not. The Euclidean algorithm proceeds in a series of steps such that the output of each step is used as an input for the next one. Let k be an integer that counts the steps of the algorithm, starting with zero. Thus, the initial step corresponds to k = 0, the next step corresponds to k = 1, k = 2, k = 3, etc.

Each step, after the first, begins with two remainders, rk − 1 and rk − 2, from the preceding step. You will notice that at each step, the remainder is smaller than the remainder from the preceding step, so that rk − 1 is less than its predecessor, rk − 2. This is intentional and central to the functioning of the algorithm. The goal of the kth step is to find a quotient qk and remainder rk such that the equation is satisfied:

```
rk - 2 = qk rk - 1 + rk
```

Here, rk < rk − 1. In other words, multiples of the smaller number rk − 1 are subtracted from the larger number rk − 2 until the remainder is smaller than the rk − 1.

That explanation may not be entirely clear, so let us look at an example.

```
Let a = 2322, b = 654.
  2322 = 654·3 + 360     (i.e. the 360 is the remainder).
```

This now tells us that the greatest common denominator of the two initial numbers, gcd(2322, 654), is equal to the gcd(654, 360).

These are still a bit unwieldy, so let us proceed with the algorithm:

```
  654 = 360·1 + 294     (the remainder is 294).
```

This tells us that the gcd(654, 360) is equal to the gcd(360, 294).

The following steps continue this process until there are simply no further steps to go:

```
  360 = 294·1 + 66     gcd(360, 294) = gcd(294, 66)
  294 = 66·4 + 30     gcd(294, 66) = gcd(66, 30)
  66 = 30·2 + 6     gcd(66, 30) = gcd(30, 6)
  30 = 6·5     gcd(30, 6) = 6
```

Therefore, gcd(2322, 654) = 6.

This process is quite handy and can be used to find the greatest common denominator of any two numbers.

The Euclidean algorithm is important for many reasons. It is related to certain cryptography methods we will see later in this book. It also is an excellent example of a recursive algorithm. We will be revisiting this algorithm in even more detail later in this book.

4.3 Computational Complexity

Computational complexity theory is focused on computational problems and classifying them based on their difficulty. This is closely related to the previously discussed algorithm analysis. The difficulty is, in turn, defined by the resources required to solve the problem. Perhaps the most well-known such problem is the P vs. NP problem. P indicates a problem that can be solved in polynomial time, and NP are problems for which the answer (if provided) can be verified in polynomial time, but there is no known way to solve the problems in polynomial time. Put more simply: P indicates problems that are solvable by a computer in polynomial time, whereas NP are problems that are not solvable in polynomial time but maybe checked in polynomial time. The question is simple: The P vs. NP problem asks whether every problem whose solution can be quickly verified by a computer can also be quickly solved by a computer. Does P = NP? If P does equal NP, then for all the NP problems there is a way to solve them in polynomial time; we just have not discovered it. As of the date of this study, most mathematicians believe P does not equal NP, but no one has yet proven that. It is one of the millennium prize problems. You can learn more about the millennium prize problems at https://www.claymath.org/millennium-problems.

Computational complexity and algorithm analysis are less concerned with finding a solution to one specific instance of a problem than they are with finding a solution that can be applied to an entire class of problems. Therefore, the complexity of a given problem is rather important. We will examine a few measures of computational complexity in the following sections. As we will spend quite a bit of time on quantum algorithms later in this book, it is important that you have a general understanding of computational complexity of algorithms. A sample of various measures of computational complexity is given in the following sections.

4.3.1 Cyclomatic Complexity

In 1976, Thomas McCabe developed cyclomatic complexity. Cyclomatic complexity is defined as the number of linearly independent paths in a given body of code. Thus, if there are no code branches, such as in if statements, switch statements, and other decision points, then there is a cyclomatic complexity of 1. There exists only one linearly independent path through the code. This is a directed graph wherein the nodes are the basic blocks of the program or function and the edges connect those nodes. The cyclomatic complexity is defined as follows:

```
C = E - N + 2P, where:
E = the number of edges of the graph.
N = the number of nodes of the graph.
P = the number of connected components.
```

McCabe only integrated the most basic elements of graph theory; however, once one has expressed a problem as a graph, the full power of graph theory can be applied. Put another way, it would not be an overly arduous task to expand this definition to incorporate a range of graph theory elements, such as weighted nodes and edges, incidence functions relating the nodes, or even more sophisticated aspects of graph theory such as spectral graph theory. Given the focus on complexity in this current study, understanding the current methods of exploring complexity is relevant to the current study.

4.3.2 Halstead Metrics

In 1977, Maurice Halstead put forth what are now known as Halstead complexity measures or metrics. These are metrics for measuring software complexity. Halstead posited several metrics for software complexity, as shown in Table 4.1.

TABLE 4.1 Halstead Metrics

Metric	Value
n1	Number of distinct operators
n2	Number of distinct operands
N1	Total number of occurrences of operators
N2	Total number of occurrences of operands
n1*	Number of potential operators
n2*	Number of potential operands

Using these metrics, Halstead arrived at some relatively simple formulas for calculating software complexity.

Program length: $N = N1 + N2$

Program vocabulary: $n = n1 + n2$

Volume: $V = N \times \log_2 n$

Difficulty: $D = \dfrac{n_1}{2} \times \dfrac{N_2}{n_2}$

Effort: $E = D \times V$

While the mathematics presented are quite simple, the concepts are effective and useful. As one example, the program length is a function of the total number of occurrences of operators added to the total number of occurrences of operands. This approach to software complexity captures the essence of what is important in a program. It is capturing the point where activity takes place (the operands and operators). The effort calculation is also quite effective: the volume of code multiplied by the difficulty of the code. This, in turn, is predicated in the difficulty calculation, which is based on operators and operands.

4.4 Coding Theory

Coding theory is yet another central aspect of computer science. The concept is to study various codes and to improve efficiency. There are four major types of codes:

- Error control

- Data compression

- Line coding

- Cryptographic coding

Error detection and correction is central to many parts of computer science, including network communication. There are several ways of detecting errors, but two that are simple to understand are checksums and cyclic redundancy checks (CRCs). A checksum is a sum of the message, usually using modular arithmetic. The recipient can recalculate the sum and compare it to the sum the sender calculated to detect any errors. CRCs are a very similar concept. Usually a CRC will be based on the remainder of a polynomial division of the message contents.

Data compression is quite common. It is likely that you have used some data compression algorithm—perhaps WinZip, 7-Zip, or RAR. The concept is to compress the message in such a way that data is still intact when it is decompressed. There are two major types of compression. The first is lossless. As the name suggests, no bits are lost in the compression. The second type is lossy. A popular lossless algorithm is the Lempel-Ziv compression methods. Some bits are lost, but they are nonessential. JPEG, MPEG, and MP3 formats use lossy compression.

A line code is a pattern used to represent data on a transmission line. For example, if you have the typical cable-connected network access to your computer, the data has to be represented as a pattern of voltages. In fiber-optic cables, the data must be represented as light waves.

Cryptographic encoding is the process of changing a message so that it should only be recoverable with the proper key. There are two main branches of cryptographic algorithms: symmetric and asymmetric. Symmetric algorithms utilize the same key to encrypt and decrypt. Examples include AES, Serpent, Blowfish, and RC4. Asymmetric algorithms use one key to encrypt the message and another key to decrypt it. Examples include Elliptic Curve Cryptography, RSA, and NTRUEncrypt.

All of these disparate coding methods are part of coding theory. Understanding how to efficiently encode and decode information is central to most computer operations. Certainly, network communications are not possible without line encoding, and it is likely the multimedia would not be practical without compression algorithms.

4.5   Logic Gates

Logic gates play a critical role in computer science and are a central issue in quantum computing. In traditional computers, logic gates are implemented usually via transistors, or some similar object. They perform a basic logical operation on input to produce output. Keep in mind that a classical computer can only see 1s and 0s. Thus, binary numbers and binary operations are ultimately all the computer works with. You may ultimately be performing trigonometry or calculus, but the computer has to break this down into binary math steps.

Before proceeding into logic gates, a brief discussion of basic binary operations is in order. For many readers, this will be a review, but in case it is not, this is essential to understanding classical computer logic gates. The binary number system was developed in its modern form by Gottfried Leibniz. He and Isaac Newton independently discovered calculus. The three operations of interest are AND, OR, and XOR operations.

4.5.1   AND

To perform the AND operation, you take two binary numbers and compare them one place at a time. If both numbers have a 1 in both places, then the resultant number is a 1. Otherwise, the resultant number is a 0, as you see here:

```
1 1 0 0
1 0 0 1
_____
1 0 0 0
```

4.5.2   OR

The OR operation tests to determine if there is a 1 in either or both numbers in a given place. If so, then the resultant number is 1. Otherwise, the resultant number is 0, as you see here:

```
1 1 0 0
1 1 0 1
_____
1 1 0 1
```

4.5.3   XOR

The XOR operation tests if there is a 1 in a number in a given place, but *not* in both numbers at that place. If it is in one number but not the other, then the resultant number is 1. Otherwise, the resultant number is 0, as you see here:

```
1 1 0 1
1 0 0 1
_____
0 1 0 0
```

The term XOR means "exclusively OR" rather than and/or. XORing has a very interesting property in that it is reversible. If you XOR the resultant number with the second number, you get back the first number, and if you XOR the resultant number with the first number, you get the second number:

```
0  1  0  0
1  0  0  1
_____
1  1  0  1
```

In the 1930s, an engineer at NEC named Akira Nakashima introduced a switching circuit theory using two-valued Boolean algebra. This is often considered the beginning of modern logic gates. There are standards for symbols used in logic gates: first, the ANSI/IEEE Std 91-1984, then the revision, ANSI/IEEE Std 91a-1991.

4.5.4   Application of Logic Gates

The AND gate implements a truth table that uses the binary AND operation. It may be helpful to first consider the ANSI/IEEE standard diagram for an AND gate, shown in Figure 4.8.

FIGURE 4.8   The AND gate

Two inputs lead to a single output. This is done with a simple truth table, much like the one shown in Table 4.2.

TABLE 4.2   Truth Table for AND

Input A	Input B	Output
1	1	1
1	0	0
0	0	0
0	1	0

Thus, what the AND gate does is take in two bits as input and perform the binary AND operation on them. It then ends out the output.

The OR gate is quite similar. The ANSI/IEEE symbol is shown in Figure 4.9.

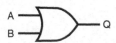

FIGURE 4.9   The OR gate

The two inputs lead to a single output. This is accomplished using a truth table, much like the one you saw in the previous table, only with the binary OR operation instead of AND (see Table 4.3).

TABLE 4.3   Truth Table for OR

Input A	Input B	Output
1	1	1
1	0	1
0	0	0
0	1	1

Of course, there is also an XOR gate for the "exclusive or" operation. This is sometimes referred to as an EOR gate or an EXOR gate. Figure 4.10 shows the ANSI/IEEE symbol for the XOR gate.

FIGURE 4.10   The XOR gate

The two inputs lead to a single output. This is accomplished using a truth table much like the ones you saw in the previous two tables, only with the binary XOR operation being used rather than AND or OR (see Table 4.4).

TABLE 4.4   Truth Table for XOR

Input A	Input B	Output
1	1	0
1	0	1
0	0	0
0	1	1

These three are simple logic gates, based on the basic three binary operations; however, there are many variations. A very common gate used is the NAND gate, which is a NOT-AND gate. Basically, it outputs false, only when all of the inputs are 1 (true). There are many systems using NAND gates. Figure 4.11 shows the ANSI/IEEE symbol for the NAND gate.

FIGURE 4.11   The NAND gate

The truth table for this one essentially says that if it is NOT an AND value (i.e., not both values a 1), then output 0 (see Table 4.5).

TABLE 4.5   Truth Table for NAND

Input A	Input B	Output
1	1	0
1	0	1
0	0	1
0	1	1

The NAND gate is very important because any Boolean function can be implemented using some combination of NAND gates. Another gate that has this property is the NOT-OR (or NOR) gate. Figure 4.12 shows the ANSI/IEEE symbol for a NOR gate.

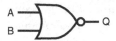

FIGURE 4.12   The NOR gate

The truth table for this one essentially says that if it is NOT an OR value (i.e., neither value is a 1), then output 0 (see Table 4.6).

TABLE 4.6   Truth Table for NOR

Input A	Input B	Output
1	1	0
1	0	0
0	0	1
0	1	0

Because either NOR gates or NAND gates can be used to create any Boolean function, they are called *universal gates*.

You might be wondering how explicitly 1s and 0s are implemented in circuitry. A common method is for a high voltage value to be a 1, and low to be a 0. So, you can see how ultimately mathematical operations are reduced to electricity flowing through logic gates and binary operations being performed on them.

The Hadamard gate is one of the more common logic gates utilized by a quantum computer. We will discuss these gates and others in more detail in later chapters. However, a brief introduction here provides a contrast to classical logic gates. The Hadamard gate acts on a single qubit and is a one-qubit version of the quantum Fourier transform. It is often denoted by the Hadamard matrix shown in Equation 4.1.

$$H = \frac{1}{\sqrt{2}} \begin{bmatrix} 1 & 1 \\ 1 & -1 \end{bmatrix}$$

EQUATION 4.1   The Hadamard Matrix

Hadamard matrices are named after the mathematician Jacques Hadamard. They are square matrices whose rows are orthogonal. They are used in quantum computing to represent a logical gate, the Hadamard gate.

4.6   Computer Architecture

Computer architecture is how we design and describe computer systems. Instruction set architecture is a substantial subtopic of computer architecture. While human programs deal with programming languages such as C++ and Java, the machine has instruction sets that are used for low-level actions. If you have ever looked at assembly language, you have seen something quite close to the actual computer instructions on the microprocessors. Assembly gets its name from the fact that software named an assembler translates the assembly code into machine code.

There are several subtopics in the field of computer architecture. Instruction Set Architecture (ISA) is the model of the architecture that is realized in things like the central processing unit. The ISA defines data types, registers, addressing, virtual memory, and other fundamental features of the computer. There are many different ways to classify architecture. Two common ways are the CISC (complex instruction set) and RISC (reduced instruction set). CISC processors have a large number of specialized instruction, whereas RISC implements a smaller set of instructions. This, of course, brings us to the question, what is an instruction? An instruction is a simple statement of what the processor should do. It often involves moving small pieces of data into and out of registers in the CPU. For example, in basic arithmetic, the contents of two registers are used and the result is then stored in a register. There are also control flow operations such as branching to another location (including conditionally branching) and calling some other block of code.

Assembly code is how one directly programs code for a CPU. The code tends to be substantially longer than other programming languages such as Java, Python, C, etc. This is because the programmer must issue every step of a command. To show the difference, "Hello, World!" in C is written like this:

```
printf("Hello, World!");
```

In Java, the program is written like this:

```
System.out.println("Hello, World!");
```

In assembly code, however, it is written like this:

```
        global    _start

        section   .text
_start: mov       rax, 1        ; system call for write
        mov       rdi, 1           ; file handle 1 is stdout
        mov       rsi, message  ; address of string to output
        mov       rdx, 13          ; number of bytes
        syscall                     ; invoke system to write
        mov       rax, 60
        xor       rdi, rdi         ; exit code 0
        syscall                  ; invoke system  to exit
        section   .data
message: db       "Hello, World", 10    ; note the newline at the end
```

The reason for this apparent complexity is that the programmer has to literally move data onto and off of specific CPU registries. Programming assembly gives one a really good understanding of CPU architecture.

Microarchitecture deals with how a processor is actually organized. This is the computer engineering of the processing chip, and it generally leads to diagrams such as the one shown in Figure 4.13.

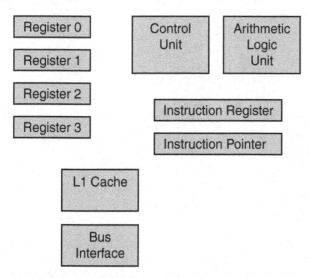

FIGURE 4.13 The CPU architecture

The image in Figure 4.13 is a very simplified CPU architecture, but it is useful for getting the general idea of microarchitecture. The idea is to design the various processing pathways. In Figure 4.13, we see just the general overview of the CPU. Memory is mapped out similarly, as are the various components of a motherboard, including the bus. The bus is the communication pathway for data transfer inside of a computer.

When designing computers, one has a number of factors to consider. Power requirements, capacity, and latency are three such factors. Computer performance is often measured by instructions per cycle (also called instructions per clock). This is the mean number of instructions that can be executed each clock cycle. The clock signal oscillates between a high state and a low state, thus the need to use the arithmetic mean to measure it. Taking the instructions per cycle and multiplying that by the clock rate (cycles per second, measured in Hertz) will produce the number of instructions per second a processor handle.

This is relevant to quantum computing; as we will see in later chapters, the design of quantum computers is a critical element of quantum computing. The two major divisions we will explore later in this book (particularly in Chapter 8, "Quantum Architecture") are adiabatic quantum computing and gate-based quantum computing. These two different approaches to architecture are significant in the advance of quantum computing.

4.7 Summary

This chapter provided an overview of the fundamental concepts of computer science. Perhaps the most important topic in this chapter to help you understand quantum computing is logic gates. A close second is the topic of algorithms. Ensure that you completely understand both before proceeding. However, we also reviewed the basics of computer architecture and examined data structures. There was also a brief coverage of computational complexity. All of these topics will help you understand the quantum computing topics we will explore in later chapters.

Algorithm analysis and data structures are critical to quantum computing as well as classical computing. Understanding basic computer architecture is also important to understanding any form of computing, and you cannot really understand quantum logic gates without some understanding of classical logical gates. The material in this chapter will provide a foundation for understanding quantum architecture and quantum logic gates.

Test Your Skills

REVIEW QUESTIONS

1. With a structure that's a list of data, where is data added?

   a. In a sequential fashion

   b. At the top

   c. Anywhere

   d. At the bottom

2. With a queue, how is data added?

   a. In a sequential fashion

   b. At the top

   c. Anywhere

   d. At the bottom

3. Which algorithm analysis method gives the best case of the algorithm?

   a. Omega

   b. Big O

   c. Theta

   d. Cyclomatic complexity

4. Which algorithm analysis method gives the average case of the algorithm?

   a. Omega

   b. Big O

   c. Theta

   d. Cyclomatic complexity

5. Which sorting algorithm is the slowest?

   a. Bubble sort

   b. Quick sort

   c. Merge sort

   d. It depends on the implementation.

6. Which of the following logic gates is most commonly used in computers?

   a. NAND

   b. OR

   c. AND

   d. XOR

7. The following symbol is used for which gate?

   a. NAND

   b. OR

   c. AND

   d. XOR

8. Which gate will output false only when all the inputs are true (1)?

   a. AND

   b. OR

   c. XOR

   d. NAND

9. Why are NOR and NAND gates referred to as universal gates?

   a. They are so widely used.

   b. They are not; XOR is the universal gate.

   c. They can be used to create any Boolean function.

   d. They are used in all architectures.

10. The _____ defines data types, registers, addressing, virtual memory, and other fundamental features of the computer.

    a. complex instruction set

    b. microarchitecture

    c. instruction register

    d. Instruction Set Architecture

Chapter | **5**

Basic Information Theory

Chapter Objectives

After reading this chapter and completing the review questions, you will be able to do the following:

- Understand basic information theory
- Calculate information entropy
- Recognize information diversity

Information theory is central to computer science, and it is important in quantum computing. The topic of information theory was introduced by Claude Shannon in his 1948 paper, "A Mathematical Theory of Communication." Shannon was primarily concerned with signal processing, data compression, and related topics. However, the field of information theory has grown since then. The focus of information theory is quantifying and communicating information. The field of information theory is closely related to data compression, machine learning, complexity science, and many other topics.

We will take a somewhat different approach in this chapter. First, you will be introduced to the basics of probability and set theory. These are needed to understand information theory. It is quite likely that for many readers, these sections will simply be reviews. However, if you don't have a basic grasp of probability and set theory, these sections are quite essential for understanding information theory.

These topics are all quite important to understanding quantum computing. All too often it is assumed the reader is familiar with them. Probability is important first because, as you will see throughout this book, quantum physics is largely probabilistic rather than deterministic. Information theory is important to understanding any aspect of computing, including quantum computing.

5.1 Basic Probability

There is a strong relationship between information theory and probability. Even the formula for calculating information entropy uses probability. Therefore, it is important to have a general understanding of probability to fully understand information theory. It is most likely that this section will be a review for most readers.

The first task is to define what *probability* is. In simplest terms, it is a ratio between the number of outcomes of interest divided by the number of possible outcomes. For example, if I have a deck of cards consisting of 52 cards, made up of four suits of 13 cards each, the probability of pulling a card of a given suit is 13/52, or ¼, which equals .25. Probabilities are always between zero and one. Zero indicates absolutely no chance of an event occurring. For example, if I have removed all 13 clubs from a deck, the odds of then pulling a club are zero. A probability of 1.0 indicates the event is certain. For example, if I remove all the cards except for hearts, then the probability of drawing a heart is 1.0. The probability of event A is a numerical measure of the likelihood of the event occurring. In the next subsection, we will examine some basic probability rules that will be explored.

5.1.1 Basic Probability Rules

The probability of any event will be between zero and one, or $0 <= P <= 1.0$.

The complement of an event is simply that event not occurring. If I pick a card from a deck, the probability of it being a heart can be easily calculated. The probability of it not being a heart is the complement of that probability. The probability of the complement of an event is equal to 1 minus the probability of the event—or put another way: $P(A^c) = 1 - P(A)$. This means that if the probability of a given event A is .45, then its complement is $1 - .45$, or .55.

Related to complements is the rule of unions. This applies to two events that are not mutually exclusive. This rule states that the probability of a union of events is the probability of event A plus the probability of event B minus the probability of their intersection (or joint probability). This can be expressed as shown in Equation 5.1.

$$P(A \cup B) = P(A) + P(B) - P(A \cap B)$$

EQUATION 5.1 Union of Events That Are Not Mutually Exclusive

This is very similar to the set theory discussed in Chapter 1, "Introduction to Essential Linear Algebra." When you see terms such as union and intersection, they have the same meaning used in set theory.

For two mutually exclusive events, the probability of their union is simply the probability of event A plus the probability of event B, as shown in Equation 5.2.

$$P(A \cup B) = P(A) + P(B)$$

EQUATION 5.2 Union of Events That Are Mutually Exclusive

What about the probability of two independent events occurring? This is referred to as the joint probability of independent events. The calculation for the joint probability of independent events is simply the probability of event A multiplied by the probability of event B, but this applies only if the events are independent. If one event is dependent on the other, then different rules apply, as shown in Equation 5.3.

P(A and B) = P(A) * P(B)

EQUATION 5.3   Probability of Two Independent Events

So, if two events are independent and event A has a probability of .45 and event B has a probability of .85, then the probability of both events occurring is .45 * .85 = .3825.

Independent events are events whose probability has no relationship at all. Put another way, two events are independent if the following are true (conversely, the following statements are true if the two events are independent):

P (A|B) = P(A)

P (B|A) = P(B)

Conditional probability refers to the likelihood of an event occurring, given some other event occurring. The likelihood of event A occurring, given event B has occurred, is equal to the probability of the intersection of event A and event B divided by the probability of event B. This is shown in Equation 5.4.

$$P(A|B) = \frac{P(A \cap B)}{PB} = \frac{P(B|A)p(A)}{P(B)}$$

EQUATION 5.4   Conditional Probability

This rule obviously is not referring to situations where event B must follow event A, but where event A can lead to event B. For example, if it is cold, there is a certain probability that I will wear a jacket, but it does not absolutely follow that I will wear a jacket.

These are basic rules of probability. Information theory, as you will see, depends on probability, and as we have discussed in previous chapters, quantum physics is probabilistic rather than deterministic.

5.2   Set Theory

Probability often uses set theory; therefore, our discussion of probability will also integrate a basic overview of set theory. There was some discussion of set theory in Chapter 1, which will be expanded here. A *set* is a collection of objects, and these objects are called the members or elements of that set. If we have a set, we say that some objects belong (or do not belong) to this set or are (or are not) in the set. We also say that sets consist of their elements.

As with much of mathematics, terminology and notation are critical. So, let us begin our study of set theory in a similar fashion, building from simple concepts to more complex. The most simple I can think of is defining an element of a set. We say that x is a member of set A, which can be denoted as follows:

x ∈ A

Sets are often listed in brackets. For example, the set of all odd integers < 10 would be shown as follows:

A = {1, 3, 5, 7, 9}

And a member of that set would be denoted as follows:

3 ∈ A

Negation can be symbolized by a line through a symbol. For example,

2 ∉ A

meaning 2 is not an element of set A.

If a set is not ending, you can denote that with ellipses. For example, the set of all odd numbers (not just those less than 10) can be denoted as follows:

A = {1, 3, 5, 7, 9, 11, …}

You can also denote a set using an equation or formula that defines membership in that set. Sets can be related to each other; the most common relationships are briefly described in this section.

The union of sets is a key concept in set theory. If you have two sets, A and B, elements that are a member of A, B, or both represent the union of A and B, symbolized as A ∪ B. Figure 5.1 depicts this.

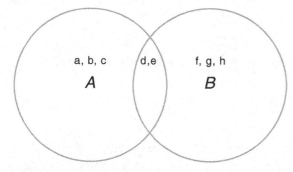

FIGURE 5.1 Union of sets

Items a, b, and c are in set A. Items f, g, and h are in set B. Items d and e are in both sets A and B. All the items, a through h, are in the union of sets A and B.

The intersection of two sets is the overlap of the two sets. If you have two sets, A and B, elements that are in both A and B are the intersection of sets A and B, symbolized as A ∩ B. Figure 5.2 illustrates this.

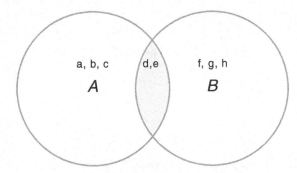

FIGURE 5.2   Intersection of sets

Only the items d and e are in the intersection of sets A and B.

If the intersection of sets A and B is empty (i.e., the two sets have no elements in common), then the two sets are said to be disjoint. Consider a deck of cards. The set of hearts has no items in common with the set of clubs. Therefore, the two sets are disjoint. Related to disjoint sets is the complement of a set. The *complement* of a set, denoted A', is the set of all elements in the given universal set U that are not in A. This is symbolized as A^c.

There is also the issue of the double complement: the complement of a set's complement is that set. In other words, the complement of A^c is A. This might seem odd at first read, but reflect on the definition of the complement of a set for just a moment. The complement of a set has no elements in that set. So, it stands to reason that to be the complement of the complement of a set, you would have to have all elements within the set.

Comparing two sets can also be of interest. This can involve determining the difference between the two sets. If you have two sets, A and B, elements that are in one set, but not both, are the difference between A and B. This is denoted as A \ B.

Now that we have covered the basic set terminology, a few additional facts about sets need to be discussed. Order is irrelevant: {1, 2, 3} is the same as {3, 2, 1} or {3, 1, 2} or {2, 1, 3}.

A common item that you will encounter is that of subsets. Set A could be a subset of set B. For example, if set A is the set of all odd numbers < 10 and set B is the set of all odd numbers < 100, then set A is a subset of set B. This is symbolized as A ⊆ B and shown in Figure 5.3.

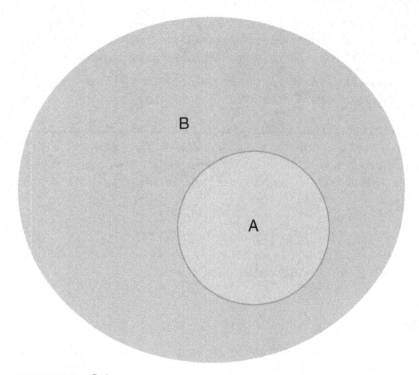

FIGURE 5.3 Subsets

Many sets may have subsets. Let us consider set A as all integers < 10. Set B is a subset; it is all prime numbers < 10. Set C is a subset of A; it is all odd numbers <10. Set D is a subset of A; it is all even numbers less than 10. We could continue this exercise making arbitrary subsets, such as E = {4, 7}, F = {1, 2, 3}, etc. The set of all subsets for a given set is called the *power set* for that set.

Sets also have properties that govern the interaction between sets. The most important of these properties are listed here:

- **Commutative law:** The intersection of set A with set B is equal to the intersection of set B with set A. The same is true for unions. Put another way, when considering intersections and unions of sets, the order in which the sets are presented is irrelevant. That is symbolized here:

    (a) $A \cap B = A \cap B$

    (b) $A \cup B = A \cup B$

- **Associative law:** Basically, if you have three sets, and the relationships between all three are all unions or all intersections, then the order does not matter. This is symbolized as follows:

    (a) $(A \cap B) \cap C = A \cap (B \cap C)$

    (b) $(A \cup B) \cup C = A \cup (B \cup C)$

- **Distributive law:** The distributive law is a bit different from the associative law, and order does not matter. The union of set A with the intersection of sets B and C is the same as taking the union of A and B intersected with the union of A and C. This is symbolized here:

    (a) $A \cup (B \cap C) = (A \cup B) \cap (A \cup C)$

    (b) $A \cap (B \cup C) = (A \cap B) \cup (A \cap C)$

- **De Morgan's laws:** These laws govern issues with unions and intersections and the complements thereof. These are more complex than the previously discussed properties. Essentially, the complement of the intersection of set A and set B is the union of the complement of A and the complement of B. The symbolism of De Morgan's laws is shown here:

    (a) $(A \cap B)^c = A^c \cup B^c$

    (b) $(A \cup B)^c = A^c \cap B^c$

These are the basic elements of set theory. Combined with probability, you should have the foundation to go deeper into information theory, which we will do in the following sections.

5.3   Information Theory

Claude Shannon is often called the father of information theory. He was a mathematician and engineer who lived from April 30, 1916 until February 24, 2001. Shannon's landmark paper was eventually expanded into a book, *The Mathematical Theory of Communication*, co-authored with Warren Weaver and published in 1963.

In his original paper, Shannon laid out some basic concepts that might seem very elementary today, particularly for those readers with an engineering or mathematics background. At the time, however, no one had ever attempted to quantify information or the process of communicating information. He began by quantifying some information concepts, with the following elementary terms that are illustrated in Figure 5.4:

- **Information source:** The producer of information. The sender of a message.
- **Transmitter:** Operates on the message to create a signal that can be sent through a channel.
- **Channel:** The medium for the signal.
- **Receiver:** Transforms the signal back into the message intended for delivery.
- **Destination:** A person or a machine for whom or for which the message is intended.

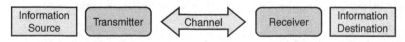

FIGURE 5.4 Information concepts

In addition to these concepts, Shannon also developed some general theorems that are important to communicating information, as described in Sections 5.3.1 and 5.3.2.

5.3.1 Theorem 1: Shannon's Source Coding Theorem

This theorem can be simply stated as follows: It is impossible to compress the data such that the code rate is less than the Shannon entropy of the source, without it being virtually certain that information will be lost. *Code rate* is a term from telecommunications and information theory. It refers to the proportion of the data that is useful. This is related to error correction codes. Error correction is important, as we will see later, and relevant to quantum computing.

In information theory, *entropy* is a measure of the uncertainty associated with a random variable. What this theorem is stating is that if you compress data in a way that the rate of coding is less than the information content, then it is very likely that you will lose some information. Shannon's coding theorem is important when compressing data.

5.3.2 Theorem 2: Noisy Channel Theorem

This theorem can be simply stated as follows: For any given degree of noise contamination of a communication channel, it is possible to communicate discrete data (digital information) nearly error-free up to a computable maximum rate through the channel. This theorem addresses the issue of noise on a given channel. Whether it is a radio signal or a network signal traveling through a twisted pair cable, there is usually noise involved in signal transmission. This theorem essentially states that even if there is noise, you can communicate digital information; however, there is some maximum rate at which you can compute information. That rate is computable and is related to how much noise there is in the channel.

5.3.3 Information Entropy

Information entropy is a key part of information theory. Shannon's landmark paper had an entire section, titled "Choice, Uncertainty and Entropy," that explored this topic in a very rigorous fashion. Entropy has a different meaning in information theory than it does in physics. Entropy, in the context of information, is a way of quantifying information content. There are two difficulties people have in mastering this concept, and I would like to address both. The first difficulty lies in confusing information entropy with thermodynamic entropy, which you probably encountered in elementary physics courses. In such courses, entropy is often described as the measure of disorder in a system. This is usually followed by a discussion of the second law of thermodynamics, which states that in a closed system, entropy tends to increase. In other words, without the addition of energy, a closed system will become more disordered over time. Before we can proceed to discuss information entropy, you need to firmly grasp that information entropy and thermodynamic entropy are simply not the same things. You should take the entropy definition you received in your freshman physics courses and put it out of your mind, at least for the time being.

The second problem you might have with understanding information theory is that so many references explain the concept in different ways, some of which can seem contradictory. In this section, I will demonstrate for you some of the common ways that information entropy is often described so that you can have a complete understanding of these seemingly disparate explanations.

In information theory, entropy is the amount of information in a given message. This is simple, easy to understand, and, as you will see, it is essentially synonymous with other definitions you may encounter. One example of an alternative explanation of information entropy is that it is sometimes described as the number of bits required to communicate information. This definition simply states that if you wish to communicate a message, that message contains information, and if you represent the information in binary format, how many bits of information is contained. It is entirely possible that a message might contain some redundancy, or even data you already have (which, by definition, would not be information). Thus, the number of bits required to communicate information could be less than the total bits in the message.

Another example of a definition that might sound peculiar to you is that many texts describe entropy as the measure of uncertainty in a message. This might sound a bit like the thermodynamics entropy definition I suggested you put out of your mind—and that might seem puzzling to some readers. I have defined information entropy as "the measure of uncertainty in a message" and "the number of bits required to communicate information." How can both of these be true? Actually, they are both saying the same thing. Let us examine the definition that is most likely causing you some consternation: entropy as a measure of uncertainty. It might help you to think of it in the following manner: *only uncertainty can provide information.* For example, if I tell you that right now, you are reading this book, this does not provide you with any new information. You already knew that, and there was absolutely zero uncertainty regarding that issue. However, the content you are about to read in the remaining chapters is uncertain. You don't know what you will encounter, at least not exactly. There is, therefore, some level of uncertainty, and thus information content. Put even more directly, *uncertainty is information.* If you are already certain about a given fact, then no information is communicated to you. New information clearly requires there was the uncertainty that the information you received cleared up. Therefore, the measure of uncertainty in a message is the measure of information in a message.

Let us begin to move toward a more mathematical definition of information entropy. Consider the formula shown in Equation 5.5.

$$H = -\sum_{i} p_i \, log_2(p_i)$$

EQUATION 5.5 Shannon Entropy

The symbol p_i denotes the probability of the occurrence of the ith category of the symbol in the string being examined. The symbol H denotes the Shannon entropy. The value is given in bits, thus log_2. This formula allows you to calculate the information entropy (i.e., Shannon entropy) in a given message.

For two variables or two messages that are independent, their *joint entropy* is the sum of the two entropies. That formula is shown in Equation 5.6.

$$H(X,Y) = -\sum_{x,y} p(x,y) \, log \, p(x,y)$$

EQUATION 5.6 Joint Entropy

If the two variables are not independent, but rather variable Y depends on variable X, then instead of joint entropy, you have *conditional entropy*. That formula is shown in Equation 5.7.

$$H(X|Y) = -\sum_{x,y} p(x,y) \, log \, p(x|y)$$

EQUATION 5.7 Conditional Entropy

Mutual information is a term for the amount of information that can be obtained about one random variable by observing another. The mutual information for X relative to Y is shown in Equation 5.8.

$$I(X;Y) = \sum_{x,y} p(x,y) log \frac{p(x,y)}{p(x)p(y)}$$

EQUATION 5.8 Mutual Information

Differential entropy, sometimes called *continuous entropy*, is an extension of Shannon entropy to measure the average "surprisal" of a random variable to continuous probability distributions. Remember that the information is the level of uncertainty or "surprise" in a message. Unfortunately, Shannon's formula for this was actually not correct. Shannon's formula was adjusted to produce the limiting density of discrete points (LDDP). This formula is given in Equation 5.9.

$$\lim_{N \to \infty} H_N(X) = \log(N) - \int p(x) \log \frac{p(x)}{m(x)} \, dx.$$

EQUATION 5.9 Limiting Density of Discrete Points

This formula requires a bit of basic calculus. If you will recall in Chapter 4, "Fundamental Computer Science for Quantum Computing," we gave a brief description of integrals, and any reader with even a single semester of calculus will recognize the limit.

As was discussed earlier, information theory has developed since Claude Shannon. Another type of information is Fisher information, which measures the amount of information in an observable variable X about an unknown parameter θ of some distribution that models X.

> **Note**
>
> Fisher information is a bit more mathematically challenging than what we have covered in this chapter. The interested reader can get more information on Fisher information from https://arxiv.org/pdf/1705.01064.pdf.

It should be clear that the topic of information theory and information entropy is a rather broad topic. There are a number of formulas for quantifying information in a range of scenarios. It is important that you have a basic working knowledge of information theory in order to proceed to later chapters that will discuss quantum information theory.

Table 5.1 summarizes the formulas for information theory presented in this section.

TABLE 5.1   Information Theory Formulas

Concept	Formula
Shannon information entropy	$H = -\sum_i p_i \, log_2 \, (p_i)$
Joint entropy	$H(X,Y) = -\sum_{x,y} p(x,y) \, log \, p(x,y)$
Conditional entropy	$H(X|Y) = -\sum_{x,y} p(x,y) \, log \, p(x|y)$
Mutual information	$I(X;Y) = \sum_{x,y} p(x,y) \, log \, \dfrac{p(x,y)}{p(x)p(y)}$
Differential entropy	$\lim_{N \to \infty} H_N(X) = log(N) - \int p(x) \, log \, \dfrac{p(x)}{m(x)} \, dx$

The interested reader can find more on information theory at https://d2l.ai/chapter_appendix-mathematics-for-deep-learning/information-theory.html.

5.3.4   Information Diversity

There are different metrics utilized as specific diversity indices for particular applications. One such diversity metric is the Shannon-Weaver index. This is sometimes referred to as the Shannon diversity index. The eponymously named Shannon diversity index was posited by Claude Shannon. Shannon used this metric to quantify the informational content in a given string of text. Shannon was most interested in electronic communications transmissions. When working with information theory, the information content of a message is referred to as the *information entropy*. The formula is shown in Equation 5.10.

$$H' = -\sum_{n=1}^{n}(pi^* \ln p_\mathrm{i})$$

EQUATION 5.10 Shannon-Weaver Index

In Equation 5.10, p_i denotes the proportion of symbols that are part of the class of the ith class of symbol in the string. H' symbolizes the Shannon diversity index (also referred to as the Shannon-Weaver diversity index). This is shown in Equation 5.11.

$$H = -\sum_{i=1}^{S} p_i \ln p_i$$

EQUATION 5.11 Shannon-Weaver Index, Form 2

In Equation 5.11, S is the number of individual species found in the community being studied. The p_i is still the proportion of symbols that are part of the ith category of the symbol in the text string of interest. There are several variants of the Simpson index. Four examples of such variations are the Berger–Parker index, the Inverse Simpson index, the Dominance index, and the Gini-Simpson index.

Hartley entropy was introduced by Ralph Hartley in 1928 and thus predates Shannon's work on information theory. This is often simply called the Hartley function. If a sample from a finite set A uniformly is picked at random, the information revealed after the outcome is known is given by the Hartley function, shown in Equation 5.12.

$$H_0(A) := log_b|A|$$

EQUATION 5.12 Hartley Entropy

In Equation 5.12, $|A|$ denotes the cardinality of A. If the base of the logarithm is 2, then the unit of uncertainty is now referred to as the Shannon. If it is the natural logarithm, then the unit is the nat. Hartley used a base 10 logarithm, and with this base, the unit of information is called the Hartley in his honor. Like the Shannon-Weaver and Simpson indices, the Hartley entropy provides insight regarding the diversity in a given dataset.

Related to some of the previous entropy values discussed so far is the Rényi entropy, which generalizes the Hartley entropy, the Shannon entropy, the collision entropy, and the min-entropy, as shown in Equation 5.13.

$$H_\alpha(X) = \frac{1}{1-\alpha} \log \left(\sum_{i=1}^{n} p_i^\alpha \right)$$

EQUATION 5.13 Rényi Entropy

In Equation 5.13, X is a discrete random variable with possible outcomes (*1, 2, ..., n*) and corresponding probabilities, p_i, for *i = 1* to *n*. Because this metric is generally used in information theory, the logarithm is typically base 2, and the order, α, is $0 < \alpha < 1$.

Collision entropy is basically a special case of the Rényi entropy, where $\alpha = 0$ and where X and Y are independent and are identically distributed. The formula for collision entropy is shown in Equation 5.14.

$$H_2(X) = -log_P(X = Y)$$

EQUATION 5.14 Collision Entropy

Min-entropy is the smallest of the Rényi entropies. The min-entropy will always be less than or equal to the standard Shannon entropy discussed earlier in this section.

The Rényi entropy is a measure of the diversity in a dataset. The Rényi entropy is also important in quantum information, where it can be used as a measure of entanglement. As with other diversity metrics, this can be useful in fully understanding the data flow between two or more network nodes.

Another important measure of information entropy is Gibbs entropy. This will be directly used in the following section on quantum information. The Gibbs entropy characterizes the state of a system by the distribution of the microstates. The formula is actually rather simple and is shown in Equation 5.15.

$$s = k_b \sum_{1^1} P_i \ln p_i$$

EQUATION 5.15 Gibbs Entropy Formula

In Equation 5.15, many of the symbols should already be familiar to you. A new symbol is K_b. This is the Boltzmann constant. The Boltzmann constant relates to the average kinetic energy of particles in a gas. In this case, it is related to the particles in a given system.

5.4 Quantum Information

Now that you have been introduced to information theory, it is time to discuss a few aspects of quantum information theory. We will address some aspects of quantum information theory in this section. Others will be introduced as appropriate when we discuss quantum algorithms and related topics in later chapters, including the next chapter.

We have not yet delved into qubits. We will discuss qubits in more detail in Chapter 6, "Basic Quantum Theory," Chapter 7, "Quantum Entanglement and QKD," and Chapter 10, "Quantum Algorithms." For the time being, let us just say that these are the quantum versions of bits, and that these qubits have a probabilistic, not deterministic, outcome. The no-teleportation theory simply states than an arbitrary quantum state (the state of a qubit) cannot be converted into a sequence of classical bits. The term *teleportation*, in this application, is a bit of a misnomer. This is due, at least in part, to the Heisenberg uncertainty theorem we discussed in Chapter 3, "Basic Physics for Quantum Computing."

The no-teleportation theory is closely related to the no-cloning theorem. The no-cloning theorem states that it is not possible to create an identical copy of an arbitrary unknown quantum state. In other words, you cannot make an identical copy of a qubit with an unknown state. To better understand that, compare it to classical bits. If I know the address of a bit, or series of bits, I can certainly make an identical copy without knowing the content. However, I cannot do that with qubits.

Just as there are measures of information entropy for classical information theory, there are measures of quantum information entropy. Probably the most common entropy is the von Neumann entropy. This is an extension of classical Gibbs entropy. The von Neumann entropy formula is shown in Equation 5.16.

$$s\,(p) = -tr(p\,ln\,p)$$

EQUATION 5.16 The von Neumann Entropy Formula

The p represents the density matrix, which describes the state of a quantum system. Remember that quantum systems are probabilistic; therefore, the density matrix is describing the statistical state of the system. The tr represents the trace, which in linear algebra is the sum of the elements on the main diagonal, going from the upper left to the lower right of the matrix. The von Neumann entropy is used in a variety of different applications in quantum information theory, particularly to describe the entropy of entanglement. Chapter 7 discusses entanglement in more detail.

Another such example is the conditional relative entropy. This is a measure of the distinguishability of two quantum states. The states are represented by matrices, and the formula is shown in Equation 5.17.

$$s(A|B)p$$

EQUATION 5.17 Conditional Quantum Entropy

The p is the density matrix described in reference to the von Neumann entropy.

For readers who wish to delve more into this topic, I recommend the following resources:

https://authors.library.caltech.edu/66493/2/chap10_15.pdf

https://arxiv.org/pdf/quant-ph/0412063.pdf

https://sitp.stanford.edu/topic/quantum-information

5.5 Summary

Information theory is important for understanding quantum computing. In this chapter, you were introduced first to basic probability and set theory. Then you were given a tour of information theory, which applies probability and set theory. The most important concepts from this chapter are how to calculate probabilities and information entropy. You will find these concepts revisited later in a quantum context. We also covered some basic concepts of quantum information theory.

Test Your Skills

REVIEW QUESTIONS

1. You are concerned about the probability of two independent events occurring. Event A has a probability of .5, and event B has a probability of .2. What is the probability of both occurring?

    a. .7

    b. .1

    c. .6

    d. 1

2. If events A and B are mutually exclusive, and event A has a probability of .25 and event B has a probability of .3, what is the probability of A or B?

    a. .55

    b. .075

    c. .475

    d. .3

3. If events A and B are not mutually exclusive and event A has a probability of .25 and event B has a probability of .3, what is the probability of A or B?

    a. .55

    b. .075

    c. .475

    d. .3

4. Given A = {1, 3, 5, 7, 9}, the symbolism for the number 4 is which of the following?

    a. $4 \in A$

    b. $4 \notin A$

    c. $4 \cup A$

    d. $4 \cap A$

5. Given set A is the set of all fruit and set B is the set of all red foods, what best describes apples?

   a. The union of A and B.

   b. The intersection of A and B.

   c. B is an element of A.

   d. A and B are disjoint.

6. When 3 bits of data are sent through a CAT 6 cable, what is the transmitter?

   a. The cable

   b. The sending computer

   c. The electrical current

   d. The switch

7. This theorem essentially states that even if there is noise, you can communicate digital information. This best describes which of the following?

   a. Information entropy

   b. Source coding theorem

   c. Noisy channel theorem

   d. Rényi entropy

8. For two variables or two messages that are independent, how their joint entropy is calculated?

   a. Adding the two entropies

   b. Multiplying the two entropies

   c. Adding the two entropies and dividing by the conditional entropy

   d. Multiplying the two entropies and dividing by the conditional entropy

9. What does the following formula describe?

$$H(X,Y) = -\sum_{x,y} p(x,y) \, log \, p(x,y)$$

   a. Joint entropy

   b. von Neumann entropy

   c. Rényi entropy

   d. Shannon entropy

10. _____ describes the state of a quantum system.

   a. No-teleportation theorem

   b. No-cloning theorem

   c. The trace

   d. A density matrix

Chapter | **6**

Basic Quantum Theory

Chapter Objectives

After reading this chapter and completing the quizzes, you will be able to do the following:

- Use bra-ket notation
- Understand the Hamiltonian operator
- Have a working knowledge of wave functions and the wave function collapse
- Recognize the role of Schrödinger's equation
- Know the role of quantum decoherence and its impact on quantum computing
- Have a generalized understanding of quantum electrodynamics
- Demonstrate basic knowledge of quantum chromodynamics

This chapter will introduce you to various aspects of quantum theory. Some of these topics were briefly touched on in Chapter 3, "Basic Physics for Quantum Computing." It is essential that you have a strong grasp of Chapters 1 through 3 in order to follow along in this chapter. The first issue to address is what precisely is quantum theory? It is actually a number of related theories, including quantum field theory, quantum electrodynamics (QED), and in some physicists' opinion, even quantum chromodynamics, which deals with quarks. In this chapter, the goal is to deepen the knowledge you gained in Chapter 3 and to provide at least a brief introduction to a range of topics that all fit under the umbrella of quantum theory.

In this chapter, it is more important than ever to keep in mind our goal. Yes, I will present a fair amount of mathematics, some of which may be beyond some readers. However, unless your goal is to do actual work in the field of quantum physics or quantum computing research, then what you need is simply a general comprehension of what the equations mean. You do not need to have the level of mathematical acumen that would allow you to actually do the math. So, if you encounter some math you find daunting, simply review it a few times to ensure you get the general gist of it and move on. You can certainly work with qubits, Q#, and other quantum tools later in this book without a deep understanding of how to do the mathematics.

6.1 Further with Quantum Mechanics

Chapter 3 introduced some fundamental concepts in quantum physics. This section expands our exploration of quantum mechanics a bit. In 1932, Werner Heisenberg was awarded the Nobel Prize in Physics for the "creation of quantum mechanics." I am not sure that one person can be solely credited with the creation of quantum mechanics, but certainly Heisenberg deserves that credit as much as anyone.

The publication that earned him the Nobel Prize was titled "Quantum-Theoretical Re-interpretation of Kinematic and Mechanical Relations." This paper is rather sophisticated mathematically, and we won't be exploring it in detail here. The paper introduced a number of concepts that formed the basis of quantum physics. The interested reader can consult several resources, including the following:

https://arxiv.org/pdf/quant-ph/0404009.pdf

https://www.heisenberg-gesellschaft.de/3-the-development-of-quantum-mechanics-1925-ndash-1927.html

https://inis.iaea.org/collection/NCLCollectionStore/_Public/08/282/8282072.pdf

6.1.1 Bra-Ket Notation

Bra-ket notation was introduced a bit earlier, in Chapter 3. However, this notation is so essential to understanding quantum physics and quantum computing that we will revisit it, with more detail. Recall that quantum states are really vectors. These vectors include complex numbers. However, it is often possible to ignore the details of the vector and work with a representation of the vector. This notation is called Dirac notation or bra-ket notation.

A *bra* is denoted by $\langle V|$, and a *ket* is denoted by $|V\rangle$. Yes, the terms are intentional, meaning *braket*, or *bracket*. But what does this actually mean? A bra describes some linear function that maps each vector in V to a number in the complex plane. Bra-ket notation is really about linear operators on complex vector spaces, and it is the standard way that states are represented in quantum physics and quantum computing. One reason for this notation is to avoid confusion. The term *vector* in linear algebra is a bit different from the term *vector* in classical physics. In classical physics, a vector denotes something like velocity that has magnitude and direction; however, in quantum physics, a vector (linear algebra vector) is used to represent a quantum state, thus the need for a different notation. It is important to keep in mind that these are really just vectors. Therefore, the linear algebra that you saw in Chapter 1, "Introduction to Essential Linear Algebra," applies.

6.1.2 Hamiltonian

It is important that you be introduced to the Hamiltonian. A Hamiltonian is an operator in quantum mechanics. It represents the sum of the kinetic and potential energies (i.e., the total energy) of all the particles in a given system. The Hamiltonian can be denoted by an H, <H>, or $\hat{H}$. When one measures the total energy of a system, the set of possible outcomes is the spectrum of the Hamiltonian. The Hamiltonian is named after William Hamilton. As you may surmise, there are multiple different ways of representing the Hamiltonian. In Equation 6.1, you see a simplified version of the Hamiltonian.

$$\hat{H} = \hat{T} + \hat{v}$$

EQUATION 6.1 The Hamiltonian

The $\hat{T}$ represents the kinetic energy, and the $\hat{v}$ represents the potential energy. The T is a function of p (the momentum), and V is a function of q (the special coordinate). This simply states that the Hamiltonian is the sum of kinetic and potential energies. This particular formulation is rather simplistic and not overly helpful. It represents a one-dimensional system with one single particle of mass, m. This is a good place to start understanding the Hamiltonian. Equation 6.2 shows a better formulation.

$$H_{operator} = -\frac{-h^2}{2m}\frac{\partial^2}{\partial x^2} + v_{(x)}$$

EQUATION 6.2 The Hamiltonian (Detailed)

Let us examine this formula to understand it. The simplest part is V(x), which simply represents potential energy. The x is the coordinate in space. Also rather simple to understand is the m, which is the mass. The $-\hbar^2$, as you will recall from Chapter 3, is the reduced Planck constant, which is the Planck constant h (6.626×10^{-34} J·s) / 2π. The ∂ symbol indicates a partial derivative. For some readers, this will be quite familiar. If you are not acquainted with derivatives and partial derivatives, you need not master those topics to continue with this book, but a brief conceptual explanation is in order. It should also be noted that there are many other ways of expressing this equation. You can see an alternative way at https://support.dwavesys.com/hc/en-us/articles/360003684614-What-Is-the-Hamiltonian-.

With any function, the derivative of that function is essentially a measurement of the sensitivity of the function's output with respect to a change in the function's input. A classic example is calculating an object's position with respect to change in time, which provides the velocity. A partial derivative is a function of multiple variables, and the derivative is calculated with respect to one of those variables.

So, you should now have a general conceptual understanding of the Hamiltonian. Our previous discussion only concerned a single particle. In a system with multiple particles (as are most systems), the Hamiltonian of the system is just the sum of the individual Hamiltonians, as demonstrated in Equation 6.3.

$$\hat{H} = \sum_{n=1}^{N} \hat{T}_n + \hat{V}$$

EQUATION 6.3 Hamiltonian (Another View)

Let us delve a bit deeper into the Hamiltonian. Any operator can be written in a matrix form. Now recall our discussion of linear algebra in Chapter 1. The eigenvalues of the Hamiltonian are the energy levels of the system. For the purposes of this book, it is not critical that you understand this at a deep working level, but you should begin to see intuitively why linear algebra is so important for quantum physics.

It also is interesting to note the relationship between the Hamiltonian and the Lagrangian. First, it is necessary to define the Lagrangian. Joseph-Louis Lagrange developed Lagrangian mechanics in 1788. It is essentially a reformulation of classical mechanics. Lagrangian mechanics uses the Lagrangian function of the coordinates, the time derivatives, and the times of the particles.

In Hamiltonian mechanics, the system is described by a set of canonical coordinates. Canonical coordinates are sets of coordinates on a phase space, which can describe a system at any given point in time. You can, in fact, derive the Hamiltonian from a Lagrangian. We won't delve into that topic in this chapter, but the interested reader can learn more about that process, and other details about the Hamiltonian, at the following sources:

https://scholar.harvard.edu/files/david-morin/files/cmchap15.pdf

https://www.damtp.cam.ac.uk/user/tong/dynamics/four.pdf

https://authors.library.caltech.edu/89088/1/1.5047439.pdf

6.1.3 Wave Function Collapse

In physics, a wave function is a mathematical description of the quantum state of a quantum system. It is usually represented by the Greek letter psi, either lowercase (ψ) or uppercase (Ψ). A wave function is a function of the degrees of freedom for the quantum system. In such a system, degrees of freedom indicate the number of independent parameters that describe the system's state. As one example, photons and electrons have a spin value, and that is a discrete degree of freedom for that particle.

A wave function is a superposition of possible states. More specifically, it is a superposition of eigenstates that collapses to a single eigenstate based on interaction with the environment. Chapter 1 discussed eigenvalues and eigenvectors. An eigenstate is basically what physicists call an eigenvector.

Wave functions can be added together and even multiplied (usually by complex numbers, which you studied in Chapter 2, "Complex Numbers") to form new wave functions. Recall the dot product we discussed in Chapter 1; the inner product is just another term for the dot product. This is also sometimes called the scalar product. Recall the inner/dot product is easily calculated, as shown in Equation 6.4.

$$\sum_{i=1}^{n} X_i Y_i$$

EQUATION 6.4   Inner Product

The inner product of two wave functions is a measure of the overlap between the two wave functions' physical state.

This brings us to another important aspect of quantum mechanics: the Born rule. This postulate was formulated by Max Born and is sometimes called the Born law or the Born postulate. The postulate gives the probability that a measurement of a quantum system will produce a particular result. The simplest form of this is the probability of finding a particle at a given point. That general description will be sufficient for you to continue in this book; however, if you are interested in a deeper under-standing, we will explore it now. The Born rule more specifically states that if some observable (position, momentum, etc.) corresponding to a self-adjoint operator A is measured in a system with a normalized wave function $|\psi\rangle$, then the result will be one of the eigenvalues of A. This should help you become more comfortable with the probabilistic nature of quantum physics.

For those readers not familiar with self-adjoint operators, a brief overview is provided. Recall from Chapter 1 that matrices are often used as operators. A self-adjoint operator on a finite complex vector space, with an inner product, is a linear map from the vector to itself that is its own adjoint. Note that it is a complex vector space. This bring us to Hermitian. Recall from Chapter 2 that Hermitian refers to a square matrix that is equal to its own conjugate transpose. Conjugate transpose means first taking the transpose of the matrix and then taking the complex conjugate of the matrix. Each linear operator on a complex Hilbert space also has an adjoint operator, sometimes called a Hermitian adjoint.

Self-adjoint operators have applications in fields such as functional analysis; however, in quantum mechanics, physical observables such as position, momentum, spin, and angular momentum are repre-sented by self-adjoint operators on a Hilbert space.

This is also a good time to discuss Born's rule, which provides the probability that a measurement of a quantum system will yield a particular result. More specifically, the Born rule states that the prob-ability density of finding a particular particle at a specific point is proportional to the square of the magnitude of the particle's wave function at that point. In more detail, the Born rule states that if an observable corresponding to a self-adjoint operator is measured in a system with a normalized wave function, the result will be one of the eigenvalues of that self-adjoint operator. There are more details to the Born rule, but this should provide you enough information. The interested reader can find more information at the following sources:

https://www.math.ru.nl/~landsman/Born.pdf

https://www.quantamagazine.org/the-born-rule-has-been-derived-from-simple-physical-principles-20190213/

Now let us return to the collapse of a wave function, which takes the superposition of possible eigenstates and collapses to a single eigenstate based on interaction with the environment. What is this interaction with the environment? This is one of the aspects of quantum physics that is often misunderstood by the general public. A common interaction with the environment is a measurement, which physicists often describe as an observation. This has led many to associate intelligent observation as a necessary condition for quantum physics, and thus all of reality. That is simply not an accurate depiction of what quantum physics teaches us.

What is termed an observation is actually an interaction with the environment. When a measurement is taken, that is an interaction that causes the wave function to collapse.

The fact that a measurement causes the wave function to collapse has substantial implications for quantum computing. When one measures a particle, one changes the state. As you will see in later chapters, particularly Chapter 8, "Quantum Architecture," and Chapter 9, "Quantum Hardware," this is something that quantum computing must account for.

The wave function can be expressed as a linear combination of the eigenstates (recall this is the physics term for eigenvectors you learned in Chapter 1) of an observable (position, momentum, spin, etc.). Using the bra-ket notation discussed previously, this means a wave function has a form such as you see in Equation 6.5.

$$\psi >= \Sigma_i \, c_i \big| \phi_i$$

EQUATION 6.5 Wave Function

This is not as complex as it seems. The Greek letter psi (ψ) denotes the wave function. The Σ symbol is a summation of what is after it. The ϕi represents various possible quantum states. The i is to enumerate through those possible states, such as $\phi 1$, $\phi 2$, $\phi 3$, etc. The c_i values (i.e., c1, c2, c3, etc.) are probability coefficients. The letter c is frequently used to denote these because they are represented by complex numbers.

Recall from Chapter 1 that if two vectors are both orthogonal (i.e., perpendicular to each other) and have a unit length (length 1), the vectors are said to be orthonormal. The bra-ket $\langle \phi_i | \phi_j \rangle$ forms an orthonormal eigenvector basis. This is often written as follows:

$$\langle \phi_i | \phi_j \rangle = \delta_{ij}.$$

The symbol δ is the Kronecker delta, which is a function of two variables. If the variables are equal, the function result is 1. If they are not equal, the function result is 0. This is usually defined as shown in Equation 6.6.

$$\delta_{ij} = \begin{cases} 0 & \text{if } i \neq j, \\ 1 & \text{if } i = j. \end{cases}$$

EQUATION 6.6 Kronecker Delta

Now let us discuss the actual process of the wave collapse. Remember that for any observable, the wave function is some linear combination of the eigenbasis before the collapse. When there is some environmental interaction, such as a measurement of the observable, the function collapses to just one of the base's eigenstates. This can be described in the following rather simple formula:

$$|\psi\rangle \rightarrow |\phi_i\rangle$$

But which state will it collapse to? That is the issue with quantum mechanics being probabilistic. We can say that it will collapse to a particular eigenstate $|\phi_k\rangle$ with the Born probability (recall we discussed this earlier in this chapter) $P_k = |c_k|^2$. The value c_k is the probability amplitude for that specific eigenstate. After the measurement, all the other possible eigenstates that are not k have collapsed to 0 (put a bit more mathematically, $c_i \neq k = 0$).

Measurement has been discussed as one type of interaction with the environment. One of the challenges for quantum computing is that this is not the only type of interaction. Particles interact with other particles. In fact, such things as cosmic rays can interact with quantum states of particles. This is one reason that decoherence is such a problem for quantum computing.

6.1.4   Schrödinger's Equation

The Schrödinger equation is quite important in quantum physics. It describes the wave function of a quantum system. This equation was published by Erwin Schrödinger in 1926 and resulted in his earning the Nobel Prize in Physics in 1933. First, let us examine the equation itself and ensure you have a general grasp of it; then we can discuss more of its implications. There are various ways to present this equation; we will first examine the time-dependent version. You can see this in Equation 6.7.

$$i\hbar \frac{\partial}{\partial t}|\psi(t)\rangle = \hat{H}|\psi(t)\rangle$$

EQUATION 6.7   Schrödinger Equation

Don't let this overwhelm you. All of the symbols used have already been discussed, and I will discuss them again here to refresh your memory.

Given that we are discussing a time-dependent version of the Schrödinger equation, it should be clear to most readers that the t represents time. Remember that the ∂ symbol indicates a partial derivative. So, we can see in the denominator that there is a partial derivative with respect to time. The $\hbar$, you will recall from Chapter 3 and from earlier in this chapter, is the reduced Planck constant, which is the Planck constant h (6.626×10^{-34} j * s) / 2π. The ψ symbol we saw earlier in this chapter. You may also recall that the symbol $\hat{H}$ denotes the Hamiltonian operator, which is the total energy of the particles in a system.

Before we examine the implications of the Schrödinger equation, let us first examine another form of the equation. You can see this in Equation 6.8.

$$\frac{\partial^2 \psi}{\partial x^2} + \frac{8\pi^2 m}{h^2}\,(E - V)\psi = 0$$

EQUATION 6.8   Schrödinger (Another Form)

You already know that the ∂ symbol indicates a partial derivative. The 2 superposed above it means this is a second derivative (i.e., a derivative of a derivative). For those readers who don't have a solid calculus background, or who don't recall their calculus, a second derivative is actually common. A first derivative tells you the rate of change for some function. A second derivative tells you the rate of change for that rate of change that you found in the first derivative. Probably the most common example is acceleration. Speed is the change in position with respect to time. That is the first derivative. Acceleration is the change in speed, which is a second derivative. The ψ symbol denotes the wave function, which you should be getting quite familiar with by now. Another symbol you are familiar with is the h, for Planck's constant. Note in this form of the Schrödinger equation that it is the Planck constant, not the reduced Planck constant. The E is the kinetic energy, and the V is the potential energy of the system. The X is the position.

Remember that in the subatomic world, we have the issue of wave-particle duality. The Schrödinger equation allows us to calculate how the wave function changes in time.

6.2   Quantum Decoherence

Quantum decoherence is a very important topic and is, in fact, critical for quantum computing. Decoherence is directly related to the previous section on wave functions. Recall that a wave function is a mathematical representation of the state of a quantum system. As long as there exists a definite phase relation between the states, that system is coherent. Also, recall that interactions with the environment cause a wave function to collapse. If one could absolutely isolate a quantum system so that it had no interaction at all with any environment, it would maintain coherence indefinitely. However, only by interacting with the environment can it be measured; thus, data can be extracted.

What does it mean to have a definite phase relation between states? First, we must examine the concept of *phase space*, which is a concept from dynamical system theory. It is a space in which all the possible states of the system are represented. Each state corresponds to a unique point in the phase space. Each parameter of the system represents a degree of freedom. In turn, each degree of freedom is represented as an axis of a multidimensional space. If you have a one-dimensional system, it is a phase line. Two-dimensional systems are phase planes.

Two values, p and q, play an important role in phase space. In classical mechanics, the p is usually momentum and the q the position. Now, in quantum mechanics, this phase space is a Hilbert space. Thus, the p and q are Hermitian operators in that Hilbert space. While momentum and position are the most common observables, and are most often used to define phase space, there are other observables such as angular momentum and spin.

To refresh your memory, a Hermitian operator is also called a self-adjoint operator. Remember, we are dealing with matrices/vectors, so the operators are themselves matrices. Most operators in quantum mechanics are Hermitian. Hermitian operators have some specific properties. They always have real eigenvalues, but the eigenvectors or eigenfunctions might include complex numbers. A Hermitian operator can be "flipped" to the other side if it appears in an inner product—something like what you see here:

$$\langle f|Ag\rangle = \langle Af|g\rangle$$

Hermitian operators' eigenfunctions form a "complete set." That term denotes that any function can be written as some linear combination of the eigenfunctions.

In general, if we are dealing with a non-relativistic model, the dimensionality of a system's phase space is the number of degrees of freedom multiplied by the number of systems-free particles. Non-relativistic spacetime is conceptually rather simple. Relativistic spacetime uses n dimensional space and m dimensional time. Non-relativistic spacetime fuses that into a single continuum. Put another way, it is simply ignoring the effects of relativity. At the subatomic level that is perfectly reasonable, as relativistic effects are essentially irrelevant.

So, when the system interacts with the environment, each environmental degree of freedom contributes another dimension to the phase space of the system. Eventually, the system becomes decoupled. There is actually a formula for this called the Wigner quasi-probability distribution. This is sometimes called the Wigner-Ville distribution or just the Wigner function. The details may be a bit more than are needed in this book; however, the general outline is certainly something we can explore. Eugene Wigner first introduced this formula in 1932 to examine quantum modifications to classical mechanics. The purpose was to link the wave function we have studied in Schrödinger's equation to a probability distribution in phase space.

Equation 6.9 shows the Wigner distribution.

$$W(x,p) \overset{\text{def}}{=} \frac{1}{\pi\hbar} \int_{-\infty}^{\infty} \psi^{*}(x+y)\psi(x-y)e^{2ipy/\hbar}\,dy$$

EQUATION 6.9 Wigner Distribution

By this point, you should not be daunted by complex-looking equations, and much of this equation use symbols you already know. But let us briefly examine them. Obviously, the W is the Wigner distribution. X is usually position and p momentum, but they could be any pair (frequency and time of a signal, etc.). Of course, ψ is the wave function, and $\hbar$ is the reduced Planck constant. We discussed the $\int$ symbol earlier in the book; it denotes integration. For our purposes, you don't have to have a detailed knowledge of the Wigner distribution, nor do you have to be able to "do the math." Rather, you just need a general understanding of what is happening.

In classical mechanics, a harmonic oscillator's motion could be completely described by a point in the phase space with the particle position x and momentum p. In quantum physics, this is not the case. Recall from Chapter 3 our discussion of Heisenberg's uncertainty principle. You cannot know with precision the position and momentum simultaneously, but by measuring x, p, or their linear combination on a set of identical quantum states, you can realize a probability density associated with these observables (x and p). The Wigner function accomplishes this goal. Our goal is to understand decoherence. The Wigner distribution shows the decoupling process because it shows the probability of various states.

6.3 Quantum Electrodynamics

Quantum electrodynamics (QED) is a topic that may be considered too advanced for an introductory book. The goal is simply for you to acquire a generalized understanding of the topic, and I believe that is an achievable goal. QED is the relativistic quantum field theory that applies to electrodynamics. It is the first theory wherein quantum mechanics and relativity are in full agreement. QED provides a mathematical description of phenomena that involve electrically charged particles.

Let us begin by defining the quantum field theory (QFT). QFT combines classical field theory, special relativity, and quantum mechanics. At this point, you should have a general working knowledge of quantum mechanics. Therefore, we will turn our attention to classical field theory and special relativity, providing a brief description of each.

Classical field theory describes how one or more fields interact with matter, via field equations. An easy-to-understand example is with weather patterns. The wind velocity at a given time can be described by a vector. Each vector describes the direction and movement of the air at a particular point. The set of all such vectors in a particular area at a given point in time would be a vector field. Over time, we would expect these vectors to change. This is the essence of a classical field theory. Maxwell's equations of electromagnetic fields were among the first rigorous field theories.

Special relativity is something you are likely familiar with. In case you need a bit of a refresher, it essentially gives us two concepts. The first is that the laws of physics are invariant; there are no privileged reference points. Also, the speed of light in a vacuum is constant.

The development of quantum electrodynamics began with the study of the interaction between light and electrons. When this research began, the only field known was the electromagnetic field, so it was an obvious place to begin. The term *quantum electrodynamics* was posited by Paul Dirac in 1927 in his paper "The quantum theory of the emission and absorption of radiation."

Classical electromagnetism would describe the force between two electrons as being an electric field produced by each electron's position. The force itself can be calculated using Coulomb's law. However, quantum field theory visualizes the force between electrons arising from the exchange of virtual photons.

Quantum electrodynamics is the fundamental theory that describes the interaction of light and matter. To be a bit more mathematically robust, the charged particles that provide the source for the electromagnetic fields are described by relativistic equations of motion (more specifically, the Klein-Gordon equation for integer spin and the Dirac equation for a spin). Let us briefly examine these equations.

Keep in mind that for the purposes of this book, you need not become an expert in these equations. You only need a general understanding of what they do.

Klein-Gordon is a relativistic wave equation that is actually related to the Schrödinger equation, so it will at least look a bit familiar to you. Equation 6.10 provides the equation.

$$\frac{1}{c^2}\frac{\partial^2}{\partial t^2}\psi - \nabla^2\psi + \frac{m^2c^2}{\hbar^2}\psi = 0.$$

EQUATION 6.10   Klein-Gordon Equation

Now, much of this you already know. Refreshing your memory a bit, ψ is the wave function, $\hbar$ is the reduced Planck constant, and m is mass. We have also discussed second derivatives and partial differential equations previously in this book. The c is the velocity of light in centimeters per second. I think you can already see some connection between this and Einstein's famous $E = mc^2$. I have yet to explain one other symbol, ∇. This one actually shows up frequently in quantum physics. This is the Laplace operator, sometimes called the Laplacian. It is sometimes denoted by $\nabla\nabla$ and sometimes by ∇^2. The definition of the Laplacian might seem a bit confusing to you. It is a second-order differential operator defined as the divergence of the gradient. In this case, the term *gradient* is a vector calculus term. It refers to a scalar-valued function f of several variables that is the vector field. The Laplacian of that vector field at some point is the vector whose components are partial derivatives of the function f at point p.

Hopefully, this general explanation did not leave you totally confused. Recall from the introduction that you need not master all of the mathematics presented in this chapter. Just make sure you understand the general idea. So what is that general idea? The Klein-Gordon equation is a relativistic wave function that describes the motion for the field, as it varies in time and space.

The Dirac equation for the spin is also a relativistic wave function. It describes particles such as electrons and quarks. It should be noted that electrons and quarks are the particles that constitute ordinary matter and are known as fermions. We will have much more to say about quarks in the section on quantum chromodynamics. The spin number describes how many symmetrical facets a particle has in one full rotation. Thus, a spin of 1/2 means the particle has to be rotated twice (i.e., 720 degrees) before it has the same configuration as when it started. Protons, neutrons, electrons, neutrinos, and quarks all have a spin of 1/2, and that is enough for you to move forward with the rest of this book. However, for some readers, you not only want to see more of the math, but by this point in this text you have become accustomed to it. So, in the interest of not disappointing those readers, Equation 6.11 presents the Dirac equation as Paul Dirac originally proposed it.

$$\left(\beta mc^2 + c\sum_{n=1}^{3}\alpha_n p_n\right)\psi(x,t) = i\hbar\frac{\partial\psi(x,t)}{\partial t}$$

EQUATION 6.11   Dirac Equation

Again, you see the now-familiar partial differential symbol, the reduced Planck constant, and the wave function—all of which should be quite familiar to you by now. You also see mc², and I anticipate most readers realize this is mass and the velocity of light, just as it is in E = mc². In this equation, the x and t are space and time coordinates, respectively. The p values that are being summed (p1, p2, and p3) are components of the momentum. The symbols α and β are 4 × 4 matrices. These are 4 × 4 matrices because they have four complex components (i.e. using complex numbers). Such objects are referred to in physics as a *bispinor*.

After our rather extensive excursions into the math of QED, let us complete this section with a return to the essential facts of QED. Electrodynamics, as the name suggests, is concerned with electricity. However, quantum electrodynamics provides a relativistic explanation of how light and matter interact. It is used to understand the interactions among electrically charged elementary particles, at a fundamental level. It is a very important part of quantum physics.

6.4 Quantum Chromodynamics

Strictly speaking, one could study quantum computing without much knowledge of quantum chromodynamics (QCD). However, this underpins the very structure of matter; therefore, one should have a basic idea of the topic. QCD is the study of the strong interaction between quarks and gluons. Quarks are the particles that make up protons and neutrons (also called hadrons). At one time, it was believed that protons and neutrons were fundamental particles; however, it was discovered that they are in turn made up of quarks. The names for the quarks are frankly whimsical, and not too much attention should be paid to the meanings of the names. Quarks have properties such as electric charge, mass, spin, etc. Combining three quarks can product a proton or neutron. There are six types of quarks. The whimsical nature of nomenclature will become clear here. The types are referred to as "flavors," and these flavors are up, down, strange, charm, bottom, and top. Figure 6.1 illustrates the families of quarks.

First Generation	Second Generation	Third Generation
u Up	c Charm	t Top
d Down	s Strange	b Bottom

FIGURE 6.1 Quarks

Evidence for the existence of quarks was first found in 1968 at the Stanford Linear Accelerator Center. Since that time, experiments have confirmed all six flavors of quarks. Therefore, these are not simply hypothetical constructs, but the actual building blocks of hadrons, and have been confirmed by multiple experiments over several decades. As one example, a proton is composed of two up quarks and one down quark. The gluons mediate the forces between the quarks, thus binding them together.

The next somewhat whimsical nomenclature comes with the concept of *color charge*. This has no relation at all to the frequency of light generating visible colors. The term *color*, along with the specific labels of red, green, and blue, is being used to identify the charge of a quark. However, this term has had far-reaching impact. That is why the study of the interaction between quarks and gluons is referred to as *chromodynamics*.

There are two main properties in QCD. The first is color confinement. This is a result of the force between two color charges as they are separated. Separating the quarks in a hadron will require more energy the further you separate them. If you do indeed have enough energy to completely separate the quarks, they actually spontaneously produce a quark-antiquark pair, and the original hadron becomes two hadrons.

The second property is a bit more complex. It is called asymptotic freedom. In simple terms, it means that the strength of the interactions between quarks and gluons reduces as the distance decreases. That might seem a bit counterintuitive. And as I stated, it is complex. The discoverers of this aspect of QCD—David Gross, Frank Wilczek, and David Politzer—received the 2004 Nobel Prize in Physics for their work.

6.5   Feynman Diagram

For those readers who are a bit exhausted from all the mathematics presented in this chapter, there is help for you. Richard Feynman created the Feynman diagrams to provide a pictorial representation of the mathematical expressions used to describe the behavior of subatomic particles. This is a much easier way to at least capture the essence of what is occurring. Let us first look at the basic diagram symbols used and then see how they work together (see Table 6.1).

TABLE 6.1   Feynman Diagram Symbols

Description	Symbol
A fermion (i.e., electron, positron, quark, etc.) is drawn as a straight line with an arrow pointing to the direction of the spin.	$f \longrightarrow f$
An antifermion is drawn as a straight line with an arrow pointing to the direction of the spin, with the primary difference being the line over the f.	$\overline{f} \longleftarrow \overline{f}$
A photon is drawn as a wavy line.	γ

Therefore, if you wish to draw two electrons with opposite spin, colliding and producing a photon, you can use Feynman diagrams without any math, as demonstrated in Figure 6.2.

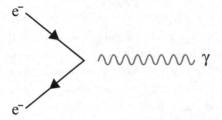

FIGURE 6.2 Feynman diagram of electrons colliding

This is just a very brief introduction to Feynman diagrams, but you will find these useful as you learn more about quantum interactions.

6.6 Summary

This chapter explored many concepts. It is really an extension of Chapter 3 and the application of some of the elements of Chapter 1. This is likely to be one of the more difficult chapters for many readers, and it is strongly suggested that you read it more than once. While many topics were explored, some are absolutely critical for your understanding of quantum computing. The bra-ket notation is used throughout quantum computing, so ensure you are quite comfortable with it. Hamiltonians also play a prominent role in quantum computing. Quantum decoherence is actually a substantial impediment to the progress of quantum computing. To fully understand decoherence, you need to understand the wave function and associated equations. Quantum electrodynamics and quantum chromodynamics were presented to help round out your basic introduction to quantum theory. However, those two topics are a bit less critical for you to move forward with quantum computing.

Test Your Skills

REVIEW QUESTIONS

1. Why does the reduced Planck constant use 2π?

    a. 2π denotes the radius of the atom.

    b. 2π is 360 degrees in radians.

    c. 2π accounts for quantum fluctuations.

    d. 2π is a derivative of Einstein's universal constant.

2. In quantum mechanics, what does the Greek letter psi represent?

    a. The Hamiltonian

    b. The reduced Planck constant

    c. The wave function

    d. Superposition of states

3. What would be most helpful in determining the probability of finding a particle at a given point?

    a. Born's rule

    b. Hamiltonian

    c. Reduced Planck constant

    d. Wave function

4. Which of the following is the most accurate description of the wave function collapse?

    a. The various possible quantum states coalesce into a single quantum state.

    b. The probabilities coalesce to a single actuality based on an observer.

    c. The bra-ket $\langle \phi_i | \phi_j \rangle$ forms an orthonormal eigenvector basis.

    d. The superposition of possible eigenstates collapses to a single eigenstate based on interaction with the environment.

5. When using the Kronecker delta and inputting two eigenstates that are the same, what will be the output?

    a. The sum of the eigenstates

    b. 1

    c. The superposition of the eigenstates

    d. 0

6. Schrödinger's equation is used to describe what?

    a. Superposition of eigenstates

    b. Eigenstates

    c. The wave function

    d. The Hamiltonian operator

7. What equation is most closely related to the decoupling that occurs during decoherence?

    a. Hamiltonian

    b. Schrödinger equation

    c. Wigner function

    d. Klein-Gordon

8. Which of the following is a wave function related to quantum electrodynamics that describes the motion for the field as it varies in time and space?

    a. Hamiltonian

    b. Schrödinger equation

    c. Wigner function

    d. Klein-Gordon

9. What is a bispinor?

    a. A 4×4 matrix with complex components

    b. Superposition of two eigenstates

    c. The product of the Dirac equation

    d. The product of the Wigner function

Chapter | 7

Quantum Entanglement and QKD

Chapter Objectives

After reading this chapter and completing the review questions, you will be able to do the following:

- Understand quantum entanglement
- Have a deeper understanding of quantum states
- Demonstrate a working knowledge of quantum key exchange protocols

Quantum entanglement is a difficult subject to understand conceptually. It is totally counterintuitive, and it took many experiments to verify that it is indeed true. However, it is a critical element of quantum physics, and in this chapter we will explore that topic. A related topic is quantum key distribution (QKD). In this chapter, you will learn the basics of QKD as well as actual implementations of QKD.

7.1 Quantum Entanglement

Quantum entanglement is one of the more odd aspects of quantum physics. It plays a critical role in some aspects of quantum key exchange, so it is important that you have a working understanding. The concept is relatively simple, but the "how" and "why" are much more complex. Essentially, quantum entanglement occurs when a pair of particles (or a group of pairs) interacts or is generated in a manner that ties (or entangles) the quantum states of each particle in the pair together. This means the measurement of polarization, momentum, spin, or other properties of one particle will be correlated with the properties of the entangled particle. If you measure, for example, the polarization of one entangled photon, you will find the other entangled photon has precisely the opposite polarization—and as far as we can tell, distance has no effect. The essence of quantum entanglement is that the properties of entangled particles are perfectly correlated—properties such as momentum, spin, polarization, etc.—such that any measurement of one entangled particle causes a wave function collapse, and both particles now have a definite state. You can see a simplified example of entanglement in Figure 7.1.

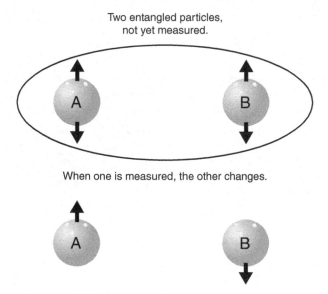

FIGURE 7.1 Entanglement

Why are the two particles entangled? Well, recall that in the previous chapters we explored the wave function in some detail. This sort of action was what Einstein termed "spooky action at a distance." Based on this and related phenomena, he believed quantum mechanics must be incomplete. Along with Boris Podolsky and Nathan Rosen, Einstein wrote a paper on what became known as the EPR paradox.

In their paper "Can Quantum-Mechanical Description of Physical Reality Be Considered Complete?", Einstein, Podolsky, and Rosen argued that quantum mechanics was simply incomplete and that there were additional elements of reality that simply were not addressed in quantum theory. In their paper, they posited a thought experiment. In this experiment, there is a pair of particles in an entangled state (it does not matter what particles are selected). If you measure one of the particles (for example, its momentum), then the measurement of the second particle would have a predictable outcome. This instantaneous effect of one entangled particle on another was disturbing, as relativity tells us that nothing can travel faster than the speed of light, and entangled particles seem to communicate information instantaneously, which is faster than the speed of light. The EPR paradox is, in essence, that the second entangled particle either is in instantaneous communication with the first particle (thus violating relativity) or already has a definite state before measurement, which violates all we know about quantum mechanics. Another term for entangled is to refer to the particles as being in a singlet state (a common state).

The EPR paradox gave rise to the concept of *nonlocality* in quantum mechanics: If two entangled particles can affect one another instantaneously, over presumably any distance, then the quantum state was not confined to the locality of either particle. I believe if you reflect on this for a time, you will realize that not only is this counterintuitive, it is counter to all classical physics.

The EPR paradox was fuel for a great deal of theoretical physics. In 1961, David Bohm proposed a variation of the EPR thought experiment. In Bohm's version, the measurements have only discrete ranges of possible outcomes. Here are some good references for more detail on Bohm's work:

https://www.nature.com/articles/milespin11

http://philsci-archive.pitt.edu/3222/1/epr.pdf

One answer to the EPR paradox was to posit that there were hidden variables we simply had not discovered. There are actually multiple "local, hidden variable" theories. Each of them posits some underlying, inaccessible variables that account for quantum entanglement and/or the probabilistic nature of quantum mechanics.

To understand Bohm's modification of the EPR paradox, assume that one has prepared a pair of spin-1/2 particles in the entangled spin singlet state, as is shown in Equation 7.1.

$$\frac{1}{\sqrt{2}}\left(|\uparrow\rangle \otimes |\downarrow\rangle - |\downarrow\rangle \otimes |\uparrow\rangle\right)$$

EQUATION 7.1 Singlet State

Also, $|\uparrow\rangle, |\downarrow\rangle$ is an orthonormal basis of the spin state space. A measurement of the spin of one of the particles along a given axis yields either the result "up" or the result "down." If you measure the spin of both particles along some given axis, then quantum theory predicts that the results obtained will be the opposite. If such measurements are carried out simultaneously on two spatially separated particles, then locality requires that any disturbance triggered by the measurement on one side cannot influence the result of the measurement on the other side. Putting that another way, nonlocality is an "incompleteness" in quantum theory, and indeed there are some hidden variables that account for the apparent nonlocality. The only way to ensure the perfect correlation between the results on the two sides is to have each particle carry a preexisting determinate value.

This brings us to an important theorem in quantum mechanics: Bell's inequality (also called Bell's theorem). In 1964, John Bell proposed a method to test for the existence of the proposed hidden variables. To gain an intuitive understanding of Bell's inequality, let us consider two photons that are entangled. Bell realized that the only way to account for the perfect correlation in quantumly entangled particles, without invoking nonlocality, was that there must be pre-existing values. Before we delve deeper into Bell's theorem, its essence is that it proves quantum physics is incompatible with the various "hidden variables" theories. This put an end to serious speculation about hidden variables as an explanation for the perceived nonlocality.

A basic intuitive understanding of Bell's inequalities is actually rather simple: Assuming hidden variables leads to strict limits on the possible values of the correlation of subsequent measurements that can be obtained from the pairs of entangled particles. However, experiments simply don't show that.

For a bit more in-depth look at Bell's theorem, let us return now to the particles in a quantum singlet state that we saw in Equation 7.1. Also, let us further suppose that these particles are now separated by some substantial distance. Measuring two particles leads to either they correlate or they don't. Using spin as the property of interest, if you measure the spin of the entangled particles along with anti-parallel directions, the results are always perfectly correlated. Measuring in perpendicular directions provides a 50% chance of correlation. These two sets of data account for two situations—parallel and anti-parallel—as illustrated here:

Pair

Anti-parallel	1	2	3	4	...	n	
Particle 1, 0°	+	−	+	+	...	−	
Particle 2, 180°	+	−	+	+	...	−	
Correlation	(+1	+1	+1	+1	...	+1)	/ n = +1
Parallel	1	2	3	4	...	n	
Particle 1, 0°	+	−	−	+	...	+	
Particle 2, 0° or 360°	−	+	+	−	...	−	
Correlation	(−1	−1	−1	−1	...	−1)	/ n = −1

But what about other angles? It turns out that the correlation is the negative cosine of the angle. Note that many sources also discuss orthogonal situations for the pair, including 90- and 270-degree angles.

Now let us look more rigorously at Bell's theorem. Consider random variables $Zi\alpha$; $i=1,2$; and $\alpha=a,b,c$ taking only the values ± 1. If these random variables are perfectly anticorrelated (i.e., if $Z1\alpha=-Z2\alpha$, for all α), then we have the formula shown in Equation 7.2.

$$P\left(Z_a^1 \neq Z_b^2\right)+P\left(Z_b^1 \neq z_c^2\right)+P\left(z_c^1 \neq Z_a^2\right)$$

EQUATION 7.2 Bell's Inequality

As you can see, this is an inequality (thus the name Bell's inequality). Let us describe these variables so that you might gain a clearer understanding of Bell's inequality. The a, b, and c represent three axes laid out such that the angle between any two of them is $2\pi / 3$. The Z value with an axis subscript indicates the spin for a given axis. Thus, Z_a^1 is indicating a spin for axis a. P indicates probability. Therefore, the first part of the equation is stating, what is the probability that $Z_a^1 \neq Z_b^2$?

Because the three ± 1-valued random variables $Z1\alpha$ can't all disagree, the union of the events {$Z1\mathbf{a}=Z1\mathbf{b}$}, {$Z1\mathbf{b}=Z1\mathbf{c}$}, and {$Z1\mathbf{c}=Z1\mathbf{a}$} is equal to the entire sample space. Thus, the sum of their probabilities must be greater than or equal to 1:

$P(Z1\mathbf{a}=Z1\mathbf{b}) + P(Z1\mathbf{b}=Z1\mathbf{c}) + P(Z1\mathbf{c}=Z1\mathbf{a}) \geq 1$

However, because $Z1\beta=-Z2\beta$, we have $P(Z1\alpha=Z1\beta)=P(Z1\alpha\neq Z2\beta)$.

Each of the three terms on the left side of the inequality must be equal to 1/4 in order to reproduce the quantum predictions. However, because 1/4 + 1/4 + 1/4 = 3/4 < 1, the full set of quantum predictions cannot be matched.

Remember that Bell's inequality is about totaling probabilities. It is sometimes helpful to look at a figure to depict this. Let us first consider the various probabilities, such as $Z_a^1 \neq Z_b^2$, to instead be probabilities of a mundane action such as whether or not it is raining, and then whether or not a person goes out into the weather. That scenario is depicted in Figure 7.2.

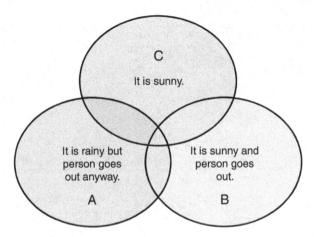

FIGURE 7.2   Bell's inequality explained simply

These are overlapping probabilities, and they can be calculated as shown in Equation 7.3.

$$P(A\cap B) \leq P(A\cap C) + P(\overline{C}\cap B)$$

EQUATION 7.3   Bell's Inequality, Simplified Explanation

In Equation 7.3, the value $\overline{C}$ is not C.

Returning to simpler terms, essentially Bell's inequality predicts that if locality holds, and hidden variables are responsible for the observed apparent nonlocality in quantum mechanics, then we should see certain outcomes of measurements. However, at least in some cases, we do not see those outcomes. Thus, hidden variables cannot account for the observed phenomena, and quantum mechanics really does include nonlocality.

While the predictions of quantum mechanics are counterintuitive, and you may agree with the opinions expressed by Einstein, Podolsky, and Rosen, these predictions have been experimentally verified numerous times. Using spin or polarization, quantumly entangled particles have been measured at separate locations, and the change in one particle does indeed create a change in the other. There are several good sources regarding experiments that have verified entanglement and the EPR paradox. Here are a few:

https://arxiv.org/abs/2004.04352

https://www.sciencedaily.com/releases/2018/04/180426141601.htm

https://www.extremetech.com/extreme/295013-scientists-capture-photographic-proof-of-quantum-entanglement

https://www.sciencemag.org/news/2018/04/einstein-s-spooky-action-distance-spotted-objects-almost-big-enough-see

Theoretical physicists have invested a great deal of thought into trying to understand how this entanglement works. For example, there is the concept of time as an emergent phenomenon due to quantum entanglement. One can certainly enjoy many hours contemplating this and other ideas. However, for our purposes, we don't need to know the cause of entanglement. That is fortunate, because while many ideas have been posited, no one actually knows the reason for entanglement.

It must be emphasized that no matter how strange entanglement might seem, it has been experimentally demonstrated with electrons, neutrinos, photons, and even molecules. It must also be emphasized how important this is to quantum physics. Schrödinger stated, "I would not call that one but rather the characteristic trait of quantum mechanics, the one that enforces its entire departure from classical lines of thought."

7.2 Interpretation

While one can study quantum computers without considering the implications of quantum mechanics, that may be a mistake because it avoids some of the wonders of quantum mechanics. Therefore, in this section, you will be introduced to some of the more well-known interpretations.

First, it is important to understand why an interpretation is needed at all. Consider two main features of quantum mechanics. The first is the issue of entanglement that we discussed in the last section. As we discussed, the EPR paradox stems from the issues that entanglement brings out. How can two particles separated by a substantial distance be synchronized? Many have posited hidden variables in the two particles, such that the values were already predetermined, and there was no need to account for the supposed paradox. However, Bell's inequality ultimately was used to show such variables don't exist. So how do we account for the entanglement?

A second issue is the fact that we only know the outcome of a quantum measurement with a certain probability, not with certainty. What does this imply about how the universe fundamentally works? It must be stressed that we know from innumerable experiments how quantum mechanics works (at least to a particular level of detail), but we really don't know *why* it works. Thus, various interpretations have been formulated, seeking an explanation.

Another point to these perspectives is to answer a very fundamental question: How does the classical world emerge from the quantum basis? Clearly, our normal world does not demonstrate wave-particle duality, entanglement, or other quantum phenomena, so physicists want to understand how we have a quantum basis for everything. After all, everything is made up of atoms that have particles that behave according to quantum mechanics, but we ultimately derive classical behavior.

7.2.1   The Copenhagen Interpretation

Entanglement necessitates at least some basic discussion of the Copenhagen interpretation of quantum mechanics. The Copenhagen interpretation was developed by Werner Heisenberg and Neils Bohr over two years, from 1925 to 1927. This interpretation asserts that quantum systems do not have definite properties until measured. Consequently, one can only predict the probability of a given quantum system having a particular value. While this view has had its critics, it is perhaps the most widely taught interpretation of the data we have from quantum mechanics.

The Copenhagen interpretation teaches that there are no hidden variables to explain quantum states and entanglement. In this view, the wave function ψ represents the state of the system, and all that is known or can be known about it before observation. This also leads to Heisenberg's uncertainty principle, which was mentioned earlier in this book. One cannot know the precise location and momentum of a particle at one time. The measuring of a quantum system causes the wave function to collapse to a particular eigenstate of the observable property that is measured.

This view leads to the rather infamous Schrödinger's cat thought experiment, which you might be familiar with. In this thought experiment, a cat is placed in a sealed box. In the box is a vial with poison gas. The vial is either open, and the cat is dead, or closed, and the cat is alive. If that vial is treated like a subatomic particle, then until it is measured, it is simply a wave function that has not yet collapsed, meaning, until someone looks in the box, the cat is in a superimposed state of being, neither alive nor dead. Then, when the box is opened, and the measurement/observation is made, the wave function collapses, and now the cat will either be alive or dead. Here are several external references should you wish to dive deeper into this topic:

https://wtamu.edu/~cbaird/sq/2013/07/30/what-did-schrodingers-cat-experiment-prove/

https://www.nationalgeographic.com/news/2013/8/130812-physics-schrodinger-erwin-google-doodle-cat-paradox-science/

https://www.iflscience.com/physics/schr%C3%B6dinger%E2%80%99s-cat-explained/

https://plato.stanford.edu/entries/qm-copenhagen/

https://www.sciencedirect.com/topics/mathematics/copenhagen-interpretation

7.2.2   The Many-Worlds Interpretation

This interpretation of quantum mechanics may indeed be the oddest thing we have yet discussed. The essence of this interpretation is that any time a quantum measurement is made, the various possible outcomes all do occur, in some alternate universe. This was first proposed by Hugh Everett in 1957 and thus is sometimes called the Everett interpretation. The implications of this view are that there are many universes, perhaps infinitely many.

For example, if one measures the polarization of a photon, one gets some specific value. Prior to the measurement, the photon was in an indeterminate state of superposition of all possible states.

7.2.3 Decoherent Histories

There are many interpretations of quantum mechanics, none quite so well known as the Copenhagen and many-worlds interpretations, but still worthy of discussion. The decoherent histories (sometimes called the consistent histories) interpretation is an attempt to generalize the Copenhagen interpretation. In this interpretation, the various possibilities for a quantum measurement are assigned to alternative histories of the system. In this way, each independent history behaves in an essentially classical manner. This interpretation does not focus on a wave function collapse.

Let us frame this interpretation in a more mathematically rigorous fashion. Consider different histories, where H_i is a specific (i) history. These are specified at different moments of time as propositions J_{ij} (j is the label for the times):

$$H_i = P_{i,1}, P_{i,2}, \ldots, P_{i,n}$$

This brings us to the propositions. A given proposition $P_{i,1}$ is true at time $t_{i,1}$, etc.

This is referred to as a homogenous history. In contrast, inhomogeneous histories have multiple time propositions that are only "or" relationships (i.e., one or the other is true). This theory is often called consistent histories. We have covered the "histories" part, but not the "consistency" part. That brings us to Equation 7.4.

$$\hat{C}_{H_i} := T \prod_{j=1}^{n_i} \hat{P}_{i,j}(t_{i,j}) = \hat{P}_{i,n_i} \cdots \hat{P}_{i,2}\, \hat{P}_{i,1}$$

EQUATION 7.4 Consistent Histories

This formula is not as daunting as it seems. The first symbol, $\hat{C}_{H_i}$, is just denoting consistent histories. The P you already know is a proposition that something is true at some specific time. The T indicates that the factors are ordered chronologically based on values of $t_{i,j}$.

7.2.4 Objective Collapse Theory

The objective collapse theory differs from the Copenhagen interpretation in that it regards the wave function and the collapse of that function to exist independent of the observer/measurement. The collapse occurs when some particular threshold is reached or randomly. The observer/measurement has no special role.

In various collapse theories, the Schrödinger equation is supplemented. There are additional terms that lead to spontaneous collapse and localize the wave function. In these models, the wave function is localized in space such that it essentially behaves like a point moving according to Newtonian physics. There are quite a few of these sorts of theories. They are all an attempt to solve what is called the measurement problem. This is the term for something we have been discussing in this chapter, and indeed in previous chapters. The measurement problem is the issue that a particle state is indeterminant until measured. These theories attempt to avoid the Schrödinger cat issues.

Table 7.1 summarizes the four major interpretations of the measurement problem.

TABLE 7.1   Interpretations

Interpretation	Description
Copenhagen interpretation	Quantum systems do not have definite properties until measured.
Many-worlds interpretation	Any time a quantum measurement is made, the various possible outcomes all do occur, in some alternate universe.
Decoherent histories	In this interpretation, the various possibilities for a quantum measurement are assigned to alternative histories of the system. In this way, each independent history behaves in an essentially classical manner. This interpretation does not focus on a wave function collapse.
Objective collapse theory	The wave function and the collapse of that function do exist independent of the observer/measurement. The collapse occurs when some particular threshold is reached or randomly. The observer/measurement has no special role.

7.3   QKE

Quantum key exchange (QKE), also called quantum key distribution, uses quantum mechanics to produce a shared secret key. One of the advantages of using quantum mechanics is the fact that measuring any particle changes its state. Thus, if two parties are using quantum key distribution, and a third party attempts to intercept the communication, that interception will be detected.

7.3.1   BB84 Protocol

Charles Bennet and Gilles Brassard developed the protocol BB84 in 1984. The name stems from the inventors' last names and the year the protocol was invented. This is a key exchange protocol that is provably secure. Let us explore how this protocol works, using the common fictitious characters Alice and Bob. Let us assume Alice would like to exchange a key with Bob. Alice begins with two strings of bits; each is some number of bits long, which we'll call n bits long. The two strings we will call a and b. The two strings of bits are encoded as a tensor product of n number of qubits.

Recall from Chapter 1 our discussion of the dot products of vectors. Now let us consider two column vectors:

$$\begin{bmatrix} 1 \\ 2 \\ 1 \end{bmatrix} \begin{bmatrix} 3 \\ 2 \\ 1 \end{bmatrix}$$

The dot product is found as follows: $(1 * 3) + (2 * 2) + (1 * 1) = 8$.

A tensor product of two vector spaces basically takes the elements and multiplies them together. Here is a representation of a tensor product:

$$\begin{bmatrix} 1 \\ 2 \\ 1 \end{bmatrix} \otimes \begin{bmatrix} 3 \\ 2 \\ 1 \end{bmatrix}$$

Figure 7.3 illustrates what occurs.

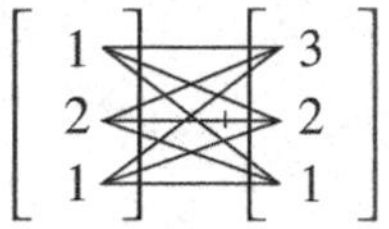

FIGURE 7.3 Tensor product

So, we have $(1 * 3)$, $(1 * 2)$, $(1 * 1)$, $(2 * 3)$, $(2 * 2)$, $(2 * 1)$, $(1 * 3)$, $(1 * 2)$, and $(1 * 1)$, but we don't just add these together; instead, they become a new vector like what is shown in Equation 7.5.

$$\begin{bmatrix} 1*3 \\ 1*2 \\ 1*1 \\ 2*3 \\ 2*2 \\ 2*1 \\ 1*3 \\ 1*2 \\ 1*1 \end{bmatrix}$$

EQUATION 7.5 Tensor Product, Step 2

This will lead to a new vector space, shown in Equation 7.6.

$$\begin{bmatrix} 3 \\ 2 \\ 1 \\ 6 \\ 4 \\ 2 \\ 3 \\ 2 \\ 1 \end{bmatrix}$$

EQUATION 7.6   Tensor Product, Step 3

Now back to the BB84 protocol. Alice first selects one of two basis states: orthogonal or rectilinear. Alice will then encode the two strings (a and b) as a tensor product. Together, a_i and b_i provide an induct to four qubit states, shown in Equation 7.7.

$$|\psi_{00}\rangle = |0\rangle$$

$$|\psi_{10}\rangle = |1\rangle$$

$$|\psi_{01}\rangle = |+\rangle = \frac{1}{\sqrt{2}}|0\rangle + \frac{1}{\sqrt{2}}|1\rangle$$

$$|\psi_{11}\rangle = |-\rangle = \frac{1}{\sqrt{2}}|0\rangle - \frac{1}{\sqrt{2}}|1\rangle$$

EQUATION 7.7   Qubit States BB84

Alice then prepares a photon polarization state depending on the bit value and basis state. The basis state can be rectilinear or orthogonal. Thus, as an example, a 0 is encoded in the rectilinear basis as a vertical polarization state, and a 1 is encoded in the diagonal basis as a 135° state. Often the + symbol is used for a rectilinear basis and the X for diagonal basis. Alice then transmits that photon in the state specified to Bob. This process is then repeated from the random bit stage, with Alice recording the state, basis, and time of each photon sent.

According to quantum mechanics, no possible measurement distinguishes between the four different polarization states, as they are not all orthogonal. The only possible measurement is between any two orthogonal states (an orthonormal basis). So, for example, measuring in the rectilinear basis gives a result of horizontal or vertical. If the photon was created as horizontal or vertical, then this measures the correct state, but if it was created as 45° or 135°, then the rectilinear measurement instead returns either horizontal or vertical at random.

Because Alice encoded the bits, there is no way for Bob to know what basis was used. Therefore, he must select a basis at random to measure in, either rectilinear or diagonal. This is done for each photon he received, and the results are recorded along with the time and measurement basis used. After Bob has measured all the photons, he notifies Alice over a traditional communication channel. Alice then sends the basis each photon was sent in, and Bob sends the basis each was measured in. They both discard photon measurements (bits) where Bob used a different basis. It turns out that on average, this will be about half the bits. The remaining half of the bits are now used as a cryptographic key. To check for the presence of an eavesdropper, Alice and Bob now compare a predetermined subset of their remaining bits. If any third party has gained any information about the photons' polarization, this introduces errors in Bob's measurements. This is because the measuring of a photon changes it. A summary of the basic steps Alice takes are given here:

Step 1. Alice begins with two strings that are n bits in length. The two strings of bits are encoded as a tensor product of n number of qubits. This will lead to a new vector space.

Step 2. Alice first selects one of two basis states: orthogonal or rectilinear. Alice will then encode the two strings (a and b) as a tensor product. Together, a_i and b_i provide an induct to four qubit states.

Step 3. Alice then prepares a photon polarization state depending on the bit value and basis state.

Step 4. Alice then transmits that photon in the state specified to Bob. This process is then repeated from the random bit stage, with Alice recording the state, basis, and time of each photon sent.

7.3.2 B92 Protocol

The B92 protocol uses two no-orthogonal states, such as |A> and |B>. This protocol was developed in 1992 by Charles Bennet, one of the inventors of the BB84 protocol.

In this case, Alice sends 0 or 1 bits. The 0 is in one basis, and the 1 is in another basis. Which of the two bases is used is chosen randomly. Bob then chooses the basis randomly (from the two possibilities). He then measures the bits received using that basis. Depending on the result he will know if he chose the correct basis. If his results are inclusive, he throws the results out. In this protocol, a substantial number of bits get excluded.

7.3.3 SARG04

SARG04 is a protocol derived from BB84. When a message is to be sent, the sending party begins with two strings of bits that are each n bits long. These are encoded as a string of n qubits, as shown in Equation 7.8.

$$|\psi\rangle = \bigotimes_{i=1}^{n} |\psi_{a_i b_i}\rangle$$

EQUATION 7.8 SARG04 Encoding

Together, a_i and b_i provide an index to four qubit states, shown in Equation 7.9.

$$|\psi_{00}\rangle = |0\rangle$$
$$|\psi_{10}\rangle = |1\rangle$$
$$|\psi_{01}\rangle = |+\rangle = \frac{1}{\sqrt{2}}|0\rangle + \frac{1}{\sqrt{2}}|1\rangle$$
$$|\psi_{11}\rangle = |-\rangle = \frac{1}{\sqrt{2}}|0\rangle + \frac{1}{\sqrt{2}}|1\rangle$$

EQUATION 7.9   SARG04 Qubit States

Note that the bit b_i is what decides which basis a_i is encoded in. The sender sends the quantum state $|\psi\rangle$ over a public channel to the recipient. The recipient receives a state εp that combines the noise of the channel ε as well as any potential interference from a third party attempting to measure the quantum state. The recipient then generates a string of bits the same length as b (from the sender) and uses those bits as a basis when measuring bits from the sender. For each qubit sent, the sender must choose one computational basis state and one Hadamard basis state so that the state of the qubit is one of these two.

To go further with the SARG04 protocol, we must first explore Hadamard basis states. The Hadamard transform (Hadamard transformation, also known as the Walsh-Hadamard transformation) plays an important role in quantum computing. This transform is often called the Hadamard gate, and we will see it again in subsequent chapters. It is a one-qubit rotation, mapping the qubit-basis states $|0\rangle$ and $|1\rangle$ to two superposition states with an equal weight of the computational basis states $|0\rangle$ and $|1\rangle$. Usually, the phases are chosen, such that Equation 7.10 is true.

$$\frac{|0\rangle + |1\rangle}{\sqrt{2}}\langle 0| + \frac{|0\rangle + |1\rangle}{\sqrt{2}}\langle 1|$$

EQUATION 7.10   Hadamard Transform

Many quantum algorithms use the Hadamard transform as an initial step, since it maps n qubits initialized with $|0\rangle$ to a superposition of all 2n orthogonal states in the $|0\rangle$, $|1\rangle$ basis with equal weight.

Now we return to SARG04. The sender will then announce the two states chosen. The recipient knows that his state is one of the two sender states and can then determine if his measurement is consistent with either state. If it is consistent with either state, then the bit is invalid because he cannot distinguish which state. If it is consistent with only one of the two candidate states, then this is a valid bit. This allows the bits of a key to be determined, which leads to a set of k valid bits. The sensor can randomly choose k/2 bits, and the sender and receiver can determine if they agree, and thus have a shared key.

7.3.4 Six-State Protocol

The six-state protocol, often simply called SSP, was published by Bechmann-Pasquinucc and Gisn in 2019 in a paper titled "Incoherent and Coherent Eavesdropping in the 6-state protocol of Quantum Cryptography." This protocol is also a variation of BB84. The main point of SSP is that it produces a higher rate of errors should someone attempt to intercept the communication. This makes it much easier to detect attempted eavesdropping. The basic algorithm is relatively simple. The sender generates a random string of qubits and encodes them using one of three bases chosen at random. That string is then sent to the recipient via some channel. The recipient then randomly chooses one of three bases for measuring the state of the received qubits. The sender and receiver will discard those qubits, wherein the recipient chooses a different basis for decoding than was chosen for encoding. The remaining qubits are the key.

7.3.5 E91

Artur Ekert, a professor of quantum physics at the Mathematical Institute, University of Oxford, implemented a different key exchange protocol named E91. E91 utilizes entangled pairs of photons. This brings us back to our previous discussion of quantum entanglement. The entangled states are correlated, and if any third party intercepts the communication, that interception will disrupt the state and be detected.

You can learn more about these protocols at these sources:

https://www.cse.wustl.edu/~jain/cse571-07/ftp/quantum/

https://eprint.iacr.org/2020/1074.pdf

https://journals.sagepub.com/doi/10.1177/1550147718778192

https://arxiv.org/abs/quant-ph/0510025

7.3.6 Implementations

There have been a number of successful implementations of quantum key exchange, and there is a definite trend toward being able to accomplish this over increasing distances. In 2007, the Los Alamos National Laboratory was able to perform quantum key exchange over 148.7 kilometers of fiber optic. In 2015, the University of Geneva and Corning, Inc., were able to perform QKE over 307 kilometers.

In the United States, the Defense Advanced Research Projects Agency (DARPA) created a quantum key distribution network consisting of ten nodes that was able to run uninterrupted for four years. In 2016, China established a QKE channel between China and Vienna, Austria (a distance of 7500 kilometers).

7.4 Summary

This chapter explored the quantum physics concept of quantum entanglement. The essential physics of this phenomenon, along with the basic math that is needed to understand it, were covered. This is an essential, though difficult to grasp, aspect of quantum physics. We also examined quantum key exchange (QKE), also known as quantum key distribution (QKD). The basic concepts were explored, along with some specific implementations and protocols.

Test Your Skills

REVIEW QUESTIONS

1. What is the primary point of studying Bell's inequality? What did it help to demonstrate?

    a. It demonstrated that hidden variables are responsible for entanglement.

    b. It demonstrated that hidden variables are not responsible for entanglement.

    c. It demonstrated a useful quantum gate.

    d. It demonstrated how to achieve entanglement.

2. Calculate the tensor product of these two vectors:

3. How many qubit states are used in BB84?

    a. 4

    b. 2

    c. As many as are needed

    d. The same as the number of qubits

4. Which QKD protocol is based on using entangled photons?

    a. BB84

    b. SARG04

    c. E91

    d. SSP

5. In the _____, the various possibilities for a quantum measurement are assigned to alternative histories of the system. In this way, each independent history behaves in an essentially classical manner. This interpretation does not focus on a wave function collapse.

    a. objective collapse theory

    b. decoherent histories interpretation

    c. many-worlds interpretation

    d. Copenhagen interpretation

6. _____ proposed a method to test for the existence of the proposed hidden variables.

    a. Erwin Schrödinger

    b. David Bohm

    c. Albert Einstein

    d. John Bell

7. _____ states that quantum systems do not have definite properties until measured.

    a. Many-worlds interpretation

    b. Bohm's interpretation

    c. Decoherent histories interpretation

    d. Copenhagen interpretation

Chapter | **8**

Quantum Architecture

Chapter Objectives

After reading this chapter and completing the review questions, you will be able to do the following:

- Explain the logical topology of quantum computers
- Articulate different qubit storage technologies
- Understand quantum gates
- Explain quantum annealing

In this chapter we delve deeper into the mechanics of quantum computing. We will deepen our exploration of qubits and cover quantum gates as well as quantum circuits. Just as importantly, we will discuss noncircuit approaches, such as those used by D-Wave. In order to fully grasp subsequent chapters, such as Chapter 9, "Quantum Hardware," and Chapter 10, "Quantum Algorithms," it is critical that you obtain a working knowledge of quantum gates and circuits. These topics are pivotal for understanding quantum hardware and algorithms.

8.1 Further with Qubits

In previous chapters, qubits were discussed; in this section, this topic will be elaborated on. A *qubit* is a quantum mechanical system based on the state of a particle. This can be the polarization of a photon, the spin of an electron, or several other properties.

The typical way to represent the quantum state of a qubit is by a linear superposition of its two orthonormal basis states, also termed *basis vectors*. Remember from Chapter 1, "Introduction to Essential

Linear Algebra," that if two vectors are both orthogonal (i.e., perpendicular to each other) and have a unit length (length 1), the vectors are said to be orthonormal. This is typically written as follows:

$$|0> = \begin{bmatrix} 1 \\ 0 \end{bmatrix} \text{ and } |1> = \begin{bmatrix} 0 \\ 1 \end{bmatrix}$$

Also, recall that the bra-ket notation, also called Dirac notation, is used to represent vectors. In this case, the two states $|0>$ and $|1>$ are both kets. These two orthonormal basis states form the computational basis of the qubit. The two kets span the two-dimensional vector space of the qubit, which is a Hilbert space.

Recall from Chapter 2, "Complex Numbers," that a Hilbert space is a vector space, like you were introduced to in Chapter 1. However, a Hilbert space extends the two-dimensional Euclidean plane and three-dimensional Euclidean space you are familiar with to any number of dimensions, including infinite dimension spaces. The German mathematician David Hilbert first described the eponymously named Hilbert spaces in his work on integral equations and Fourier series. A Hilbert space is essentially a vector space that is generalized to potentially infinite dimensions.

If one wishes to represent two qubits, there are four states to be represented:

$$|00> = \begin{bmatrix} 1 \\ 0 \\ 0 \\ 0 \end{bmatrix} \text{ and } |11> = \begin{bmatrix} 0 \\ 0 \\ 0 \\ 1 \end{bmatrix} \text{ and } |01> \begin{bmatrix} 0 \\ 1 \\ 0 \\ 0 \end{bmatrix} \text{ and } |10> \begin{bmatrix} 0 \\ 0 \\ 1 \\ 0 \end{bmatrix}$$

Keep in mind that these are the states you will have once you have measured the qubit. Until such a measurement occurs, the qubit is in a superposition of possible states. Therefore, to describe a qubit, the following formula is useful:

$$| \psi > = \alpha|0> + \beta|1>$$

The values α and β are the probability amplitudes. Usually, these probabilities are complex numbers. When we measure the qubit, Born's rule tells us the probability of outcome $|0>$ with value '0' is $|\alpha|^2$ and the probability of the outcome being $|1>$ with the value '1' is $|\beta|^2$. Remember, α and β are the probability amplitudes and are going to be complex numbers. Given that probabilities always equal to 1, we can say that

$$|\alpha|^2 + |\beta|^2 = 1$$

While this might seem a bit new to some readers, it is really fairly standard probability. With the exception that the reader needs to have some concept of the Born rule, we will now explore at least the fundamentals of the Born rule.

The Born rule (sometimes called Born's postulate or Born's law) provides us with the probability that a measurement of a quantum system (such as a qubit) will yield a particular result. This was formulated by Max Born in 1926. Among other things that Born's rule teaches us is that it states that the probability density of finding a particle at a particular point is proportional to the square of the magnitude of the particle's wave function at that point.

To understand Born's law, let us begin with some observable. That observable corresponds to a self-adjoint operator A. A has a discrete spectrum measured in a system and the system has a normalized wave function. Born's law tells us that given these circumstances, we know some specific things about this system. However, before we get to what Born's rule tells us (note that I have intentionally used both "Born's rule" and "Born's law"), you must understand what a self-adjoint operator is.

To understand self-adjoint operators, first remember that when you are using linear algebra, matrices are in fact operators. A self-adjoint operation is a linear map A from the vector space V to itself that is its own adjoint. In a complex Hilbert space, an operator's adjoint is often also called a Hermitian transpose or Hermitian conjugate. Put more simply, an adjoint in a complex Hilbert space has the same function of a complex conjugate of a complex number. Recall from Chapter 2 that a complex conjugate has the same real and imaginary parts, but with an opposite sign. So that the complex conjugate of $3 - 4i$ is $3 + 4i$.

Now, returning to what Born's rule tells us:

- The result of the measurement will be one of the eigenvalues of the self-adjoint operator A.

- The probability of the measurement resulting in a particular eigenvalue λ_i is equal to $<\psi|P_i|\psi>$, where P_i is the projection onto the eigenspace of A corresponding to λ_i.

These lead us back to the Bloch sphere discussed previously in this book and shown in Figure 8.1.

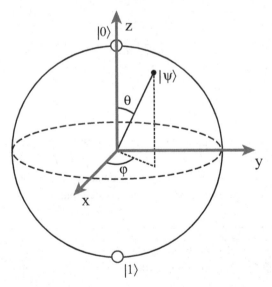

FIGURE 8.1   Bloch sphere

We can now explore the Bloch sphere representation a bit more thoroughly. First, we need to discuss the concept of degrees of freedom, as it is used in the physical sciences. A degree of freedom is an independent physical parameter of the state of a given physical system. All the possible states of a particular system constitute that system's phase space. Considered from another perspective, the dimensions of that phase space are the degrees of freedom for that specific system.

We have previously discussed the probabilities α and β. Now we can be more specific. Oftentimes the probabilities are depicted as Hopf coordinates. Hopf coordinates are part of Hopf fibration. Hopf fibration, also known as a Hopf map, describes a hypersphere in four-dimensional spaces in terms of an ordinary sphere. This was developed by the mathematician Heinz Hopf in 1931. A full discussion of Hopf's work in topology is beyond the scope of this current work; however, it is sufficient for our purposes to know that this is useful for describing locations on a sphere (like our Bloch sphere) when using complex numbers.

The Hopf fibration (also called a Hopf map) describes hypersphere (i.e., a sphere in four-dimensional space). The description consists of circles and an ordinary three-dimensional sphere. Hopf found a many-to-one continual function from the hypersphere to the normal sphere, such that each distinct point on the normal sphere is mapped from a distinct circle of the hypersphere.

Hopf's work has been important in topology and twistor theory. With that exceedingly brief description of Hopf coordinates, using them to describe the α and β is shown here:

$$\alpha = e^{i\psi} \, \cos\frac{\theta}{2}$$
$$\beta = e^{i(\psi+\varphi)} \, \sin\frac{\theta}{2}$$

The value $e^{i\psi}$ is the phase state of the qubit. Sometimes α is chosen to be real, leaving just two degrees of freedom and yielding this formula:

$$\alpha = \cos\frac{\theta}{2}$$
$$\beta = e^{i\phi} \sin\frac{\theta}{2}$$

These probabilities require a bit more explanation. To begin with, the e value is Euler's number, a transcendental number that was discussed in Chapter 2. The symbols ϕ and θ are angles.

There are two primary operations that can be performed on a qubit. The first is measurement. This is usually more formally called standard basis measurement. This operation will provide a measurement that will result in either a $|0>$ or a $|1>$ based on the aforementioned probabilities $|\alpha|^2$ and $|\beta|^2$. It is critical to realize that with qubits, the measurement is an irreversible operation, unlike classical bits. Remember, before the measurement, the qubit is in a state of superposition. After the measurement, superposition collapses to one of the two basis states.

The other operation that can be performed on a qubit is applying a quantum logic gate. We discussed classical logic gates in Chapter 4, "Fundamental Computer Science for Quantum Computing." Much of this current chapter will be devoted to exploring quantum gates and ensuring you have a working understanding of them.

As with many items we discuss in this book, the level of understanding you need to take away varies substantially based on your goals. If you simply want a generalized understanding of quantum operations, then you must understand that a given qubit will yield a 1 or 0 when measured with a particular probability. Furthermore, you must remember that before measurement, the qubit is in a superposition of these states.

If your goal is to delve deeper into quantum computing, then you should be very comfortable with everything presented in this section. It might be necessary for some readers to return to Chapters 1 and 2 to review linear algebra and complex numbers.

8.2   Quantum Gates

Chapter 4 summarized the essentials of computer science, including logic gates. Logic gates are a fundamental aspect of computing. This remains true for quantum computing, where quantum logic gates are needed.

In the circuit model of quantum computing, the basic circuit is the quantum gate (sometimes called a quantum logic gate). These quantum gates serve the same purpose in quantum computing that classical logic gates serve in digital circuits. Chapter 4 briefly discussed some of the gates used in quantum computing, but much more detail will be provided here.

Many of the gates used in classical computing are not reversible. The logical AND gate is an example of a nonreversible classical gate. The NOT gate is a classical gate that is reversible. In general, a gate is said to be reversible if the input vector can be uniquely recovered from the output vector and there is a one-to-one correspondence between its input and output assignments. This means that not only can the outputs be uniquely determined from the inputs, but also the inputs can be recovered from the outputs.

Reversible gates are necessary for effective computing. This is true of classical computers and quantum computers. A more mathematically rigorous description of classical reversible gates is as follows: An n-bit reversible gate is a bijective mapping f from the set $\{0,1\}^n$ of n-bit data onto itself. For some readers, the term *bijective* may be new. There are actually three related terms that need to be defined. Those terms are injective, surjective, and bijective. An easy way to understand these terms is to consider two sets of points, which we will call A and B, as shown in Figure 8.2.

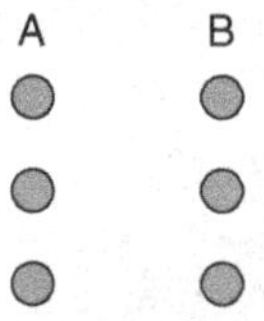

FIGURE 8.2   Two sets of points

In its simplest terms, an injection means that everything in A can be mapped to something in B, but there might be items in B with nothing matching in A. Surjective means that every B has at least one matching A, but could actually have more than one match in A. Bijective means every A has a B, and vice versa. Put more formally, it means both injective and surjective. Figure 8.3 might help you understand these three terms better.

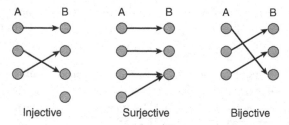

Injective   Surjective   Bijective

FIGURE 8.3   Injective, surjective, and bijective

You may be wondering what this has to do with quantum architecture. Bijective functions are invertible. This will be important when we discuss reversible gates and circuits. Unitary matrices represent quantum logic gates. You'll recall matrices from Chapter 1 (and we have seen them many times since then). A unitary matrix is one that is first a square matrix and has complex elements. Furthermore, its conjugate transpose is also its inverse. Recall from Chapter 2 that conjugate transpose simply changes a+ib to a−ib, or vice versa. You can see a unitary matrix in Equation 8.1.

$$A = \begin{bmatrix} \dfrac{1}{\sqrt{2}} & \dfrac{1}{\sqrt{2}} \\ \dfrac{1}{\sqrt{2}}i & -\dfrac{1}{\sqrt{2}}i \end{bmatrix}$$

EQUATION 8.1   Unitary Matrix

The conjugate transpose is shown in Equation 8.2.

$$A^* = \begin{matrix} \dfrac{1}{\sqrt{2}} - \dfrac{1}{\sqrt{2}}i \\ \dfrac{1}{\sqrt{2}} \ \dfrac{1}{\sqrt{2}}i \end{matrix}$$

EQUATION 8.2   Unitary Matrix Conjugate Transpose

A very good resource on unitary matrices can be found at https://www.math.tamu.edu/~dallen/m640_03c/lectures/chapter4.pdf.

8.2.1   Hadamard Gate

Perhaps the most widely discussed quantum gate is the Hadamard gate. It is represented by the Hadamard matrix shown in Equation 8.3.

$$H = \frac{1}{\sqrt{2}} \begin{bmatrix} 1 & 1 \\ 1 & -1 \end{bmatrix}$$

EQUATION 8.3   The Hadamard Matrix

This gate was briefly discussed in Chapter 4. This matrix is a square matrix with entries that are either +1 or −1. It is named after the French mathematician Jacques Hadamard. Note the Hadamard gate multiplies the Hadamard matrix by $\frac{1}{\sqrt{2}}$. Returning the matrix itself, you may note that the rows are mutually orthogonal. The Hadamard gate operates on a single qubit. It is a one-qubit version of the quantum Fourier transform. This, of course, requires us to discuss the quantum Fourier transform (QFT). For those readers who just want a general understanding of quantum computing, this is material you may wish to scan, but not be overly concerned with having a deep understanding of.

The quantum Fourier transform is a linear transformation on quantum bits. It is analogous to the classical inverse discrete transform. The quantum Fourier transform is important for many reasons. Not only is it related to the Hadamard gate, but it is actually a part of several quantum algorithms. In fact, Shor's algorithm uses the quantum Fourier transform.

Let us first review the classical discrete Fourier transform. The classical discrete Fourier transform acts on a vector $(x_0, x_1, x_2, ..., x_{n-1})$, mapping it to another vector $(y_0, y_1, y_2, ..., y_{n-1})$, when both vectors are elements of the complex space. The classical discrete Fourier transform uses the formula shown in Equation 8.4.

$$y_k = \frac{1}{\sqrt{N}} \sum_{n=0}^{N-1} x_n \omega_N^{-kn}$$

EQUATION 8.4   The Classical Discrete Fourier Transform

This is for k = 0, 1, 2, ..., n−1. In Equation 8.4, the $\omega_N = e^{2\pi i/n}$ and ω_N^n is the nth root of unity. The root of unity is any complex number that yields 1 when raised to some positive integer power n. This is sometimes called a de Moivre number after French mathematician de Moivre. He is known for the de Moivre formula that links complex numbers to trigonometry as well as his work on probability theory.

The quantum Fourier transform acts in a similar manner, operating on a quantum state. The quantum Fourier transform uses the same formula you saw in Equation 8.4. However, it is operating on quantum states such as shown in Equation 8.5.

$$|x\rangle = \sum_{i=0}^{N-1} x_i |i\rangle \rightarrow \sum_{i=0}^{N-1} y_i |i\rangle$$

EQUATION 8.5   The Quantum Discrete Fourier Transform Mapping

In Equation 8.5, the state on the left is mapped to the state on the right. Using |x> as a basic state, one can also express the quantum Fourier transform as the map shown in Equation 8.6.

$$|x\rangle \mapsto \frac{1}{\sqrt{N}} \sum_{k=0}^{N-1} \omega_N^{xk} |k\rangle$$

EQUATION 8.6 The Quantum Discrete Fourier Transform Mapping, Alternative Representation

Much more could be said about the quantum discrete Fourier transform, but this brief description is adequate for our purposes. Returning now to the Hadamard gate, it has the property that $HH^{\dagger} = I$. Put in words, the Hadamard gate multiplied by its transpose results in the identity matrix.

8.2.2 Phase Shift Gates

Phase shift gates are an interesting group of quantum gates. Phase shift gates operate on a single qubit and leave the basis state |0> unchanged but map the basis state |1> to $e^{i\varphi}$|1>. Interestingly, phase shift gates do not change the probability of measuring a |0> or |1> after they are applied. These gates, instead, modify the phase of the quantum state, thus the name. Equation 8.7 shows a generalized phase shift gate.

$$R_{\phi} = \begin{bmatrix} 1 & 0 \\ 0 & e^{i\phi} \end{bmatrix}$$

EQUATION 8.7 Phase Shift Gate

Phase shift gates are used in many places, but specifically in transmons. A transmon is a superconducting charged qubit, designed to have reduced sensitivity to interference. Here are some interesting papers on phase shift gates:

https://cds.cern.ch/record/684838/files/0311103.pdf

https://arxiv.org/pdf/1110.2998.pdf

https://arxiv.org/pdf/quant-ph/0011013.pdf

8.2.3 Pauli Gates

Recall our discussion of Pauli matrices from Chapter 2. The three matrices are

$$\begin{bmatrix} 0 & 1 \\ 1 & 0 \end{bmatrix}$$

$$\begin{bmatrix} 0 & -i \\ i & 0 \end{bmatrix}$$

$$\begin{bmatrix} 1 & 0 \\ 0 & -1 \end{bmatrix}$$

These are usually represented with the σ notation, thus:

$$\sigma_1 = \begin{bmatrix} 0 & 1 \\ 1 & 0 \end{bmatrix}$$

$$\sigma_2 = \begin{bmatrix} 0 & -i \\ i & 0 \end{bmatrix}$$

$$\sigma_3 = \begin{bmatrix} 1 & 0 \\ 0 & -1 \end{bmatrix}$$

It should not surprise you that there are Pauli gates. In fact, there are three such gates: Pauli-X, Pauli-Y, and Pauli-Z. Each of these operates on a single qubit, transforming it.

The Pauli-X gate is the quantum equivalent of the classical NOT gate. It is the equivalent of a rotation around the x-axis of the Bloch sphere by π radians. It will transform |0> to |1>, and vice versa. And as you can probably guess, the Pauli-X matrix represents it:

$$X = \begin{bmatrix} 0 & 1 \\ 1 & 0 \end{bmatrix}$$

The Pauli-Y gate is the equivalent of a rotation around the y-axis by π radians. It will transform |0> to i|1> and |1> to −i|0>. It is represented by the Pauli-Y matrix:

$$Y = \begin{bmatrix} 0 & -i \\ i & 0 \end{bmatrix}$$

Finally, we come to the Pauli-Z gate. You can probably guess that it is the equivalent of rotating about the z-axis of the Bloch sphere. It is a special case of a phase shift gate. It leaves the |0> basis state unchanged, but maps the basis state |1> to −|1>. It is represented by the Pauli-Z matrix:

$$Z = \begin{bmatrix} 1 & 0 \\ 0 & -1 \end{bmatrix}$$

8.2.4   Swap Gates

Unlike the gates we previously discussed in this section, swap gates operate on two qubits. As the name suggests, they swap the qubits. It is represented by the matrix shown in Figure 8.4.

$$\text{SWAP} = \begin{bmatrix} 1 & 0 & 0 & 0 \\ 0 & 0 & 1 & 0 \\ 0 & 1 & 0 & 0 \\ 0 & 0 & 0 & 1 \end{bmatrix}$$

FIGURE 8.4 Swap gate

There is another interesting variation of the swap gate—the square root of swap gate. This intriguing gate essentially performs a halfway swap. What makes it more interesting is that it is a universal gate. As discussed briefly in Chapter 4, that means one can construct other gates using the square root of swap gate. Considering a two-qubit system, the square root of swap gate is shown in Figure 8.4.

8.2.5 Fredkin Gate

A Fredkin gate is a classical computational circuit invented by Edward Fredkin. It is a universal gate. Recall this means that any logical or arithmetical operation can be constructed entirely from Fredkin gates. The quantum version of the Fredkin gate is a 3-bit gate that performs a controlled swap; therefore, it is sometimes called a CSWAP gate or a cS gate.

8.2.6 Toffoli Gates

Toffoli gates are eponymously named after the inventor Tommaso Toffoli. These gates are also called CCNOT gates and are universal reversible logic gates for classical computers; they are not for quantum applications. They have three inputs and three outputs.

Essentially, a Toffoli gate works by examining the inputs. If the first two qubits are in the state |1>, then it applies a Pauli-X on the third bit. Otherwise, it does nothing. This is a controlled gate.

8.2.7 Controlled Gates

While there are other forms of controlled gates, the general class of controlled gates operating on qubits using specific operations is widely used. For example, the controlled NOT gate (often called the cNOT or cX gate) acts on two qubits. If the first qubit is |1>, then the NOT operation is performed on the second qubit. If the first qubit is not |1>, then the second qubit is unchanged. Assuming the basis states |00>, |01>, |10>, and |11>, the cX gate can be represented by the matrix shown in Equation 8.8.

$$\begin{bmatrix} 1 & 0 & 0 & 0 \\ 0 & 1 & 0 & 0 \\ 0 & 0 & 0 & 1 \\ 0 & 0 & 1 & 0 \end{bmatrix}$$

EQUATION 8.8 cX Gate Matrix

There is also the controlled-U gate. This gate also operates on two qubits, and the first qubit is a control (thus the name). The mapping of the controlled-U gate is shown here:

$$|00> \rightarrow |00>$$

$$|01> \rightarrow |01>$$

Note that if the first qubit is zero, nothing is changed.

There are more complex gates, such as this one:

$$|10> \rightarrow |1> \otimes U|0> = |1> \otimes (u_{00}|0> + u_{10}|1>)$$

Before continuing, we must examine what this means, because some of it might seem quite odd. The U stands for one of the Pauli matrices ($\sigma_x \sigma_y \sigma_z$). If it is the Pauli-Z matrix, then it is a controlled Z gate. Thus, u00 means $|00>$ input into a particular Pauli matrix. Now with that explanation, we can complete our description.

We now show Pauli matrices used in a more complex gate.

$$|11> \rightarrow |1> \otimes U|1> = |1> \otimes (u_{01}|0> + u_{11}|1>)$$

As you can see, this is a bit more of a complex gate than some of the others we have discussed. However, you can view it as a controlled Pauli gate, if that helps you to understand it.

The quantum CNOT (controlled NOT) gate operates much like what you see in Figure 8.5.

Input	Output
$|00\rangle$	$|00\rangle$
$|01\rangle$	$|01\rangle$
$|10\rangle$	$|11\rangle$
$|11\rangle$	$|10\rangle$

FIGURE 8.5   Quantum CNOT

8.2.8   Ising Gates

Ising gates are very interesting gates. There are actually three of them: XX, YY, and ZZ gates. These are in fact often called Ising coupling gates. These are named after Ernst Ising, who developed the eponymously named Ising model. The Ising model represents the magnetic dipole moments of atomic spins.

Ising gates are two qubit gates that are implemented by some quantum computers, particularly those that operate with trapped ions. We will be discussing more hardware-specific issues, such as trapped ions, in Chapter 9. These gates are more complex than the gates we have previously discussed in this chapter. For the casual reader, it is sufficient to understand that these are quantum gates. For the reader wishing a bit more depth, let us first look at the matrices for these gates. These are shown in Equation 8.9 through Equation 8.11.

$$\begin{bmatrix} \cos(\phi) & 0 & 0 & -i\sin(\phi) \\ 0 & \cos(\phi) & -i\sin(\phi) & 0 \\ 0 & -i\sin(\phi) & \cos(\phi) & 0 \\ -i\sin(\phi) & 0 & 0 & \cos(\phi) \end{bmatrix}$$

EQUATION 8.9   Ising XX Coupling Gate

$$\begin{bmatrix} \cos(\phi) & 0 & 0 & i\sin(\phi) \\ 0 & \cos(\phi) & -i\sin(\phi) & 0 \\ 0 & i\sin(\phi) & \cos(\phi) & 0 \\ i\sin(\phi) & 0 & 0 & \cos(\phi) \end{bmatrix}$$

EQUATION 8.10   Ising YY Coupling Gate

$$\begin{bmatrix} e^{i\phi/2} & 0 & 0 & 0 \\ 0 & e^{-i\phi/2} & 0 & 0 \\ 0 & 0 & e^{-i\phi/2} & 0 \\ 0 & 0 & 0 & e^{i\phi/2} \end{bmatrix}$$

EQUATION 8.11   Ising ZZ Coupling Gate

As you can see, these are all 4×4 matrices. To refresh your memory, e is Euler's number, ϕ is the azimuthal angle, and, of course, i is the base imaginary number. The trigonometric function you are certainly familiar with already.

8.2.9   Gottesman–Knill Theorem

When discussing quantum gates, we must also discuss the Gottesman–Knill theorem. This was proposed by Daniel Gottesman and Emanuel Knill and states that circuits that consist only of gates from the qubit Pauli group's normalizer can be perfectly simulated in polynomial time on a classic probabilistic computer. This requires us to define a few terms we have not previously encountered in this book. Pauli group is probably the easiest to define. It is a group that consists of the identity matrix and all of the Pauli matrices. Next, we must define what a normalizer is, for those readers not familiar with group theory. A normalizer can be any one of the following three equivalent items:

1. The largest intermediate subgroup in which the subgroup is normal.

2. The set of all elements in that group that commute with the subgroup.

3. The set of all elements in the group for which the induced inner automorphism restricts to the group's automorphism.

That third definition is probably quite daunting for readers who do not have a strong mathematical background. Fortunately, the more casual reader doesn't need to have a deep understanding of what a normalizer is. What is important is that the Pauli group (sometimes termed a Clifford group) can be generated using only CNOT, Hadamard, and phase gates. Therefore, stabilizer circuits can be constructed using only these gates.

What the Gottesman–Knill theorem tells us is that a quantum circuit, meeting specific criteria, can be simulated on a classical computer in an efficient manner. This is actually the basis of some current research wherein quantum problems are explored on classical computers. This is the most important thing to know about the Gottesman–Knill theorem.

8.3 More with Gates

Now that we have discussed, at least in general terms, some of the more common quantum gates, let us delve a bit deeper into the concept of quantum logic gates. This section is a bit more technical. Depending on your goals in reading this text, this subsection may or may not be critical for you to fully master.

Reflecting back on the material from Chapter 4, as well as what has been discussed thus far in this chapter, it should be clear what a logical gate is. It essentially takes in bits (or qubits) and puts out bits (or qubits). Ultimately, all computer operations must be reduced to gate operations. In the classical computing world, this means eventually reduced to binary logical operations. In the quantum computing world, this is reduced to actions on quantum gates. Input qubits enter the gate, which then produces output qubits. Notice that I intentionally did not state that the qubits were replaced. In some operations, an input may remain unchanged.

In the quantum gate world, we need gates that are always reversible. The specific reversibility is called a *unitary mapping*. Now drawing on all the mathematics covered previously in this book, let us put this in a more rigorous form. A quantum gate provides a linear transformation of a complex inner product space that preserves the Hermitian inner product. Recall that the inner product is also called the dot product. The inner product of two vectors is simply the two vectors multiplied. Consider vectors X and Y. The inner product is shown in Equation 8.12.

$$\sum_{i=1}^{n} X_i Y_i$$

EQUATION 8.12 Inner Product

Also recall from Chapter 2 that Hermitian refers to a square matrix that is equal to its own conjugate transpose. Conjugate transpose means first taking the transpose of the matrix and then taking the matrix's complex conjugate.

8.4 Quantum Circuits

Now that we have covered, at least in a general manner, quantum gates, it is time to discuss quantum circuits. The simplest explanation is that a quantum circuit is a sequence of quantum gates.

Since we discussed reversible quantum gates in the previous section, it is natural to consider reversible quantum circuits. Consider a scenario where you have to reverse the gates of n bits. We will call these gates A and B. If you put them together, such that k outputs of A are mapped to k inputs for B, you have a reversible circuit that operates on n+n–k bits. This is a basic structure for a reversible quantum circuit.

We can now begin to discuss how to diagram such quantum circuits. We first need to include notation for all the various quantum gates we may wish to use. Table 8.1 shows the various symbols for quantum gates we discussed in the previous sections.

TABLE 8.1 Common Gate Symbols

Gate	Symbol
Hadamard	$-\boxed{\text{H}}-$
Pauli-X	$-\boxed{\text{X}}-$
Pauli-Y	$-\boxed{\text{Y}}-$
Pauli-Z	$-\boxed{\text{Z}}-$
SWAP	✕
Phase shift	$-\boxed{\text{S}}-$
Toffoli	⊕

Gate	Symbol
Fredkin	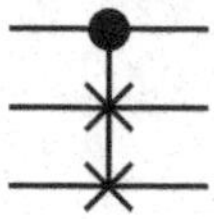
Controlled	ΛG
Controlled Not (CNOT, CX)	
Controlled Z	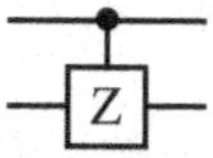 Z

Table 8.1 shows the most common gate symbols. Now we can begin to discuss quantum circuits. Let us begin with a quite simple circuit—one that does not actually do much other than have a single measurement on an input, and doesn't even have any gates. This is shown in Figure 8.6.

$|0\rangle$ ———[⊿]— $= |0\rangle$

FIGURE 8.6   Simplest circuit

Figure 8.6 presents a symbol we have not discussed before. That is the measurement symbol, which is shown in Figure 8.7.

FIGURE 8.7   The measurement symbol

So, what Figure 8.7 is telling us is that we have a qubit in state $|0\rangle$ that is measured and remains in state $|0\rangle$. Next, let us get a bit more complicated. We have a qubit that is put through a Hadamard gate and then measured to produce some value. This is shown in Figure 8.8.

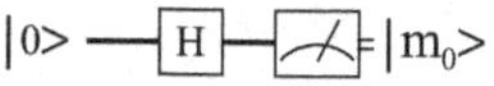

$|0\rangle$ ———[H]——[⊿]= $|m_0\rangle$

FIGURE 8.8   A simple Hadamard gate circuit

The symbol $|m_0\rangle$ just means the result of the measurement. It could be $|0\rangle$ or $|1\rangle$.

Now we can expand this a bit more. What about circuits with multiple gates? That is easy to diagram, regardless of where the measurement takes place. For now, let's ignore the "why" part, as in why you would want to combine particular gates, and simply consider how to diagram them. Figure 8.9 shows a simple two-gate diagram.

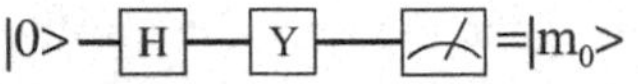

$|0> - \boxed{H} - \boxed{Y} - \boxed{\measuredangle} = |m_0>$

FIGURE 8.9 Two-gate diagram

One can also have gates in parallel. For example, one might have a Pauli-X gate and a Pauli-Y gate in parallel, as shown in Figure 8.10.

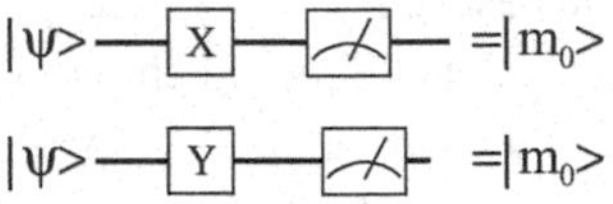

$|\psi> - \boxed{X} - \boxed{\measuredangle} - = |m_0>$

$|\psi> - \boxed{Y} - \boxed{\measuredangle} - = |m_0>$

FIGURE 8.10 Another two-gate diagram

In Figure 8.10, each qubit is put through its gate and then measured, yielding some value (either $|1>$ or $|0>$).

8.5 The D-Wave Quantum Architecture

This section explores, at a high level, the D-Wave architecture. This is due to two reasons:

- D-Wave takes a different approach to quantum computing than do other vendors.

- D-Wave is so prominent in quantum computing, its architecture bears some scrutiny.

While this section will only explore the D-Wave architecture at a high level, D-Wave itself provides a great deal of detail on its website, including numerous documents anyone can read.

D-Wave's first processor was a superconducting integrated circuit that utilized flux qubits. Flux qubits are very small, usually micrometer, loops of superconducting metal with a number of Josephson junctions functioning as the qubits. Josephson junctions use a thin layer of non-superconducting material between two layers of superconducting material. These devices are named after Brian Josephson, who was awarded the 1973 Nobel Prize in Physics for his work.

In May 2011, D-Wave announced the D-Wave One, with a 128-qubit processor. In 2012, a 512-bit D-Wave computer was released. In 2019, D-Wave announced the next-generation Pegasus quantum processing chip.

The D-Wave systems use a fundamentally different process than gate-based quantum computers. To begin with, the qubits are superconducting chips, not actual quantum states of particles such as photons. Secondly, the approach to computing is a bit different. D-Wave utilizes something called quantum annealing, which is a process of finding the global minimum of a given function over a set of candidate solutions. The process starts from a quantum-mechanical superposition of all the candidate states; it then uses a time-dependent equation to evolve towards a solution.

It may also be informative for you to view D-Wave's own description of quantum annealing in the following excerpt[1]:

> "Quantum annealing processors naturally return low-energy solutions; some applications require the real minimum energy (optimization problems) and others require good low-energy samples (probabilistic sampling problems).
>
> "**Optimization problems.** In an optimization problem, we search for the best of many possible combinations. Optimization problems include scheduling challenges, such as 'Should I ship this package on this truck or the next one?' or 'What is the most efficient route a traveling salesperson should take to visit different cities?'
>
> "Physics can help solve these sorts of problems because we can frame them as energy minimization problems. A fundamental rule of physics is that everything tends to seek a minimum energy state. Objects slide down hills; hot things cool down over time. This behavior is also true in the world of quantum physics. Quantum annealing simply uses quantum physics to find low-energy states of a problem and, therefore the optimal or near-optimal combination of elements.
>
> "**Sampling problems.** Sampling from many low-energy states and characterizing the shape of the energy landscape is useful for machine learning problems where we want to build a probabilistic model of reality. The samples give us information about the model state for a given set of parameters, which can then be used to improve the model.
>
> Probabilistic models explicitly handle uncertainty by accounting for gaps in our knowledge and errors."

8.5.1   SQUID

At the heart of D-Wave's approach is the superconducting qubit (SQUID). This is the equivalent of the classical computer transistor. The term SQUID comes from the full name Superconducting QUantum Interference Device. SQUIDs use the aforementioned Josephson junction. There are two SQUID types: the direct current (DC) and radio frequency (RF).

Again, it may be useful to consider D-Wave's own description of SQUID, found in this excerpt:

> "Quantum computers have similarities to and differences from this CMOS transistor idea. Figure 1 shows a schematic illustration of what is known as a superconducting qubit (also called a SQUID), which is the basic building block of a quantum computer (a quantum 'transistor', if you like). The name SQUID comes from the phrase Superconducting QUantum Interference Device. The term 'Interference' refers to the electrons—which behave as waves inside quantum waves, interference patterns which give rise to the quantum effects. The reason that quantum effects such as electron waves are supported in such a structure—allowing it to behave as a qubit—is due to the properties of the material from which it is made. The large loop in the

---

1. https://docs.dwavesys.com/docs/latest/c_gs_2.html

diagram is made from a metal called niobium (in contrast to conventional transistors which are mostly made from silicon). When this metal is cooled down, it becomes what is known as a superconductor, and it starts to exhibit quantum mechanical effects.

"A regular transistor allows you to encode 2 different states (using voltages). The superconducting qubit structure instead encodes 2 states as tiny magnetic fields, which either point up or down. We call these states +1 and −1, and they correspond to the two states that the qubit can 'choose' between. Using the quantum mechanics that is accessible with these structures, we can control this object so that we can put the qubit into a superposition of these two states as described earlier. So by adjusting a control knob on the quantum computer, you can put all the qubits into a superposition state where it hasn't yet decided which of those +1, −1 states to be.

"In order to go from a single qubit to a multi-qubit processor, the qubits must be connected together such that they can exchange information. This is achieved through the use of elements known as couplers. The couplers are also made from superconducting loops. By putting many such elements (qubits and couplers) together, we can start to build up a fabric of quantum devices that are programmable. Figure 2 shows a schematic of 8 connected qubits. The loop shown in the previous diagram has now been stretched out to form one of the long gold rectangles. At the points where the rectangles cross, the couplers have been shown schematically as blue dots."

The most important thing to realize about the D-Wave approach is that while it is radically different from other approaches, it has had remarkable success in producing stable working systems.

8.6 Summary

In this chapter, we explored the fundamentals of quantum architecture. Our main focus was on quantum gates and circuits. However, we also explored quantum annealing and related approaches. The material in this chapter sets the stage for Chapters 9 and 10. It is important that you be comfortable with the added details on qubits, as well as have a working knowledge of quantum gates and circuits, before continuing to the next chapter.

Test Your Skills

REVIEW QUESTIONS

1. _____ operate on a single qubit and leave the basis state $|0>$ unchanged but map the basis state $|1>$ to $e^{i\phi} |>$.

   a. Hadamard gates

   b. Phase shift gates

   c. Pauli gates

   d. Toffoli gates

2. What property(ies) is/are required for two vectors to be considered orthonormal?

   a. Unit length

   b. Use of bra-ket notation

   c. Normalized

   d. Orthonormal

3. _____ states that the probability density of finding a particle at a particular point is proportional to the square of the magnitude of the particle's wave function at that point.

   a. Hilbert space

   b. Hilbert rule

   c. Schrödinger's equation

   d. Born's rule

4. _____states that circuits that consist only of gates from the normalizer of the qubit Pauli group can be perfectly simulated in polynomial time on a probabilistic classic computer.

   a. Schrödinger's equation

   b. Gottesman–Knill Theorem

   c. Born's rule

   d. Phase shifting

5. A _____ gate provides a linear transformation of a complex inner product space that preserves the Hermitian inner product.

    a. Hadamard

    b. Pauli

    c. Quantum

    d. Ising

6. What does the following symbol denote?

    a. Hadamard gate

    b. Measurement

    c. Toffoli gate

    d. Phase shift

Chapter | **9**

Quantum Hardware

Chapter Objectives

After reading this chapter and completing the review questions, you will be able to do the following:

- Articulate different qubit storage technologies
- Understand decoherence
- Explain methods to mitigate decoherence
- Demonstrate a working knowledge of quantum networking

This chapter explores the physical implementation of quantum computers. In previous chapters we have explored qubits; in this chapter, we will explore the physical implementation of quantum computers. Decoherence will also be covered. Understanding the implementation of qubits and the role of decoherence are the most important topics in this chapter.

In addition to those fundamental aspects of quantum computing, we will also explore quantum networking and currently theoretical topics such as topological quantum computing. This chapter should provide you with a general understanding of the physical elements of quantum computing.

9.1 Qubits

Chapter 8, "Quantum Architecture," discussed qubits at some length, from a mathematical perspective; however, it did not address the issue of how the qubits are actually physically realized. What is needed is any quantum mechanical system that has two states. The two states will be used to represent a 1 or a 0. This section addresses a few specific approaches to physically implementing qubits.

Before we examine specific physical realizations of qubits, a few general facts about qubits should be discussed. As has been covered in detail throughout this book, qubits are probabilistic by their very nature. This means that they are prone to errors in calculations. We will explore error correction algorithms in Chapter 10, "Quantum Algorithms." Beyond the probabilistic nature of qubits, there is their sensitivity to environmental noise, which we will explore later in this chapter.

An important fact we must address now is how many physical qubits are needed to implement a logical qubit. You might naturally suppose that it is a one-to-one relationship; however, that supposition would be inaccurate. There is not a specific correlation formula; however, it typically takes several *physical* qubits to implement one *logical* qubit. As an example, Shor's error correction code works by encoding a single logical qubit in nine physical qubits. The system is predicated on repetition codes in groups of three qubits. Equation 9.1 illustrates the general definitions of logical states.

$$|0_L\rangle = \big(|000\rangle + |111\rangle\big) \otimes \big(|000\rangle + |111\rangle\big) \otimes \big(|000\rangle + |111\rangle\big)$$
$$|1_L\rangle = \big(|000\rangle - |111\rangle\big) \otimes \big(|000\rangle - |111\rangle\big) \otimes \big(|000\rangle - |111\rangle\big)$$

EQUATION 9.1 Shor's Error Correction Code

Essentially, the process works by a type of "majority voting" so that any accidental bit or phase flips are discovered. Again, this is not a formula that can be applied to all situations. You will not always need nine physical qubits to create one logical qubit. However, it is quite common to require multiple physical qubits to make one logical qubit work.

Chapter 8 discussed logical qubits and gates; however, there is not a one-to-one comparison to physical qubits. In other words, one logical qubit does not equal one physical qubit. The exact number of physical qubits to embody a logical qubit varies. For example, Shor's error correction code, also called the repetition code, works by encoding a logical qubit into nine physical qubits. Some other scenarios use as little as three physical qubits for one logical qubit. The issue is error correction. Physical qubits are very error prone.

9.1.1 Photons

Photons are commonly used for creating physical qubits, with the data (1 or 0) determined by the polarization. The horizontal polarization is |0> and vertical is |1>. The polarization method is a common method for using photons for qubits. This is the essence of using polarization for encoding qubits.

Photons can be described as having a horizontal or vertical polarization. Some sources refer to a right or left circular polarization. In general, polarization specifies a geometrical orientation for a transverse wave. A transverse wave is a wave with oscillations that are perpendicular to the direction of the wave. The term *perpendicular*, in this instance, is synonymous with transverse. The motion of a transverse wave can be described in the following formula:

$$s(p,t) = Au\,sin\left(\frac{t-(p-0)\frac{d}{v}}{T}+\varphi\right)$$

In this formula, the values are as follows:

- d is the direction of propagation.
- o is a reference point in the medium of propagation.
- A is the wave amplitude.
- v is the velocity of propagation.
- T is the period.
- φ is the phase at the reference point o.
- p is a location/point.
- t is the time.

This is primarily a description of linear polarization.

Circular polarization allows for multiple independent displacement directions along with the direction d. While the light is commonly used in discussions of polarization, any electromagnetic wave can have polarization.

There are also forms of polarization other than circular or linear (for example, elliptical polarization). Any electromagnetic wave that is polarized, such that the tip of the field vector defines an ellipse that is in a fixed intersecting plan and is perpendicular to the direction of propagation, is elliptically polarized.

Another method used with photons is to encode the qubit using time-bin encoding. The process involves having a single photon be processed through a Mach-Zehnder interferometer. This interferometer is a device that takes two beams derived from splitting a single light source and determines the relative phase shift variations between them. When a photon enters the interferometer, it will be guided along one of two paths. One path is longer than the other, and the difference between the two paths must be longer than the photon's coherence length. Coherence length is the propagation distance over which a coherent electromagnetic wave can maintain a particular degree of coherence.

The photon takes one of the two paths. The shorter path (i.e., the earlier arrival of the photon) designates the state |0>, and the longer path designates state |1>.

A variation of using photons is Linear Optical Quantum Computing (LOQC). This is a system rather than a single qubit, and it uses photon detectors along with other optical instruments such as mirrors and waveplates. The photons are still the carriers of information. The interested reader can learn more about LOQC at the following sources:

https://arxiv.org/abs/quant-ph/0512071

https://arxiv.org/abs/1305.3592

https://inspirehep.net/literature/773113

In 2020, researchers at Harvard University proposed a novel method for using photons for qubits. The qubit would be a single atom in their proposed approach, with the atom's photons as information carriers. In order to use photons in quantum computation, the photons must interact; however, under normal conditions, photons don't interact with themselves. The Harvard team proposed using a mirror to reflect photons produced by the atom back to the atom so they would interact with the atom. As of this writing, this is a theoretical proposal and has not yet been realized in a physical device.

9.1.2 Electron

Electrons and photons are two of the most obvious ways to implement a qubit. Electron qubits use some property, such as electron spin, to indicate the state of the qubit. For example, an up spin can designate state |0> and a down spin can designate |1>.

There are other variations of using electrons to store qubits. In 1997, David DiVencenzo and Daniel Loss proposed a type of quantum computer that uses the spin of freedom of electrons, which are confined to quantum dots, to physically implement a qubit. This is now called a Loss-DiVincenzo quantum computer. The term *quantum dot* actually comes from nanotechnology. A device that is only of nanometer scale in one dimension is referred to as a quantum well. A device that is of nanometer scale in two dimensions is called a quantum wire. A device that is of nanometer scale in all three dimensions is known as a quantum dot. The Loss-DiVencenzo uses electrons confined to a three-dimensional nano device to implement qubits.

Other researchers have focused on quantum states of electrons in particular mediums. For example, the Okinawa Institute of Science and Technology has worked on using electrons in liquid helium. Data suggests that electron spin states in liquid helium would maintain coherence longer. Reading the data in the qubit is based on detecting different Rydberg states. Rydberg states are excited states that follow the Rydberg formula. This, of course, requires the understanding of a few additional terms. An *excited state* is any quantum state that has a higher energy than the absolute minimum (i.e., the ground state). The work of Johannes Rydberg, the Rydberg formula, calculates the wavelengths of a spectral line in a chemical element. This model was later refined by Neils Bohr.

The details of the Rydberg formula are not absolutely necessary for you to understand qubits, but for those interested readers, those details are given. First, the formula depends on the Rydberg constant, symbolized as RH for hydrogen. Then, the Rydberg formula (again using hydrogen as an exemplar) is shown here:

$$\frac{1}{\lambda} = R_H \left(\frac{1}{n_1^2} - \frac{1}{n_2^2} \right)$$

In this formula, the values are as follows:

- RH is the Rydberg constant.
- λ is the wavelength of electromagnetic radiation in a vacuum.

- n1 is the principal quantum number of an energy level.

- n2 is the principal quantum number of an energy level for atomic electron transition.

Put in simpler terms, the Rydberg formula predicts the wavelength of light resulting from an electron changing energy levels in an atom. You may recall principle quantum numbers from Chapter 3, "Basic Physics for Quantum Computing."

In 2020, researchers at the University of New South Wales, working with colleagues at the Université de Sherbrooke in Quebec and Aalto University in Finland, announced a rather novel approach to qubits. The researchers created artificial atoms that have normal electron shells (see Chapter 3 for a review of electron shells) but no nucleus. Because there is no nucleus, and thus no positive charge, the team used an electrode to provide the positive charge. The qubit was implemented in a quantum dot (recall this is a device that is nanoscale in all three dimensions) of 10 nanometers in diameter. The researchers postulate that having multiple electrons as the qubit rather than a single electron will provide a more robust qubit.

9.1.3 Ions

Trapped ions can also be used as the physical implementation of qubits. The qubit value is stored as an electronic state for each ion. This of course requires stable ions. Fortunately, there are a number of such stable ions. A common approach used in trapped ions for quantum computing is the Paul ion trap, named after Wolfgang Paul. No, for those astute readers, this is not a misspelling of Wolfgang Pauli. These are two different physicists. Wolfgang Pauli received his Nobel Prize in Physics for the Pauli Exclusion Principle in 1945. Wolfgang Paul received his Nobel Prize in Physics in 1989 for the development of methods to isolate atoms and subatomic particles for study, which is directly related to our current interests.

Trapping ions is a bit more challenging than one might first suspect. One has to consider Earnshaw's theorem, proven by Samuel Earnshaw in 1842. This theorem essentially states that a charged particle cannot be held in a stable equilibrium by electrostatic forces alone. For those readers who wish a more rigorous mathematical description, let us put this more formally: The Laplace has no solution with local minima or maxima in free space. There are saddle points, which are points in the graph of a function where the derivatives (i.e., the slopes) in orthogonal directions are all zero but are not a local extrema of the function. What all that means is that using electrostatic forces alone, there cannot be a stable equilibrium.

This takes us back to the Paul ion trap. This trap uses an electric field oscillating at radio frequency. Assuming the frequency has the right oscillation frequency and field strength, the charged particle is trapped at the aforementioned saddle point. For those readers who wish a bit more detail on how Paul ion traps and saddle points work, there is the Mathieu function. The motion of the ion in the saddle point is described by Mathieu functions. These functions are solutions to Mathieu's differential equations, first introduced by Emile Mathieu. The differential equation is

$$\frac{d^2y}{dx^2} + \left(a - 2q\ cos\ 2x\right)y = 0$$

where a and q are parameters specific to the particular application.

This is not material you absolutely must master to follow this book, but it is provided for the reader who wishes to delve a bit deeper. This also demonstrates that there is a limit to how deeply one can pursue quantum computing without more substantial mathematics, including differential equations. For more details on the Mathieu differential equations, the interested reader can consult the following sources:

http://pi.math.cornell.edu/~rand/randpdf/AMR.pdf

https://cds.cern.ch/record/828858/files/978-3-540-26576-4_BookBackMatter.pdf

Paul ion traps are not the very first ion traps. The first implementation was proposed by Ignacio Cirac and Peter Zollar in 1995. They provided a mechanism for implementing a controlled-NOT gate using a trapped ion system.

9.1.4 NMRQC

Nuclear magnetic resonance quantum computing (NMRQC) is a very interesting approach to physically implementing quantum computers. This approach uses spin states of nuclei within molecules to represent the qubits. The states are probed using nuclear magnetic resonances, thus the name. This system is fundamentally a variation on nuclear magnetic resonance spectroscopy.

There are two approaches to this process. Originally, the molecules were in a liquid state, and this was known as liquid state nuclear magnetic resonance. However, molecules in a solid state are now more commonly used. This is referred to as solid state nuclear magnetic resonance. One example is nitrogen in a diamond lattice. The crystalline structure makes it much easier to localize the individual qubits. This variation depends on nitrogen vacancy centers. One type of point defect in a diamond occurs when the nearest neighbor pair of a nitrogen atom substitutes for a carbon atom, causing a vacancy in the lattice.

Whether using liquid or solid state, the use of nuclear spins for quantum computing was proposed in 1997. In 2001, IBM was able to implement Shor's algorithm on a seven-qubit NMRQC.

In 1998, Bruce Kane proposed a quantum computer that was essentially a hybrid between the quantum dot (which will be discussed later in this chapter) and the NMRQC. You can learn more about the Kane quantum computer at the following sources:

https://www.nature.com/articles/30156

https://permalink.lanl.gov/object/tr?what=info:lanl-repo/lareport/LA-UR-02-4626

9.1.5 Bose-Einstein Condensate Quantum Computing

One fascinating approach to quantum computing is the use of Bose-Einstein condensates to communicate among multiple small quantum computers. The concept is similar to current multicore processors. A Bose-Einstein condensate (BEC) is a state of matter formed when a gas consisting of bosons is cooled to temperatures quite close to absolute zero. Bosons are particles that can be either elementary particles or composite particles. Bosons are particles that carry a force and have a whole number spin. There are four gauge bosons in the standard model that carry specific forces:

- Photon

- Gluon (there are actually different types of gluons)

- Charged weak bosons (there are two types of these)

- Neutral weak bosons

In addition, there is the Higgs boson, which you have undoubtedly heard of. Gauge bosons are simply bosons that carry some fundamental force. As you can see from the preceding list, there is a different gauge boson for each of the fundamental forces.

Just to clarify some of the particle physics involved, a brief overview of the various particles is given here. There are three basic types of elementary particles: hadrons, bosons, and fermions. These can be further subdivided. For example, fermions include all quarks and leptons. We have discussed quarks in previous chapters. Leptons are fundamental particles that have a half integer spin. Examples are the electron, muon, and tau. In fact, there are two families of leptons, as shown in Table 9.1.

TABLE 9.1   Leptons

Charged	Neutral
Electron	Electron neutrino
Muon	Muon neutrino
Tau	Tau neutrino

Hadrons are made up of quarks and/or antiquarks. You are undoubtably familiar with hadrons. The two most common examples are the proton and neutron.

Returning to bosons, they are either elementary or composite. Photons are a good example of elementary bosons. Mesons are composite bosons—essentially particles made up of quarks and/or antiquarks.

Now that we have covered some basic facts about particles, let us return to BEC computing. The concept in this approach to quantum computing is to divide computational problems among multiple small quantum computers. Each individual quantum computer communicates information using BEC clouds. This approach is believed to ameliorate the decoherence problem. The interested reader can dive deeper into BEC computing at the following sources:

https://physics.gatech.edu/news/bose-einstein-condensates-evaluated-communicating-among-quantum-computers

https://physicsworld.com/a/citizen-scientists-excel-at-creating-bose-einstein-condensates/

https://cds.cern.ch/record/403945/files/9910073.pdf

9.1.6   GaAs Quantum Dots

Gallium arsenide (GaAs) is often used to create quantum dots. A quantum dot is a device that is nanoscale in all three dimensions. The electron spin in the GaAs quantum dot is subject to an effective magnetic field. This field is called an Overhauser field. The Overhauser effect is a nuclear effect that occurs when the nuclear spin polarization of one population of nuclei is transferred to another. This is accomplished via cross-relaxation. The details of cross-relaxation are beyond the scope of our current discussion; however, the general process is that an RF (Radio Frequency) pulse (or series of pulses) is applied to some sample in a homogeneous magnetic field, and the resonance frequency of the nuclei is transferred to another population of nuclei.

Typically, the field has a random magnitude and direction, and measurements occur by averaging multiple experimental runs. It happens that the nuclear spins evolve slower than the electron spins, which means that over a sufficiently short period of time, the Overhauser field is static. This allows the electron spin to be used for information purposes. There have been numerous single-qubit experiments utilizing this technique.

Table 9.2 summarizes the different methods of physically implementing qubits we have discussed.

TABLE 9.2   Physical Qubits

Method	Brief Description
Photons	The horizontal polarization is |0> and vertical is |1>. The polarization method is a common method for using photons for qubits.
Linear Optical Quantum Computing (LOQC)	This is a system rather than a single qubit, and it uses photon detectors along with other optical instruments such as mirrors and waveplates. The photons are still the carriers of information
Electrons	Electron qubits use some property, such as electron spin, to indicate the state of the qubit. For example, an up spin can designate state |0>, and a down spin can designate |1>.
Ions	The qubit value is stored as an electronic state for each ion.
Nuclear magnetic resonance quantum computing	This approach uses spin states of nuclei within molecules to represent the qubits. The states are probed using nuclear magnetic resonances, thus the name.
Bose-Einstein condensate quantum computing	Bose-Einstein condensates are used to communicate among multiple small quantum computers, much like a multiprocessor computer.
GaAs quantum dots	A quantum dot is a device that is nanoscale in all three dimensions. The electron spin in the GaAs quantum dot is subject to an effective magnetic field.

9.2   How Many Qubits Are Needed?

This question is difficult to answer due to the fact that numerous variables affect the answer. However, some general guidelines can be given. In general, it is believed that we will need approximately 4000 qubits to crack 2048-bit RSA. It is also believed that 1000 qubits are necessary for effective machine learning. We will discuss the breaking of RSA in more depth in Chapter 11, "Current Asymmetric Algorithms."

Of course, how many qubits are needed also depends on how fast one wishes to crack the algorithm in question. Researchers Craig Gidney of Google and Martin Ekera from the Swedish Royal Institute of Technology demonstrated that 20 million qubits could crack 2048-bit RSA in eight hours. You can find more about their work at https://cacm.acm.org/news/237303-how-quantum-computer-could-break-2048-bit-rsa-encryption-in-8-hours/fulltext.

This is actually far better than previous estimates. It had been estimated that one billion qubits would be needed to break 2048-bit RSA keys. For breaking RSA, it is all about factoring. As early as 2012, researchers used four qubits to factor the number 143—the point being that any answer to the question "How many qubits are needed to do X?" is necessarily a very rough estimate. A number of parameters need to be considered; however, the fact remains that, as of this writing, the quantum computers we have are simply not powerful enough.

9.3   Addressing Decoherence

We have discussed decoherence several times in this book, particularly in Chapter 6, "Basic Quantum Theory." This section dives a bit deeper into decoherence and then examines how it can be mitigated in quantum computing. In Chapter 10, we will examine error-correcting algorithms, but in this chapter we will consider physical mechanisms to mitigate decoherence.

To better understand decoherence, consider a system of N particles, where x_i is a point in three-dimensional space. That system can be represented by a wave function:

$$\psi\left(x_1, x_2, x_3 \cdots x_n\right)$$

Recall that ψ is the wave function.

Chapter 6 discussed the wave function, which is shown in Equation 9.2 and briefly described again in the paragraph that follows.

$$\psi> = \sum_i c_i |\phi i$$

EQUATION 9.2   The Wave Function

Again, the ψ symbol denotes the wave function. The Σ symbol is the summation of what is after it. The ϕi represents the possible quantum states. The i is to enumerate through those possible states, such as $\phi 3$ $\phi 2$, $\phi 3$, etc. The ci values (c1, c2, c3, etc.) are probability coefficients. The letter c is used because the values are represented by complex numbers.

Thus, for an N particle system, there is a wave function for each particle. The effective dimensionality of a system's phase space is the number of degrees of freedom. To better understand degrees of freedom, let us first consider a very simple example. Consider a system that is, effectively, one dimensional—a ball in a tube, as illustrated in Figure 9.1. Of course, we know that the ball and tube are both three-dimensional objects, but the ball can only move along one dimension.

FIGURE 9.1   Ball moving in one dimension

This ball can be completely described with two parameters: position and velocity. Thus, it has two degrees of freedom. You should note that some texts use only the position as degrees of freedom and describe position and velocity as the dimensionality of the phase space.

If we continue our analogy and allow the ball to move in three dimensions, as is shown in Figure 9.2, we now have six degrees of freedom.

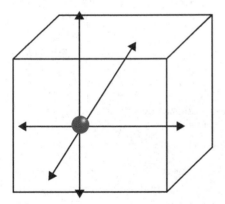

FIGURE 9.2   Ball moving in three dimensions

Now if we replace the ball with a particle, then each particle in a system has six degrees of freedom. Thus far we have simply considered the "ball" as a single point. We know that particles are actually wave functions.

When two systems interact, their state vectors are no longer constrained to their own phase space. Also, note that the environment can itself be a system. In fact, it is when the environment serves as the second system that the greatest interference occurs. When a system is interacting with the external environment, the dimensionality of the joint state vector (that of both systems) increases substantially. This is when the Wigner distribution becomes a factor.

Recall from Chapter 6 that the Wigner distribution is used to link the wave function in Schrödinger's equation to a probability distribution in phase space. This is shown in Equation 9.3.

$$W(x,p) \overset{\text{def}}{=} \frac{1}{\pi\hbar} \int\limits_{-\infty}^{\infty} \psi^*(x+y)\psi(x-y)e^{2ipy/\hbar} \, dy$$

EQUATION 9.3 Wigner Distribution

Also, recall from Chapter 6 the description of this formula. The W simply represents the Wigner distribution. The x value is usually position and p momentum, but they could be any pair of values (frequency and time of a signal, etc.). You know that ψ is the wave function and $\hbar$ is the reduced Planck constant. You should also recall that the $\int$ symbol denotes integration.

What all of this means is that, at some point, decoherence in a quantum system is inevitable. Recall the two-slit experiment discussed in Chapter 3. Interference, and thus decoherence, can occur quite easily. This leads to the very substantial problem of trying to mitigate decoherence. To make matters even more challenging, in 2020, it was discovered that cosmic rays can interfere with quantum states, and thus lead to decoherence in at least some scenarios.

Theoretically, a quantum system could maintain coherence indefinitely if it were completely isolated from the external environment; however, no system is perfectly isolated from its environment. It has even been demonstrated that cosmic rays and background environmental radiation can contribute to decoherence in quantum computers. Even entanglements can occur between the quantum computing system and its environment.

In addition to the external environment, the system itself can be an issue. For example, the physical equipment needed for things like implementing quantum gates is constructed of atoms and particles that have quantum properties. In general, many systems are only able to maintain coherence for a matter of microseconds to a few seconds.

The issue of controlling decoherence is closely related to the issue of quantum error correction. We will be exploring quantum error correction in Chapter 10; however, both decoherence and error correction affect the reliability of quantum computations. The problem is whether quantum computers can perform lengthy computations without noise (be it from decoherence or other sources) rendering the output useless. Remember that qubits are, by their very nature, probabilistic.

The problem of decoherence only increases as quantum computing sizes increase. The more qubits and quantum gates a system has, the more susceptible it is to decoherence. That is due to the fact that there are more components that can interfere with each other. This is why the sizes for quantum computers, such as IBM announcing a 53-qubit system in October 2019, are so important. The size is only part of the issue, however. How long those qubits can fend off decoherence is equally important. Clearly, a quantum computer must maintain coherence long enough to perform meaningful calculations.

9.3.1 Supercooling

One method used to help combat decoherence is supercooling to just a fraction of one kelvin. In fact, some systems cool to a few nanokelvins. If you are not familiar, or don't recall the kelvin scale, 0 kelvin is the equivalent to –273.15 Celsius or –459.67 Fahrenheit. This is not arbitrary. The point 0 kelvin is absolute zero, which implies no thermal energy at all. Thus, a nanokelvin is literally a fraction of a degree above absolute zero. To provide some context, temperatures in space are often around 2.7 kelvin. Obviously, proximity to heat sources such as stars can alter that. The surface of Pluto plummets to about 40 kelvin. So, quantum computing relies on temperatures that are much colder than Pluto, and even colder than deep space.

The reason supercooling is needed is expressed in the following quote:

> "At extremely cold temperatures, atoms and molecules simply move around less. Generally speaking, the lower a temperature is, the more stable a molecule becomes. Less movement means less energy being expelled. At a molecular level, that means that less energy is flying around, and consequently (since voltage and energy are directly related) less volatility in the voltage. This in turn means there is less of a chance that something outside of a human's control will cause a qubit's voltage to spike, causing the qubit to flip from one quantum state to another. Thus, keeping the computer cold introduces less energy into the system. This minimizes the chances of qubits incorrectly flipping in between quantum states."[1]

To give you some idea of temperatures actually used in quantum computing, consider temperatures of existing systems. As of October 2020, the IBM 50-qubit computer begins at about 800 millikelvin and cools to 10 millikelvin. D-Wave operates about 0.1833 kelvin. As we have seen, these temperatures are colder than deep space.

In 2020, researchers in Australia at the University of New South Wales were able to perform quantum computing at 1.5 kelvin.[2] This was referred to as "hot" qubits. As you can probably surmise, it takes substantial power to maintain such low temperatures. Also, in 2020, researchers developed quantum chips running at 1 kelvin.[3]

9.3.2 Dealing with Noise

Closely related to decoherence is the concept of noise. In fact, some sources use noise and decoherence synonymously. As you can probably surmise, this is not a reference to actual audio signals. In a more general sense, noise is any issue that has a deleterious impact on computing results. This can be errors, faults, or, yes, decoherence.

Scientists at IBM have an interesting approach to the problem of noise. Their approach is counterintuitive. They have found that the use of a noise amplification technique helps improve the accuracy of a quantum computer. What this literally means is that they repeat a particular computation at varying levels of noise. This allows them to estimate, with high accuracy, what the result would have been

1. https://www.qats.com/cms/2019/08/02/quantum-computing-cooling/
2. https://www.engadget.com/2018-01-09-this-is-what-a-50-qubit-quantum-computer-looks-like.html
3. https://www.newscientist.com/article/2240539-quantum-computer-chips-demonstrated-at-the-highest-temperatures-ever/

in the complete absence of noise. The interested reader can learn more about this technique at the following resources:

https://www.ibm.com/blogs/research/2019/03/noise-amplification-quantum-processors/

https://venturebeat.com/2019/03/27/ibms-quantum-computation-technique-mitigates-noise-and-improves-accuracy/

9.3.3   Filtering Noise

Another interesting method for mitigating decoherence was proposed by a team of researchers in Israel. The researchers began by firing single photons at atoms and studying the results. When photons strike an atom, they are deflected. If the photon spin was not aligned with its path, then the photon and atom became entangled. However, if the photon spin was aligned with its path, the photon did not become entangled with the atom. This experiment suggests that creating some filtering mechanism for incoming radiation (i.e., light, cosmic rays, etc.) could substantially reduce the probability of those incoming particles becoming entangled with qubits and causing decoherence.

9.4   Topological Quantum Computing

Topological quantum computing is, at least for now, theoretical; however, it has substantial potential and should therefore be examined. To understand topological quantum computers, you must first have at least some general understanding of braid theory. The details of this are rather advanced mathematically. It is not critical that you have all of the details just to have a general understanding of topological quantum computing. Therefore, this topic will be divided into two sections. The first section will be the essentials you need to know. The second section will provide more details for those readers who are interested. Obviously, the first section will be comparatively brief.

9.4.1   Basic Braid Theory

Braid theory is often explained considering lines or strings. Consider two planes, A and B, with points a1, a2; b1, b2; etc. Then consider stings attaching the points in the planes, as illustrated in Figure 9.3.

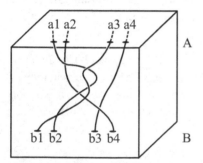

FIGURE 9.3   Braids

Consider the lines connecting points in A to points in B as strings. A braid is an intertwining of n strings attached to one surface (in this case, plane A) to another surface (in this case, plane B), such that each string never traces back to its origin. Think of the strings as "falling" from plane A to plane B. A braid group is a group of braids that are equivalent. What does it mean to be equivalent? While you might twist them in different ways, if the strings are connecting the same origin and endpoint, they are equivalent.

9.4.2 More on Braid Theory

Braid theory is based on braid groups. Braids are groups formed by their equivalence classes of n-braids and generations of these groups. A braid group is based on n-strands and is thus denoted Bn. Let us begin by considering a connected manifold of at least two dimensions. We will call this manifold X. Manifolds are topological spaces that resemble Euclidean space near each point. The term "resembles" is a bit imprecise. It is more precise to state that it is homeomorphic. A homeomorphism is a continuous function between topological spaces that has a continuous inverse function. Put more simply, if two spaces are homeomorphic, there is a mapping between the two spaces that preserves all the topological properties. Thus, an n-dimensional manifold (called an n-manifold) is a topological space such that each point has a neighborhood that is homeomorphic to the Euclidean space of dimension n.

9.4.3 More on Topological Computing

Now that we have some generalized working knowledge of what braids are, we can return to discussing topological computing. This type of computing uses quasiparticles called anyons.

Quasiparticles are not electrons, protons, or neutrons. You may have guessed that from the name. These are emergent phenomena that occur when a system such as a solid behaves as if it contained different weakly interacting particles in some vacuum. Quasiparticles exist only in a system that has many interacting particles. Anyons are specific types of quasiparticles found only in two-dimensional systems.

Topological computing uses anyons' world lines to form braids. A world line is the path an object traces in four-dimensional spacetime. Unlike simply discussing trajectory, the world line includes the temporal dimension, as is implied by the name. These braids are then utilized as logic gates. Topical quantum computers are believed to be more stable than other approaches to quantum computing. There has not yet been a physical realization of a topological computer; as of now, it is theoretical.

9.5 Quantum Essentials

A quantum computer contains multiple elements, each of which will be explored in this section. These are general components that would be common to all quantum computers.

9.5.1 Quantum Data Plane

Simply put, the quantum data plane is where the physical qubits reside. This also requires the hardware and circuitry necessary to support the qubits and quantum gate operations. In addition to physically representing the qubits, the quantum data plane also must contain support structures.

9.5.2   Measurement Plane

Some would consider the measurement plane to be part of the quantum data plane; however, it is at least conceptually separate. This is the hardware responsible for measuring qubits. This is also sometimes called the control and measurement plane. This measurement plane is responsible for control signals needed to perform operations on the qubits and for receiving and processing the output of measurements on the qubits.

9.5.3   Control Processor Plane

The layer identifies and triggers specific gate operations as well as measurements. Put another way, the control processor plane will execute program code that is provided by a host processor. Some sources call this the control process plan and host process, due to the tight coupling with a processor.

9.6   Quantum Networking

Quantum networks are closely related to quantum computers. This is much the same as the relationship between classical computers and traditional computer networks. The concept behind quantum networks is to transmit information using quantum physics. The nodes on a quantum network are quantum processors of one or more qubits. The communication lines can vary, but fiber optics have been used. If one is to communicate with more than just two nodes, a switching mechanism will be required.

Chapter 7, "Quantum Entanglement and QKD," discussed quantum key exchange. Similar technology can also be used for quantum communications. Rather than the bits of a cipher key being exchanged, the bits of a message are exchanged.

9.6.1   Tokyo QKD

The Tokyo QKD network is an example of a quantum network using technologies similar to quantum key exchange. This network has a three-layer architecture. The quantum layer consists of point-to-point quantum links that generate secure keys. There is a middle layer responsible for key management. Then, the communication layer handles standard communications such as secure video links. In essence, this network depends on the quantum layer for security. This has been demonstrated by setting up a secure TV conference between Otemachi, a district in Tokyo, and Koganei. This is a distance of 28 kilometers, and is shown on the map in Figure 9.4.

FIGURE 9.4   Tokyo QKD

9.6.2 Beijing-Shanghai Quantum Link

In 2017, China announced a 2000-kilometer quantum fiber link connection between Beijing and Shanghai, as illustrated on the map in Figure 9.5.

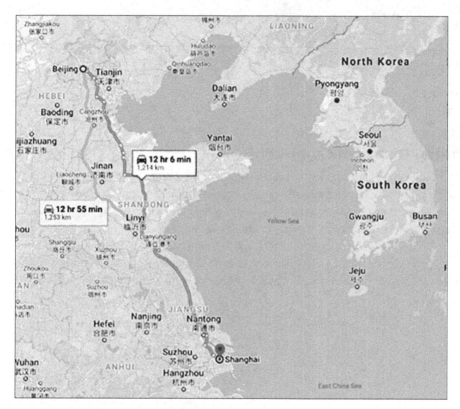

FIGURE 9.5   Beijing–Shanghai Link

During the initial demonstration of this link, the president of the Chinese Academy of Sciences made several video phone calls over the quantum link. This is one of many similar projects going on in China.

9.6.3 Micius Satellite

In 2016, China launched the Micius satellite. The purpose of this satellite was to facilitate quantum communication. This project began with the work of physicist Jian-Wei Pan of the University of Science and Technology of China. In 2017, the satellite was used to set up a secure video conference between Beijing and Vienna, Austria. The satellite was used for key exchange to facilitate a secure video conference. That is a distance of 7456 kilometers. To put this in perspective, consider the map shown in Figure 9.6.

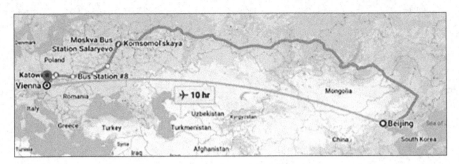

FIGURE 9.6   Beijing–Vienna

9.6.4 Distributed Quantum Computing

Distributed quantum computing is an application of quantum networking for a slightly different purpose. Rather than the goal being to communicate data, it is to coordinate computation. Essentially, quantum processors are linked through some quantum network. This allows the constituent processors to exchange qubits between them. In essence, this is creating quantum cluster computing. Not only is this readily scalable, as with classical computer clusters, but it might aid in combating decoherence. As quantum processors grow more complex, decoherence is more difficult to control. Having smaller quantum processors that share data makes controlling each processor's coherence more manageable.

9.7   Summary

In this chapter, we delved into the physical aspects of quantum computing. Understanding the physical implementation of qubits is the foundation of quantum computing. We also delved into decoherence and quantum networking. These are core concepts in quantum computing that you should be familiar with as you move forward in your learning of quantum computing.

Test Your Skills

REVIEW QUESTIONS

1. What is the purpose of time-bin encoding?

   a. To facilitate storing qubits in trapped ions

   b. To facilitate storing qubits in electrons

   c. To facilitate storing qubits in photons

   d. To facilitate storing qubits in any boson

2. When using time-bin encoding, what does the earlier arrival designate?

   a. State |0>

   b. State |1>

   c. An error

   d. A superposition

3. What do Mathieu functions describe?

   a. The wave function

   b. The motion of the ion in the saddle point

   c. The behavior of qubits in Bose-Einstein condensate quantum computing

   d. The wave function collapse

4. A particle that can move in only two dimensions should have how many degrees of freedom?

   a. 4

   b. 2

   c. 1

   d. 6

5. Where would one find circuitry to measure the qubits states?

   a. Quantum data plane

   b. Measurement plan

   c. Control plane

   d. State plane

6. Which of the following is closest to a normal temperature for a hot qubit?

   a. Above 0 Celsius

   b. Room temperature

   c. A degree or more kelvin above absolute zero

   d. Above normal room temperature

7. Nuclear magnetic resonance quantum computing most frequently uses _____.

   a. gaseous state

   b. solid state

   c. liquid state

   d. plasma state

## Chapter 10

Quantum Algorithms

Chapter Objectives

After reading this chapter and completing the review questions, you will be able to do the following:

- Understand basic quantum algorithms
- Examine algorithm structure
- Explain the purpose and structure of quantum algorithms

The entire point of quantum computing is to execute quantum algorithms. It should therefore come as no surprise to you that this chapter is rather important. In Chapter 16, "Working with Q#," and Chapter 17, "Working with QASM," you will explore quantum computer programming, but that is predicated on some knowledge of quantum algorithms.

In this chapter, we will first explore what an algorithm is. This will be an expansion of what was presented in Chapter 4, "Fundamental Computer Science for Quantum Computing." We will also go through rather detailed discussions of several prominent quantum algorithms. This should provide you a reasonably effective understanding of quantum algorithms. Some of these algorithms are rather complex. You may finish this chapter with only a generalized understanding of them; however, do not let that concern you. In Chapters 16 and 17, you will actually program some of these algorithms, and that should help solidify your understanding.

10.1   What Is an Algorithm?

Although this might seem like an overly pedantic topic, it is not the case that all readers will have had a rigorous computer science background and be familiar with topics such as algorithms and algorithm analysis. Chapter 4 provided you with a simplistic definition of algorithms and a basic understanding of algorithm analysis. Before delving into quantum algorithms, it is important to deepen your understanding of algorithms (or for some readers, review).

Chapter 4 provided a colloquial definition of an algorithm as essentially a recipe. Although not inaccurate, it's simply too informal. In mathematics, an algorithm is a finite sequence of well-defined instructions to solve a problem or class of problems. To quote from one of my favorite algorithm textbooks, "Informally, an algorithm is any well-defined computational procedure that takes some value, or set of values, as input and produces some value, or set of values, as output. An algorithm is thus a sequence of computational steps that transform the input into the output."[1]

Algorithms must be unambiguous. What is meant by this is that the steps are clear and very well-defined, and the output is predictable based on the inputs. This comports with the recipe analogy of Chapter 4. An algorithm provides a clear, step-by-step process for accomplishing some task. The specific steps of an algorithm must be a well-defined and finite sequence of steps.

Now that you have a clearer understanding of what an algorithm is, let us address a few questions regarding algorithms. Whether or not the algorithm is correct is actually a remarkably simple question. If, for every input, the algorithm ceases when the correct output is consistently found, then the algorithm is correct. In fact, the term *consistently* might be a bit too anemic. An algorithm should be reliable and *always* produce a correct output. Consistently does not necessarily imply "every time," and an algorithm should function every time.

Obviously, our interest is in computer algorithms, and as we progress through this section we will examine a few algorithms—more specifically, quantum algorithms. However, it must be noted that an algorithm can be expressed in many forms, including using words from your preferred language. The aforementioned recipe is an algorithm. A specific set of steps to accomplish any task is an algorithm.

The Euclidean algorithm is a classic algorithm that illustrates the essence of algorithms. For mathematics and computer science students, this will be quite familiar. The Euclidean algorithm is a method for discovering the greatest common divisor of two integers. This might seem like a trivial task, but as integers get larger, the problem quickly becomes substantial. The Euclidean algorithm proceeds in a series of well-defined steps such that the output of each step is used as the input for the next one. Let n be an integer that counts the steps of the algorithm, starting with zero. Thus, the initial step corresponds to $n = 0$, the next step corresponds to $n = 1$, etc.

Each step, after the first, begins with two remainders, r_{n-1} and r_{n-2}, from the preceding step. You will notice that at each step the remainder is smaller than the remainder from the preceding step, such that r_{n-1} is less than its predecessor r_{n-2}. This is deliberate and central to the functioning of the algorithm. The goal of the nth step is to find a quotient qn and remainder r_n such that the equation

$$r_{n-2} = q_n r_{n-1} + r_n$$

---

1. Cormen, Thomas H.; Leiserson, Charles E.; Rivest, Ronald L.; Stein, Clifford. *Introduction to Algorithms, Third Edition* (p. 27). MIT Press, 2009.

is satisfied, where $r_n < r_{n-1}$. In other words, multiples of the smaller number r_{n-1} are subtracted from the larger number r_{n-2} until the remainder is smaller than the r_{n-1}.

Some readers might still be a bit unclear, so let us use a concrete example:

Let a = 1864, b = 326.

1864 = 326 * 5 + 234 (234 is the remainder)

326 = 234 * 1 + 92 (92 is the remainder)

234 = 92 * 2 + 50 (50 is the remainder)

92 = 50 * 1 + 42 (42 is the remainder)

50 = 42 * 1 + 8 (8 is the remainder)

42 = 8 * 5 + 2 (2 is the remainder)

8 = 2 * 4

4 = 2 * 2

gcd(4, 2) = 2

Therefore, gcd(1864, 326) = 2.

The specifics of this algorithm and its application are not critical to your understanding of quantum algorithms, but the Euclidean algorithm provides a very good example of an algorithm. You can see that it is a finite series of well-defined steps that solves a problem. If the previous example was not clear enough, Figure 10.1 provides a flow chart of the Euclidean algorithm.

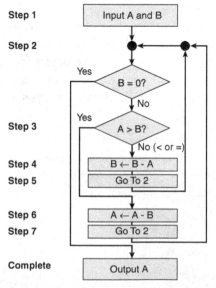

FIGURE 10.1   Euclidean algorithm flow chart

You may have noticed the line that is quite a bit thicker than the other lines in the flow chart. This was done to draw your attention to it. This represents recursion. *Recursion*, a common technique in algorithms, means to call oneself again. When a computer function is recursive, it calls itself repeatedly. A classic example is a function to calculate the factorial of an integer. This is usually implemented recursively, as shown here:

```
int fact(int n)
{
    if (n < = 1) // base case
        return 1;
    else
        return n*fact(n-1);
}
```

Therefore, a quantum algorithm is a finite sequence of well-defined instructions to solve a problem or class of problems, executed on qubits and quantum gates. The most widely known quantum algorithms are Shor's algorithm and Grover's algorithm, which we will discuss in detail in this chapter. These algorithms are just like classical computing algorithms, except they have at least a portion that is dependent on calculations using quantum computing. That last part might seem odd to some readers. Many quantum algorithms actually have a substantial part of the algorithm that can be executed in a classical computing manner, with only a portion being executed in qubits.

10.2 Deutsch's Algorithm

Deutsch's algorithm is one of the easiest-to-understand quantum algorithms, which makes it an excellent choice for our starting point. This algorithm was created by Professor David Deutsch of the University of Oxford. This algorithm might seem to be solving a problem that is a bit contrived, and that may be accurate. Therefore, it might help you to not dwell too much on the practicality of the problem in question. Here is the problem: You have four functions; each takes as input a 1 or 0 and outputs a 1 or 0, as illustrated in Figure 10.2.

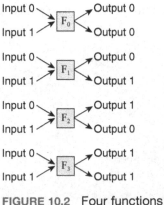

FIGURE 10.2 Four functions

The functions are traditionally labeled f_0, f_1, f_2, and f_3. This leaves us with the question of what these functions actually do; put another way, what is Figure 10.2 showing us? What is depicted in Figure 10.2 is that functions f_0 and f_3 set the output to the same value (either 0,0 or 1,1), no matter what the input is. Function f_1 sets 0 to 0 and 1 to 1. Function f_2 sets 0 to 1 and 1 to 0. Functions f_0 and f_3 are called *constant* (i.e., the output is always predictable, regardless of the input). Functions f_1 and f_2 are called *balanced*, as their output is always a balance of 1 and 0.

So, what is the problem to be solved? If we have a black box that we send input to and get output from, how do we determine if that particular black box contains a constant function (f_0 or f_3) or a balanced function (f_1 or f_2)?

Using classical computers to answer the question, we have to make two evaluations. The first evaluation involves inputting a 0 and determining the output. The second evaluation is to input a 1 and determine the output. After those two operations, we will know definitively if the black box contains a balanced or constant function.

Using a quantum algorithm, namely Deutsch's algorithm, we can determine what is in the black box in a single step. Deutsch envisioned a quantum circuit, much like what is depicted in Figure 10.3.

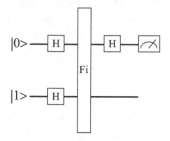

FIGURE 10.3 Deutsch circuit

You may have noticed that we only measure the first output qubit, not the second. Recall from Chapter 8, "Quantum Architecture," that the gates depicted are Hadamard gates. The F_i denotes that we have a function that is one of the previously discussed F functions, but we don't know which one. The qubits $|0> \otimes |1>$ are input into the circuit, more specifically going through the Hadamard gates. Equation 10.1 shows a Hadamard gate, if you need a refresher.

$$H = \frac{1}{\sqrt{2}}\begin{bmatrix} 1 & 1 \\ 1 & -1 \end{bmatrix}$$

EQUATION 10.1 Hadamard Gate

By putting our input qubits through a Hadamard gate, the state is changed to what's shown in Equation 10.2.

$$\frac{1}{\sqrt{2}}\big(|0\rangle + |1\rangle\big) \otimes \frac{1}{\sqrt{2}}\big(|0\rangle - |1\rangle\big) = \frac{1}{2}\big(|00\rangle - |01\rangle + |10\rangle - |11\rangle\big)$$

EQUATION 10.2 State after the Hadamard Gate

Next, we will put the qubits into the F_i function. Remember, we don't know which of the four F functions this actually is. This changes the state to what is shown in Equation 10.3.

$$\frac{1}{2}\big(|0\rangle \otimes |f_i(0)\rangle - |0\rangle \otimes |f_i(0) \oplus 1\rangle + |1\rangle \otimes |f_i(1)\rangle - |1\rangle \otimes |f_i(1) \oplus 1\rangle\big)$$

EQUATION 10.3 State after the F_i Function

The state is either |0> − |1> or |1> − |0>. With a bit of algebra, this can be rearranged to what you see in Equation 10.4.

$$\frac{1}{\sqrt{2}}\big((-1)^{fi(0)}|0\rangle + (-1)^{fi(1)}|1\rangle\big) \otimes \frac{1}{\sqrt{2}}\big(|0\rangle - |1\rangle\big)$$

EQUATION 10.4 State after the F_i Function, Rearranged

However, recall from Figure 10.3 that we are not done. We have another Hadamard gate followed by a measurement. If the result of our measurement is 0, the F_i is either F_0 or F_3, a constant function. If it is 1, then F_i is either F_1 or F_2, a balanced function. So, with one measurement, we discover the nature of the F_i black box, as opposed to two measurements with a classical computer.

As stated earlier, this might seem like a bit of a contrived example; however, it is relatively easy to follow, and thus a good place to start examining quantum algorithms. Make sure you follow this algorithm before moving on to more complicated algorithms.

10.3 Deutsch-Jozsa Algorithm

This algorithm is quite interesting and important in quantum computing. Obviously, it is a modification of the Deutsch algorithm. The issue is actually rather straightforward. The Deutsch algorithm looks at the functions of one variable, whereas the Deutsch-Jozsa algorithm generalizes this to functions of n variables. First, consider the Deutsch-Jozsa problem. We begin with a black-box quantum computer that implements some function that takes in n-digit binary values and produces either a 0 or 1 for the output of each such value. The output will either be balanced (an equal number of 1s and 0s) or constant (either all 1s or all 0s). We wish to determine if the function is constant or balanced. This quantum black box is also referred to as an *oracle*. In computational theory, an oracle is an abstract machine that can be visualized as a black box that produces some result.

The actual algorithm begins with the first n bits in state |0>, and the final bit is in the state |1>. Then a Hadamard transform, shown in Equation 10.5 (and introduced in Chapter 8), is applied to each bit.

$$H_m = \frac{1}{\sqrt{2}}\begin{pmatrix} H_{m-1} & H_{m-1} \\ H_{m-1} & -H_{m-1} \end{pmatrix}$$

EQUATION 10.5   Hadamard Transform

The application of the Hadamard transform to each bit will produce the state depicted in Equation 10.6.

$$\frac{1}{\sqrt{2^{n+1}}} \sum_{x=0}^{2^n-1} |x\rangle\big(|0\rangle - |1\rangle\big)$$

EQUATION 10.6   Post Hadamard Transform State

Thus far, this seems not that different from the standard Deutsch's algorithm. However, we now have a function, which we will call f(x). This function maps the state |x>|y| to |x>|y $\oplus$ f(x)>. In this case, the symbol $\oplus$ denotes addition modulo 2. For the f(x) function, it has to be a function that does not decohere x. The function f(x) is a quantum oracle (described previously). As the values of x are put through the oracle f(x), either a 1 or 0 is produced. Also, keep in mind that each of the Hadamard gates will affect the state of the qubit. This, the Deutsch-Jozsa algorithm, can be described as shown in Figure 10.4.

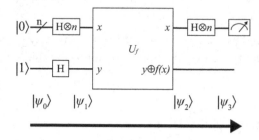

FIGURE 10.4   Deutsch-Jozsa algorithm

The arrow at the bottom represents the states changing from ψ_0 to ψ_1. The output will be 0 if f(x) is balanced and 1 if f(x) is constant. For n bits of input, the final output will be n 0s if f(x) is constant. Any other output (any combination of 0s and 1s, or all 1s) indicates that f(x) is balanced. Like the Deutsch algorithm, the problem the Deutsch-Jozsa algorithm solves is a bit contrived and might not appeal to you. The main point in describing both algorithms is that they are relatively easy to understand when compared with the other algorithms we will discuss.

10.4   Bernstein-Vazirani Algorithm

The Bernstein-Vazirani algorithm is less well-known than some of the other algorithms we cover in this chapter. In fact, this algorithm is often overlooked in introductory quantum computing books. However, it is not terribly difficult to understand and is related to the Deutsch-Jozsa algorithm. It is essentially a variation on the Deutsch-Jozsa algorithm. That might be a reason why it is often not covered in introductory texts. However, our goal is to ensure you understand quantum algorithms. Therefore, covering another algorithm that is not only inherently easier to understand, but also based on two other algorithms we have covered, seems like an excellent way to achieve that goal.

Much like the Deutsch and Deutsch-Jozsa algorithms, the Bernstein-Vazirani algorithm is solving a rather contrived problem. Unlike the Deutsch algorithms, Bernstein-Vazirani is not trying to distinguish between two types of functions; instead, it is working to learn a string-encoded function. In fact, it is working to prove a separation between two complexity classes. For those readers not familiar with the complexity classes this algorithm is referencing, they will be described briefly.

There are two complexity classes being considered by Bernstein-Vazirani. Bounded-error probabilistic polynomial time (BPP) is a class of problems that are solvable, in polynomial time, by a probabilistic Turing machine with an error probability that is bounded by an error probability of less than 1/3. This is a subset of problems that are called PP, which is an acronym for probabilistically polynomial. That simply means they provide a probabilistic answer in polynomial time. Polynomial time means that the upper bound of the algorithm's runtime is a polynomial expression related to the size of the algorithm. There are probabilistically polynomial problems that only provide a probable answer, and there are deterministic polynomial algorithms. The latter provide a deterministic answer with a running time whose upper bound is expressed by a polynomial related to the input.

PP are problems that are probabilistically solvable in polynomial time with an error probability of less than ½. BQP is bounded-error quantum polynomial time. These are problems that are solvable by a quantum computer in polynomial time with an error probability of less than 1/3.

Now that you have a general concept of the problem that Bernstein-Vazirani is solving, let us look at the actual algorithm. Given some secret string that will be $s \in \{1,2\}^n$ modulo 2 and a function $f\{0,1\}^n$, where $f(x)$ is the dot product between x and the secret string s, find s. Put more simply, the Bernstein-Vazirani algorithm takes a string of bits (s) and puts them through a black-box function f(s) that returns either a 0 or 1. What we want to do is find out what the string of bits was.

So, what is it that Bernstein-Vazirani can do better than classical algorithms? A classical algorithm needs at least n queries of the function to find out what s is. However, the Bernstein-Vazirani algorithm can use a quantum computer to find the s value in only a single query. That is undoubtedly a substantial improvement. The algorithm's steps are not overly complicated. First, you begin with the n qubit state:

$$|0\rangle^{\otimes n}$$

You will apply a Hadamard transform to that state as you see here:

$$\frac{1}{\sqrt{2^{n+1}}} \sum_{x=0}^{2^n-1} |x\rangle$$

Remember from previous chapters that the Hadamard gate makes a transformation on a single qubit, as shown here:

$$H|0\rangle = \frac{1}{\sqrt{2}}\left(|0\rangle + |1\rangle\right)$$

$$H|1\rangle = \frac{1}{\sqrt{2}}\left(|0\rangle - |1\rangle\right)$$

You can use summation notation to represent both of those, as follows:

$$H|a\rangle = \frac{1}{\sqrt{2}} \sum_{x \in \{0,1\}} (-1)^{a \cdot x} |x\rangle$$

Now we have the quantum oracle U_f. This oracle transforms the input $|x\rangle$ into $(-1)^{f(x)} |x\rangle$. Application of this quantum oracle transforms the superposition, yielding

$$\frac{1}{\sqrt{2^n}} \sum_{x=0}^{2^n-1} (-1)^{f(x)} |x\rangle$$

Then the Hadamard gate is applied again. Now a measurement is taken of the resulting qubits. That measurement yields the secret string. This is a bit simplified discussion of the Bernstein-Vazirani algorithm. The goal is to ensure you have a generalized understanding of how to use qubits and quantum gates—we can essentially accomplish in one step what would take classical algorithms more than one step.

10.5   Simon's Algorithm

As with all the algorithms we have discussed so far, Simon's algorithm is designed to solve a particular class of problems. Suppose you have some function f that takes in binary strings of length n and outputs binary strings of length n. Put more simply, it takes in a string of binary digits, performs some operation on them, and outputs a string of the same length that has been altered by the operation. The operation is the exclusive or (XOR), sometimes simply called addition modulo 2. This can be reworded in the opposite direction, given that the binary XOR operation is reversible:

x ⊕ y = s

Now we wish to find s.

To summarize, if you put string x into the function, you will get out string y. This was done via x ⊕ s. We wish to find out what the string s is. With a classical computer and classical algorithm, there will need to be at most (i.e., worst-case scenario) $s^{n-1} + 1$ function evaluations.

Before we can adequately evaluate the quantum solution to this (i.e., Simon's algorithm), we need to first discuss a preliminary issue. If you have two binary strings, we will call them x $(x_1, x_2, ..., x_n)$ and y $(y_1, y_2, ..., y_n)$, the dot product of these two stings is simply x * y, with * simply denoting standard multiplication. So, it would be $x_1 * y_1$; $x_2 * y_2$, etc. This is quite simple to understand.

Simon's algorithm has the following steps:

Step 1.   Initialize two n-qubit registers to the zero state.

Step 2.   Apply a Hadamard transform to the first register.

Step 3.   Apply the query function. This query function acts on both quantum registers.

Step 4.   Measure the second register.

Step 5.   Apply a Hadamard transform to the first register.

Figure 10.5, with the circuit, might clarify this for you.

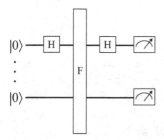

FIGURE 10.5   Simon's algorithm circuit

There is a bit of post-processing done by classical computing. You may have noticed that many current "quantum" algorithms combine some classical and some quantum operations.

10.6   Shor's Algorithm

This is perhaps the most important quantum algorithm we will study in this chapter. Some sources say it is also the most complicated. That is why some texts deal with it last. However, once you have become comfortable with the previous three algorithms, you should be able to move forward with Shor's algorithm, which was invented by Peter Shor, a professor of applied mathematics at MIT. The problem addressed by Shor's algorithm is how to factor some integer N. The algorithm itself consists of two parts. The first part is purely classical; the second part is quantum.

This process works best if N is odd, the reason being that we are seeking a non-trivial divisor of N, and for all N that are even, 2 is a trivial divisor.

The first step is to select some pseudo-random number that is less than N (the number you wish to factor). Now you should compute the greatest common denominator for a and N. One way to accomplish this would be with the Euclidean algorithm, covered earlier in this chapter. As you can see, the selection of the Euclidean algorithm to explain the broader concept of algorithms was intentional. Why are we computing the gcd of a and N? Because if the gcd (a, N) = 1, then the two integers are relatively prime. We need for a to be relatively prime for the rest of this to operate successfully.

Now that we have computed the greatest common denominator of a and N, we must ask a question, is it not equal to 1? In other words, if the gcd = 1, then we continue; if not, we are done. If the gcd (a, N) ! = 1, then a is a non-trivial factor of N, and this phase is complete.

If we are moving forward, then we need to use a period-finding function to identify the period of the function:

$$fa, N(x) = a^x \bmod N$$

Put in less rigorous mathematical terms, we are seeking some r for which f(x + r) = f(x). For those readers who do not recall modulus arithmetic, let us briefly discuss it here.

The simplest explanation of modulus operations is one often used by computer programmers. To use the modulus operator, simply divide A by N and return the remainder.

Thus, 7 mod 2 = 1

And 12 mod 5 = 2

This provides a functional understanding of using the modulus operator but lacks an understanding of what modulus arithmetic is. One way to think about modulus arithmetic is to imagine doing any integer math you might normally do but bound your answers by some number. A classic example is the clock. It has numbers 1 through 12, so any arithmetic operation you do has to have an answer that is 12 or less. If it is currently 6 o'clock and I ask you to meet me in 7 hours, simple math would say I am asking you to meet me at 13 o'clock. But that is not possible because our clock is bounded by the number 12! The answer is simple, take your answer and use the mod operator with a modulus of 12 and look at the remainder.

13 mod 12 = 1

I am actually asking you to meet me at 1 o'clock (whether that is a.m. or p.m. depends on what the original 6 o'clock was, but that is really irrelevant to understanding the concepts of modular arithmetic). This is an example of how you use modular arithmetic every day.

While the basic concepts of modular arithmetic dates back to Euclid, who wrote about modular arithmetic in his book *Elements*, the modern approach to modular arithmetic was published by Carl Gauss in 1801.

Congruence in modulus operations is a very important topic, and you will see it frequently applied in modern cryptographic algorithms. In fact, this will be used in Shor's algorithm in this chapter and in RSA in Chapter 11, "Current Asymmetric Algorithms." Two numbers, a and b, are said to be "congruent modulo n" if

(a mod n) = (b mod n) → a ≡ b(mod n)

The symbol $\equiv$ is used to denote congruence in mathematics. In many programming languages, the % symbol is used to perform the modulo operation (i.e., to divide the first number by the second, and only return the remainder).

If two numbers are congruent modulo n, then the difference between a and b will be some multiple of n. To make this clear, let us return to the clock analogy used earlier in this chapter: 14 and 2 are congruent modulo, and it turns out that the difference between 14 and 2 is 12, a multiple of n (1 × 12). We also know that 14, or 1400 hours on the 24-hour clock, is 2 o'clock. So, when we say that 14 and 2 are congruent modulo 12, we are stating that, at least in reference to modulo 12, 14 and 2 are the same. Let us look at another example: 17 and 5 are congruent modulo 12, and the difference between them is 12. Again, using the 24-hour clock to test our conclusions, we find that 1700 hours is the same as 5 p.m.

There are some basic properties of congruences that you should be aware of:

a $\equiv$ b (mod n) if n|(a–b)

a $\equiv$ b (mod n) implies b $\equiv$ a (mod n)

a $\equiv$ b (mod n) and b $\equiv$ c (mod n) imply a $\equiv$ c (mod n)

A congruence class is a group of numbers that are all congruent for some given modulus. Another name for congruence classes is residue classes. So, let us consider an example where the modulus is 5. What numbers are congruent modulo 5? Let's begin with 7. 7 mod 5 = 2. So now we ask what other numbers mod 5 = 2. We will arrive at an infinite series of numbers: 12, 17, 22, 27, 32, etc. You should also note that this works the other way (i.e., with integers smaller than the modulus, including negatives). We know that 7 mod 5 = 2, but 2 mod 5 = 2 (the nearest multiple of 5 would be 0; 0 *5, thus 2 mod 5 = 2). Make sure you fully understand why 2 mod 5 = 2, and then we can proceed to examine negative numbers. Our next multiple of 5 after 0, going backwards, is –5 (5 * –1). So, –3 mod 5 = 2. We can now expand the elements of our congruence class to include –3, 0, 2, 7, 12, 17, 22, 27, 32, etc.

Now that we have reviewed modulus arithmetic, let us consider an example common in introductory texts on quantum computing. We will consider N = 15 and a = 2. These numbers are chosen frequently (or some similar integers) because they are small, and the calculations are easy.

Table 10.1 shows some values of x and a.

TABLE 10.1 Example Values

x	0	1	2	3	4	5	6	7
f a,N(x) for a=2	1	2	4	8	1	2	4	8
f a,N(x) for a=4	1	4	1	4	1	4	1	4

Just to ensure this is clear to you, let us look at a few of the entries. Consider x = 4 and a = 2:

$$fa, N(x) = a^x \; mod \; N$$

or

$$fa, N(x) = 2^4 \; mod \; 15$$

which leads to

$$= 16 \; mod \; 15$$
$$= 1$$

Let us consider one more example, where x = 5 and a = 4:

$$fa, N(x) = a^x \; mod \; N$$

or

$$fa, N(x) = 4^5 \; mod \; 15$$

which leads to

$$= 1024 \; mod \; 15$$
$$= 4$$

This part requires the second phase of the algorithm. This is the quantum period-finding algorithm, which is described in the next subsection.

Returning from the period function, we continue the factoring process. If the value we find for r is odd, then we return to step 1, selecting a different pseudo-random number a. Also, if

$$a \; r / 2 \equiv -1$$

we return to step 1 and select a different a.

However, if we have succeeded, then gcd ($a^{r/2}$ + 1, N) and we have found the factors of N.

10.6.1   The Quantum Period-Finding Function

This section is rather technical. It is not critical that all readers master this section. If you understand the general outline of Shor's algorithm, that should be adequate. You may choose to treat this portion as a black box. However, for those who wish to understand more, details are provided.

The heart of the quantum portion of Shor's algorithm is that each choice of N and each choice of a used in f(x) = a^x mod N have their own quantum circuit. Given some N (the integer we wish to factor), first find Q = 2q such that $N^2 < Q < 2N^2$. Q is the number of states. This, in turn, implies that

Q/r > N (remember we are looking for the period r). Here is where the quantum issues come into play. The qubit registers need to hold superpositions of the values from 0 to Q − 1. That, in turn, indicates the number of qubits needed.

The first step of the quantum portion of this algorithm is to initialize the registers (note that the ⊗ in the equations that follow is for tensor product). Equation 10.7 shows the initialization of the registers. Remember, the Q is the number of states.

The circuits used for the period function are chosen depending on the choice of N. That means there could be different circuits used for Shor's algorithm. What we are trying to find is given the value N (the number we wish to factor), find a $Q = 2^q$ such that the following holds true:

$$N^2 \leq Q < 2N^2$$

The registers are initialized to the state depicted in Equation 10.7.

$$\frac{1}{\sqrt{Q}} \sum_{x=0}^{Q-1} |x>$$

EQUATION 10.7   Initializing Registers for Shor's Algorithm

The summation notation is used here (i.e., the Σ), but it is the tensor product being used to combine the individual items x = 0 to Q − 1. The initial state is a superposition of Q states. This is accomplished by creating q independent qubits, each in a superposition of 0 and 1 states.

Now that the registers are initialized, we construct a quantum function f(x) that will produce an entanglement of the input and output bits (see Equation 10.8).

$$U_f \frac{1}{\sqrt{Q}} \sum_{x=0}^{Q-1} |x, 0^q> = \frac{1}{\sqrt{Q}} \sum_{x=0}^{Q-1} |x, f(x)>$$

EQUATION 10.8   Quantum Function

This leads to a situation where the Q input bits and the n output bits are entangled. The next step is to apply the inverse quantum Fourier transform to the input register. Again, for the casual reader, this detail is not necessary, but for the interested reader, a brief description is provided.

The quantum Fourier transform operates on some quantum state |x> and maps it to a quantum state |y> using the formula shown in Equation 10.9.

$$y_k = \frac{1}{\sqrt{N}} \sum_{n=0}^{N-1} x_n \omega_N^{nk}$$

EQUATION 10.9   Quantum Fourier Transform

In Equation 10.9, the n value will increment from 0 to N − 1. The ω_N^n is a rotation, and N is the length of vectors where $N = 2^n$. The inverse quantum Fourier transform is quite similar and is shown in Equation 10.10.

$$n = \frac{1}{\sqrt{N}} \sum_{n=0}^{N-1} y_k \omega_N^{-nk}$$

EQUATION 10.10   Inverse Quantum Fourier Transform

The inverse quantum Fourier transform is applied to the input register using a Qth root of unity. For those readers not familiar with it, a root of unity is any complex number that, when raised to some positive integer power n, yields 1. This is sometimes called a de Moivre number, named after the French mathematician Abraham de Moivre.

Now a measurement is performed, and some outcome y is obtained in the input register and some outcome z in the output register. Our next step is to perform continued fraction expansion (classical operation) on $\frac{y}{Q}$ to find approximations of $\frac{d}{s}$ that satisfy two conditions:

1. $s < N$

2. $\left| \frac{y}{Q} - \frac{d}{5} \right| < \frac{1}{2Q}$

If we have these two conditions, then s is probably the period r or at least a factor of it. We can then check to see if our f(x) works as it should. If it does, we are then done; otherwise, we have to obtain more candidates for r and try again.

Now with that mathematical interlude concluded, we can return to the steps of Shor's algorithm. As was stated, we apply the inverse quantum Fourier transform to the input register. We could delve deeper into what occurs when this transform is applied, but the issue for our purposes is that it produces a sum where each term represents a different path to the same result. Now we move forward and perform a measurement. This will lead to some value x in the input register and some value y in the output register. This, in turn, leads to checking classically to see if we have an answer (i.e., a factor). If we do, we are done. If we don't, we obtain more candidates for r and repeat.

Now for those readers who wish to know even more details, particularly the "why" behind these calculations, we can explore those here. The issue with r has to do with a fact about integers. Recall that the goal of Shor's algorithm is to factor integers. The order of an integer x modulo M is the smallest integer $r > 0$ such that $x^r = 1 \bmod M$. If no such integer r exists, then the order is said to be infinite. The steps are summarized here:

Step 1.   Pick a random number a between 1 and N (the N is what you wish to factor).

Step 2.   Compute gcd (a,N).

Step 3.   If gcd (a,N) != 1, you are done.

Step 4. If gcd (a,N) = 1, you used the quantum period subroutine to find r. The quantum period function substeps are given here:

Quantum Step 1: Initialize the registers.

Quantum Step 2: Construct the f(x) quantum function and apply it to the state.

Quantum Step 3: Apply the inverse quantum Fourier transform to the input register.

Quantum Step 4: Measure.

Quantum Step 5: Perform classical continued fraction expansion to find approximations.

Quantum Step 6: Check whether you have found the period; if you have, you are done.

Quantum Step 7: Otherwise, obtain more candidates for r.

Step 5. If r is odd, go back to step 1.

Step 6. If $a^{r/2} \equiv -1 \pmod{N}$, then go back to step 1.

Step 7. Otherwise, you have found nontrivial factors of N and you are done.

As should be clear to you at this point, we don't have a stable working quantum computer that can avoid decoherence long enough to factor large integers, such as would be found in RSA algorithms used in practice. However, there have been multiple demonstrations of Shor's algorithm with smaller integers.

10.7 Grover's Algorithm

Grover's algorithm is essentially a search algorithm. It was developed by Lov Grover in 1996. There are certainly other descriptions of it that we will explore a bit later in this section, but for the time being, you can view it as a search algorithm. To explain how the algorithm works, consider some unsorted data store that has N entries. Given N elements, the worst-case scenario for classical queries is that it will take n queries. The average case is N / 2. Grover's algorithm works in $\sqrt{N}$, which is a substantial improvement over classical methods.

Now to work with Grover's algorithm on our N element data store, we must perform a bit of initial setup. There must be an N-dimension state space, which is provided by log2N qubits. We will call this state space H. Now we number each entry in the data store from 0 to N – 1, much like any standard array in programming. Then we have to select some observable that acts on the state space H. Many sources denote this observable with the symbol Ω. This observable must have N eigenvalues, all of which are known. Each eigenstate of Ω encodes one of the entries in the database. The eigenstates are denoted using the bra-ket notation:

{|0>, |1>, |2>, ..., |N – 1>}

And, of course, the eigenvalues are denoted in much the same way:

$\{\lambda_0, \lambda_1, \lambda_2, ..., \lambda_{N-1}.\}$

Now we need an operator that functions to compare database entries based on some criterion. Grover's algorithm does not specify the operator or its criteria. That will be selected based on the particular data store and search. However, the operator must be a quantum subroutine that functions via a superposition of states. The operator is often designated as Uω.

Our operator has the following property when applied to the previously mentioned eigenstates (which we will denote as $|\omega\rangle$):

$$U\omega|\omega\rangle = -|\omega\rangle$$

However, for all x that are not ω, we want the following:

$$U\omega|x\rangle = |x\rangle$$

Put another way, we are trying to identify the particular eigenstate $|\omega\rangle$ that Uω acts on in a manner different from the other eigenstates. Alternatively, we may identify the eigenvalue associated with the eigenstate. This operator, U_ω, is often referred to as a quantum oracle. It is some unitary operator that operates on two qubits. That defines the U_ω operator.

There is a second operator, the U_s. The s is a superposition of possible states (which we will be discussing in detail in just a moment). The operator is

$$Us = 1|s\rangle \langle s|-I$$

Now that we have the preliminary items established, let us examine the specific steps of the algorithm. The first step is to initialize the system to a state. That state will be a superposition of states often denoted as follows:

$$|s \geq \frac{1}{\sqrt{N}} \sum_{x=0}^{N-1} |x\rangle$$

Don't let this seemingly complex formula discourage you. We are simply stating that the state $|s\rangle$ is a superposition of all possible states $|x\rangle$.

Now we perform a step called the Grover iteration r and we do this N times. This step r is simply to apply the operator U_ω and apply the operator U_s. Both operators were described previously.

Now the third step is to perform the measurement of the observable Ω. This measurement will provide some eigenvalue λ_ω. As we iterate through the process, we eventually get to the proper answer. The steps are summarized here:

Step 1. Initialize the system to a state.

Step 2. Perform the iteration r(N) times.

Step 3. Perform the measurement.

The efficacy of Grover's algorithm has been proven mathematically in multiple ways. It is one of the algorithms that confirm the power we will realize from quantum computers once decoherence is solved.

10.8 Summary

This chapter examined several quantum algorithms. This chapter is likely to be one that was difficult for many readers. You might need to read it more than once before continuing. Many of these algorithms you will see again in later chapters, and actually coding them might clarify the algorithms for you. The algorithms most important for you to understand from this chapter are Deutsch, Shor, and Grover's algorithms.

Test Your Skills

REVIEW QUESTIONS

1. What algorithm is described in the following question: "If we have a black box that we send input to and get output from, how do we determine if that particular black box contains a constant function or a balanced function?"

   a. Simon's algorithm

   b. Grover's algorithm

   c. Deutsch's algorithm

   d. Shor's algorithm

2. Which of the following is a quantum search algorithm?

   a. Simon's algorithm

   b. Grover's algorithm

   c. Deutsch's algorithm

   d. Shor's algorithm

3. How many Hadamard gates are used in the Deutsch-Jozsa algorithm as described in this chapter?

   a. One

   b. Two

   c. Three

   d. Four

4. What part of Shor's algorithm is quantum?

   a. All of it

   b. The period-finding portion

   c. The congruence portion

   d. The modulus portion

Chapter | **11**

Current Asymmetric Algorithms

Chapter Objectives

After reading this chapter and completing the review questions, you will be able to do the following:

- Understand current asymmetric algorithms
- Explain why quantum computing poses a threat to these algorithms
- Recognize the importance of quantum computing for cryptography

In order to fully understand the impact quantum computers have on cryptography, it is useful to have a solid understanding of current asymmetric algorithms. This chapter explores current, commonly used asymmetric algorithms. These algorithms are widely used today in e-commerce, online banking, virtual private networks, and a host of secure communication scenarios. However, all of these algorithms are susceptible to attacks from quantum computers. This chapter explains the algorithms and why quantum computers render them obsolete.

Current asymmetric algorithms are all based on some mathematical problem that is computationally hard to solve. In more precise terms, that means a problem that cannot be solved in polynomial time. However, it has already been shown that many of these problems can be solved in polynomial time by a quantum computer. That poses a substantial threat to current cybersecurity. In subsequent chapters, we will explore algorithms that have been proposed as quantum-resistant standards. In this chapter, we explore, in some detail, the most current and widely implemented asymmetric algorithms. This will allow you to have a full understanding of the issues.

Some readers might not be entirely clear on what polynomial time is. An algorithm is solvable in polynomial time if the number of steps needed to complete the algorithm is $O(n^k)$ for some nonnegative integer k. The n denotes the complexity of the input. Recall from Chapter 4, "Fundamental Computer

Science for Quantum Computing," our discussion of arrays. Many algorithms that work with arrays use n as the array size. Any problem that can be solved by an algorithm in polynomial time is considered to be tractable.

11.1 RSA

RSA is perhaps the most commonly used asymmetric algorithm today. It is undoubtedly one of the most well-recognized. This algorithm was first published in 1977 by Ron Rivest, Adi Shamir, and Leonard Adleman. The name RSA is taken from the first letter of each mathematician's surname. The algorithm is based on the difficulty of factoring a large number into its prime factors. With current classical computers, the most efficient known factoring algorithm for large integers is the general number sieve. Recall the discussion from Chapter 4 on computational complexity and the Big O notation. The general number sieve has the following complexity:

$$O\left\{ exp\left[C(log\ n)^{\frac{2}{3}} (log\ log\ n)^{\frac{2}{3}} \right] \right\}$$

The important thing to keep in mind, even if that notation seems a bit daunting, is that it is not an efficient algorithm. This is why RSA is secure enough for current use. Now let us examine RSA in some depth to better understand why factoring integers is key to RSA security. For those readers interested in knowing more about the general number sieve, it is the most efficient classical algorithm for factoring large integers. For more details you can consult these resources:

https://citeseerx.ist.psu.edu/viewdoc/download?doi=10.1.1.219.2389&rep=rep1&type=pdf

https://mathworld.wolfram.com/NumberFieldSieve.html

To examine RSA, let us begin with the key generation. To create the public and private key pair, the first step is to generate two large random primes, p and q, of approximately equal size. You will need to select two numbers so that when multiplied together, the product will be the size you want (i.e., 2048 bits, 4096 bits, etc.).

The next step is to multiply p and q to get n. This is a rather simple equation:

n = pq

The third step is to multiply Euler's totient for each of these primes (p and q) in order to get the Euler's totient of n.

If you are not familiar with Euler's totient, it is a relatively simple concept. Two numbers are considered co-prime if they have no common factors. Consider the integers 15 and 8, which are co-prime. The factors of 15 are 3 and 5, and the factors of 8 are 2 and 4. The integers 15 and 8 have no common factors, so they are considered co-prime. Euler's totient asks how many numbers smaller than n are co-prime to n. We call that number Euler's totient, or just the totient. It just so happens that for prime numbers, this is always the number minus 1. As one example, the prime number 11 has 10 integers that are smaller than 11 and are co-prime to 11.

Now that you have a basic understanding of Euler's totient, we can continue. When we multiply two primes together, it should be obvious we get a composite number—and there is no easy way to determine the Euler's totient of a composite number. Euler found that if you multiple any two prime numbers together, the Euler's totient of that product is the Euler's totient of each prime multiplied together. Thus, the next step is

$$m = (p-1)(q-1)$$

This leads to m, which is the Euler's totient of n.

For the fourth step, we are going to select another number, which we will call e. We want to pick e so that it is co-prime to m. Frequently, a prime number is chosen for e. That way, if e does not evenly divide m, then we are confident that e and m are co-prime, as e does not have any factors to consider.

At this point, we have almost completed generating the key. Now we just find a number d that when multiplied by e and modulo m would yield a 1:

Find d, such that $de \bmod m \equiv 1$

This completes the key generation. We will publish e and n as the public key and keep d as the secret key. The following steps summarize the key generation process:

Step 1. Generate two large random primes, p and q, of approximately equal size.

Step 2. Multiply p and q to get n.

Step 3. Multiply Euler's totient for each of these primes (p and q) in order to get the Euler's totient of n.

Step 4. Select another number, which we will call e. We want to pick e so that it is co-prime to m.

Step 5. Find d, such that $de \bmod m \equiv 1$.

To encrypt, you simply take your message raised to the e power and modulo n:

$$C = M^e \bmod n$$

To decrypt, you take the cipher text and raise it to the d power modulo n:

$$P = C^d \bmod n$$

Next, we'll look at two examples of RSA using very small integers. These integers are too small to be effective; however, this should help you to understand the process involved.

11.1.1   RSA Example 1

Let's look at an example that might help you understand the process. Of course, RSA would be done with very large integers. To make the math easy to follow, we will use small integers in the following example (which is taken from Wikipedia):

1. Choose two distinct prime numbers, such as $p = 61$ and $q = 53$.

2. Compute $n = pq$, giving n $= 61 \cdot 53 = 3233$.

3. Compute the totient of the product as $\varphi(n) = (p - 1)(q - 1)$, giving $\varphi(3233) = (61 - 1)(53 - 1) = 3120$.

4. Choose any number $1 < e < 3120$ that is co-prime to 3120. Choosing a prime number for e leaves us only to check that e is not a divisor of 3120. Let $e = 17$.

5. Compute d, the modular multiplicative inverse yielding $d = 2753$.

6. The public key is ($n = 3233$, $e = 17$). For a padded plaintext message m, the encryption function is m^{17} (mod 3233).

7. The private key is ($n = 3233$, $d = 2753$). For an encrypted ciphertext c, the decryption function is c^{2753} (mod 3233).

11.1.2   RSA Example 2

For those readers new to RSA, or new to cryptography in general, it might be helpful to see one more example, with even smaller numbers:

1. Select primes: $p = 17$ and $q = 11$.

2. Compute $n = p\, q = 17 \times 11 = 187$.

3. Compute $\phi(n) = (p - 1)(q - 1) = 16 \times 10 = 160$.

4. Select e: gcd(e,160) = 1. Choose $e = 7$.

5. Determine d: $de = 1$ mod 160 and $d < 160$. Value is d = 23 since $23 \times 7 = 161 = 10 \times 160 + 1$.

6. Publish the public key (7 and 187).

7. Keep secret the private key (23).

These two RSA examples are relatively simple. The prime numbers used are so small that the key would easily be cracked, even with low-end classical computers. However, the small prime numbers make the mathematics quite manageable, so you can easily master the concepts. If this is new information to you, you might find it worthwhile to work through these examples a few times yourself.

11.1.3 Factoring RSA Keys

Factoring is the cornerstone of RSA security. Clearly, one could, at least hypothetically, factor the n value to retrieve p and q and then regenerate the private key. However, it turns out that factoring really large numbers into their prime factors is extremely difficult, at least for classical computers. A more technical description would be to state that it is "computationally infeasible." There is no efficient algorithm for doing it. And we're talking about really large numbers: RSA can use 1024-, 2048-, 4096-, 8192-bit, and larger keys. Those are extremely large numbers. Let us look at an example. Here is a 2048-bit number represented in decimal format:

> 51483247893254789632147780069501356699875410025145630214586147855148324789325477896321477800695015148324789325478963214778006950135669987541002514563021458614785514832478932547896321477800695013256666312458863144587702335658896350232358658900145221478533654 7

In most modern RSA implementations, at least as of this writing, 2048 bits is the smallest RSA key used. Now reflect on the preceding number and contemplate attempting to factor it. I believe you will agree this is quite a daunting task, and we have already discussed the use of the general number sieve.

There are mathematical techniques that will enhance the process, but nothing that makes factoring such large numbers a viable endeavor, at least on classical computers. Of course, should anyone ever invent an efficient algorithm that will factor a large number into its prime factors, RSA would be dead. There certainly have been incidents where someone was able to factor a small RSA key. In 2009, Benjamin Moody factored a 512-bit RSA key in 73 days. In 2010, researchers were able to factor a 768-bit RSA key. Due to these advances in factorization, modern implementations of RSA use larger key sizes.

Now we come to the issue related to quantum computing. Recall the discussion of Shor's algorithm from Chapter 10, "Quantum Algorithms." Shor's algorithm was invented in 1994 by mathematician Peter Shor. He demonstrated that a quantum computer can find the prime factors of an integer N in polynomial time. In fact, the time needed is log N. This does not mean that a quantum computer can immediately read any ciphertext encrypted with RSA. It will take time to factor the public key. However, that time is within a practical timeframe using Shor's algorithm on a quantum computer. Given the ubiquitous nature of RSA, this is a severe issue for security.

11.2 Diffie-Hellman

While some security textbooks state that RSA was the first asymmetric algorithm, this is not accurate. Developed by Whitfield Diffie and Martin Hellman in 1976, Diffie-Hellman was the first publicly described asymmetric algorithm. This is a cryptographic protocol that allows two entities to exchange a symmetric key through some unsecure medium, such as the Internet.

The Diffie-Hellman protocol has two parameters, called p and g. Parameter p is a prime number and parameter g (typically referred to as a generator) is an integer less than p, with the following property: for every number n between 1 and $p-1$ inclusive, there is a power k of g such that $n = gk$ mod p. Let us continue the standard cryptographic practice of using Alice and Bob to illustrate this.

Alice generates a random private value a and Bob generates a random private value b. Both a and b are drawn from the set of integers.

They derive their public values using parameters p and g and their private values. Alice's public value is g^a mod p and Bob's public value is g^b mod p.

They exchange their public values.

Alice computes $g^{ab} = (g^b)^a$ mod p, and Bob computes $g^{ba} = (g^a)^b$ mod p.

Because $g^{ab} = g^{ba} = k$, Alice and Bob now have a shared secret key, k.

Figure 11.1 illustrates this process.

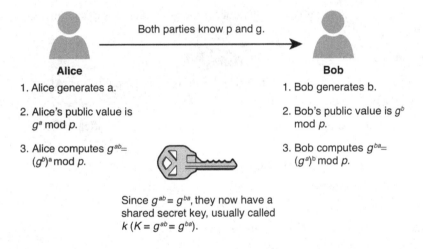

Both parties know p and g.

Alice

1. Alice generates a.

2. Alice's public value is g^a mod p.

3. Alice computes $g^{ab} = (g^b)^a$ mod p.

Bob

1. Bob generates b.

2. Bob's public value is g^b mod p.

3. Bob computes $g^{ba} = (g^a)^b$ mod p.

Since $g^{ab} = g^{ba}$, they now have a shared secret key, usually called k ($K = g^{ab} = g^{ba}$).

FIGURE 11.1   Diffie-Hellman

If you examine this process, you should note that the security of Diffie-Hellman is predicated on the difficulty of solving the discrete logarithm problem. Shor's algorithm can also be applied to discrete logarithms. This means that given a quantum computer running Shor's algorithm, Diffie-Hellman can be broken in a reasonable time period.

11.2.1   Elgamal

Elgamal is one of many improvements made to Diffie-Hellman. Taher Elgamal first described it in 1984. Elgamal is based on the Diffie-Hellman key exchange algorithm.

The Elgamal algorithm has three parts:

- Key generator
- Encryption algorithm
- Decryption algorithm

Continuing with the example of Alice and Bob, we can easily describe the Elgamal key generation process:

1. Alice generates an efficient description of a multiplicative cyclic group G of order q with generator g.

2. Alice chooses a random from x from a set of numbers {0, ..., q–1).

3. Then Alice computes h = gx. Recall that g is the generator for the group and x is a random number from within the group.

    Also, h, G, q, and g are the public key, and x is the private key.

4. If Bob wishes to encrypt a message m and send it to Alice, he starts with the public key Alice generated. The process for Bob to encrypt a message is as follows:

    a. Bob generates a random number y chosen from {0, ..., q–1}. Y is often called an ephemeral key.

    b. Bob will calculate c1. That calculation is simple: $c1 = g^y$.

    c. A shared secret, $s = h^y$, is computed.

    d. The message m is converted to m′ of G.

    e. Bob must calculate c2. That calculation is relatively easy: c2 = m′ * s.

    f. Bob can now send c1 and c2 as the encrypted text.

5. To decrypt a message m with the private key that Alice generated, the following process is done:

    a. The recipient calculates $s = c1^x$.

    b. The recipient calculates $m′ = c2 * s^{-1}$.

    c. Finally, m′ is converted back to the plaintext m.

The structure should look only moderately similar to Diffie-Hellman; however, it is still based on the same security presumptions as Diffie-Hellman. This means that given a working quantum computer, Elgamal will also be susceptible to attacks that can succeed in polynomial time.

11.2.2 MQV

Much like Diffie-Hellman, Menezes-Qu-Vanstone (MQV) is a protocol for key agreement and is, in fact, based on Diffie-Hellman. It was first proposed by Menezes, Qu, and Vanstone in 1995 and then modified in 1998. MQV is incorporated in the public-key standard IEEE P1363. HMQV (Hash MQV) is an improved version. Like Diffie-Hellman, the security of MQV is predicated on the difficulty classical computers have solving the discrete logarithm problem. Quantum computers, as we have seen, have no such difficulty.

MQV uses elliptic curves, which will be discussed in detail in the next section; however, the general steps are given here. There are some preliminary items needed before we start the MQV steps. The two parties have a public and private key pair. Alice's is usually designated as A being her public key and a being her private key. Bob's keys are similar: B is his public key and b is his private key. These will be used in the following steps for Alice and Bob to exchange a new key to use. There is also a value h that is a cofactor from the elliptic curve they are both using. There is one more value that you need to know about, and it's a bit more complex. You will see it in steps 4 and 5.

Step 1. The person starting the key exchange, traditionally called Alice, generates a key pair using a randomly chosen value x and then calculating $X = xP$, where P is some point on an elliptic curve. The key pair is (X, x).

Step 2. The other party, usually called Bob, also generates a key pair. His key pair is (Y, y), which is generated by using a randomly chosen y and then calculating $Y = yP$.

Step 3. Alice now calculates a value $Sa = X + \overline{X}a$ modulo n. She then sends her X to Bob.

Step 4. Bob calculates $Sb = y + \overline{Y}b \bmod n$ and sends the Y to Alice.

Step 5. Alice then calculates $K = h * Sz(Y + \overline{Y}B)$ while Bob calculates $K = h * Sb(X + \overline{X}A)$.

You might wonder why they would go through all this trouble. Don't Alice and Bob already have a public and private key? Can they not just simply use these keys? They could; however, two things are occurring in MQV. First, the public key of each party is really being used to authenticate that party, not to encrypt data. Second, a new symmetric key is used every time they run this algorithm. Therefore, Alice and Bob could potentially have a different, new symmetric key for every message.

11.3 Elliptic Curve

Elliptic curve cryptography is a bit more mathematically complex than RSA. Elliptic curves can be used to form groups and thus are suitable for cryptographic purposes. There are two types of elliptic curve groups. The two most common (and the ones used in cryptography) are elliptic curve groups based on F_p, where p is prime, and those based on $F2^m$. F is the field being used, and m is some integer value. Elliptic curve cryptography is an approach to public-key cryptography based on elliptic curves over finite fields.

Elliptic curves applied to cryptography were first described in 1985 by Victor Miller (of IBM) and Neil Koblitz. The security of elliptic curve cryptography is based on the fact that finding the discrete logarithm of a random elliptic curve element with respect to a publicly known base point is difficult to the point of being impractical to do. An elliptic curve is the set of points that satisfy a specific mathematical equation. The equation for an elliptic curve is as follows:

$$y^2 = x^3 + Ax + B$$

Figure 11.2 illustrates a common way to depict the graph of this equation.

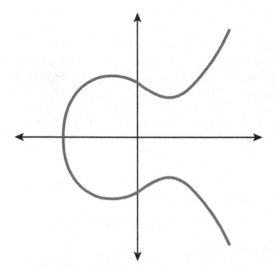

FIGURE 11.2   Elliptic curve graph

There are other ways to represent an elliptic curve, but Figure 11.2 is the most common, and perhaps the easiest to understand. Another way to describe an elliptic curve is that it is simply the set of points that satisfy an equation that has two variables in the second degree and one variable in the third degree. The first thing you should notice from the graph in Figure 11.2 is the horizontal symmetry. Any point on the curve can be reflected about the x-axis without changing the shape of the curve.

Lawrence Washington of the University of Maryland describes an elliptic curve a bit more formally: "an elliptic curve E is the graph of an equation of the form where A and B are constants. This will be referred to as the Weierstrass equation for an elliptic curve. We will need to specify what set A, B, x, and y belong to. Usually, they will be taken to be elements of a field, for example, the real numbers R, the complex numbers C, the rational numbers Q, one of the finite fields Fp (=Zp) for a prime p, or one of the finite fields Fq, where q=pk with k1." These values will make more sense as we go deeper into ECC.

The operation used with the elliptic curve is addition (recall that a group's definition requires a set along with an operation). Thus, elliptic curves form additive groups.

The members of the elliptic curve field are integer points on the elliptic curve. You can perform addition with points on an elliptic curve. Throughout most of the literature on the elliptic curve, we consider two points, P and Q. The negative of a point P = (xP, yP) is its reflection in the x-axis: the point –P is (xP, –yP). Notice that for each point P on an elliptic curve, the point –P is also on the curve. Suppose that P and Q are two distinct points on an elliptic curve, and assume that P is not merely the inverse of Q. To add the points P and Q, you draw a line through the two points. This line will intersect the elliptic curve at exactly one more point, called –R. The point –R is reflected in the x-axis to the point R. The law for addition in an elliptic curve group is P + Q = R.

The line through P and –P is a vertical one that does not intersect the elliptic curve at a third point; therefore, the points P and –P cannot be added as done previously. For this reason, the elliptic curve group includes the point at infinity O. By definition, P + (–P) = O. As a result of this equation, P + O = P in the elliptic curve group. O is called the additive identity of the elliptic curve group; all elliptic curves have an additive identity. You can see this in Figure 11.3.

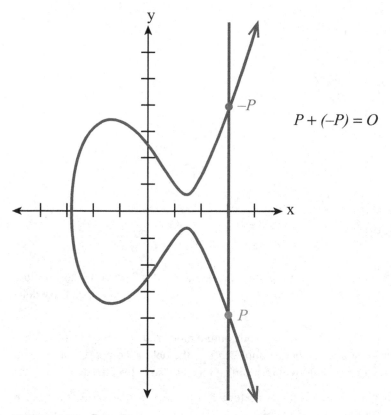

$$P + (-P) = O$$

FIGURE 11.3 P + –P

To add a point P to itself, a tangent line to the curve is drawn at the point P. If yP is not 0, then the tangent line intersects the elliptic curve at exactly one other point, –R, and –R is reflected in the x-axis to R. This operation is called "doubling the point P," as illustrated by Figure 11.4.

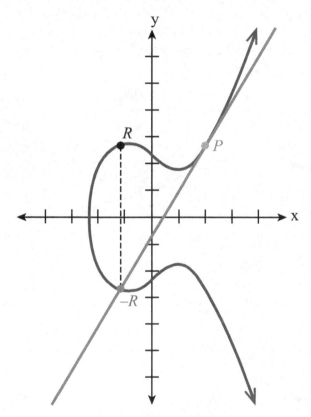

FIGURE 11.4 Doubling the point P

The tangent from P is always vertical if yP = 0. If a point P is such that yP = 0, then the tangent line to the elliptic curve at P is vertical and does not intersect the elliptic curve at any other point. By definition, 2P = O for such a point P.

Recall that the field Fp uses the numbers from 0 to p − 1, and computations end by taking the remainder on division by p (i.e., the modulus operations). For example, in F_{23}, the field is composed of integers from 0 to 22, and any operation within this field will result in an integer also between 0 and 22.

An elliptic curve with the underlying field of Fp can be formed by choosing the variables a and b within the field of F_p. The elliptic curve includes all points (x,y) that satisfy the elliptic curve equation modulo p (where x and y are numbers in F_p). For example, y^2 mod p = x^3 + ax + b mod p has an Fp's underlying field if a and b are in Fp.

If $x^3 + ax + b$ contains no repeating factors, then the elliptic curve can be used to form a group. An elliptic curve group over Fp consists of the points on the corresponding elliptic curve, together with a special point O called the point at infinity. There are finitely many points on such an elliptic curve.

At the foundation of every asymmetric cryptosystem is a hard mathematical problem that is computationally infeasible to solve. The discrete logarithm problem is the basis for the security of many cryptosystems, including the Elliptic Curve Cryptosystem. More specifically, the ECC relies upon the difficulty of the Elliptic Curve Discrete Logarithm Problem (ECDLP).

Recall that we examined two geometrically defined operations over certain elliptic curve groups. These two operations were point addition and point doubling. By selecting a point in an elliptic curve group, one can double it to obtain the point 2P. After that, one can add the point P to the point 2P to obtain the point 3P. The determination of a point nP in this manner is referred to as scalar multiplication of a point. The ECDLP is based upon the intractability of scalar multiplication products.

In the multiplicative group Zp*, the discrete logarithm problem is as follows: given elements r and q of the group, and a prime p, find a number k such that r = qk mod p. If the elliptic curve groups are described using multiplicative notation, then the elliptic curve discrete logarithm problem is as follows: given points P and Q in the group, find a number such that Pk = Q, where k is called the discrete logarithm of Q to the base P. When the elliptic curve group is described using additive notation, the elliptic curve discrete logarithm problem is the following: given points P and Q in the group, find a number k such that Pk = Q.

The following is a common example, used in many textbooks, papers, and web pages. It uses rather small numbers that you can easily work with but still makes the general point of how elliptic curve cryptography works.

In the elliptic curve group defined by

y2 = x3 + 9x + 17 over F23

what is the discrete logarithm k of Q = (4,5) to the base P = (16,5)?

One way to find k is to compute multiples of P until Q is found. The first few multiples of P are shown here:

P = (16,5) 2P = (20,20) 3P = (14,14) 4P = (19,20) 5P = (13,10)

6P = (7,3) 7P = (8,7) 8P = (12,17) 9P = (4,5)

Because 9P = (4,5) = Q, the discrete logarithm of Q to the base P is k = 9.

In a real application, k would be large enough such that it would be infeasible to determine k in this manner. This is the essence of elliptic curve cryptography; obviously, we use much larger fields. For more information, an excellent online tutorial can be found at http://arstechnica.com/security/2013/10/a-relatively-easy-to-understand-primer-on-elliptic-curve-cryptography/.

Elliptic curve cryptosystems (ECC) rely on the difficulty of the Elliptic Curve Discrete Logarithm Problem (ECDLP). This is a problem that cannot be solved in polynomial time on a classical computer. As you might have already surmised, this means that ECC is susceptible to attacks from quantum computers.

As you can see from the previous sections, elliptic curves form groups, and those groups can be used just as any other algebraic group. The practical implication of this is that one can adapt various algorithms to elliptic curve groups. There are many permutations of elliptic curve cryptography, including the following:

- Elliptic Curve Diffie-Hellman (used for key exchange)

- Elliptic Curve Digital Signature Algorithm (ECDSA)

- Elliptic Curve MQV key agreement protocol

- Elliptic Curve Integrated Encryption Scheme (ECIES)

In this section, we will take a closer look at two of these: ECC Diffie-Hellman and ECDSA.

11.3.1 ECC Diffie-Hellman

Diffie-Hellman, which we examined earlier in this chapter, is the oldest key exchange protocol. It is a natural to modify for elliptic curves. Elliptic curve Diffie-Hellman (ECDH) is a key exchange or key agreement protocol used to establish a shared secret over an insecure medium. That shared secret is then either used directly or as the basis to derive another key. In the case of ECDH, the public-private key pairs are based on elliptic curves.

- **Public:** Elliptic curve and point (x,y) on curve
- **Secret:** Alice's A and Bob's B
    - Alice computes A(B(x,y)).
    - Bob computes B(A(x,y)).
    - These are the same since AB = BA.
- **Public:** Curve $y^2 = x^3 + 7x + b \pmod{37}$ and point $(2,5) \Rightarrow b = 3$
- **Alice's secret:** A = 4
- **Bob's secret:** B = 7
    - Alice sends Bob 4(2,5) = (7,32).
    - Bob sends Alice 7(2,5) = (18,35).
    - Alice computes 4(18,35) = (22,1).
    - Bob computes 7(7,32) = (22,1).

For more details, consult NIST Special Publication 800-56A, Revision 2, at http://csrc.nist.gov/ publications/nistpubs/800-56A/SP800-56A_Revision1_Mar08-2007.pdf.

11.3.2 ECDSA

The Digital Signature Algorithm was invented specifically for digitally signing messages. Of course, one can utilize any asymmetric algorithm to sign a message, but the Digital Signature Algorithm was designed for that purpose. As you might expect, there is an elliptic curve variant on this algorithm.

To illustrate how this works, we will consider the fictitious characters Bob and Alice once again. First, the two parties must agree on some parameters: the curve, denoted as E, the base point/generator of the elliptic curve, denoted as G, and the order of G (an integer), denoted by n. Now to sign a message, Alice takes the following steps:

Step 1. Select a random integer k that is less than n (i.e., K>1; k< n).

Step 2. Compute $kG = (x_1, y_1)$ and $r = x_1$ mod n. If $r = 0$, then go to step 1.

Step 3. Compute k^{-1} mod n.

Step 4. Compute e = SHA-1(m). Most digital signature algorithms use a hash; in this case, the hash is usually SHA-1. Therefore, this is stating that Alice computes the SHA-1 hash of the message.

Step 5. Compute $s = k^{-1}\{e + d_A \cdot r\}$ mod n.

Step 6. If s = 0, then go to step 1. In other words, Alice keeps repeating the process until s ! = 0. This is not usually time consuming and could happen on the first attempt.

Step 7. Alice's signature for the message m is (r, s).

In order for Bob to verify Alice's signature (r,s), he will execute the following steps:

Step 1. Verify that r and s are integers in [1, n–1].

Step 2. Compute e = SHA-1(m).

Step 3. Compute $w = s^{-1}$ mod n.

Step 4. Compute $u_1 = ew$ mod n and $u_2 = rw$ mod n.

Step 5. Compute $(x_1, y_1) = u_1 G + u_2 Q_A$.

Step 6. Compute $v = x_1$ mod n.

Step 7. Accept the signature if and only if v = r.

Figure 11.5 summarizes the process.

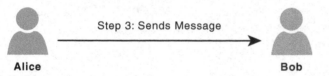

Step 3: Sends Message

Alice

Bob

Step 1: Generates her signature r, s

Step 4: Verifies signature

Step 2: Signs message

FIGURE 11.5   ECDSA

This is like the traditional Digital Signature Algorithm, except that it uses elliptic curve groups. ECDSA is quite secure, at least against classical computer attacks; however, it is susceptible to attacks by quantum computers.

11.4 Summary

In this chapter, we examined some classical asymmetric algorithms in use today. These algorithms are widely used in e-commerce, online banking, and many other applications. None of these algorithms is resistant to quantum computing–based attacks. For this reason, it is important that newer, quantum-resistant algorithms are tested for use. The next four chapters will explore the issues of quantum computing and cryptography. It is important that you have an understanding of how current algorithms function and why they are not resistant to quantum computing–based attacks.

Test Your Skills

REVIEW QUESTIONS

1. Shor's algorithm can factor an integer N in what time?

   a. N^2

   b. log(N)

   c. ln(N)

   d. N!

2. Which of the following equations is most related to elliptic curve cryptography?

   a. Me % n

   b. P = Cd % n

   c. Ce % n

   d. y2 = x3 + Ax + B

3. What is a discrete logarithm?

4. Explain the basic setup of Diffie-Hellman (the basic math, including key generation).

5. What is the formula for encrypting with RSA?

6. Explain RSA key generation.

Chapter | **12**

The Impact of Quantum Computing on Cryptography

Chapter Objectives

After reading this chapter and completing the review questions, you will be able to do the following:

- Understand how quantum computing will impact asymmetric cryptography
- Explain how symmetric cryptography will change after quantum computing
- Appreciate the changes to applications of cryptography that quantum computing will necessitate

Even before starting this book, you were very likely aware that quantum computing would have a substantial impact on cryptography and cybersecurity. In fact, that may have been your impetus for learning more about quantum computing. The most obvious impact of quantum computing will be on asymmetric cryptography. However, that is not to say there is no impact on other areas of cryptography. We will explore that impact in this chapter.

The primary concern for cryptography stems from the nature of current asymmetric cryptographic algorithms. Even if quantum computing had no impact at all on symmetric ciphers or cryptographic hashes, which is not the case, the impact on asymmetric cryptography alone would be troublesome. Virtually all aspects of network security depend, at least to some degree, on asymmetric cryptography. This includes e-commerce, VPNs, and many authentication protocols. Currently used asymmetric algorithms are secure because they are based on mathematical problems that are difficult to solve. By "difficult," we mean that they cannot be solved in practical time using classical (i.e., non-quantum) computers. RSA is based on the difficulty of factoring numbers into their prime factors. Diffie-Hellman is based on the difficulty of solving the discrete logarithm problem. The various improvements to Diffie-Hellman, such as Elgamal and MQV, are also based on the difficulty of solving the discrete logarithm problem. Elliptic curve cryptography, which includes several algorithms, is based on the difficulty of solving discrete logarithm problems of a random elliptic curve element with respect to a publicly known base point. The problem for cybersecurity is that it has already been proven that these mathematical problems can be solved with quantum computers.

The question is not "will quantum computers impact cryptography?" but rather "how soon?" Because it has been proven that quantum algorithms can solve the problems that form the basis for current asymmetric cryptography, in a time that is practical, quantum computing will eventually render existing asymmetric or public key algorithms obsolete and ineffective. This means that the cryptography used for key exchange in VPNs, digital certificates, all e-commerce solutions, and even some network authentication protocols, will no longer be secure. Transport Layer Security (TLS), which is widely used to secure Internet traffic, including web traffic, email, and even voice over IP, will no longer be secure. While these dangers to cybersecurity are not immediate, because quantum computing is not yet a practical, usable reality, it is important for anyone in cybersecurity to be aware of the problem and to be familiar with the progress toward solutions.

There are many terms used for quantum-resistant cryptography. Sometimes the term *post-quantum cryptography* is used, and sometimes *quantum-safe cryptography*. Whatever the term, the concept is the same: cryptographic algorithms that are based on mathematics that is not readily solvable by quantum computers. In addition to the United States National Institute of Standards quantum-resistant cryptography standard project, the European Telecommunications Standards Institute along with the Institute for Quantum Computing have been hosting workshops on quantum-safe cryptography. The various approaches to quantum-safe cryptography will be discussed in detail in Chapter 13, "Lattice-based Cryptography," Chapter 14, "Multivariate Cryptography," and Chapter 15, "Other Approaches to Post-Quantum Cryptography." You can read about the NIST quantum-safe cryptography standards at https://csrc.nist.gov/projects/post-quantum-cryptography.

12.1   Asymmetric Cryptography

Our examination of the impact of quantum computing should begin with the place it will have the most obvious effect—asymmetric cryptography. You have undoubtedly become familiar with some of these issues as you have progressed through the chapters in this book. Classical asymmetric cryptography is based on particular problems in number theory, such as the factoring problem or the discrete logarithm problem.

The answer to quantum computing's threat to asymmetric cryptography is to utilize asymmetric algorithms based on different mathematical problems. Particularly, problems that, at least thus far, have not been shown to be vulnerable to quantum computing attacks. There are several such families of algorithms. We will explore them in some detail in coming chapters. These families of algorithms include lattice-based cryptography, multivariate cryptography, super-singular elliptic curve isogeny cryptography, and hash-based cryptography.

Lattice-based cryptography is simply cryptographic systems based on some problem in lattice-based mathematics. One of the most commonly used problems for lattice cryptography is the Shortest Vector Problem (SVP). Essentially, this problem is that given a particular lattice, how do you find the shortest vector within the lattice? More specifically, the SVP involves finding the shortest nonzero vector in the vector space V, as measured by a norm, N. Recall from Chapter 1, "Introduction to Essential Linear Algebra," that a norm is a function that assigns a strictly positive length or size to each vector in a vector space. The SVP is a good choice for post-quantum computing.

Another problem used in latticed-based cryptography is the Closest Vector Problem (CVP). This problem is summarized as follows: given a vector space V and a metric M for a lattice L and a vector v that is in the vector space V, but not necessarily in the lattice L, find the vector in the lattice L that is closest to the vector v. Chapter 13 examines this concept in more detail.

Multivariate cryptography, as the name suggests, is based on mathematical problems with multiple variables. More specifically, these algorithms are often based on multivariate polynomials over a finite field. There are encryption schemes as well as digital signature methods based on multivariate cryptography.

Super-singular elliptic curve isogeny cryptography is, as the name suggests, a particular variation of elliptic curve cryptography. Super-singular elliptic curves are a particular class of elliptic curves over a field. Chapter 14 explores these algorithms in some detail.

There are also hash-based cryptographic algorithms. The first hash-based digital signatures were developed by Ralph Merkle in the 1970s. It should also be noted that the Merkle-Damgaard construction is used in many hashing algorithms. Current hash-based algorithms that are being considered for post-quantum cryptography include Leighton-Micali Signatures (LMS) and eXtended Merkle Signature Scheme (XMSS). Chapter 15 examines hash-based cryptographic solutions in more detail.

Code-based cryptography has a bit different approach. These are systems that rely on error-correcting codes. One such system is the McEliece cryptosystem published in 1978 by Robert McEliece. This algorithm was not widely used in classical cryptography but has been a candidate for post-quantum cryptography. The McEliece system has already been shown to be resistant to Shor's algorithm, which makes it quite attractive. Chapter 15 explores this algorithm in more detail.

12.1.1   How Many Qubits Are Needed?

As discussed in Chapter 9, "Quantum Hardware," a rough estimate of 4000 qubits is necessary for breaking RSA using 2048-bit. This estimate is not without basis in experiment. The issue is how fast a quantum computer can factor a number. In 2014, physicists used a quantum computer to factor the number 56,153. Now, that number is obviously much smaller than typical RSA keys. To provide some perspective, a 2048-bit key, changed to decimal numbers, would be 256 digits long. To put this in perspective, here is a 256-digit number:

9,123,456,789,321,654,987,111,222,333,444,555,666,777,888,999, 321,785,828,499,202,001,039,
231,943,294,122,098,992,909,098,

461,654,843,513,213,651,488,351,315,654,684,643,513,513,167,

879,841,294,872,617,124,598,248,547,555,666,777,685,987,654,

123,456,828,499,202,001,039,231,943,294,122,098,992,909,098,

548,548,477,658,987,899,845,965,599,458

You can agree that this is a rather large number. Thus, cracking five-digit numbers does not bring us to the point where RSA is currently in danger. What has been shown, however, is that once quantum computers have reached a point of stability (i.e., decoherence is controlled) and we have been able to expand the number of stable qubits available, RSA will no longer be secure.

12.2 Specific Algorithms

Perhaps the most important question regarding quantum computing, from a cybersecurity perspective, is what impact quantum computing will have on specific cryptographic algorithms. We have covered this topic, at least on a surface level, previously in this book and in this chapter. In this section, we will examine specific algorithms and how vulnerable they are to quantum computing attacks.

12.2.1 RSA

Chapter 11, "Current Asymmetric Algorithms," explained the details of RSA with examples. This was to ensure you understood why Shor's algorithm had such a substantial impact on RSA. As discussed in Chapter 10, "Quantum Algorithms," Shor's algorithm is able to factor integers in polynomial time. This means it will be able to derive the RSA private key from the public key within a practical time period.

12.2.2 Diffie-Hellman

As you learned in Chapter 11, Diffie-Hellman is based on the difficulty of solving the Discrete Logarithm Problem. There have been numerous improvements on Diffie-Hellman, such as ElGamal and MQV, but the security of these algorithms is also predicated on the difficulty of solving the Discrete Logarithm Problem.

Chapter 10 explored Shor's algorithm and demonstrated that in addition to being able to factor integers, the algorithm can be used in solving the Discrete Logarithm Problem. Thus, Shor's algorithm alone makes the Diffie-Hellman family of algorithms insecure to quantum computing–based attacks.

Shor's algorithm is not the only threat to algorithms whose security is based on the difficulty of solving the Discrete Logarithm Problem, however. In 2016, Martin Ekera introduced a modified version of Shor's algorithm that was specifically used to solve what is termed the *Short Discrete Logarithm Problem*. This problem is used in Diffie-Hellman as implemented in TLS and IKE protocols, which we will discuss in more detail later in this chapter. There have been further refinements of Ekera's work since 2016.

12.2.3 ECC

In the previous section we discussed the discrete logarithm problem. As you know from Chapter 11, elliptic curve cryptography is based on the Elliptic Curve Discrete Logarithm Problem (ECDLP). This means that all the variations of elliptic curve cryptography are not quantum safe.

12.2.4 Symmetric Ciphers

Most of the impact discussed in the literature involves the effect of quantum algorithms on asymmetric cryptography. However, there is also an effect on symmetric cryptography. That effect is definitely less impactful but still is an effect. As an example, consider Grover's algorithm, which we also discussed in Chapter 10. It can "guess" symmetric keys in a number of iterations that is roughly one half the key space. Therefore, if one is considering AES 128-bit, Grover's algorithm can guess the key in 2^{64} iterations. How long might that take? With current technology, it would still be prohibitively long. However, it does mean that simply increasing symmetric keys, perhaps simply doubling key size, should be adequate to protect against quantum attacks.

The general consenses of the cryptographic community is that symmetric ciphers will be quantum safe with slight modification. That slight modification will most often simply be a doubling of key size. So rather than utilize AES 128-bit, one should use AES 256-bit. If one is already using AES 256-bit, then a 512-bit key should be considered. The actual AES standard only allows for the three key sizes of 128, 192, and 256 bits. However, the Rijndael algorithm itself has no such limitation and can accommodate 512-bit keys. This doubling of key size would apply to all symmetric ciphers, including Blowfish, Serpent, CAST, IDEA, etc.

The reason these algorithms are not in danger from quantum computers is actually rather simple. Symmetric ciphers, as the name itself suggests, have a single key. That, in turn, means that the algorithms' security is not based on relating two keys. Asymmetric ciphers work only because the two separate keys (public and private key) are related through some underlying math. That math is secure only because of the difficulty of solving a particular mathematical problem; however, symmetric ciphers' security is not built on the security of some underlying mathematical problem. Essentially, there is no fundamental mathematics problem for the quantum computer to solve in order to break the symmetric cipher. The best a quantum computer can do is perhaps speed up brute-force attacks.

12.2.5 Cryptographic Hashes

Cryptographic hashes, like symmetric ciphers, are not based on the difficulty of solving particular mathematical problems. At least not most cryptographic hashing algorithms. The most commonly used cryptographic hash functions are simply implementations of the information theoretic concepts of confusion and diffusions. The Merkle-Damgaard construction is used in quite a few hash functions. Thus, SHA-2, SHA-3, Whirlpool, GOST, RIPEMD, and other commonly used cryptographic hash functions are unlikely to be impacted by quantum computing. One might, in an abundance of caution, choose to implement larger digest sizes. This would mean using SHA-2 512-bit rather than 256-bit, or perhaps RIPEMD 320 rather than 160. Other than these modest changes, there is no immediate indication of substantial security threats to most cryptographic hashes.

12.3 Specific Applications

Ultimately, all computing is about applications. While a computer scientist may derive gratification from simply solving intellectual problems, the goal is to provide some useful application. This is true of cryptography as well. In this section, you will see common applications of cryptography explained. The specific changes needed for these applications to be quantum resistant will also be explored.

12.3.1 Digital Certificates

Digital certificates are of paramount importance in applied cryptography. They are the way in which one retrieves someone's public key. Digital certificates are integral to secure communications such as Transport Layer Security (TLS), and they perform a role in many forms of authentication. X.509 is an international standard for the format and information included in a digital certificate. X.509 is the most common type of digital certificate in the world. It is a digital document that contains a public key signed by the trusted third party who issued the certificate, which is known as a Certificate Authority (CA). The X.509 standard was first published in 1988. It has been revised since then, with the most recent version being X.509 v3, specified in RFC 5280.[1] This system supports not only getting information about the certificate holder but validating that information with a trusted third party. This is key to secure protocols such as SSL and TLS, as we will see later in this chapter.

The content of an X.509 certificate is as follows:

- **Version**: What version of X.509 is being used. Today that is most likely going to be version 3.

- **Certificate holder's public key**: This is the public key of the certificate holder. Essentially, this is how public keys are disseminated.

- **Serial number**: This is a unique identifier that identifies this certificate.

- **Certificate holder's distinguished name**: A distinguished or unique name for the certificate holder—usually a URL for a website or an email address.

- **Certificate's validity period**: Most certificates are issued for one year, but the exact validity period is reflected in this field.

- **Unique name of certificate issuer**: This identifies the trusted third party who issued the certificate. Public Certificate Authorities include Thawte, Verisign, GoDaddy, and others.

- **Digital signature of issuer**: How do you know that this certificate was really issued by the Certificate Authority it claims to have been issued by? That is by having a digital signature.

---

1. "RFC 5280," IETF, https://www.rfc-editor.org/info/rfc5280.

- **Signature algorithm identifier**: In order to verify the signer's digital signature, you will need the signer's public key and what algorithm they used.

There are other optional fields, but those just listed are the required fields. Notice that the last three items are all related to the ability to validate this certificate. One of the advantages of the X.509 digital certificate is the system for validating the certificate holder. This is critical to secure communications, not just encrypting the transmissions but verifying the identity of the parties involved.

The question to address now is, what impact will quantum computers have on digital certificates? Fortunately, the actual certificates won't require a substantial change. The infrastructure used to manage certificates will require substantial change, and we will discuss that later in this chapter. The format of the X.509 certificate can remain the same. The difference is the digital signature algorithm listed in the certificate and the public key that is in the certificate. These will need to be quantum-resistant algorithms.

12.3.2 SSL/TLS

It is not an overstatement to assert that SSL/TLS provided the framework for the Internet as we know it today. The ability to conduct e-commerce, have secure communications, and safely send data is, in large part, contingent upon SSL/TLS. When the web first began, security was not a concern. Hypertext Transfer Protocol (HTTP) is inherently quite insecure. As the web grew more popular, it quickly became apparent that security was needed in order to use the web for sensitive communications such as financial data. Netscape invented the Secure Sockets Layer (SSL) protocol, beginning with version 1.0. It was never released due to significant security flaws; however, version 2.0 was released in 1995 and began to be widely used. Unfortunately, SSL version 2.0 had security flaws, and it was subsequently supplanted with SSL version 3.0 in 1996. Version 3.0 was not just a minor improvement over past versions; it was a complete overhaul. It was published as RFC 6101.

TLS 1.0 was released in 1999. It was essentially an upgrade to SSL 3.0; however, it was not compatible with SSL 3.0. TLS 1.0[2] also added support for GOST hashing algorithm as an option for message authentication and integrity. Previous versions supported only MD5 and SHA-1 as hashing message authentication codes.

TLS 1.0 was eventually supplanted by TLS 1.1, released in April 2006. It had a number of specific cryptographic improvements, including improved initialization vectors as well as supporting cipher block chaining for AES.

In August of 2008, TLS 1.2 was released as RFC 5246, and it had many improvements over previous versions, including replacing MD5 and SHAQ with SHA-256. Then TLS 1.3 was released in August 2018, with additional improvements, and defined by RFC 8446.

---

2. "What Is TLS/SSL?" Microsoft TechNet article, https://technet.microsoft.com/en-us/library/cc784450(v=ws.10).aspx.

As quantum computers become more stable and widely used, there will eventually need to be an alteration of the TLS standard to accommodate quantum-safe cryptography. This will likely include different asymmetric algorithms than are currently used as well as increased key sizes for symmetric algorithms. Such a new standard will likely include a larger digest sized for hashes.

12.3.2.1 The Handshake Step-by-Step

In order to fully understand SSL/TLS, it might be useful to understand how a secure connection is established. The process of establishing an SSL/TLS connection is rather complex, but the general process is summarized here:

1. Communication begins with the client sending a Hello message. That message contains the client's SSL version number, cipher settings (i.e., what algorithms can the client support), session-specific data, and other information that the server needs to communicate with the client using SSL.

2. The server responds with a server Hello message. That message contains the server's SSL version number, cipher settings (i.e., what algorithms the server can support), session-specific data, and other information that the client needs to communicate with the server over SSL. The server also sends the client the server's X.509 certificate. The client can use this to authenticate the server and then use the server's public key. In some optional configurations, client authentication is required. In that case, part of the server Hello message is a request for the client's certificate. Client authentication is not generally used in e-commerce, as it would require each and every client to have an X.509 certificate from a well-known and trusted Certificate Authority. I suspect that most of you reading this book do not have such a certificate. If e-commerce sites did request such a certificate, it might reduce online fraud, but would also add an extra burden and cost to consumers. Consumers would have to purchase a certificate, at an average cost of $19.95 per year.

3. Now the client uses the server's X.509 certificate to authenticate the server. It does this by retrieving the public key of the certificate authority who issued this X.509 certificate and using that to verify the CA's digital signature on the X.509 certificate. Assuming authentication works, the client can now proceed with confidence that the server is indeed who it claims to be.

4. Using all data generated in the handshake thus far, the client creates the pre-master secret for the session, encrypts it with the server's public key (obtained from the server's certificate, sent in step 2), and then sends the pre-master secret to the server.

5. If the server is configured to require client authentication, then at this point the server requires the client to send to the server the client's X.509 certificate. The server will use this to attempt to authenticate the client.

6. If client authentication is required and the client cannot be authenticated, the session ends. If the client can be successfully authenticated, the server uses its private key to decrypt the pre-master secret that the client sent to it.

7. Both the client and the server use the pre-master secret that was sent from the client to the server, to generate the session keys. The session keys are symmetric keys and use whatever algorithm the client and server have agreed upon in steps 1 and 2 of the handshake process.

8. Once the client has finished generating the symmetric key from the pre-master secret, the client sends a message to the server stating that future messages from the client will be encrypted with the session key. It then sends an encrypted message indicating that the client portion of the handshake is finished.

9. Once the server has finished generating the symmetric key from the pre-master secret, the server sends a message to the client informing it that future messages from the server will be encrypted with the session key. The server then sends an encrypted message indicating that the server portion of the handshake is finished.

The handshake process itself will not need substantial changes to accommodate quantum-safe cryptography. The issues will be changing the asymmetric algorithms used and the key/digest sizes. However, it is important that preparations are made for these changes to occur.

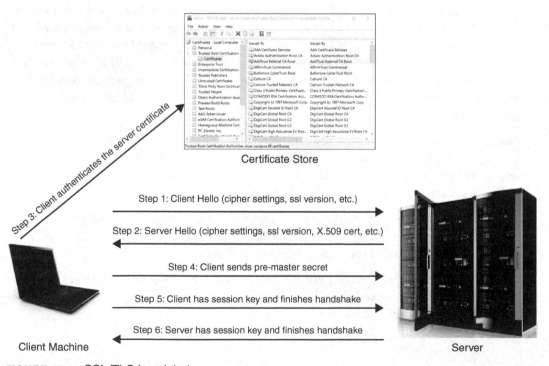

FIGURE 12.1 SSL/TLS handshake summary

12.3.4 Public Key Infrastructure (PKI)

Digital certificates will require small changes in order to accommodate quantum resistant cryptography; however, the public key infrastructure that is used to generate, distribute, and validate certificates will require more substantial improvements.

It is beneficial to first understand the public key infrastructure (PKI), then specific changes to address quantum computing, can be discussed. The PKI is fundamentally the infrastructure needed to create, distribute, and manage digital certificates. Because digital certificates are the means by which public keys for asymmetric algorithms are disseminated, the PKI is a key part of any implementation of asymmetric cryptography.

One role of the PKI is to bind public keys with some user's identity via a certificate authority. In other words, it is not adequate to simply have public keys widely available. There needs to be some mechanism to validate that a specific public key is associated with a specific user. With PKI, this is done via a CA that validates the identity of the user.

There are several parts to the PKI. Each certificate issuer must be trusted by the other certificate issuers for the certificates to be interchangeable. Consider the process of visiting an online banking site. The site has a digital certificate issued by some certificate authority. That certificate authority needs to be one that you and the bank both trust. Then later, perhaps you visit an e-commerce website. This website might use an entirely different certificate authority, but it must also be one that you trust.

The Certificate Authority is responsible for issuing and managing certificates.[3] This includes revoking certificates. Revoking certificates is accomplished in one of two ways:

- **Certificate revocation list (CRL)**: This is simply a list of certificates that have been revoked. A certificate can be revoked for many reasons, as we already mentioned. There are two ways these lists are distributed:

    - **Push model**: CA automatically sends the CRL out at regular intervals.

    - **Pull model**: The CRL is downloaded from the CA by those who want to see it to verify a certificate.

        Neither model provides instant, real-time updates.

- **Status checking**: Given that CRLs are not real time, Online Certificate Status Checking Protocol (OCSP) was invented. OCSP is a real-time protocol that can be used to verify whether a certificate is still valid. OCSP is described in RFC 6960. OCSP uses HTTP to communicate messages. It is supported in Internet Explorer 7 (and beyond), Microsoft Edge, Safari, and Mozilla Firefox 3 (and later).

---

3. "Public Key Infrastructure," Microsoft Developer Network, https://msdn.microsoft.com/en-us/library/windows/desktop/bb427432(v=vs.85).aspx.

The CA is often assisted by a Registration Authority (RA). The RA is responsible for verifying the person/entity requesting a digital certificate. Once that identity has been verified, the RA informs the CA that a certificate can be used.

The *Public-Key Infrastructure X.509 (PKIX)* is the working group formed by the IETF to develop standards and models for the public key infrastructure. Among other things, this working group is responsible for updates to the X.509 standard.

The *Public-Key Cryptography Standards (PKCS)* is a set of voluntary standards created by RSA along with several other companies, including Microsoft and Apple. At press time, there are 15 published PKCS standards:

- PKCS #1: RSA Cryptography Standard
- PKCS #2: Incorporated in PKCS #1
- PKCS #3: Diffie-Hellman Key Agreement Standard
- PKCS #4: Incorporated in PKCS #1
- PKCS #5: Password-Based Cryptography Standard
- PKCS #6: Extended-Certificate Syntax Standard
- PKCS #7: Cryptographic Message Syntax Standard
- PKCS #8: Private-Key Information Syntax Standard
- PKCS #9: Selected Attribute Types
- PKCS #10: Certification Request Syntax Standard
- PKCS #11: Cryptographic Token Interface Standard
- PKCS #12: Personal Information Exchange Syntax Standard
- PKCS #13: Elliptic Curve Cryptography Standard
- PKCS #14: Pseudorandom Number Generators
- PKCS #15: Cryptographic Token Information Format Standard

These standards are formed by the working group, which involves experts from around the world, each contributing input to the standard.

Now that you have an understanding of how the PKI functions, the issues related to quantum computing can be addressed. There will be little or no change required for the registration authorities. Their roles won't change; however, key generation for certificates will need to change substantially. It is an entirely different process to generate a key for NTRU or GGH (see Chapter 13) than it is for RSA. The digital signature algorithms will also need to be changed. These changes will require reconfiguration of the various servers used in the PKI. Thus, the PKI changes might be the most substantial.

12.3.5 VPN

Virtual private networks (VPNs), like SSL/TLS, depend on both symmetric and asymmetric cryptographic algorithms. This means there will be changes needed to accommodate quantum computers. Before we delve into those details, it is worthwhile to briefly summarize VPN technology.

The concept of a VPN is to emulate an actual physical network connection. This requires the VPN to provide both the same level of access and the same level of security as a traditional, physical network connection. In order to emulate a dedicated point-to-point link, data is encapsulated, or wrapped, with a header that provides routing information, allowing it to transmit across the Internet to reach its destination. This creates a virtual network connection between the two points, but this connection only provides a virtual network. Next, the data is also encrypted, thus making that virtual network private.

This leads naturally to the technologies involved in authentication and encryption on VPNs. There are several technologies that can facilitate establishing a VPN, each of which works in a slightly different manner. We will examine each of these in this chapter. Despite the differences in the protocols, the end goals are the same: authenticate the user first, verify that this user is who they claim to be, and then exchange cryptographic information, such as what algorithms to use.

Internet Protocol Security (IPsec) is widely used to create VPNs. According to some sources, it is the most widely used VPN protocol; therefore, it is worthy of some additional study. IPsec is used in addition to the IP protocol to add security and privacy to TCP/IP communication. IPsec is incorporated with Microsoft operating systems as well as many other operating systems. For example, the security settings in the Internet Connection Firewall that ships with Windows 10 enables users to turn on IPsec for transmissions. IPsec is a set of protocols developed by the IETF (Internet Engineering Task Force, www.ietf.org) to support secure exchange of packets. IPsec has been deployed widely to implement VPNs.

IPsec has two encryption modes: transport and tunnel. The transport mode works by encrypting the data in each packet but leaves the header unencrypted. This means that the source and destination address, as well as other header information, are not encrypted. The tunnel mode encrypts both the header and the data. This is more secure than transport mode but can work more slowly. At the receiving end, an IPsec-compliant device decrypts each packet. For IPsec to work, the sending and receiving devices must share a key, an indication that IPsec is a single-key encryption technology. IPsec also offers two other protocols beyond the two modes already described. Those protocols are AH (Authentication Header) and ESP (Encapsulated Security Payload).

IPsec will require substantial changes in order to accommodate quantum computers. The entire suite of cryptographic algorithms used in IPsec will require changes. Furthermore, key exchange protocols will need to be modified. It is possible that an entirely new quantum-resistant VPN will be used instead. For widespread use, it is more practical to simply upgrade existing VPN technologies such as IPsec to better accommodate quantum-resistant cryptography.

12.3.6 SSH

Secure remote communications to servers is a common need particularly for network administrators who often need to remotely connect to the servers they administer. Secure Shell (SSH) is the most common way to securely connect remotely with a server. As with other applications of cryptography, quantum computing will require some changes to this protocol.

Unix and Unix-based systems such as Linux utilize SSH to connect to a target server. The SSH standard uses asymmetric cryptography to authenticate the remote computer and, when mutual authentication is required, to authenticate the client. SSH was first released in 1995 and was developed by Tatu Ylonen, at Helsinki University of Technology. His goal was to replace insecure protocols such as Telnet, rsh, and rlogin. SSH version 1 was released as freeware. By 1999, OpenSSH had been released and is still a very popular version of SSH.

SSH version 2 has an internal architecture with specific layers responsible for particular functions:

- The transport layer handles the key exchange and authentication of the server. Keys are re-exchanged usually after either one hour of time has passed or 1 gigabyte of data has been transmitted. This renegotiation of keys is a significant strength for SSH.

- The user authentication layer is responsible for authenticating the client. There are a few ways this can be done—the two most common are password and public key. The password method simply checks the user's password. The public key method uses either DSA or RSA key pairs to verify the client's identity, and can also support X.509 certificates.

- Generic Security Service Application Program Interface (GSSAPI) authentication is variation of SSH authentication to allow for the use of either Kerberos or NTLM to authenticate. While not all versions of SSH support GSSAPI, OpenSSH does.

SSH can be used to provide secure file transfer with technologies such as Secure Copy (SCP), SSH File Transfer Protocol (SFTP), and Files transferred over SSH (FISH).

SSH can be configured to use several different symmetric algorithms, including AES, Blowfish, 3DES, CAST-128, and RC4. The specific algorithm is configured for each SSH implementation. The first issue quantum computing will alter is the use of particular symmetric algorithms. I anticipate that 3DES and CAST-128 will no longer be supported. Blowfish and AES should be supported but with larger key sizes. Of course, the asymmetric algorithms used in key exchange and authentication will also need to be changed. Given that SSH is distributed with most Linux distributions, this will require alterations to Linux for most vendors such as Red Hat, Mint, Ubuntu, etc.

Summary

This chapter discussed the practical implications of quantum computing on cryptographic implementations. Specific algorithms were explored, including the impact that quantum computing will have on the use of those algorithms. Perhaps most importantly, common applications of cryptography were explored, and the necessary changes to accommodate quantum-safe cryptography were discussed.

Test Your Skills

REVIEW QUESTIONS

1. Assuming practical, working quantum computers, what change will be needed for AES?

   a. None. It will not be affected.

   b. It will need to be replaced.

   c. It will need larger key sizes.

   d. It will have to be combined with a hashing algorithm.

2. Assuming practical, working quantum computers, what change will be needed for CAST-128?

   a. None. It will not be affected.

   b. It will need to be replaced.

   c. It will need larger key sizes.

   d. It will have to be combined with a hashing algorithm.

3. The ability to solve the Discrete Logarithm Problem impacts which algorithm(s)?

   a. RSA

   b. DH

   c. ECC

   d. AES

4. Once quantum computers become a practical reality, how much change will the X.509 standard require?

   a. None

   b. Minimal

   c. Substantial overhaul

   d. It will need to be replaced.

5. Why are symmetric algorithms less impacted by quantum computing than asymmetric?

   a. Their long key sizes make them quantum safe.

   b. Their use of confusion and diffusion makes them quantum safe.

   c. They are impacted as much as or more than asymmetric algorithms.

   d. They are not predicated on specific mathematical problems that a quantum computer can solve.

Chapter 13

Lattice-based Cryptography

Chapter Objectives

After reading this chapter and completing the review questions, you will be able to do the following:

- Understand the basis for lattice-based cryptography
- Demonstrate a working knowledge of specific algorithms
- Comprehend how these algorithms can be quantum resistant
- Appreciate the principles of lattice reduction attacks

In previous chapters, we covered the fundamentals of quantum computing. Chapter 12, "The Impact of Quantum Computing on Cryptography," explored the impact of quantum computing on cryptography and cybersecurity. This chapter explores a potential answer to the impact of quantum computing on cryptography. Lattice-based algorithms have been proposed as quantum-resistant asymmetric algorithms.

Lattice-based algorithms are cryptographic algorithms predicated on mathematical problems related to lattices. Recall that the security of RSA is based on the computational difficulty of factoring an integer into its prime factors. Diffie-Hellman, and its variations, have security based on the computational difficulty of solving the discrete logarithm problems. The various elliptic curve–based algorithms depend on the difficulty of solving the discrete logarithm in reference to an elliptic curve and a point not on the curve. All of these currently used algorithms have security predicated on some mathematical problem. Lattice-based algorithms have security based on mathematical problems related to lattices.

Before we explore specific problems, then algorithms, it is important to understand lattices. Presumably you recall the material from Chapter 1, "Introduction to Essential Linear Algebra." If you are not completely clear on those topics, you should review that chapter before continuing with this one. Lattices are matrices and can be any number of dimensions, though for ease of presentation, most books demonstrate two-dimensional matrices. Each column represents a vector. The matrices used in lattice-based cryptography are much larger than the matrices one typically sees in textbooks; otherwise, solving mathematical problems based on a lattice would be a trivial task to solve, and encryption based on lattices would be easily broken.

This chapter explores the mathematical basis for lattice-based cryptography in more detail, but first a brief introduction. Lattice-based cryptography is simply cryptographic systems based on some problem in lattice-based mathematics. One of the most commonly used problems for lattice-based cryptography is the Shortest Vector Problem (SVP). Essentially, this problem is, given a particular lattice, how do you find the shortest vector within the lattice? More specifically, the SVP involves finding the shortest nonzero vector in the vector space V, as measured by a norm, N. A norm is a function that assigns a strictly positive length or size to each vector in a vector space. The SVP is a good choice for post-quantum computing.

Asymmetric cryptography is based on mathematical problems that are difficult to solve. In fact, the problems are so difficult to solve that no solution can be found within a practical period of time.

Another mathematical problem for lattices is the Closest Vector Problem (CVP). This problem is summarized as, given a vector space V, and a metric M for a lattice L and a vector v that is in the vector space V, but not necessarily in the lattice L, find the vector in the lattice L that is closest to the vector v. This problem is related to the previously discussed Shortest Vector Problem and is also difficult to solve.

13.1   Lattice-Based Mathematical Problems

A lattice can be defined as a set of points in some space having n dimensions, which has a periodic structure. The basis vectors of the lattice are used to generate the lattice. Equation 13.1 provides a mathematical description of a lattice.

$$\mathcal{L}\left(b_4 \ldots bn\right) = \left\{ \sum_{i=1}^{r} x_i b_i : x_i \in z \right\}$$

EQUATION 13.1   Definition of a Lattice

In Equation 13.1, the values b1...bn are basis vectors. Alternatively, this can be expressed as the sum (Σ) of the vectors x that are all elements of the set of integers (Z).

A lattice consists of vectors. Lattices use linearly independent vectors. A set of vectors is described as *linearly dependent* if any one of the vectors in the set can be defined as a linear combination of the other vectors. Conversely, if there is no vector in the set that can be defined in this manner, then the vectors are described as *linearly independent*. These vectors form the basis for a lattice.

This is one aspect of the definition of a lattice, but not the only one. Lattices also appear in geometry and group theory. Consider the real numbers R^n. A lattice is a subgroup of the group R^n, which is isomorphic to the integer group Z^n. This, of course, requires that we define what a subgroup is. In group theory, a subgroup is defined as follows: if G is a group under some operation, and H is a subset of G that also forms a group under that operation, then H is a subgroup of G. Consider the group of integers under the operation of addition. This is clearly a subgroup of the group of rational numbers under the operation of integers.

It is also important that you understand the term *isomorphic* in this context. One often sees that term used in connection with graph theory; however, it has applications in group theory and other areas of mathematics. In any area of mathematics, an isomorphism is a mapping between two structures that preserves the structures and can be reversed via an inverse mapping. Isomorphisms are important because two isomorphic structures will also have the same properties.

One, somewhat trivial example is the group of real numbers with respect to addition (R,+). This group is isomorphic with the group of positive real numbers with multiplication (R$^+$,×).

Now that we have defined the concept of lattices from two different perspectives, we can explore lattices a bit further. Some of this material is new and some is a brief review of some concepts in Chapter 1. These are critical concepts in order for you to understand lattice-based cryptography.

The term *vector space* is quite central to lattice-based cryptography. First, consider a vector. A vector is a group of values. The values can be real numbers, complex numbers, integers, etc. A set of such vectors that is closed under vector addition and closed under scalar multiplication is a vector space. Put a bit more formally, consider a set of vectors V, and within that set select any two vectors, w and v, and a scalar α. The following must be true for V to be a vector space:

- Given v, w $\in$ V, v + w $\in$ V
- Given v $\in$ V and a scalar α, αv $\in$ V

These are not the only property of vector spaces. There are a number of associativity and commutativity properties. However, the two properties just listed are generally the ones that limit some set of vectors to being a vector space or not. However, in the interest of completeness, here are the additional properties given vectors v and w in vector space V along with scalar α:

- v + w = w + v (commutativity of addition).
- (u + v) + w = u + (w + v) (associativity of addition).
- α (v + w) = αv + αw (distributive).
- (α + β)v = αv + βv (distributive).
- There is a vector z $\in$ V such that z + v = v (i.e., a zero vector).
- For each v, there is a −v $\in$ V such that v + (−v) = z (additive inverse).

Vectors have a number of practical applications, but for our current purpose we can simply consider them as mathematical objects. The dimension of a vector space V is the number of vectors over its base field. This is often called the cardinality of the vector space V. A set of vectors B form a basis in a vector space V, if every vector in V can be written as a finite linear combination of the vectors in B. Then B is the set of basis vectors for the vector space V. It is certainly possible that a vector space V can have more than one basis set B. However, all such bases must have the same number of elements, as that is the dimension of the vector space V.

Another concept from linear algebra that is used frequently in lattice-based cryptography is orthogonality. Two elements in a vector space (u and v) are said to be orthogonal if their dot product is zero. A dot product is the sum of the products of the corresponding elements of the two vertices. Essentially, the dot product is used to produce a single number, a scalar, from two vertices or two matrices. This is contrasted with the tensor product. In math, a tensor is an object with multiple indices, such as a vertex or array. The tensor product of two vector spaces V and W, $V \otimes W$, is also a vector space.

Unimodular matrices are also used in some lattice-based algorithms. A unimodular matrix is a square matrix of integers with a determinant of +1 or −1. A determinant is a value that is computed from the elements of a square matrix. The determinant of a matrix A is denoted by $|A|$. Here is an example of a unimodular matrix:

$$\begin{bmatrix} 2 & 3 & 2 \\ 4 & 2 & 3 \\ 9 & 6 & 7 \end{bmatrix}$$

Recall from Chapter 1 that we take three submatrix determinants to get the determinant of this matrix:

$$2\begin{bmatrix} 2 & 3 \\ 6 & 7 \end{bmatrix} - 3\begin{bmatrix} 4 & 3 \\ 9 & 7 \end{bmatrix} + 2\begin{bmatrix} 4 & 2 \\ 9 & 6 \end{bmatrix}$$

Recall that each determinant is computed by $ad - bc$. Thus, we have

$2[(2 * 7) - (3 * 6)] - 3[(4 * 7) - (3 * 9)] + 2[(4 * 6) - (2 * 9)]$

which in turn gives us

$2[14 - 18] - 3[28 - 27] + 2[24 - 18]$

which is

$-8 - (3) + 12$

$= 1$

Cyclic lattices are also used in some cryptographic applications. A cyclic lattice is a lattice that is closed under a rotational shift operator. Equation 13.2 provides a more rigorous definition.

A Lattice $L \subseteq Z^n$ is cyclic if $\forall x \in L: rot(x) \in L$

EQUATION 13.2   Definition of Cyclic Lattice

13.1.1   Shortest Integer Problem

The Shortest Integer Problem, sometimes called Short Integer Solution (SIS), is as follows: Given an $m \times n$ lattice A, which is composed of m uniformly random vectors (which are integers), also stated as $A \in z_q^{nxm}$, find a nonzero short integer vector v such that $Ax = 0$ mod q. This problem forms the basis for Ajtai cryptographic primitive. There are other ways of stating this problem that you will find in some of the literature; however, this form is used here because it is the clearest.

13.1.2   Shortest Vector Problem

The Shortest Vector Problem (SVP) is frequently used as a basis for lattice-based cryptographic systems. This problem is, given a particular lattice and a norm N for a lattice L, find the shortest nonzero vector in V as measured by N in L. Put more formally, the SVP is to find the shortest vector in the vector space V, as measured by a norm, N. Remember that a *norm* is a mathematical function that assigns a positive integer to each vector in a vector space, which is the vector's length or size. The shortest vector must be a nonzero vector.

Put even more formally, given lattice L, vector v, and norm n, then

$$N(v) = \lambda L$$

where λL denotes the length of the shortest nonzero vector in the lattice L.

There are several different approaches to solving this problem, none of which solve the problem in a time that is of practical use, even with a quantum computer. This means that the SVP is a good foundation for lattice-based cryptography. Later in this chapter, we will review the methods for solving lattice-based problems. Keep in mind that the lattices used are so large that one cannot simply look and find the solution to this or other lattice-based problems.

A variation of the Shortest Vector Problem is the Gap Shortest Vector Problem (GapSVP). This problem begins with a fixed function of the dimension of the lattice N. We will refer to this function as β, which is a fixed function of the dimension of the lattice L. Given a basis for the lattice, the algorithm is attempting to determine if $\lambda(L) \leq 1$ or $\lambda > \beta$.

13.1.3   Closest Vector Problem

Another mathematical problem used in lattice-based cryptography is the Closest Vector Problem (CVP). This problem is, given a particular vector space V, along with a metric M for a lattice L and a vector v that is in the vector space V, but not necessarily in the lattice L, how does one find the vector in the lattice L that is closest to the vector v? This problem is related to the previously discussed Shortest Vector Problem and is also computationally hard to solve. In fact, the CVP is a generalization of the SVP.

Given the relationship of the CVP to the SVP, you might assume there is a GapCVP, much as there is a GapSVP. If you assume that, you are indeed correct. With GapSVP, the input consists of a lattice basis and a vector v, and the algorithm must determine if one of the following is correct:

- There is a lattice vector w such that the distance between w and v is at most 1.

- Every vector in the lattice is at a distance greater than β from v.

13.2 Cryptographic Algorithms

Lattice problems are effective for forming cryptographic algorithms. In 1996, the first lattice-based cryptographic algorithm was published. This was created by Milos Ajtai and based on the Short Integer Solution (SIS). This algorithm has been shown to have various vulnerabilities, so it is not actually used for cryptography today. However, it was the first demonstration of the application of lattices to cryptography and thus is usually mentioned in any discussion of lattice-based cryptography. In this section, we will review the three most widely used lattice-based cryptographic algorithms.

13.2.1 NTRU

NTRU (N-th degree Truncated polynomial Ring Units) was first publicly described in 1996 by Jeffery Hoffstein, Jill Pipher, and Joseph Silverman. There have also been additional variants of this algorithm developed since its initial publication. NTRU can best be defined as a group of related cryptographic algorithms. This group of algorithms has been one of the most studied lattice-based cryptosystems. It is a very important group of algorithms, particularly due to the fact that two variations of NTRU have made it past round two of the NIST project to find a quantum-resistant cryptography standard.

NTRU is based on the Shortest Vector Problem in a lattice. The security of NTRU is predicated on the computational difficulty of factoring certain polynomials in a given truncated polynomial ring. This requires that we briefly explore the concept of polynomial rings, for those readers who might not be familiar with them.

A polynomial ring is a ring formed from the set of polynomials in one or more indeterminates (i.e., variables) with coefficients in another ring. Recall the discussion of rings in Chapter 1. A ring is a set with two operations, an identity element, and the inverse operation of the first operation. A polynomial is an expression that consists of variables and coefficients. Another term for the variable is indeterminate, as it was in the definition of a polynomial ring.

Consider, as an example of a polynomial ring, the ring R[X]. This is a ring in X over a field r with the coefficients of p. This can be defined as follows:

$$p = p_0 + p_1X + p_2X^2 + \dots + p_{n-1}X^{n-1} + p_nX^n$$

A truncated polynomial ring is a ring made up of polynomials only up to some set degree. Essentially, the degree of the polynomial is limited or truncated.

For those readers who would like a more rigorous mathematical treatment of polynomial rings, I recommend the following resources:

https://people.seas.harvard.edu/~salil/am106/fall09/lec16.pdf

http://www.math.umd.edu/~immortal/MATH403/lecturenotes/ch16.pdf

Now with that preliminary mathematical information covered, we can return to the NTRU algorithm. NTRU specifically utilizes the truncated polynomial ring shown in Equation 13.3.

$$R = Z[x]/(x^N - 1)$$

EQUATION 13.3 NTRU's Truncated Polynomial Ring

Z is the set of integers, with X being an element of the set of integers.

N is understood to be prime. The key generation process begins with the selection of N, followed by the selection of p and q that must satisfy the criteria that $\gcd(p,q) = 1$. q is often some power of 2, and p is usually relatively small.

The next step is the generation of two polynomials, usually labeled f and g, each having a degree at most N−1. The two polynomials have coefficients in $\{-1,0,1\}$ (e.g., $-x^3$, $-x^2+x-1$). The polynomial f must also have inverses for both modulo p and modulo q. If f does not have inverses both for modulo p and q, then a different f value must be selected. The next step is to actually calculate the inverse of f mod p and f mod q. These are usually designated as f_p and f_q, respectively. The public key is generated according to Equation 13.4.

$$h = pf_q g(mod\ q)$$

EQUATION 13.4 NTRU Key Generation, Step 2

The h is the public key. The polynomials f, fp, and g are the private key. Now that we have a key, how do we apply it to encryption and decryption? We will use the traditional Alice and Bob for this discussion. Assume some message m that is in the form of a polynomial. We already have h and q. Alice wants to encrypt the message m and send it to Bob. Alice now chooses some random polynomial r, usually with small coefficients. Now to encrypt, Alice performs the equation shown in Equation 13.5.

$$e = r * h + m\ (mod\ q)$$

EQUATION 13.5 NTRU Key Generation, Step 3

When Bob receives this message, he will need to decrypt it. Bob takes the encrypted message e and uses Equation 13.6 to decrypt.

$$a = f * e\ (mod\ q)$$

EQUATION 13.6 NTRU Key Generation, Step 4

Note that a in Equation 13.6 represents an intermediate step to the plaintext we wish to retrieve. Keep in mind that e is just r * h + m and that f, fp, and g are private keys. This means we could rewrite Equation 13.6 as shown in Equation 13.7.

$$a = f * (r * h + m) \pmod{q}$$

EQUATION 13.7 NTRU Key Generation, Step 5

The key generation process should tell you that h is really $pf_q g(mod\ q)$, so we can rewrite Equation 13.7 to what you see in Equation 13.8.

$$a = f * (r * pfq * g + m) \pmod{q}$$

EQUATION 13.8 NTRU Key Generation, Step 6

You don't have to consider the permutation of the decryption equation. You can stay with the $a = f * e$ $(mod\ q)$ version. It was just important that you fully understand the process. Now Bob will need to calculate a polynomial, typically called b, that satisfies Equation 13.9.

$$b = a \pmod{p}$$

EQUATION 13.9 NTRU Key Generation, Step 7

Recall Bob's secret key was f, fp, and g, and we have not used all of those values yet. Now, using Equation 13.10, Bob will use them to get back the message m that Alice sent.

$$m = f_p * b \pmod{p}$$

EQUATION 13.10 NTRU Key Generation, Step 8

As was discussed previously, NTRU is actually a family of algorithms. What has just been described is NTRUEncrypt. You now have a solid understanding of NTRUEncrypt key generation, encryption, and decryption. There are many reasons this algorithm has received so much attention as a candidate for quantum-resistant cryptography. The first is that, as of this writing, it has not been shown to be susceptible to any quantum attacks, such as Shor's algorithm. Furthermore, NTRU performs faster than RSA. Performance is crucial in real-world applications.

In addition to the aforementioned NIST standards project, there are other standards that are evaluating NTRU variations. The European Union's PQCRYPTO project is examining the Stehlé-Steinfeld version of NTRU as a possible European standard. This version is provably secure but is less efficient than the original NTRU.

IEEE 1363.1 is the IEEE standard for public key cryptographic techniques based on hard problems over lattices. This standard was published in 2008 and is no longer an active standard; however, when this standard was active, it specifically recommended NTRUEncrypt.

There are also public, open-source NTRU libraries. There is an entire NTRU open-source project on GitHub (https://github.com/NTRUOpenSourceProject). You can also find open-source Java implementations of NTRU on GitHub (https://github.com/tbuktu/ntru). The Cipher EX V1.5 project for .NET includes NTRU libraries (https://www.codeproject.com/Articles/828477/Cipher-EX-V).

There have been multiple cryptanalysis studies of NTRU algorithms, including NTRU signature schemes dating back many years. However, all of these are predicated on attacks involving the implementation of NTRU rather than fundamental mathematics. All of these attacks also focus on NTRU signature algorithms. All cryptographic algorithms are predicated on correct implementation. Incorrect implementation can significantly degrade the performance of any cryptographic algorithm.

More recent cryptanalysis studies have focused on the mathematical assumptions underpinning NTRU. These studies have demonstrated the resilience of NTRU against a range of cryptographic attacks. The newer studies of NTRU taken in light of the earlier studies indicate NTRU is mathematically sound but can be weakened by improper implementation.

13.2.2 GGH

The GGH algorithm, which is named after the surnames of its inventors, Oded Goldreich, Shafi Goldwasser, and Shai Halevi, is a widely studied lattice-based cryptosystem. It is an asymmetric algorithm that has been demonstrated to be resistant to cryptanalysis. This algorithm was first publicly described in 1997. The algorithm was constructed using the Closest Vector Problem (CVP). The private key is a basis vector B of the lattice L and a unimodular matrix U (recall the discussion of unimodular matrices earlier in this chapter).

This basis vector has certain properties, such as vectors that are nearly orthogonal vectors and a matrix U, which is unimodular. The public key is another basis of the same lattice of the form B' = UB. The message M is a message space that consists of the vector $(m_1, ..., m_n)$ in a range of $-M < m_i < M$.

The message is encrypted by multiplying the message vector by the public key B'. This is shown mathematically in Equation 13.11.

$$v = \sum m_i b_i'$$

EQUATION 13.11   GGH, Step 1

Remember that m consists of integer values, whereas B' is a lattice point. This means we can describe the cipher text as listed in Equation 13.12.

$c = v + e$

EQUATION 13.12   GGH, Step 2

The e is an error correcting vector, $(1, -1)$. To decrypt the message, the cipher text, c, is multiplied by the inverse of B, B^{-1}. Here it is put mathematically:

$$M = c \, B^{-1}$$

This is a relatively easy-to-understand algorithm. While it is well studied, there have been successful cryptanalytical attacks. H. Lee and C. Hahn, in 2010, demonstrated that partial information of the plaintext can aid in decrypting the GGH algorithm ciphertext. While their method was applied against the highest dimension of GGH being proposed at the time, it also required coupling with Nguyen's attack. The Lee and Han method also required some knowledge of the plaintext; thus, it can be argued this cryptanalysis of GGH is intriguing but unlikely to represent real-world cryptanalysis conditions.

The study conducted by Charles de Barros and L. M. Schechter in 2015 suggested enhancements to GGH. The authors began by describing GGH succinctly, as follows:

> "Its main idea is to encode a message into a lattice vector v, add some small perturbation r and generate the ciphertext c= v+r. The norm of the vector r must be sufficiently small, so the v is the lattice vector closest to c."

They then described the most direct way of attacking GGH, which is to reduce the public key in order to find a basis to apply Babai's algorithm. de Barros and Schechter further stated that even if the private key cannot be derived, the message may be retrievable.

Zeroizing attacks have been successful against several variations of GGH. In their 2015 paper " Cryptanalysis of the Quadratic Zero-Testing of GGH," Brakerski et al. described these types of attacks as follows:

> "Roughly speaking, Zeroizing attacks proceed by honestly computing many top-level encoding of zero, then using the prescribed zero-testing procedure to setup and solve a system of multilinear equations in the secret parameters of the scheme. These attacks rely crucially on the linearity of the zero-testing procedure, and so some attempts were made recently to devise alternative zero-testing procedures which are non-linear."

13.2.3   Peikert's Ring

The Peikert's Ring algorithm is for key distribution, much like Diffie-Hellman, which you saw in Chapter 11, "Current Asymmetric Algorithms." There are variations, such as the Ring Learning With Errors Key Exchange algorithm (RLWE-KEX). This algorithm is designed to be secure against quantum computer attacks.

Ring Learning With Errors (RLWE) works with a ring of polynomials modulo some polynomial. Recall our discussion of polynomial rings earlier in this chapter. The polynomial is often represented with the symbol Φ (x). The coefficients are in the field of integers mod q. Multiplication and addition are reduced mod Φ (x). The key exchange algorithm can be generally described as follows:

There is some polynomial often expressed as

$$a(x) = a_0 + a_1x + a_2x^2 + \ldots a_{n-3}x^{n-3} + a_{n-2}X^{n-2} + a_{n-1}X^{n-1}.$$

The coefficients of this polynomial are integers mod q. The polynomial itself is a cyclotomic polynomial. For those readers not familiar with cyclotomic polynomials, this topic is a bit more rigorous mathematically. You don't necessarily need to have a full understanding of it to have a general working knowledge of RLWE. However, for the sake of completeness, it will be described here.

The short definition is that cyclotomic polynomials are polynomials whose complex roots are primitive roots of unity. However, that is only helpful if one is familiar with roots of unity, and roots in general. The nth root of unity, where n is a positive integer, is some number x that satisfies the rather simple equation shown in Equation 13.13.

$x^n = 1$

EQUATION 13.13 Roots of Unity

This explains roots of unity, and I suspect that is rather simpler than you might have feared. However, it does not explain the primitive roots of unity. A given root of unity, we will call it n, is said to be primitive if it is not the mth root of unity for some smaller m. To put this another way, assume you have found a root of unity ($x^n = 1$). In order to be considered a primitive root of unity, it must also satisfy the condition shown in Equation 13.14.

$x^m \neq 1$ for m = 1, 2, 3, 4, ..., x–1.

EQUATION 13.14 Primitive Root of Unity

Now for those readers seeking an even more rigorous mathematical definition, the nth cyclotomic polynomial is the polynomial given by the formula shown in Equation 13.15.

$$\Phi_n(x) = \prod_\zeta (x - \zeta)$$

EQUATION 13.15 Nth Cyclotomic Polynomial

Do not be overly concerned if this explanation is still rather opaque to you. This is completely normal if you don't have a solid background in number theory. However, you can certainly continue on and understand the gist of RLWE, even with a rather hazy understanding of roots of unity.

Now, continuing with key generation, there is usually an initiator for the key exchange; we will use the symbol I to represent that party. Then there is a respondent we will represent with R. Both parties know the values q, n, and a(x) and can generate small polynomials according to the distribution Xα with parameter α. The value q is a prime number. The value a(x) is a fixed polynomial shared by both the initiator I and the respondent R. Now we can address the steps of key generation:

1. Generate two polynomials with small coefficients.

   These polynomials will generally be called s_I and e_I (yes, the $_I$ subscript is for initiator, and as you will see shortly, the $_R$ subscript is for responder).

2. Compute $p_I = as_I + 2e_I$.

   Now the initiator sends that p_I to the responder. At this point, the responder will generate two polynomials, s_R and e_r.

3. Compute $p_R = as_R + 2 e_R$.

   The recipient will then generate a small $e`_R$ from X_α.

4. Compute $k_R = p_I s_R + 2e`_R$.

5. Compute $k_R = as_I s_R + 2e_I s_R + 2 e`_R$.

Next, the signal function will be used. This function has not yet been described. The signal function is rather complex. If you don't fully grasp it, that won't be an impediment to following the rest of key generation. However, again, in the interest of completion, the signal function works as follows:

First, you define a subset we will call E:

$$E := \left\{ -\lfloor \frac{q}{4} \rfloor, \ldots, \lfloor \frac{q}{4} \rfloor \right\} \text{ of } Zq = \left\{ -\frac{q-1}{2}, \ldots, \frac{q-1}{2} \right\}$$

The function is the characteristic function of the complement of E. The term *characteristic function* can have different meanings in different contexts. In this case, it is an indicator function of a subset. The term *indicator function* means the function indicates membership in the subset. A 1 is returned if the value is a member of the subset, and a 0 is returned if the value is not a member of the subset. The actual signal function (S) is this:

$S(v) = 1$ if $v \in E$; $S(v) = 0$ if $v \notin E$

Continuing on with key generation, we now use the signal function we just described by applying it to each coefficient of k_R:

$w = S(k_R)$

The respondent's key stream sk_R is calculated by

$sk_R = Mod2(k_R, w)$

Now the respondent will send the w and the p_R to the initiator.

The initiator receives those two values and now will take a sample $e`_I$ from $X\alpha$ and compute

$K_I = p_R s_I + 2e`_I$

The $sK_I \bmod 2(K_I, w)$ is the initiator's key stream.

You might be thinking this is quite a complex series of steps—and you would be correct. This is clearly more complex than key generation in GGH or NTRU. It is also more complex than key generation for Diffie-Hellman, which you saw in Chapter 11.

The security of this key exchange algorithm will depend on the sizes of the parameters. Frequently, sizes such as n = 1024, q = 40961, and $\Phi(x) = x^{1024} + 1$ are suggested (or similar sizes). There has been a substantial amount of research focusing on variations in parameter sizes in order to achieve an acceptable level of security, while also preserving an adequate efficiency.

13.3   Solving Lattice Problems

Lattice basis reduction algorithms such as Lenstra-Lenstra-Lovász (LLL) or Block-Korkine-Zolotarev (BKZ) are then applied, with the goal of reducing the B matrix basis to a different basis that forms the same lattice, but with smaller "length" of the basis. Lattice reduction algorithms are generally based on Gram-Schmidt orthogonalization and decomposition.

The concept of lattice basis reduction is relatively simple. Given some integer lattice basis as input, try to find another basis with shorter vectors that are nearly orthogonal. Recall our previous discussion on basis vector. What is being attempted is to find another basis vector that is shorter but otherwise quite similar to the one used for this lattice. This creates a mathematical problem that is easier to solve than the original problem. When applied to cryptography, it presents a method for having a probability of deriving the private key.

The goal of this chapter is not to focus on lattice reduction, but rather to introduce you to the process as it applies to lattice-based cryptography. For the reader's edification, an entire subsection on LLL with substantial detail is provided; however, that is only one lattice reduction algorithm. There are others, such as Block-Korkine-Zolotarev (BKZ), Seysen Reduction, and others. There is also a rather large body of research on such algorithms.

13.3.1   Lenstra-Lenstra-Lovász (LLL)

LLL, which finds an approximately short vector—guaranteed to be within a factor (2/3) n of the actual shortest vector—in polynomial time. LLL produces a "reduced" basis of a lattice, with an approximately short basis vector as a result. The details of this algorithm will also be rather complex, but not such that most readers cannot follow the general outline. A few preliminaries are in order. There is a lattice L and a basis $B = \{b_1, b_2, ..., b_d\}$ that has n-dimensional integer coordinates with $d \le n$. The LLL algorithm calculates a reduced lattice basis.

This Gram-Schmidt orthogonal basis can be represented as follows:

B* = {b1*, b2*, ..., bn*}

Once you have the basis B, the next step is to define its Gram-Schmidt process orthogonal basis. For those readers not familiar with it, Gram-Schmidt is a process for orthonormalizing a set of vectors. The Gram-Schmidt process takes a finite, linearly independent set of vectors and generates an orthogonal set of vectors that spans the same k-dimensional subspace as the original set.

Next is the use of a projection operator. In linear algebra, a projection is a linear transformation P from a vector space to itself, such that if the projector P is applied twice, it provides the same result as if it was applied once P2 = P. This type of operation is referred to as *idempotent*. Idempotence is the property of an operator that can be applied multiple times, with the result not changing after the first application. Incidentally, the word *idempotent* stems from *idem*, meaning "same," and *potent*, indicating strength or power. Thus, the word literally means "the same strength."

Equation 13.16 shows the Gram-Schmidt process projection operator.

$$\text{proj}_u (v) = \frac{\langle u, v \rangle}{\langle u, u \rangle} u$$

EQUATION 13.16 Gram-Schmidt Process Projection Operator

In Equation 13.16, <u, v> represents the inner product of the vectors u and v. This projection projects the vector v orthogonally onto the line spanned by vector u.

The Gram-Schmidt process then goes through a series of projection steps, the details of which are not critical for us in this discussion. However, the Gram-Schmidt coefficients are relevant and are shown in Equation 13.17.

$$\mu_{i,j} = \frac{\langle b_i, b_j^* \rangle}{\langle b_j^*, b_j^* \rangle}, \text{for any } 1 \le j < i \le n$$

EQUATION 13.17 Gram-Schmidt Coefficients

Then the LLL algorithm will reduce the basis B if there is a parameter, usually denoted by δ, such that

1. For $1 \le j \le i \le n$: $|\mu_{i,j}| \le 0.5$
2. For k = 2, 3, ..., n: $\delta \|bk^*\|^2 + \mu_{k,k-1}^2 \|b_{k-1}^*\|^2$

This might seem rather convoluted and not really clear to some readers. So, let us explore it just a bit. The first issue is the parameter δ. The key to LLL is finding the correct parameter. Lenstra, Lenstra, and Lovász originally used $\delta = 3/4$. Others have used $\delta = 1$ and $\delta = 1/4$. Finding the right parameter is part of the issue of getting LLL to work properly. Next, let us address B and B*. B is the set of basic vectors for the lattice L. B* is the Gram-Schmidt process orthogonal basis. The concept is to find reduced basis vectors so that one can solve the lattice problem and potentially break a cryptographic algorithm that depends on that lattice problem.

It is also worth noting that lattice reduction in general and LLL in particular are not guaranteed to work in breaking an algorithm. They simply have a probability of doing so. And even when these methods do work, they are not instantaneous. In fact, they can take substantial time. The focus on these algorithms is that they can break a lattice-based cryptographic algorithm in less time than would otherwise be required. The key to take away from this discussion of LLL is that any proposed lattice-based algorithm should be thoroughly analyzed in light of lattice reduction algorithms. For those readers familiar with Mathematica, it has a function called LatticeReduce that uses LLL. There is also a standalone implementation of LLL in fplll available on GitHub https://github.com/fplll/fplll.

13.4 Summary

This chapter introduced lattice-based problems and lattice-based cryptographic algorithms. These are important issues to understand, as they are part of the work to find cryptographic algorithms that are resistant to quantum computer attacks. While the focus of this book is on quantum computing itself, quantum-resistant cryptography is part of that topic. You also saw a brief introduction to lattice reduction methods for attacking lattice-based cryptography.

Test Your Skills

REVIEW QUESTIONS

1. Which of the following is the most accurate definition of a subgroup?

    a. If G is a group under some operation, and H is a subset of G that also forms a group under that operation, then H is a subgroup of G.

    b. If G is a group under some operation and its inverse, and H is a subset of G, then H also forms a group under that operation, and H is a subgroup of G.

    c. If G completely contains H, then H is a subgroup of G.

    d. If H has the elements all in G and has the same operations as G, then H is a subgroup of G.

2. Which of the following is a property required for V to be a vector space?

    a. Given $v, w \in V, v + w \in V$.

    b. Given $v, w \in V, vw \in V$.

    c. Given $v \in V$ and a scalar $\alpha, \alpha v \in V$.

    d. Given $v \in V$ and $w \notin V, vw \notin V$.

3. A _____ lattice is a lattice that is closed under a rotational ____ operator.

    a. unitary, shift

    b. unimodular, scalar

    c. cyclic, scalar

    d. cyclic, shift

4. What does the following describe? Given an m × n lattice A, which is composed of m uniformly random vectors (which are integers), also stated as $A \in z_q^{nxm}$, find a nonzero short integer vector v satisfying such that $Ax = 0 \bmod q$.

    a. Shortest Vector Problem

    b. Closest Vector Problem

    c. Shortest Integer Problem

    d. Closest Integer Problem

5. _____ was first publicly described in 1996 by Jeffery Hoffstein, Jill Pipher, and Joseph Silverman. There have also been additional variants of this algorithm developed since its initial publication.

   a. Ajtai

   b. NTRU

   c. GGH

   d. Peikert's Ring

6. _____ was the first lattice-based cryptographic algorithm published.

   a. Ajtai

   b. NTRU

   c. GGH

   d. Peikert's Ring

7. The equation $R = z[x]/(x^N - 1)$ is most closely associated with what algorithm?

   a. Ajtai

   b. NTRU

   c. GGH

   d. Peikert's Ring

Chapter | **14**

Multivariate Cryptography

Chapter Objectives

After reading this chapter and completing the review questions, you will be able to do the following:

- Understand the basis for multivariate cryptography
- Demonstrate a working knowledge of specific algorithms
- Comprehend how these algorithms function

The term *multivariate cryptography* refers to cryptographic primitives that are based on multivariate polynomials over a finite field F. These algorithms have been proposed as quantum resistant. Some of these algorithms are part of the NIST project seeking a quantum-resistant standard. You can visit that website at https://csrc.nist.gov/projects/post-quantum-cryptography.

14.1 Mathematics

The algorithms in this chapter require you to use some mathematics we have covered in previous chapters as well as some that may be new to some readers. For this reason, we have this brief section introducing you to mathematical concepts you will need. We also review briefly the critical mathematics needed with regard to specific algorithms in the sections on those algorithms.

Recall from Chapter 1, "Introduction to Essential Linear Algebra," that a field is an algebraic system consisting of a set, an identity element for each operation, two operations, and their respective inverse operations. You can think of a field as a group that has two operations rather than one, and it has an inverse for both of those operations. A finite field is just a field that is limited or finite. Chapter 11, "Current Asymmetric Algorithms," discussed finite fields in relationship to elliptic curve cryptography.

One new concept we need to explore is that of an extension field. If we have a field F, then we have a field $E \subseteq F$, such that the operations of E are those of F, and we can say that E is a subfield of F and that F is an extension field of E.

A polynomial is an expression consisting of variables and coefficients, such as you see in Equation 14.1.

$$x^2 + 3x - 12$$

EQUATION 14.1 A Polynomial

The polynomial shown in Equation 14.1 is a univariate polynomial as it has only one variable (also called an indeterminate). A multivariable polynomial has more than one variable as demonstrated in Equation 14.2.

$$x2 + 3y - 12z$$

EQUATION 14.2 A Polynomial with Multiple Variables

Equation 14.2 is a multivariable polynomial. More precisely, it is trivariate, as it has three variables. *Multivariate cryptography* is the general term for cryptographic algorithms based on multivariable polynomials.

The essence of the system of multivariate quadratic equations problem (MQ) is to solve a system $p1(x) = p2(x) = \ldots pm(x) = 0$ where each pi is a quadratic in $x + (x1, \ldots, xn)$, where all the coefficients and variables are in a field Fq with q elements.

Multivariate cryptography uses trapdoor one-way functions that take the form of a multivariate quadratic polynomial. The public key is given by a public set of quadratic polynomials, as follows:

$$P = (p1(w1, \ldots, wn), \ldots pm(w1, \ldots, wn))$$

Each p_i is a nonlinear polynomial in $w = (w1, \ldots, wn)$.

A trapdoor function is a function that is relatively easy to compute in one direction but computationally infeasible to compute in the other direction. Essentially, without knowing specifics about the inputs to the algorithm, it would take so much time and computing resources to solve the problem that it is impractical to do so. Trapdoor functions are the key to many cryptographic algorithms. The discrete logarithm and integer factorization that we saw in Chapter 11 are examples. Consider integer factorization. It is quite easy to multiply two primes and get an integer. It is much more difficult to factor that integer into its prime factors.

In addition to the term *polynomial*, you will see the term *irreducible polynomial* rather frequently. This actually means precisely what the name suggests. This is a polynomial that cannot be factored into the product of two other polynomials. In other words, it cannot be reduced any further.

Recall from Chapter 8, "Quantum Architecture," that we discussed the following three terms: injective, surjective, and bijective. In its simplest terms, *injective* means that everything in A can be mapped to something in B, but there might be items in B with nothing matching in A. *Surjective* means that every B has at least one matching A, but could actually have more than one match in A. *Bijective* means every A has a B, and vice versa. Figure 14.1, repeated from Chapter 8, should refresh your memory.

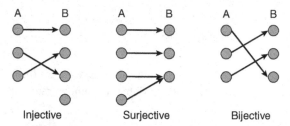

FIGURE 14.1   Injective, surjective, and bijective

Affine transformations are used by some of these algorithms. Generally speaking, an affine transformation is an automorphism of an affine space. For some readers, that definition might not bring any clarity. It might be helpful to consider the case of geometry. In Euclidean geometry, an affine transformation is a geometric transformation that will preserve the lines and any parallelism but won't necessarily preserve angles and distances. As you can tell from the definition, this term has its origins in geometry.

The term *isomorphism* comes up frequently in multivariate cryptography, as discussed briefly in previous chapters. An isomorphism is a mapping between two structures that preserves the structure and can be inverted. The term *structure* is used intentionally because it is rather vague. Isomorphisms can apply to graphs in graph theory, topology structures, algebraic structures, and others.

14.2   Matsumoto-Imai

Published by Tsutomu Matsumoto and Hideki Imai in 1988, the Matsumoto-Imai cryptographic algorithm was one of the first published multivariate systems, which makes it important to study. This cryptographic system was later broken, so it is not currently used; however, its importance in the history of multivariate cryptography warrants a brief examination.

The system begins with a finite field we will call F, with q elements. Then we have g(X), which is an irreducible polynomial of degree n over the field F. Then we have a second field, which we will call E. E is an extension of F, of degree n. Here it is put another way:

$E = F[x]/g(x).$

Next, we identify an isomorphism between the vector space F^n and the extension field E. We will designate this isomorphism as ϕ. Equation 14.3 describes this isomorphism.

$$\phi\,(x_1,\,x_2,\,\ldots,\,x_n) = \sum_{i=1}^{n} x_i x^{i-1}$$

EQUATION 14.3 Matsumoto-Imai Isomorphism

There is a bijective map of F: E → E over the extension field E, as defined in Equation 14.4.

$$F(Y) = Y^{q^{\theta}+1}$$

EQUATION 14.4 Matsumoto-Imai Bijective Map

The value of θ in Equation 14.4 is $0 < \theta < n$, and the gcd $(q^n - 1,\ q^{\theta} + 1) = 1$.

To be able to invert the map F, the extended Euclidian algorithm is used to compute an integer h such that $h(q^{\theta} + 1) = 1 \bmod (q^n - 1)$. Using the Euclidean algorithm (discussed in Chapter 10) to invert F (to get F^{-1}), we have what is shown in Equation 14.5.

$$F^{-1}(x) = x^h = y^{h(q\theta\,+1)} - y^{k(qn\,-1)} = y$$

EQUATION 14.5 Matsumoto-Imai Inverted Field

The public key is the composed map shown in Equation 14.5.

P = S F T with two invertible linear maps:

$S: F^n \rightarrow F^n$

$T: F^n \rightarrow F^n$

The private key is S, h, and T.

To encrypt a message M, which is represented as a vector $z = (z_1,\,z_2,\,\ldots,\,z_n)$, you use Equation 14.6.

$$w = P(z) \in F^n$$

EQUATION 14.6 Matsumoto-Imai Encryption

To decrypt the process is a bit more involved. There are steps to be taken, beginning with the ciphertext w:

1. $x = S^{-1}(w) \in F^n$

2. $X = \phi\,(x)$

3. $Y = F - 1\,(X)$

4. $y = \phi^{-1}\,(Y)$

5. $z = T\,(y)$

Figure 14.2 shows the general relationship of the elements in the system.

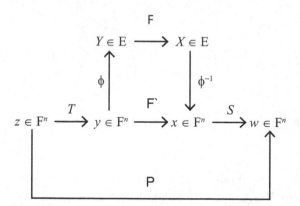

FIGURE 14.2 Matsumoto-Imai cryptosystem

The Matsumoto-Imai cryptosystem, while shown to have security flaws, did pave the way for other multivariate algorithms. As you will see later in this chapter, many of those are robust and could potentially be quantum-resistant algorithms. It is also noteworthy that many algorithms have been created that are variations of Matsumoto-Imai.

14.3 Hidden Field Equations

Hidden Field Equations (HFE) is a public key cryptography system that was invented by Jacques Patarin and first publicized at Eurocrypt in 1996. The cryptographic security is based on the difficulty of finding solutions to a system of multivariate quadratic equations, sometimes referred to as the MQ problem. This algorithm was created as an improvement of the Matsumoto-Imai system.

The basis of the mathematics for this particular cryptography algorithm is not overly complex, but a few new concepts will need to be introduced. We begin with a base field we will call Fq. Then we have two extension fields over that base field. Our extension fields are F_q^n and F_q^m. Let us briefly review extension fields. First, keep in mind the definition of a field discussed in Chapter 1 and reviewed in the introduction to this chapter. If we have a field F, then we have a field $E \subseteq F$, such that the operations of E are those of F, and we can say that E is a subfield of F and that F is an extension field of E.

Let us examine this in slightly different terminology. Consider our previous field E. We also have a field F that contains all of E, plus additional elements. However, the operations in E and F are the same. This would make field F an extension of field E.

First, consider some finite field F_q, with q as a power of two, and some extension field G. The basis of G is $B_1, B_2, ..., B_n$.

Next, consider some value h such that $h = q^\theta + 1$ for some value of θ and $0 < h < q^n$. And along with $h = q^\theta + 1$, consider the greatest common denominator, gcd $(h, q^n - 1) = 1$. Put in other terms, h and

$q^n - 1$ have no common factor other than 1 and are thus co-prime or relatively prime. This all leads to a map of $u \rightarrow u^h$ on G that is one to one. The inverse map is $u \rightarrow u^{h'}$, where h' is the multiplicative inverse of h mod $q^n - 1$.

The concept of the HFE cryptosystem is to build the secret key, beginning with a polynomial P in one unknown x over some finite field F_q^n. It should be noted that in actual practice, $q = 2$ is commonly used, though n can be any number (preferably quite large). Now that we have this field F_q^n and we have a polynomial P, one can find solutions to the equation $P(x) = y$, if such solutions exist. The polynomial $(p_1, p_2, ..., p_n)$ is transformed so that the public information hides the structure and prevents inverting it. This is accomplished by using the finite fields F_q^n as a vector space over F_q and selecting two linear affine transformations.

The values of S, P, and T constitute the private key. Just as a refresher, our polynomial P, along with our two affine transformations, S and T, are the private key. The public key is the $(p_1, ..., p_n)$ of a finite field F_q.

To encrypt a message M, it needs to be transferred from the field F_q^n to F_q^n. The message M is then a vector $(x_1, x_2, ..., x_n) \in F_q^n$. The ciphertext is generated by evaluating each of the polynomials p_i at each of the vector elements. This is shown in Equation 14.7.

$$c = p_1(x_1, x_2, ..., x_n), p_2(x_1, x_2, ..., x_n), ..., p_n(x_1, x_2, ..., x_n) \in F_q^n$$

EQUATION 14.7   HFE Encryption

This can be described more compactly, as shown in Equation 14.8.

$$c = P(z) \in F_q^n$$

EQUATION 14.8   HFE Encryption Compact Expression

Decryption is a bit more complex, much as it was on the Matsumoto-Imai system. Recall we have S, P, and T as private keys. We begin with inverting the affine map S, which can be expressed as shown in Equation 14.9.

$$x = S^{-1}(c) \in F_q^n$$

EQUATION 14.9   HFE Decryption, Step 1

This can also be expressed as shown in Equation 14.10.

$$X = \phi(x)$$

EQUATION 14.10   HFE Decryption, Step 1 (Alternate Expression)

The next step is to find the solutions $Y_1, ..., Y_k$ of $F(Y) = X$. This is shown in Equation 14.11.

$$y = \{Y \in E : F(Y) = X\}$$

EQUATION 14.11   HFE Decryption, Step 2

The third step involves Equation 14.12.

$$y_i = \phi^{-1}(Y_i)$$

EQUATION 14.12   HFE Decryption, Step 3

The plaintext is then generated by Equation 14.13.

$$z_i = T^{-1}(y_i)$$

EQUATION 14.13   HFE Decryption, Final Step

There have been several variations of HFE, each of which has its own strengths and weaknesses; however, the existence of these variations further illustrates the value of HFE.

14.4   Multivariate Quadratic Digital Signature Scheme (MQDSS)

This algorithm, as the name suggests, is used explicitly for digital signatures. It is based entirely on the MQ problem. The multivariate quadratic (MQ) polynomial problem was mentioned briefly earlier in this chapter. The details of the MQ problem are not as important as understanding how difficult it is to solve. The difficulty of solving the MQ problem is contingent upon a number of parameters, such as the number of variables, the number of equations, the size of the base field, etc. For those readers who wish to explore the mathematical details of this problem, there is an excellent paper from the International Association of Cryptological Research (IACR) titled "MQ Challenge: Hardness Evaluation of Solving Multivariate Quadratic Problems" (https://eprint.iacr.org/2015/275.pdf).

The MQDSS is based on a multivariate quadratic system, shown in Equation 14.14.

$$P : F^n \rightarrow F^m$$

EQUATION 14.14   MQDSS System

The coefficients are chosen randomly. Those coefficients are then fixed for the users utilizing this particular implementation of MQDSS. Each user then choses a random vector s from the F^n as his or her private key. Put more clearly, the users choose an s such that

$$s \in F^n$$

The public key is computed as follows:

$$k = P(s) \in F^m$$

To be verified, a user of the system will need to demonstrate he or she knows a solution of the quadratic system $P(x) = v$ without revealing any information about his or her private key, s. The specifics of how that is proved are not really necessary for our current purposes. The issue to understand is that this system is provably secure.

14.5 SFLASH

The SFLASH algorithm was created for the New European Schemes for Signatures, Integrity and Encryption (NESSIE) project. NESSIE was a European project from 2000 to 2003 to identify secure cryptography algorithms. The project reviewed symmetric, asymmetric, and hashing algorithms.

SFLASH was designed as a digital signature algorithm. The first item of note about this algorithm is that it is substantially faster than RSA. It is important to keep in mind that security is only one aspect of a successful algorithm. In order to be of practical use, the algorithm must also be efficient. To better understand this, imagine there is an asymmetric algorithm that is measurably more secure than RSA, Elliptic Curve Cryptography, NTRU, and GGH; however, that algorithm requires 30 minutes to encrypt a message. How could such an algorithm be used for applications like e-commerce? Consumers are unlikely to embrace an e-commerce website that requires 30 minutes for checkout.

SFLASH is a variant of Matsumoto-Imai. Thus, understanding the mathematics of that algorithm will aid you in understanding the SFLASH algorithm. The idea is to remove a small number of equations from the public key. As with Matsumoto-Imai, we begin with a finite field F that has q elements. We also have an extension field E of n degrees. Then we define an isomorphism, $\phi\ F^n \rightarrow E$. Key generation is very similar to the key generation of Matsumoto-Imai. There is a parameter θ such that $(q^n - 1, q^\theta + 1) = 1$.

The next step is to define a univariate map shown in Equation 14.15.

$F: E \rightarrow E, F(Y) = Y^{q\theta+1}$

EQUATION 14.15 SFLASH Univariate Map

The extended Euclidean algorithm is used to compute the signing exponent h, shown in Equation 14.16.

$H(1 + q^\theta) = 1 \bmod q^{n-1}$

EQUATION 14.16 SFLASH Exponent h

As with Matsumoto-Imai, there is an affine transformation, $T: F^n \rightarrow F^n$, and a randomly chosen invertible affine transformation over the vector space F^n is selected: $S: F^n \rightarrow F^{n-a}$.

The private key consists of the two maps S and T and the signing exponent h. The public key P is the composed map shown in Equation 14.17.

$S \circ \phi^{-1}$

EQUATION 14.17 SFLASH Public Key

This algorithm, as you can see, is somewhat similar to Matsumoto-Imai. As was stated at the beginning of this chapter, many algorithms have been created that are variations or improvements of Matsumoto-Imai.

Table 14.1 summarizes the algorithms explored in this chapter.

TABLE 14.1 Summary of Algorithms

Algorithm	Mathematical Basics
Matsumoto-Imai	A finite field F with q elements. g(X) is an irreducible polynomial of degree in n over the field F. An isomorphism between the vector space F^n and the extension field E. A bijective map F: E $\rightarrow$ E over the extension field E.
Hidden Field Equations (HFE)	A base field we will call F_q. Two extension fields, F_q^n and F_q^m. A polynomial P in one unknown x over some finite field F_q^n. S, P, and T constitute the private key.
Multivariate Quadratic Digital Signature (MQDSS)	$P : F^n \rightarrow F^m$. The users choose an s such that s ϵ F^n. k = P(s) ϵ F^m.
SFLASH	An isomorphism, ϕ $F^n \rightarrow$ E. Univariate map F: E $\rightarrow$ E, $F(Y) = Y^{q^{\theta}+1}$.

14.6 Summary

This chapter focused on multivariate cryptography. Some of the mathematics might have been new for some readers. The algorithms in this chapter are all viable candidates for quantum resistant cryptography and thus worthy of study. Combining this chapter with Chapter 13, "Lattice-based Cryptography," and Chapter 15, "Other Approaches to Post-Quantum Cryptography," will provide you with a solid general understanding of quantum computing–resistant cryptographic algorithms.

Test Your Skills

REVIEW QUESTIONS

1. Which of the following is the most accurate description of a field?

   a. A set, an identity element for one operation, one operation, and its inverse operation

   b. A set, an identity element for each operation, two operations, and an inverse for one of those operations

   c. A set, an identity element for one operation, two operations, and their respective inverse operations

   d. A set, an identity element for each operation, two operations, and their respective inverse operations

2. A bijective map F: E → E over the extension field E is most closely associated with which algorithm?

   a. Matsumoto-Imai

   b. Hidden Field Equations

   c. SFLASH

   d. MQDSS

3. gcd (h, qn − 1) = 1 is most closely associated with which algorithm?

   a. Matsumoto-Imai

   b. Hidden Field Equations

   c. SFLASH

   d. MQDSS

4. Which algorithm has a public key k = P(s) ϵ Fm?

   a. Matsumoto-Imai

   b. Hidden Field Equations

   c. SFLASH

   d. MQDSS

5. _____signature algorithm is substantially faster than RSA.

   a. Matsumoto-Imai

   b. Hidden Field Equations

   c. SFLASH

   d. MQDSS

## Chapter 15

Other Approaches to Quantum Resistant Cryptography

Chapter Objectives

After reading this chapter and completing the review questions, you will be able to do the following:

- Understand the basis for hash-based cryptographic algorithms
- Demonstrate a working knowledge of code-based cryptography
- Explain the concepts of supersingular isogeny key exchange
- Comprehend the details of a few exemplary algorithms

Chapter 13, "Lattice-based Cryptography," and Chapter 14, "Multivariate Cryptography," introduced you to various types of cryptographic algorithms that have been posited as quantum resistant. This chapter presents you with an assortment of cryptographic algorithms that do not fit neatly into one of those two categories.

15.1 Hash Functions

Before we can explore how hashing algorithms can be used for quantum-resistant cryptography, it is important to have a firm understanding of cryptographic hashes. In order to be a cryptographic hash function, an algorithm needs to have three properties.

- **The function is one-way.** This means this function cannot be "unhashed." In other words, it is not reversible. That is contrary to encryption algorithms, which must be reversible in order to decrypt.

- **A variable-length input produces a fixed-length output.** This means that regardless of the input, be it 1 bit or 1 terabyte, the algorithm will output the same size hash (also called a message digest). Each particular cryptographic hash algorithm has a specific size output. For example, SHA-1 produces a 160-bit hash.

- **The algorithm must be collision resistant.** A collision is defined as two different inputs producing the same output. If you use SHA-1, then you have a 160-bit output. Therefore, there are 2^{160} possible outputs. Obviously, you could have trillions of different inputs and never see a collision. It should be noted that the size of the output (also called a digest or message digest) is only one factor in collision resistance. The nature of the algorithm itself also has an impact on collision resistance.

Cryptographic hashes have been used for message and file integrity, forensic image integrity, and password storage; however, there are also ways to use a hash as a basis for an encryption/decryption algorithm. These types of algorithms will be explored in this chapter.

15.1.1   Merkle-Damgaard

Many cryptographic hashing algorithms have at their core a Merkle-Damgaard construction. First described in Ralph Merkle's doctoral dissertation published in 1979, a Merkle-Damgaard function (also called a Merkle-Damgaard construction) is a method for building hash functions. Merkle-Damgaard functions form the basis for MD5, SHA-1, SHA-2, and other hashing algorithms.

The Merkle-Damgaard starts by applying a padding function to create an output that is of some particular size (256 bits, 512 bits, 1024 bits, etc.). The specific size will vary between algorithms, but 512 bits is a common size that many algorithms use. The function then processes blocks, one at a time, combining the new block of input with the previous round block. As an example, consider a 1024-bit message that you break into four separate 256-bit blocks. Block 1 will be processed, and then its output is combined with block 2 before block 2 is processed. Then that output is combined with block 3 before it is processed. Finally, that output is combined with block 4 before that block is processed. Thus, Merkle-Damgaard is often referred to as a compression function, as it compresses all the message into a single output block. The algorithm will start with some initial value or initialization vector that is specific to the implementation. The final message block is always padded to the appropriate size (256 bits, 512 bits, etc.) and includes a 64-bit integer that indicates the size of the original message.

15.1.2   SWIFFT

Sliding Windowed Infinite Fast Fourier Transform (SWIFFT) is actually not a single algorithm but rather a collection of functions. These are provably secure hash functions. The SWIFFT functions are all based on the fast Fourier transform (FFT). Therefore, a logical place for us to begin is a brief exploration of the FFT.

An FFT is an algorithm that computes the discrete Fourier transform of a sequence to a representation in the frequency domain. It is called "fast" because it reduces the number of computations needed for N points from $2N^2$ to $2^N \log_2 N$.

Now let us walk through this algorithm, step by step.

The first step is to select a polynomial variable. This is often denoted with the symbol α.

Now you will input the message you wish to encrypt. That message is frequently denoted with a capital M and has a length of mn. The values of mn are defined by the length of M, as you will see in the next steps.

The next step is to convert the message M into a collection of m polynomials. These polynomials are denoted by p_i and are polynomials within some polynomial ring R. Recall the definition of a polynomial ring from Chapter 13: A polynomial ring is a ring formed from the set of polynomials in one or more indeterminates with coefficients in another ring. Recall that we discussed rings in Chapter 1, "Introduction to Essential Linear Algebra." A ring is a set with two operations, an identity element, and the inverse operation of the first operation. A polynomial is an expression that consists of variables and coefficients. Another term for variable is indeterminate, as it was in the definition of a polynomial ring.

The next step is to compute the Fourier coefficients of each p_i. These Fourier coefficients are defined as a_i and are fixed.

For the next step, you perform pointwise multiplication of the Fourier coefficients p_i with the Fourier coefficients of a_i, for each i. This will then be followed by using an inverse fast Fourier transform to yield m polynomials f_n, each of a degree less than 2n.

For the next step, you will compute the following formula:

$$f = \sum_{i=1}^{m}(f_i)\ mod\,p \text{ and } \alpha^n + 1$$

Finally, you convert the f to n log(p) bits and output those bits.

The steps are summarized as follows:

STEP 1. Select a polynomial variable.

STEP 2. Input the message you wish to encrypt.

STEP 3. Convert the messages into a collection of m polynomials.

STEP 4. Compute the Fourier coefficients.

STEP 5. Perform pointwise multiplication of the Fourier coefficients p_i with the Fourier coefficients of a_i.

STEP 6. Compute the formula $f = \sum_{i=1}^{m}(f_i)\ mod\,p$ and $\alpha^n + 1$.

SWIFFT, unlike many other provably secure algorithms, is considered fast. There are some known attacks on SWIFFT. Two are the generalized birthday attack and the inversion attack. The generalized birthday attack requires 2^{106} operations to succeed. Inversion attacks take 2^{445} operations. This means that it is impractical to break SWIFFT.

For those readers who would like to delve deeper into SWIFFT, the following link may be helpful: https://www.alonrosen.net/PAPERS/lattices/swifft.pdf.

Birthday attacks are quite important in cryptography, and there is a mathematical puzzle that can help those readers not familiar with these attacks. It is called the birthday paradox (sometimes called the birthday problem). The issue is this: how many people would you need to have in a room to have a strong likelihood that two would have the same birthday (i.e., month and day, not year). Obviously, if you put 367 people in a room, at least two of them must have the same birthday, because there are only 365 days in a year (plus February 29 on leap year). However, we are not asking how many people you need to *guarantee* a match, just how many you need to have a strong probability. It just so happens that with even 23 people in the room, you have a 50% chance that two have the same birthday.

How is this possible? How is it that such a low number can work? Basic probability tells us that when events are independent of each other, the probability of all of the events occurring is equal to a product of each of the events' probabilities. Therefore, the probability that the first person does not share a birthday with any previous person is 100%, because no previous people are in the set. That can be written as 365/365. Now, for the second person, there is only one preceding person, and the odds that the second person has a different birthday than the first are 364/365. For the third person, there are two preceding people he or she might share a birthday with, so the odds of having a different birthday than either of the two preceding people are 363/365. Because each of these is independent, we can compute the probability as follows:

365/365 * 364/365 * 363/365 * 362/365 ... * 342/365 (342 is the probability of the 23rd person sharing a birthday with a preceding person.).

Let us convert these to decimal values, which yields (truncating at the third decimal point) the following:

* 0.997 * .994 * .991 * .989 * .986 * ... * .936 = .49, or 49%.

This 49% is the probability that they will not have any birthdays in common, thus there is a 51% (better than even odds) chance that two of the 23 will have a birthday in common.

Just for reference, if you have 30 people in the room, the probability that two have the same birthday is 70.6%. If you have 50 people, the probability rises to 97%, which is quite high. This does not simply apply to birthdays. The same concept can be applied to any set of data. It is often used in cryptography and cryptanalysis. The birthday paradox represents a guideline for how one might get a collision in a hashing algorithm.

In reference to cryptographic hash functions, the goal is to find two different inputs that produce the same output. When two inputs produce the same output from a cryptographic hash, this is referred to as a collision. It just so happens that the number of samples from any set of n elements required to get a match or collision is $1.174 \sqrt{n}$. Returning to the preceding birthday problem, $1.174 \sqrt{365} = 22.49$.

15.1.3 Lamport Signature

Published in 1979 by Leslie Lamport, the Lamport signature algorithm has been around for quite some time. One can create a Lamport signature using any cryptographically secure one-way function. Based on the earlier discussion of hash functions, it should be clear that cryptographic hash functions are often used for this purpose.

The algorithm begins with generating a key pair. One party uses a pseudo-random-number generator to create 256 pairs of random numbers. Each number generated is also 256 bits in size. Thus, a total of approximately 128 kilobytes is generated—i.e., (2 * 256 * 256) / 1024. This 128-kilobyte number is kept as a private key.

In order to generate the public key, each of these 512 random numbers (2 * 256) is hashed. This leads to a total of 512 hashes, each of 256 kilobytes in size. This is the public key that is shared with anyone who might wish it.

As the name suggests, this algorithm is for digital signatures. The purpose of digital signatures is not to preserve message confidentiality but to ensure message integrity. For example, when an email is signed, that does not prevent someone other than the intended recipient from reading it. However, it does allow the recipient to be able to verify who sent it.

The sender who generated the keys now wishes to sign a message. The first step is to hash the message so that a 256-bit hash or digest is produced. Then for each bit in the hash, one number from the pairs that make up the private key is selected. This usually means if the bit is 0, the first number is used; if it is 1, the second number is used. This will produce a sequence of 256 numbers, each one 256 bits long. Thus, the signature is 64 kilobytes. What makes this different from some other signature algorithms is that the signature is used one time only. The sender will then destroy the private keys used.

To verify the signature, the recipient will also hash the message to get a 256-bit hash/digest. Then the recipient uses the bits in that hash/digest to select out 256 of the hashes in the sender's public key. He uses the same selection method that the sender utilized (i.e., if it is 0, use the first hash; if it is 1, use the second). Now the recipient will hash each of the 256 random numbers in the sender's signature. If all of these exactly match the 256 hashes selected from the sender's public key, the signature is verified. If any don't match, the signature is rejected. These steps are summarized in Figure 15.1.

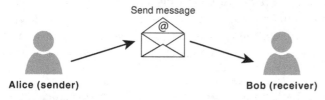

Send message

Alice (sender)   **Bob (receiver)**

1. Generate 128 KB private key
2. Hash message = 256 bit
3. Each bit in the hash = 1 number from the private key
4. This produces 256 numbers 64 KB in size

5. Select 256 hashes of sender's public key
6. Hash each number in sender's signature
7. Match hashes

FIGURE 15.1 Lamport signature

15.2 Code-Based Cryptography

The term *code-based cryptography* refers to cryptosystems that rely on error-correcting codes as their basis. Some of these algorithms have been around for quite some time, even decades. They have received renewed interest as quantum computing progresses. There is a clear interest in quantum-resistant cryptography.

15.2.1 McEliece

The McEliece cryptosystem is eponymously named after its inventor, Robert McEliece. This algorithm was published in 1978. That makes it perhaps the oldest algorithm being proposed as quantum resistant. Despite its age, this algorithm has already been shown to be immune to Shor's algorithm.

The security of McEliece is based on the difficulty of decoding a general linear code. For those readers not familiar with the topic, a brief description of a general linear code is provided. A linear code is used for error correction. There is a linear combination of codes. Linear codes are frequently used in forward error correction. Hamming codes are a classic example of a linear code. Hamming codes can detect errors and correct them.

The algorithm has some parts that might seem vague. This is because there is some flexibility in the linear codes one can choose. Thus, the specifics of the linear code are not delineated in the algorithm. We will begin with key generation, which is often the most complex part of an asymmetric algorithm:

1. The person generating the key must select a linear code, which we will call C. Linear codes often have functions that generate matrices; we call those generators. So, there will be a generator G for the linear code C. The C chosen should also give rise to a decoding algorithm we will call A. The code is able to correct t errors.

2. The person generating the key must select a random k × k binary nonsingular matrix we will call S. Recall that a nonsingular matrix is a square matrix that is invertible.

3. The person generating the key chooses a random n × n permutation matrix, which we will call P. A permutation matrix is a square binary matrix that has exactly one entry of 1 in each row and each column and 0s elsewhere.

4. The person generating the key needs to compute a k × n matrix, which we will call H. This is computed by SGP (i.e., the nonsingular matrix multiplied by the generator, then that product multiplied by the permutation matrix).

The public key is (H, t), and the private key is (SPA).

Now to encrypt is relatively simple. The sender takes a message, m, that has a binary length k. The sender then computes this simple formula:

$$c` = mH$$

Next, the sender generates a random n-big vector we will call z that contains exactly t ones. The cipher text $c = c` + z$.

The recipient will decrypt with the following steps:

1. Compute the inverse of P. We will call this P^{-1}.

2. Compute $d = cP^{-1}$.

3. The decoding algorithm A is used to decode d to m`.

The original message, m, is then decrypted using this rather simple formula:

$m = m`S^{-1}$

As you can see, the general process is not as complex as some of the algorithms we have examined, both in this chapter and in Chapters 13 and 14. However, there are issues that we did not define. This is due to the fact that the McEliece cryptosystem does not define what code C you must select, and that selection will, in turn, determine the generator matrix G and the decoding algorithm A. Therefore, when describing McEliece, these aspects are not explicitly defined.

It is not critical that you have a deep understanding of these codes, but for the interested reader, let us explore one type of code that is often used in applications of the McEliece cryptosystem. These are binary Goppa codes. Binary Goppa codes are a subset of the class of Goppa codes eponymously named after Valerii Goppa.

A binary Goppa code is defined by a polynomial $g(x)$ of degree t over some finite field, usually denoted as $GF(2^m)$ and a sequence of n distinct elements from $GF(2^m)$ that are not roots of the polynomial.

The McEliece cryptosystem originally used parameters n = 1024, k = 524, and t = 50. Recent cryptanalyses suggest larger parameters such as n = 2048, k = 1751, t = 27, or even larger. For true resistance against quantum computers, parameters of n = 6960, k = 5413, and t = 119, or larger, are suggested. This yields a rather large public key of 8,373,911 bits. The most important thing to remember about McEliece is that, like NTRU described in Chapter 13, this algorithm has made it to round three of the NIST quantum computing standards selection process.

15.2.2   Niederreiter Cryptosystem

Developed in 1986 by Harald Niederreiter, the Niederreiter cryptosystem is a variation of the McEliece cryptosystem. It is probably a good idea to make sure you are quite familiar with McEliece before continuing with this section.

The Niederreiter cryptosystem security is relatively the same as McEliece; however, its encryption process is faster than McEliece, which has made it interesting for cryptography. It also usually uses the binary Goppa code, as discussed earlier. The key generation is quite similar to McEliece:

1. Select a binary (n, k)-linear Goppa code, G, capable of correcting t errors. This code has a decoding algorithm A.

2. Generate an $(n - k) \times n$ parity check matrix, H, for the code, G.

3. Select a random $(n - k) \times (n - k)$ binary nonsingular matrix, S.

4. Select a random $n \times n$ permutation matrix; we will again call this P.

5. Compute the $(n - k) \times n$ matrix, $H^p = SHP$.

The public key is (H^p, t) and the private key is (S, H, P).

In order to encrypt a message, m, as a binary string, e^m, that is a string of length t, the cipher text is generated with this formula:

$c = H^p e^t$

While the encryption is a bit simpler than with the McEliece system, the decryption is quite reminiscent of the McEliece decryption:

1. Compute $S^{-1}c$ from HPm^t (i.e., $S^{-1}c = HPm^t$).

2. Use the decoding algorithm for G to recover Pm^t.

3. The message $m = P^{-1}Pm^T$.

Another use of the Niederreiter cryptosystem is for digital signatures, which is in fact a common application of Niederreiter.

15.3 Supersingular Isogeny Key Exchange

The name of this particular algorithm might seem rather daunting, but its full name might give you some relief: supersingular isogeny Diffie-Hellman key exchange. If you recall the descriptions of Diffie-Hellman from Chapter 11, "Current Asymmetric Algorithms," and bear in mind the purpose of this algorithm is key exchange, it might be a bit easier for you to understand.

This is a newer algorithm, having been published in 2011. It begins with elliptic curve operations, which you were briefly introduced to in Chapter 11. In this chapter, we will first expand upon that knowledge of elliptic curves and then describe this algorithm.

15.3.1 Elliptic Curves

Elliptic curves can be used to form groups and therefore are appropriate for cryptographic purposes. There are two types of elliptic curve groups. The two most common (and the ones used in cryptography) are elliptic curve groups based on F_p, where p is prime, and those based on $F2^m$. F, as you will see in this chapter, is the field being used. F is used because we are describing a field. Elliptic curve cryptography is an approach to public key cryptography based on elliptic curves over finite fields.

Remember that a field is an algebraic system consisting of a set, an identity element for each operation, two operations, and their respective inverse operations. A finite field, also called a Galois field, is a field with a finite number of elements. That number is called the order of the field. Elliptic curves used for cryptographic purposes were first described in 1985 by Victor Miller and Neil Koblitz. The security of elliptic curve cryptography is based on the fact that finding the discrete logarithm of a random elliptic curve element with respect to a publicly known base point is difficult to the point of being impractical to do.

An elliptic curve is the set of points that satisfy a specific mathematical equation. The equation for an elliptic curve looks something like this:

$$y^2 = x^3 + Ax + B$$

You can see this equation graphed in Figure 15.2.

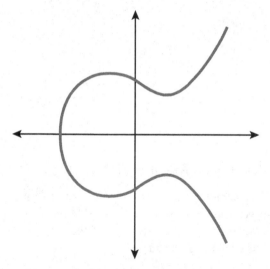

FIGURE 15.2 The graph of an elliptic curve

The operation used with the elliptic curve is addition (remember the definition of a group requires a set along with an operation). Thus, elliptic curves form additive groups.

Recall from earlier in this book that a group is an algebraic system consisting of a set, an identity element, one operation, and its inverse operation. An abelian group or commutative group has an additional axiom: $a + b = b + a$ if the operation is addition, or $ab = ba$ if the operation is multiplication. A cyclic group is a group that has elements that are all powers of one of its elements.

The members of the elliptic curve field are integer points on the elliptic curve. You can perform addition with points on an elliptic curve. Throughout this chapter, as well as most of the literature on elliptic curve, we consider two points: P and Q. The negative of a point $P = (xP, yP)$ is its reflection in the x-axis: the point $-P$ is $(xP, -yP)$. Notice that for each point P on an elliptic curve, the point $-P$

is also on the curve. Suppose that P and Q are two distinct points on an elliptic curve, and assume that P is not merely the inverse of Q. To add the points P and Q, a line is drawn through the two points. This line will intersect the elliptic curve in exactly one more point, called −R. The point −R is reflected in the x-axis to the point R. The law for addition in an elliptic curve group is P + Q = R (Bos, et al., 2004).

The line through P and −P is a vertical line that does not intersect the elliptic curve at a third point; thus, the points P and −P cannot be added as previously. It is for this reason that the elliptic curve group includes the point at infinity, O. By definition, P + (−P) = O. As a result of this equation, P + O = P in the elliptic curve group. O is called the additive identity of the elliptic curve group; all elliptic curves have an additive identity (see Figure 15.3).

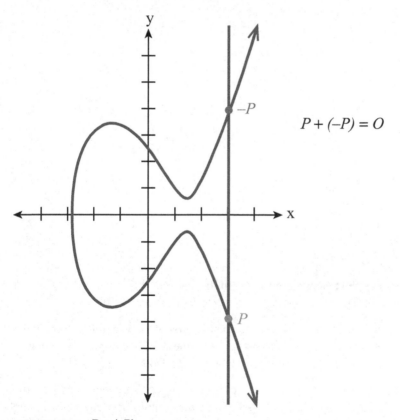

FIGURE 15.3 P + (−P)

To add a point P to itself, a tangent line to the curve is drawn at the point P. If yP is not 0, then the tangent line intersects the elliptic curve at exactly one other point, −R, which is reflected in the x-axis to R. This operation is called doubling the point P and can be seen in Figure 15.4.

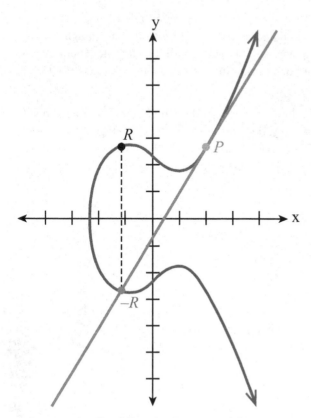

FIGURE 15.4   Doubling the P

The tangent from P is always vertical if yP = 0.

If a point P is such that yP = 0, then the tangent line to the elliptic curve at P is vertical and does not intersect the elliptic curve at any other point. By definition, 2P = O for such a point P.

Recall that the field Fp uses the numbers from 0 to p − 1, and computations end by taking the remainder of division by p (i.e., the modulus operations). For example, in F_{23}, the field is composed of integers from 0 to 22, and any operation within this field will result in an integer also between 0 and 22.

An elliptic curve with an underlying field of F_p can be formed by choosing the variables a and b within the field of F_p. The elliptic curve includes all points (x,y) that satisfy the elliptic curve equation modulo p (where x and y are numbers in F_p).

For example, y^2 mod p = x^3 + ax + b mod p has an underlying field of Fp if a and b are in Fp.

If x^3 + ax + b contains no repeating factors, then the elliptic curve can be used to form a group. An elliptic curve group over Fp consists of the points on the corresponding elliptic curve, together with a special point O called the point at infinity. There are finitely many points on such an elliptic curve.

15.3.2 SIDH

Now that you have reviewed the basics of elliptic curves, we can move forward to discuss supersingular isogeny Diffie Hellman (SIDH). We will have to add a few additional concepts. First, consider the equation of an elliptic curve:

$$y^2 = x^3 + ax + b$$

Now we add a new concept: the j-invariant of an elliptic curve. Let us approach this a bit differently than some texts do. We will start from the interpretation and then work on the math. Consider a model for an elliptic curve $E \subset P^2$. P is an element of E (i.e., $P \in E$). Recall from our previous discussions of elliptic curves that one can draw lines through the curve. There are lines the go through P and are tangent to E. These lines are invariant.

The j-invariant for an elliptic curve described by the function $y^2 = x^3 + ax + b$ is given by this formula:

$$j(E) = 1728 \frac{4a^3}{4a^3 + 27b}$$

When curves are isometric, they will have the same j-invariant over a closed field. In this case, the term *isometric* means that there is a function between two groups that establishes a one-to-one correspondence between the group's elements. Furthermore, the function respects the given group operations. In Chapter 11, when we discussed elliptic curve cryptography, we stated that the elliptic curves from algebraic groups. So, what is being discussed here is the fact that if two curves are isometric, they will have the same j-invariant (over a closed field).

This still leaves the term *isogeny* unexplored. In this context, an isogeny is a morphism of algebraic groups that is surjective and has a finite kernel. Kernels are an aspect of algebra we have yet to explore. For our purposes now, all you need to know is that when you have a homomorphism (and an isomorphism is a type of homomorphism), then the kernel is the inverse image of 0. This requires a bit of explanation as to what an inverse image is. Consider some function f that is a function from X to Y (the particulars of the function are immaterial for our discussion). Now consider a set $S \subseteq Y$. The inverse of S is the subset T, which is defined in the following way:

$$f^{-1}|S| = \{x \in T | f(x) \in S\}$$

Recall from Chapter 8, "Quantum Architecture," that *surjective* refers to a function that for every element in Y, there is at least one element in X, and that need not be unique. Figure 15.5, which originally appeared in Chapter 8 (and was also used in Chapter 14), should refresh your memory.

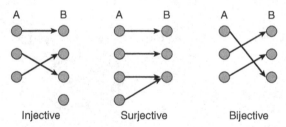

A B	A B	A B
Injective	Surjective	Bijective

FIGURE 15.5   Injective, surjective, and bijective

Supersingular isogeny Diffie-Hellman does involve some mathematics beyond the scope of this introductory book. However, it is important that you have a general idea of the more basic mathematical aspects, and that you understand SIDH is a key exchange algorithm. However, for those readers with a more rigorous mathematical background, the math will be presented here.

The fictional characters of Alice and Bob, who you might recall from Chapter 11, have been used in demonstrating asymmetric cryptography since the publication of the original paper on RSA in 1977. Alice and Bob will each have a prime number of a particular form. These forms are shown here:

$$E\left[L^e A^A\right] \text{ and } E\left[L_B^{eB}\right]$$

It should be relatively clear that the capital A represents Alice's values, and the capital B represents Bob's. Alice and Bob will each select a random cyclic subgroup (this will be secret) of their respective torsion subgroup and compute the corresponding isogeny.

That step might have included several items you are not familiar with. You should recall the discussion of groups and abelian groups from Chapter 1. Recall that a group is an algebraic system consisting of a set, an identity element, one operation, and its inverse operation. An abelian group adds to those requirements the commutative property. A torsion subgroup is a subgroup of an abelian group that consists of all the elements of the abelian group that have finite order. In this case, *order* is a term that comes from group theory and means cardinality (i.e., the number of elements). If it happens that all the elements in the abelian group have finite order (i.e., number of elements), then the group is called torsion. Finally, recall that a cyclic group is a group that has elements that are all powers of one of its elements. So, for example if you start with element x, then the members of a cyclic group would be as follows:

$$x^{-2}, x^{-1}, x^0, x^1, x^2, x^3, \ldots$$

Back to our discussion of what Bob and Alice do: They will now publish the equation of the target curve of their isogeny. This allows both parties to privately (and more importantly, secretly) calculate new isogenies from E, so they will both have the same shared secret. Why will they arrive at the same shared secret? Because the curves have a common j-invariant and are therefore isomorphic.

Let us summarize the steps. First, we have the setup process that both Alice and Bob complete:

1. A prime of the form $E\left[L^e A^A\right] * E\left[L_B^{eB}\right] * f \pm 1$.

2. A super singular elliptic curve E over fp^2 (a finite field).

3. Fixed elliptic points on the curve E, those points being P_A, Q_A, P_B, Q_B (remember P and Q as points in an elliptic curve).

4. The order of P_A and Q_A is $(lA)^{eA}$. The order of P_B and Q_B is $(lB)^{eB}$.

This will allow both Alice and Bob to have the necessary material for the key exchange. Next, we have a series of steps in the key exchange. Some are performed by Alice and some by Bob.

Alice generates two random integers: m_A, $n_A < (lA)^{eA}$. Alice generates $R_A := m_A * (P_A) + n_A$ (Q_A). Recall from Chapter 2, "Complex Numbers," that the symbol := means "is defined to be." Alice uses the point R_A, which was created in the preceding step, to create an isogeny mapping $E \rightarrow E_A$, which we will call ϕ_A, and curve E_A, which is isogenous to the curve E. Alice now applies the mapping, ϕ_A, that was just created to P_B and Q_B (remember Bob created these) to form two points on the curve E_A. Those points are $\phi_A P_B$ and $\phi_A Q_B$. Alice sends three things to Bob: E_A, $\phi_A P_B$, and $\phi_A Q_B$. Now it is time for Bob to perform his steps so that the two parties have a shared secret key. Bob will essentially do the same things Alice did; only the subscripts will be the reverse of what Alice used:

1. Bob generates two random integers: m_B, n_B $(lB)^{eB}$.

2. Bob generates $R_B := m_B * (P_B) + n_B (Q_B)$.

3. Bob uses the point R_B, which was created in the preceding step, to create an isogeny mapping $E \rightarrow E_B$, which we will call ϕB_A, and curve E_B, which is isogenous to the curve E.

4. Bob now applies the mapping, ϕ_B, that was just created to P_A and Q_A (remember Alice created these) to form two points on the curve E_B. Those points are $\phi_B P_A$ and $\phi_B Q_A$.

5. Bob now sends three things to Alice: E_B, $\phi_A P_B$, and $\phi_B Q_A$.

Now both Alice and Bob have exchanged materials, so they can create a shared secret key.

Alice can use the parts she received from Bob as well as items she generated, as follows:

1. $m_A (\phi_B (P_A)) + n_A (\phi_B (Q_A.)) = S_{BA}$.

2. Alice uses S_{BA} to create an isogeny mapping, which we will call ψ_{BA}.

3. Alice uses ψ_{BA} to create an elliptic curve, E_{BA}, which is isogenous to E.

4. Alice computes the j-invariant of the curve E_{BA}. We can call this j-invariant K (you will see why in just a moment).

Bob will do something almost identical:

1. $m_B(\phi_A (P_B)) + n_B(\phi_A (Q_B.)) = S_{BA}$.

2. Bob uses S_{AB} to create an isogeny mapping we will call ψ_{AB}.

3. Bob uses ψ_{AB} to create an elliptic curve, E_{AB}, which is isogenous to E.

4. Bob computes the j-invariant of the curve E_{AB}. We can call this j-invariant K. We call it K because if the curves are isogenous, they generate the same j-invariant, and now we have a common key for Alice and Bob to use.

Yes, this is a rather long process, with many steps. It also may stretch the mathematics of some readers. However, it is one of the contenders for a quantum-computer-resistant key exchange algorithm. Therefore, it is worthwhile to reread this section a few times, if needed, to ensure you are at least generally comfortable with the outline of the algorithm.

For those readers who want to delve more into this algorithm, there is an excellent paper from the International Association of Cryptologic Research (IACR) that will go into more depth: https://eprint.iacr.org/2019/1321.pdf. It is often helpful when learning something new, particularly something that is relatively challenging, to read two or more different explanations.

15.4 Summary

In this chapter, we have examined different types of algorithms that have been proposed for quantum-resistant solutions. We have examined hash functions, code-based cryptography, and supersingular isogeny key exchange. Some of the math in this chapter might have been a bit rigorous for some readers. Keep in mind that unless you intend to be working in the field of quantum-resistant cryptography, it is not critical that you have every nuance of every algorithm clear in your mind. As long as you have a general understanding, that will be sufficient.

Test Your Skills

REVIEW QUESTIONS

1. At the core of many cryptographic hash functions is a(n) _____.

    a. Merkle-Damgaard construction

    b. pseudo-random-number generator

    c. isogeny

    d. error correction code

2. Which of the following algorithms has a private key of (SPA)?

    a. SWIFFT

    b. SIDH

    c. Lamport

    d. McEliece

3. The _____ cryptosystem originally used parameters n = 1024, k = 524, and t = 50.

    a. SWIFFT

    b. SIDH

    c. Lamport

    d. McEliece

4. The_____ cryptosystem usually uses the binary Goppa code.

    a. Niederreiter

    b. McEliece

    c. Lamport

    d. SWIFFT

5. A finite field, also called a _____, is a field with a finite number of elements.

   a. torsion group

   b. Galois field

   c. abelian group

   d. torsion field

6. When curves are _____, they will have the same j-invariant over a closed field.

   a. isomorphic

   b. isometric

   c. surjective

   d. bijective

Chapter | **16**

Working with Q#

Chapter Objectives

After reading this chapter and completing the review questions, you will be able to do the following:

- Understand the fundamentals of Q#
- Write Q# programs
- Create quantum simulations with Q#

Microsoft developed Q# as a relatively easy-to-use quantum programming language. Microsoft first announced Q# in September 2018, and by December 2018 it was released. Q# is based on C# for syntax structure but includes the ability to create quantum logic gates as well as to simulate entanglement.

If you have no experience in programming, do not be overly concerned. In the section "Getting Started with Q#," we will approach a basic Q# program assuming you have no experience programming at all. There is also a section titled "Basic Programming Concepts," which is where we'll begin.

16.1   Basic Programming Concepts

This section is for those readers who have very limited programming experience. If you have experience in programming, particularly in C#, then you may wish to skim this section to at least get some of the Q#-specific items.

16.1.1   Variables and Statements

In general, all programs handle data of some sort. Regardless of the purpose of the program, it must process data. Data must be temporarily stored in the program. This is accomplished via variables. A variable is simply a place in memory set aside to hold data of a particular type. This is called a variable because its value or content can change or vary. When you create a variable, you are actually setting aside a small piece of memory for storage purposes. The name you give the variable is actually a label for that address in memory. For example, you declare a variable in this manner:

```
int j;
```

In this case, you have just allocated 4 bytes of memory (the amount used by integers), and you are using the variable j to refer to those 4 bytes of memory. Now whenever you reference j in your code, you are actually referencing a specific address in memory. Table 16.1 lists and describes the basic data types available in Q#.

TABLE 16.1 Q# Data Types

Data Type	Description
Unit	Represents a singleton type whose only value is ().
Int	Represents a 64-bit (4 byte) signed integer. Values range from –9,223,372,036,854,775,808 to 9,223,372,036,854,775,807.
BigInt	Represents signed integer values of any size.
Double	Represents a double-precision 64-bit floating point number. Values range from –1.79769313486232e308 to 1.79769313486232e308.
Bool	Represents Boolean values (true/false).
String	Represents text as values that consist of a sequence of UTF-16 (2 byte) code units.
Qubit	Represents a qubit. Values of type Qubit are instantiated via allocation.
Result	Represents the result of a projective measurement onto the eigenspaces of a quantum operator with eigenvalues ±1. Possible values are 0 and 1.
Pauli	Represents a single-qubit Pauli matrix. Possible values are PauliI, PauliX, PauliY, and PauliZ.
Range	Represents an ordered sequence of equally spaced Int values, in ascending or descending order.
Array	Represents values that each contain a sequence of values of the same type.
Tuple	Represents values that each contain a fixed number of items of different types. Tuples containing a single element are equivalent to the element they contain.

Once you have variables, the next building block is a statement. A statement is simply a single line of code that performs some action. That action might be to declare a variable, add two numbers, compare two values, or just about anything at all. All statements/expressions end with a semicolon. This is true in many programming languages, including Java, C, and C#. A few example statements will help clarify this for you:

```
int acctnum;
acctnum = 555555;
acctnum = acctnum + 5;
```

Each statement performs a different action, but it does perform some action, and it ends with a semi-colon. In many programming languages, the terms *statement* and *expression* are used interchangeably. In Q#, an expression is a special type of statement. Q# has some very specific statements. Table 16.2 shows the possible statement types.

TABLE 16.2 Q# Statement Types

Statement Type	Description
Variable declaration	Defines one or more local variables that will be valid for the remainder of the current scope, and it binds them to the specified values. There are also variable reassignment statements that change a variable's value.
Expression statement	An expression statement consists of an operation or function call returning a Unit. The invoked callable needs to satisfy the requirements imposed by the current context.
Return statement	A return statement terminates the execution within the current callable context and returns control to the caller.
Fail statement	A fail statement aborts the execution of the entire program, collecting information about the current program state before terminating in an error.
Iteration	An iteration is a loop-like statement that during each iteration assigns the declared loop variables to the next item in a sequence (a value of Array or Range type) and executes a specified block of statements.
Repeat statement	Quantum-specific loop that breaks based on a condition. The statement consists of an initial block of statements that is executed before a specified condition is evaluated. If the condition evaluates to false, an optional subsequent fixup-block is executed before entering the next iteration of the loop.
Conjugation	A conjugation is a special quantum-specific statement, where a block of statements that applies a unitary transformation to the quantum state is executed, followed by another statement block, before the transformation applied by the first block is reverted again. In mathematical notation, conjugations describe transformations of the form U†VU to the quantum state.
Qubit allocation	Instantiates and initializes qubits and/or arrays of qubits and then binds them to the declared variables. Executes a block of statements. The instantiated qubits are available for the duration of the block and will be automatically released when the statement terminates.

There is another special type in Q# called *immutable*. As the name suggests, it cannot change. It is like a constant in other programming languages. If you use the `let` statement, then you are making the type an immutable. Therefore, if you say

```
let myvar =3
```

then `myvar` has the value 3 and cannot be changed.

Now that you have seen variable declaration and statements, it is time to examine the basic structure of a Q# program. All programs, regardless of the programming language, have components. In Q#, as with many programming languages, the components are defined by brackets, {}. Here is the "Hello World" application written in Q#:

```
@EntryPoint()
operation Hello() : Unit {
    Message("Hello quantum world!");
}
```

Note that we have an operation we call `Hello`. This particular program has a single function/operation named `Hello`. Note that there is nothing in the parentheses. Inside the parentheses is where you place arguments (also called parameters) for the function. A parameter is what you pass to the function in order for it to work. For example, in this case, in order to square a number, we have to give it the number to square. Students often ask me, what do I need to put as parameters? Do I even need any parameters for this function? I will tell you the same thing I tell them. Ask yourself this question: If I wanted some person to do this task for me, would I need to give them anything? And if so, what? If you wanted a person to square a number for you, you would have to give them that number; however, if you just wanted them to say "hi," you would not have to give them anything. So, a function that squares a number should take one parameter, and a function that displays "hi" on the screen might not take any parameters.

This operation has a single statement in it. It simply displays the message "Hello quantum world!" Note that like all statements, it ends with a semicolon. Also note there are brackets at the beginning of the operation and at the end. Any coherent block of code—including functions, if statements, and loops—begins and ends with brackets {}.

16.1.2 Control Structures

The most common type of decision structure is the `if` statement. These statements exist in all programming languages but are implemented slightly differently. An `if` statement literally says, "if some condition exists, then execute this certain code." Let's look at how you do that in Q#. Here is a basic example that we can dissect to help you learn about `if` statements:

```
if( age == 65)
{
   Message ("You can retire!");
}
```

Notice we use ==, not =. A single = assigns a value, whereas == evaluates if something is true.

The `for` loop is perhaps the most commonly encountered loop in all programming. It is quite useful when you need to repeatedly execute a code segment a certain number of times. The concept is simple.

You tell the loop where to start, when to stop, and how much to increase its counter by each loop. Here is the basic format:

```
for (qubit in qubits)
{
 H(qubit);
}
```

You can also iterate from 1 to some value, as shown here:

```
for (index in 1 .. length(qubits)) {
    set results += [(index-1, M(qubits[index]))];
}
```

Either example will iterate through the code within the brackets a finite number of times. The differences are simply in how those iterations are counted.

Also, using statements are frequently seen in Q#. Concerning using statements, Microsoft states the following:

> "It is used to allocate qubits for use in a block of code. In Q#, all qubits are dynamically allocated and released, rather than being fixed resources that are there for the entire lifetime of a complex algorithm. A using statement allocates a set of qubits at the start, and releases those qubits at the end of the block."[1]

Many programming languages have using statements. A using statement basically means that, in the section denoted, we are "using" the item we named. Here is an example of a using statement wherein we are using qubit:

```
using (qubit = Qubit()) {

            for (test in 1..count) {
                SetQubitState(initial, qubit);
                let res = M(qubit);

                // Count the number of ones we saw:
                if (res == One) {
                    set numOnes += 1;
                }
            }

            SetQubitState(Zero, qubit);
    }
```

---

1. https://docs.microsoft.com/en-us/quantum/tutorials/explore-entanglement

16.1.3 Object-Oriented Programming

A great deal in Q# is object oriented. Therefore, you should be at least basically familiar with object-oriented programming concepts. An *object* is a programming abstraction that groups data with the code that operates on it. All programs contain data of different types. An object simply wraps all that up in a single place, called an object.

In object-oriented programming, four concepts are integral to the entire process of object-oriented programming:

- **Abstraction** is basically the ability to think about concepts in an abstract way. You can create a class for an employee, without having to think about a specific employee. It is abstract and can apply to any employee.

- **Encapsulation** is really the heart of object-oriented programming. This is simply the act of taking the data, and the functions that work on that data, and putting them together in a single class. Consider the use strings in any programming language. They are usually represented by a `string` class. The `string` class has the data you need to work on (i.e., the particular string in question) as well as the various functions you might use on that data, all wrapped into one class.

- **Inheritance** is a process whereby one class inherits, or gets, the public properties and methods of another class. The classic example is to create a class called `animal`. This class has properties such as `weight`, and methods such as `move` and `eat`. All animals would share these same properties and methods. When you wish to create a class for, say a monkey, you then have class `monkey` inherit from class `animal`, and it will have the same methods and properties that `animal` has. This is one way in which object-oriented programming supports code reuse.

- **Polymorphism** literally means "many forms." When you inherit the properties and methods of a class, you need not leave them as you find them. You can alter them in your own class. This will allow you to change the form those methods and properties take.

The term *class* is one you see a lot in object-oriented programming. It is a template for instantiating objects. Think of it as the blueprint for the objects you will need. It defines the properties and methods of that object. Q# has several objects that are built in, such as the `qubit` object.

In this section, you have been given a brief introduction to programming, Q#, and object-oriented concepts. These basic programming concepts should give you a general understanding of programming as well as Q#. Additional concepts will be described as they are introduced in the remainder of this chapter.

16.2   Getting Started with Q#

You can use Q# locally as part of Visual Studio Code, or you can use the online version. First, the local installation will be explored. The first step is to download and install VS Code. You can download the setup file from https://code.visualstudio.com/download#.

The next step is to install the Microsoft Quantum Development Kit for Visual Studio Code. You can get that from https://marketplace.visualstudio.com/items?itemName=quantum.quantum-devkit-vscode. You must have VS Code installed, but closed. The install for the Quantum Development Kit will open VS Code, as shown in Figure 16.1.

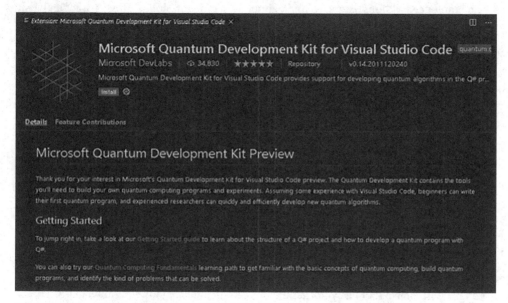

FIGURE 16.1   Microsoft QDK for Visual Studio Code

Click **View > Command Palette** and select **Q#: Create new project** from the screen shown in Figure 16.2.

Note that the first time you run this, Visual Studio Code will need to download some items. You might also be prompted to allow Visual Studio Code to communicate through your firewall.

Click **Standalone console application**.

Navigate to the location to save the project. Enter the project name and click **Create Project**. When the project is successfully created, click **Open new project...** in the lower right.

FIGURE 16.2 New Q# program in Visual Studio Code

You will be prompted for a new location for your project, as shown in Figure 16.3.

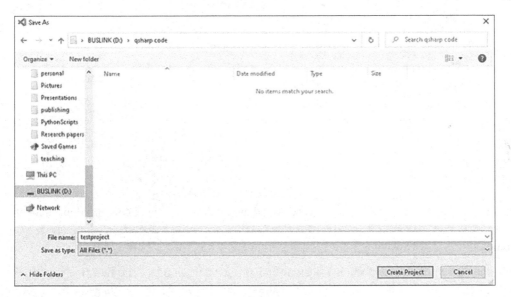

FIGURE 16.3 Save the program in Visual Studio Code

If you have Visual Studio 2017 or 2019, you can install the Microsoft Quantum Development Kit for Visual Studio from https://marketplace.visualstudio.com/items?itemName=quantum.quantum-devkit-vscode.

You also have the option of using the Quantum Development Kit online for free at https://www.microsoft.com/en-us/quantum/development-kit. The Binder option is the free version. When you launch it, you will immediately see samples, as shown in Figure 16.4. This is a great way to get started.

Quantum Development Kit Samples

These samples demonstrate the use of Q# and the Quantum Development Kit for a variety of different quantum computing tasks.

Many samples can be used directly in your browser using either Q# on its own, or Q# togther with Python. Alternatively, you can create a new terminal to run most Q# standalone samples, as well as samples that demonstrate how to use Q# together with Python or .NET.

A small number of the samples have additional installation requirements beyond those for the rest of the Quantum Development Kit. These a README.md files for each sample, along with complete installation instructions.

	Sample	Run in browser...		Run at command line...
Getting started:	Intro to IQ#	Q# notebook		
	Measurement		Q# standalone	
	Quantum random number generator		Q# standalone	
	Simple quantum algorithms		Q# standalone	
	Teleportation		Q# standalone	
Algorithms:	CHSH Game		Q# + Python	Q# + .NET
	Database Search	Q# notebook	Q# + Python	Q# + .NET
	Integer factorization		Q# + Python	Q# + .NET
	Oracle synthesis		Q# standalone	
	Order finding		Q# standalone	
	Repeat Until-Success (RUS)		Q# standalone	
	Reversible Logic Synthesis		Q# + Python	Q# standalone
	Simple Grover's Algorithm		Q# standalone	
Arithmetic:	Adder	Q# notebook		
Characterization:	Bayesian Phase Estimation		Q# standalone	
Chemistry:	Hamiltonian analysis		Q# + Python	Q# + .NET
	Hubbard model (data model)			Q# + .NET
	Hubbard model (simulation)			Q# + .NET

FIGURE 16.4   QDK Samples

Let us begin by examining a random-number generator done in Visual Studio Code. Random-number generators are common tutorial code samples for Q#. You can see the entire code in Figure 16.5. We will then break it down by explaining it.

We will assume you have no programming background and explain all of it. The first line states the namespace and then has the name of your project (whatever you selected when you created the project). A namespace allows you to group related classes together.

Next, you see several open statements, as shown in Figure 16.6.

FIGURE 16.5   Q# random-number generator

```
open Microsoft.Quantum.Canon;
open Microsoft.Quantum.Intrinsic;
open Microsoft.Quantum.Convert;
open Microsoft.Quantum.Math;
open Microsoft.Quantum.Measurement;
```

FIGURE 16.6   Q# open statements

A brief description of these namespaces is provided here:

- `Microsoft.Quantum.Canon` contains the fundamental items needed in quantum programming.

- `Microsoft.Quantum.Convert` has functions for converting from one Q# data type to another.

- `Microsoft.Quantum.Math` contains mathematical data types and functions.

- `Microsoft.Quantum.Measurement` contains the objects/functions necessary to measure qubits.

What this is doing is opening some of the namespaces that are part of the Microsoft Quantum Development Kit. These namespaces include classes/objects you can use.

After the comments, you see the first operation, as shown in Figure 16.7.

```
operation QuantumPseudoRandomNumberGenerator() : Result {
    using (q = Qubit()) {  // Allocate a qubit.
        H(q);              // Put the qubit to superposition. It now has a 50% chance of being 0 or 1.
        return MResetZ(q); // Measure the qubit value.
    }
}
```

FIGURE 16.7   Operation `QuantumPseudoRandomNumberGenerator`

The first thing to note is this operation does not take in any parameters. It does implement a `using` statement, which we discussed earlier in this chapter. It is using a single instance of the `Qubit` class we simply called a.

The next thing you see is some text preceded by `//`, and it appears in green in Visual Studio or Visual Studio Code. This is called a comment. Comments are text that will be ignored by Visual Studio but are there to provide information to whoever is reading them. It is a good idea to comment on your code to indicate what it is you are trying to accomplish. Also, when you are new to programming, or new to a particular language such as Q#, a good tip for learning it is to get sample code and heavily comment it. Go through all the sample code, commenting every line. This can help you to understand every line. If you don't understand a given part of the code, put a comment stating as much. Then make it a point to go back and seek out answers to all the code you don't yet understand.

The function `QuantumPseudoRandomNumberGenerator` is actually called from the function `RandomNumberInRange`. Therefore, we should examine that operation next (note we are using the terms *function* and *operation* interchangeably). You can see this function in Figure 16.8.

```
operation RandomNumberInRange(max : Int) : Int {
    mutable bits = new Result[0];
    for (idxBit in 1..BitSizeI(max)) {
        set bits += [QuantumPseudoRandomNumberGenerator()];
    }
    let sample = ResultArrayAsInt(bits);
    return sample > max
        ? RandomNumberInRange(max)
        | sample;
}
```

FIGURE 16.8   Operation `RandomNumberInRange`

This operation does have a single parameter. It is an integer we name `max`. That is the maximal range. We then create an array of type Result that we call `bits`. Notice that it is preceded by the keyword `mutable`, indicating that it is indeed mutable/changeable.

We next have a `for` loop (also discussed earlier in this chapter). This `for` loop will add to the result array bits, the value retrieved from `QuantumPseudoRandomNumberGenerator`. Now we can more clearly see the purpose of the algorithm. It is to return a bit. That bit is then put in an array to create a set of random bits.

Then we come to the function `SampleRandomNumber`, as shown in Figure 16.9.

```
@EntryPoint()
operation SampleRandomNumber() : Int {
    let max = 50;
    Message($"Sampling a random number between 0 and {max}: ");
    return RandomNumberInRange(max);
}
```

FIGURE 16.9 Operation `SampleRandomNumber`

This operation is preceded by the `@EntryPoint()` directive, which tells us that this is the starting point for this program. It has only two things it does. The first is to set a `max` (in this case, 50). The next is to call the function `RandomNumberInRange`, passing it the value `max`.

It is recommended that you write this program yourself and then execute it. It is common to have some configuration issues with whatever tool you are using (Visual Studio 2017/2019, Visual Studio Code, or the online Quantum Development Kit). It is best to get those issues sorted out now before you move on to more complex programs. Also, once you get this program to execute as written, experiment with changing a single line (perhaps start with the `max` value) to see what happens. You should take the time to become very comfortable with this simple program before you move forward into more complex examples.

16.3 Grover's Algorithm

You may wish to review the presentation of Grover's algorithm from Chapter 10, "Quantum Algorithms." However, a brief review is presented before we delve into the code.

16.3.1 Grover's Algorithm Reviewed

Recall that Grover's algorithm is a search algorithm. There must be an N-dimension state space, which we will call H, that is provided by log2N qubits. Then the entries in the data store are numbered from 0 to N−1. Then there is an observable, Ω, that acts on the state space H. Ω must have eigenvalues, all of which are known. Each eigenstate of Ω encodes one of the entries in the database. The eigenstates are denoted using bra-ket notation:

$$\{|0>, |1>, |2>, ..., |N-1>\}$$

And, of course, the eigenvalues are denoted in much the same way:

$$\{\lambda_0, \lambda_1, \lambda_2, ..., \lambda_{N-1}\}.$$

The next step is to determine some operator that functions to compare database entries based on some criterion. Grover's algorithm does not specify the operator or its criteria. That will be selected based on the particular data store and search; however, the operator must be a quantum subroutine that functions via a superposition of states. The operator is often designated as Uω.

Our operator has the following property when applied to the previously mentioned eigenstates (which we will denote as $|\omega>$):

$$U\omega|\omega> = -|\omega>$$

However, for all x that are not ω, we want the following:

$$U\omega|x> = |x>$$

Put another way, we are trying to identify the particular eigenstate $|\omega>$ that $U\omega$ acts on in a manner different from the other eigenstates. This operator, U_ω, is often referred to as a *quantum oracle*. It is some unitary operator that operates on two qubits. That defines the U_ω operator. There is a second operator called U_s. The s is a superposition of possible states. The operator is as follows:

$$Us = 1|s> <s|-I$$

The first step is to initialize the system to a state. That state will be a superposition of states, often denoted as follows:

$$|s \geq \frac{1}{\sqrt{N}} \sum_{x=0}^{N-1} |x>$$

We are simply stating that the state $|s>$ is a superposition of all possible states $|x>$.

The next step is called the Grover iteration, r, and is executed N times. This step r is simply to apply the operator U_ω and apply the operator U_s.

The third step is to perform the measurement of the observable Ω. This measurement will provide some eigenvalue λ_ω. As we iterate through the process, we eventually get to the proper answer.

This review should help refresh your memory of Grover's algorithm. In the next section, we look at code that implements a simple version of Grover's algorithm.

16.3.2   The Code for Grover's Algorithm

The code will be presented in sections, each described in light of the review of Grover's algorithm. Some of this depends on objects that are part of the Quantum Development Kit. So, the first item to examine is the open statements, as shown in Figure 16.10.

```
namespace GroversAlgorithm{
    open Microsoft.Quantum.Intrinsic;
    open Microsoft.Quantum.Convert;
    open Microsoft.Quantum.Math;
    open Microsoft.Quantum.Canon;
    open Microsoft.Quantum.Arrays;
    open Microsoft.Quantum.Measurement;
```

FIGURE 16.10   The open statements in Grover's algorithm code

You might notice that there are more here than were in the random-number generator discussed earlier in this chapter. Specifically, there are two that were not in the previous code:

```
open Microsoft.Quantum.Intrinsic;
open Microsoft.Quantum.Arrays;
```

These are included because they contain specific classes we will need in implementing Grover's algorithm. The next part of the code is the function `ReflectMarked`. As you can see in Figure 16.11, it is preceded by comments, which are given to help explain what the function is doing.

```
// Recall the description of the algorithm earlier in this book
// This code reflects around the basis state using alternating zeros and ones
// then defines what input we are attempting to find in the main search
// The  OutQubits is initialized t to (|0⟩ - |1⟩) / √2,

operation ReflectMarked(InQubits : Qubit[]) : Unit {
    Message("Reflecting about marked state...");
    using (OutQubits = Qubit()) {
        within {
            X(OutQubits);
            H(OutQubits);
            // Flip the OutQubits for marked states.
            // This producing the state with alternating 0s and 1s by using
            // the X instruction on every other qubit.
            ApplyToEachA(X, InQubits[...2...]);
        } apply {
            Controlled X(InQubits, OutQubits);
        }
    }
}
```

FIGURE 16.11 `ReflectMarked`

This function takes in a Qubit array we named `InQubits`. The message portion is not strictly necessary, but it is a good idea to tell the user what is happening. Notice we have X and H. Those are quantum gates that are part of the Q# Quantum Development Kit. This is one of the reasons using the Quantum Development Kit is so useful. The various gates you need are already built in.

H is the Hadamard gate and is part of the `Microsoft.Quantum.Intrinsic` namespace. There are other gates included in this namespace. Some that you will see frequently are shown in Table 16.3.

TABLE 16.3 Operations in `Microsoft.Quantum.Intrinsic`

X, Y, and Z	Pauli-X, -Y, and -Z gates.
T	The T gate.
Rx, Ry, and Rz	These are rotations about the x-, y-, and z-axes.
R	This applies rotation about a given Pauli axis.
M	This performs a measurement of a single qubit in the Pauli-Z basis.
Measure	Performs a joint measurement of one or more qubits in the specified Pauli bases.
CNOT	This applies a controlled (not) gate.

We also see something new—the `ApplyToEach` operation. This is part of the `Microsoft.Quantum.Canon` namespace. It applies a single qubit operation to each element in a given register.

Then we move on to the next function in the code, `ReflectUniform`, shown in Figure 16.12.

```
/// Reflects about the superposition state.
operation ReflectUniform(InQubits : Qubit[]) : Unit {
    within {
        // Transform the uniform superposition to all-zero.
        Adjoint PerpareUniformZeros(InQubits);
        // Transform the all-zero state to all-ones
        SetAllOnes(InQubits);
    } apply {
        // Now that we've transformed the uniform superposition to t
        // all-ones state, reflect about the all-ones state, then le
        // the within/apply block transform us back.
        ReflectAboutAllOnes(InQubits);
    }
}
```

FIGURE 16.12 `ReflectUniform`

You can see that this calls two functions: `SetAllOnes` and `ReflectAboutAllOnes`. Both of these are passed an array, `InQubits`. We also see something called `Adjoint`. This is a functor. Functors (not functions) are something specific to Q#. To quote from Microsoft:

> "Functors are factories that allow to access particular specialization implementations of a callable. Q# currently supports two functors; the Adjoint and the Controlled functor, both of which can be applied to operations that provide the necessary specialization(s)."[2]

The `Adjoint` functor defines a unitary transformation of the quantum state. This is often represented as U (unitary transformation).

There are three more functions in the preparation of the data to search, and we have seen these called in previous code segments. These functions are shown in Figure 16.13.

```
/// Reflects about the all-ones state.
operation ReflectAboutAllOnes(InQubits : Qubit[]) : Unit {
    Controlled Z(Most(InQubits), Tail(InQubits));
}

operation PerpareUniformZeros(InQubits : Qubit[]) : Unit is Adj + Ctl {
    ApplyToEachCA(H, InQubits);
}

operation SetAllOnes(InQubits : Qubit[]) : Unit is Adj + Ctl {
    ApplyToEachCA(X, InQubits);
}
```

FIGURE 16.13 Additional functions for Grover's algorithm

---

2. https://docs.microsoft.com/en-us/quantum/user-guide/language/expressions/functorapplication#functor-application

Note that `ReflectAboutAllOnes` simply uses the controlled Z gate. `PrepareUniformZeros` and `SetAllOnes` each use the function `ApplyToEach`. Recall that this function applies a single qubit operation to each element in a given register.

Now we have the function to actually search for input. This is shown in Figure 16.14.

```
    @EntryPoint()
operation SearchForMarkedInput(nQubits : Int) : Result[] {
    using (qubits = Qubit[nQubits]) {
        // Initialize a uniform superposition over all possible inputs.
        PerpareUniformZeros(qubits);
        // The search itself consists of repeatedly reflecting about the
        // marked state and our start state, which we can write out in Q#
        // as a for loop.
        for (idxIteration in 0..NumberofIterations(nQubits) - 1) {
            ReflectMarked(qubits);
            ReflectUniform(qubits);
        }
        // Measure and return the answer.
        return ForEach(MResetZ, qubits);
    }
}
```

FIGURE 16.14 Entry point for Grover's algorithm

Notice this is the entry point for the program, and it should help demonstrate for you how the other functions are used. First, we initialize a uniform superposition, and then we search via reflecting operations. Finally, we measure each qubit.

There is one more function that will simply tell you how many iterations are needed to find a single marked item. This function was called in `NumberofIterations` and is shown in Figure 16.15.

```
function NumberofIterations(nQubits : Int) : Int {
    let iItems = 1 <<< nQubits; // 2^numQubits
    // compute number of iterations:
    let angle = ArcSin(1. / Sqrt(IntAsDouble(iItems)));
    let iIterations = Round(0.25 * PI() / angle - 0.5);
    return iIterations;
}
```

FIGURE 16.15 The `NumberofIterations` function

As with the random-number generator, it is recommended you actually code this and then get it to execute. After you get it executed, work with different variations. Alter small bits of code and see what happens. This will help you to understand the code better.

16.4 Deutsch-Jozsa Algorithm

This is another algorithm from Chapter 10. We will briefly review it here and then work through code that implements this algorithm.

16.4.1   Deutsch-Jozsa Algorithm Reviewed

Recall from Chapter 10 that this is a modification of the Deutsch algorithm. The issue is actually rather straightforward. The Deutsch algorithm looks at functions of one variable. The Deutsch-Jozsa algorithm generalizes this to functions of n variables. Recall this problem involves a black-box quantum computer that implements some function that takes in n-digit binary values and produces either a 0 or 1 for the output of each such value. The output will either be balanced (an equal number of 1s and 0s) or constant (either all 1s or all 0s). The goal of the algorithm is to determine if the function is constant or balanced.

The actual algorithm begins with the first n bits in state $|0\rangle$, and the final bit is in the state $|1\rangle$. Then a Hadamard transform is applied to each bit. Now we have a function we will call f(x). This function maps the state $|x\rangle|y\rangle$ to $|x\rangle|y \oplus f(x)\rangle$. In this case, the symbol $\oplus$ denotes addition modulo 2. As the values of x are put through the oracle f(x), either a 1 or 0 is produced. The output will be 0 if f(x) is balanced and 1 if f(x) is constant. For n bits input, the final output will be n 0s if f(x) is constant. Any other output (any combination of 0s and 1s, or all 1s) indicates that f(x) is balanced.

16.4.2   The Code for Deutsch-Jozsa Algorithm

We begin with the namespace opening and the open statements for other namespaces. This is shown in Figure 16.16.

```
namespace DeutschJozsa {
    open Microsoft.Quantum.Intrinsic;
    open Microsoft.Quantum.Canon;
    open Microsoft.Quantum.Arrays;
    open Microsoft.Quantum.Convert;
    open Microsoft.Quantum.Measurement;
```

FIGURE 16.16   Beginning of Deutsch-Jozsa

Let us begin at the entry point, shown in Figure 16.17.

```
@EntryPoint()
operation RunDeutschJozsa(iQubits : Int, mElements : Int[]) : Bool {
    return IsConstant(
        BooleanFunction(iQubits, mElements), iQubits
    );
}
```

FIGURE 16.17   Deutsch-Jozsa entry point

This function simply calls the function IsConstant, passing it another function, BooleanFunction, along with the parameters to BooleanFunction (iQubits, mElements) and the remaining parameter to IsConstant.

Next, let us look at the function IsConstant. This will return if the value is constant or not (i.e., not balanced). The function is shown in Figure 16.18.

```
operation IsConstant (Uf : ((Qubit[], Qubit) => Unit), n : Int) : Bool {

    using ((queryRegister, target) = (Qubit[n], Qubit())) {

        X(target);
        H(target);

        within {

            ApplyToEachA(H, queryRegister);
        } apply {
            Uf(queryRegister, target);
        }

        let resultArray = ForEach(MResetZ, queryRegister);

        Reset(target);

        return All(IsResultZero, resultArray);
    }
}
```

FIGURE 16.18 The IsConstant function

Much of this you have seen earlier in this chapter. We have the two gates, X and H. We are also using the ApplyToEach operation. Note that this function takes in another function, Uf. In this case, that function is one we name BooleanFunction. That requires the two parameters for BooleanFunction, and those are shown as well.

There are two other functions in our code: BooleanFunction and a function named UnitaryOperation. Those are both shown in Figure 16.19.

```
internal operation UnitaryOperation(n : Int, mElements : Int[], query : Qubit[], target : Qubit) : Unit {
    // This operation applies the unitary Operation

    for (markedElement in mElements) {

        ControlledOnInt(markedElement, ApplyToEachCA(X, _))(query, [target]);
    }
}

function BooleanFunction (iQubits : Int, mElements : Int[]) : ((Qubit[], Qubit) => Unit) {
    return UnitaryOperation(iQubits, mElements, _, _);
}
```

FIGURE 16.19 Remaining functions for Deutsch-Jozsa

As you can see, the `BooleanFunction`, in turn, calls the `UnitaryOperation` function. If you carefully studied the previous code samples and reviewed the Deutsch-Jozsa algorithm, this code example should help you to better understand both the algorithm and Q# programming.

16.5   Bit Flipping

Let us try one more example. This code simply demonstrates bit flipping. This example is quite similar to one found on Microsoft's website at https://docs.microsoft.com/en-us/quantum/tutorials/explore-entanglement. The code on the Microsoft site goes further and simulates entanglement. You should consider working through that example as well.

First, let's look at the code. In this case, all the code is shown in Figure 16.20.

```
≡ entangled.qs > ...
1    namespace EntangleMent {
2        open Microsoft.Quantum.Canon;
3        open Microsoft.Quantum.Intrinsic;
4
5        operation SetQubitState(desired : Result, target : Qubit) : Unit {
6            if (desired != M(target)) {
7                X(target);
8            }
9        }
10
11       @EntryPoint()
12       operation TestState(count : Int, initial : Result) : (Int, Int) {
13
14           mutable numOnes = 0;
15           using (qubit = Qubit()) {
16
17               for (test in 1..count) {
18                   SetQubitState(initial, qubit);
19                   let res = M(qubit);
20
21                   // Count the number of ones we saw:
22                   if (res == One) {
23                       set numOnes += 1;
24                   }
25               }
26
27               SetQubitState(Zero, qubit);
28           }
29
30
31           return (count - numOnes, numOnes);
32       }
33   }
```

FIGURE 16.20   Entanglement

First notice that this code depends a great deal on gates and measurements. You see the X operation and the M operation that were discussed previously in this chapter. Recall that X flips the state, and M measures it. The entry point is the operation `TestState`, which tests the state of some qubit.

The function simply takes in a number of iterations to go through and an initial value. Then it will go through flipping bits and outputting the result. This is a rather simple program, but it will help you get more comfortable with Q#.

16.6 Summary

In this chapter, you finally applied the knowledge you have learned to actual programming tasks. If you worked through the projects in this chapter, you should now have a basic working knowledge of Q#. Furthermore, actually programming some of these algorithms should aid you in understanding those algorithms better. There are also numerous sources on the Internet you can consult:

- **Microsoft's Quantum Computing Foundations:** https://docs.microsoft.com/en-us/learn/paths/quantum-computing-fundamentals/
- **Microsoft Quantum Katas:** https://docs.microsoft.com/en-us/quantum/tutorials/intro-to-katas
- **Microsoft Q# User Guide:** https://docs.microsoft.com/en-us/quantum/user-guide/

Test Your Skills

REVIEW QUESTIONS

1. In Q#, what data type represents the result of a projective measurement onto the eigenspaces of a quantum operator with eigenvalues ±1?

    a. EigenReturn

    b. Return

    c. Result

    d. EigenResult

2. A(n) _____ is a loop-like statement that during each iteration assigns the declared loop variables to the next item in a sequence (a value of Array or Range type) and executes a specified block of statements.

    a. iteration

    b. repeat

    c. for-next

    d. while

3. _____ is the act of taking the data, and the functions that work on that data, and putting them together in a single class.

    a. Abstraction

    b. Encapsulation

    c. Inheritance

    d. Polymorphism

4. What namespace are Pauli gates found in?

   a. `Microsoft.Quantum.Intrinsic`

   b. `Microsoft.Quantum.Canon`

   c. `Microsoft.Quantum.Gates`

   d. `Microsoft.Quantum.Measurement`

5. What does the Quantum Development Kit's R operation do?

   a. Rotate about the x-, y-, or z-axis.

   b. Reset a given qubit.

   c. Reset a given gate.

   d. Rotate about a given Pauli axis.

## Chapter 17

Working with QASM

Chapter Objectives

After reading this chapter and completing the review questions, you will be able to do the following:

- Understand the fundamentals of QASM
- Write QASM programs
- Create quantum simulations with QASM

Quantum Assembly Language (QASM) is a programming language specifically for quantum programs. It is used to simulate quantum gates and quantum algorithms. You use an online editor (https://www.quantum-inspire.com/projects/6923062) to write QASM code. That editor is shown in Figure 17.1.

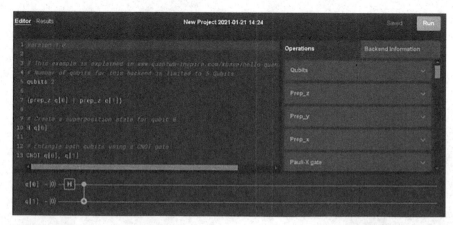

FIGURE 17.1 Quantum Inspire Editor

This programming language is meant to allow you to experiment with various quantum gates and circuits. It is an ideal tool to translate your theoretical knowledge of quantum computing into practice. In fact, it is probably easier to set up quantum simulations in QASM than in Q# (see Chapter 16, "Working with Q#").

If you have no experience in programming, do not be overly concerned. We will approach a basic QASM program assuming you have no experience programming at all. There is also a section titled "Basic Programming Concepts," which is where we'll start.

17.1   Basic Programming Concepts

QASM does not have many of the structures found in other programming languages. This section introduces the programming concepts associated with QASM.

17.1.1   Instructions

QASM is based on instructions, and the various instructions are related specifically to quantum operations and structures. The fact that so much of what you need for quantum computing is built into the QASM language makes it an excellent choice for learning quantum computing. For example, the command `qubits n` initializes a qubit register of size n. By default, all qubits are initialized in the $|0\rangle$ state.

There are three `prep` statements. With the `prep` instruction, qubits will be explicitly initialized in the $|0\rangle$ state of a specific basis:

- `prep_z`
- `prep_y`
- `prep_x`

The Pauli gates are also prearranged for you in QASM. There are three:

- Pauli-X
- Pauli-Y
- Pauli-Z

Several other gates and measurements are available to you. Table 17.1 summarizes the most important ones.

TABLE 17.1   QASM Instructions

Instruction	Meaning
Pauli-X	To use the Pauli-X gate on the first qubit, you use this syntax: `X q[0]`
Pauli-Y	The Y gate is similar: `Y q[0]`
Pauli-Z	And here's the Z gate: `Z q[0]`

Hadamard	To execute the Hadamard gate against the first qubit is much like the Pauli gates:
	`H q[0]`
	Here's how to execute the Hadamard (or any other gate) against the first two qubits:
	`H q[0,1]`

Identity	I is the identity matrix/gate.
Rx	This is the rotation operator; in this case, rotation about the x-axis. Then use this on the first qubit: `Rx q[0]`
Ry	This is the rotation operator; in this case, rotation about the y-axis. Then use this on the first qubit: `Ry q[0]`
Rz	This is the rotation operator; in this case, rotation about the z-axis. Then use this on the first qubit: `Rx Z[0]`
T gate	Here's how to execute the T gate on the first qubit: `T q[0]`
CNOT gate	The CNOT gate is a two-qubit operation, where the first qubit is usually referred to as the control qubit and the second qubit as the target qubit. This can be used to entangle two qubits, as follows: `CNOT q[0], q[1]`
SWAP gate	The SWAP gate is a two-qubit operation. Expressed in basis states, the SWAP gate swaps the state of the two qubits involved in the operation: `SWAP q[0], q[1]`
Toffoli gate	Recall that this gate is sometimes called the Controlled-Controlled NOT gate. Here's an example: `Toffoli q[1], q[2], q[3]`
`measure_x`	All measurements measure in some basis. The `measure_x` command will measure the qubit in the x-basis.
`measure_y`	All measurements measure in some basis. The `measure_y` command will measure the qubit in the y-basis.
`measure_z`	All measurements measure in some basis. The `measure_z` command will measure the qubit in the z-basis.
`measure_all`	This command will measure all the qubits in parallel using the z-basis.

If you start the editor and define two qubits, you see the screen shown in Figure 17.2.

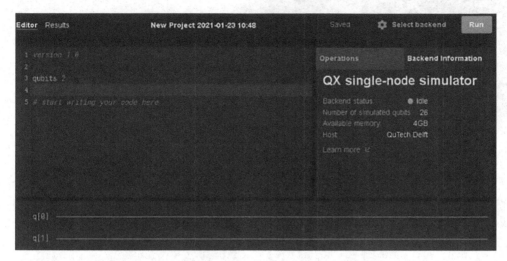

FIGURE 17.2 Two qubits

Pay attention to the bottom of the screen, where you can see q[0] and q[1], the two qubits. If you add any gates, you will see they get added at the bottom. Adding a CNOT gate produces the change you see in Figure 17.3.

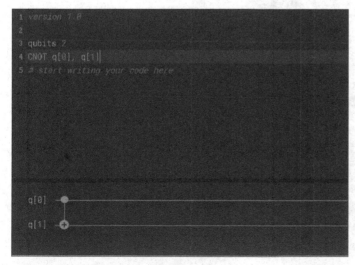

FIGURE 17.3 CNOT gate

If rather than using a CNOT gate you had used a Hadamard gate on the first qubit and a Pauli-X gate on the second, you would get the result shown in Figure 17.4.

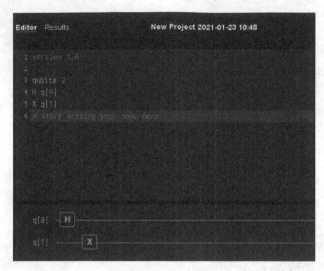

FIGURE 17.4   Hadamard gate

You can also execute multiple gates on a single qubit. In Figure 17.5, you see multiple gates on each qubit and then gates on both. These are not done to fulfill any particular algorithm, just to represent what you can do with QASM.

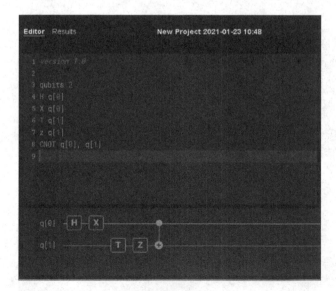

FIGURE 17.5   Multiple gates

This is one of the most powerful aspects of using QASM. You can see the circuits you are building graphically. That makes it quite easy to visualize what you are constructing. Also, as you can see, writing the code is very straightforward. You may find the implementations of algorithms in this chapter easier to follow than those in Chapter 16.

17.1.2   Commands

QASM does have a number of commands for various tasks. In this section, we examine some of the more common commands you will need to use. Table 17.2 describes the commands you will need to know.

TABLE 17.2   QASM Commands

Command	Definition
`display`	The display outputs writes the current state of the qubit register.
`error_model depolarizing_ channel, 0.001`	The depolarizing channel error model causes a random error between each operation on a qubit.
`display_binary`	`display_binary` obtains the contents of the binary register.
`number of shots`	Algorithms can be deterministic or nondeterministic. If they are deterministic, they are single shot (number of shots (N=1)) or multi-shot (number of shots (N>1)).

With these instructions and commands, you will be able to follow along with the code presented in this chapter. In fact, much of it may be almost obvious to you. That is the power of QASM.

17.2   Getting Started with QASM

Once you set up your free Quantum Inspire account at https://www.quantum-inspire.com, you can start new projects. Figure 17.6 shows the first step.

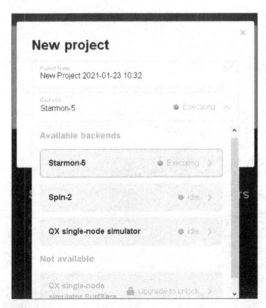

FIGURE 17.6   Starting a new project

This will then open the editor with your new project, as shown in Figure 17.7.

FIGURE 17.7   New project editor

Selecting the backend will determine much of what you can do. Only some backends are available with the free version. Quantum Inspire has two quantum processors in addition to emulators. There are some restrictions on what you can do with the actual processors. For more details, it is best to refer to the documentation on this issue available at https://www.quantum-inspire.com/kbase/hardware-backends/.

17.3   Quantum Error Correction

It is clearly important to have some level of error correction in quantum algorithms. In fact, quantum error correction is a rich field of research. The example shown here is a very simple error correction algorithm. It is not terribly efficient, but it does demonstrate the basic concepts. In this case, we encode one logical qubit with three physical qubits.

The concept is simple. Let us assume you have a single qubit and perform the operation shown in Equation 17.1.

$$|\psi> = \alpha|0> + \beta\;|1>$$

EQUATION 17.1   Quantum Error Basic Equation

How will you detect errors? That is indeed a serious problem. Now our solution here is effective, but inelegant. We will simply use two extra bits; that way, we easily detect if there was a bit-flipping error. So now we use the equation shown in Equation 17.2.

$$|\psi> = \alpha\,|000> + \beta\,|111>$$

EQUATION 17.2 Error Correcting Equation

The code is shown here:

```
version 1.0
qubits 5

.Encoding
cnot q[0],q[1]
cnot q[0],q[2]

.Introduce_Error
x q[1]

.Error_Detection
cnot q[0],q[3]
cnot q[1],q[3]
cnot q[0],q[4]
cnot q[2],q[4]
measure q[3,4]

.Error_Correction
# Both b[3]=b[4]=0
#do nothing

# b[3]=b[4]=1
c-x b[3,4], q[0]

# b[3]=1,b[4]=0
not b[4]
c-x b[3,4],q[1]
not b[4]

# b[3]=0,b[4]=1
not b[3]
c-x b[3,4],q[2]
not b[3]

.Measurement
measure q[0:2]
```

In the editor, this code looks like what you see in Figure 17.8.

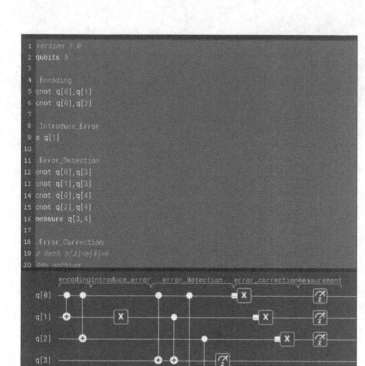

FIGURE 17.8 Error correction

The concept again is quite simple, but inefficient. By using three qubits, if there is no error, we should have all three give the same result. If one has an error, then we will have a single qubit that does not match. Due to the obvious inefficiency of this approach, it is not recommended for actual quantum computing; however, it is an excellent way for you to become familiar with the concept. It also gives you practice working with QASM.

17.4 Grover's Algorithm

You may wish to review the presentation of Grover's algorithm from Chapter 10, "Quantum Algorithms." However, a brief review is presented before we delve into the code.

17.4.1 Grover's Algorithm Reviewed

Recall that Grover's algorithm is a search algorithm. There must be an N-dimension state space, which we will call H, that is provided by log2N qubits. Then the entries in the data store are numbered from 0 to N–1. Then there is an observable, Ω, that acts on the state space H. Ω must have eigenvalues, all of which are known. Each eigenstate of Ω encodes one of the entries in the database. The eigenstates are denoted using bra-ket notation:

$$\{\,|0>,\ |1>,\ |2>,\ ...,\ |N{-}1>\}$$

And, of course, the eigenvalues are denoted in much the same way:

$$\{\lambda_0,\ \lambda_1,\ \lambda_2,\ ...,\ \lambda_{N-1}.$$

The next step is to determine some operator that functions to compare database entries based on some criterion. Grover's algorithm does not specify the operator or its criteria. That will be selected based on the particular data store and search; however, the operator must be a quantum subroutine that functions via a superposition of states. The operator is often designated as $U\omega$.

Our operator has the following property when applied to the previously mentioned eigenstates (which we will denote as $|\omega>$):

$$U\omega\,|\omega> = -|\omega>$$

However, for all x that are not ω, we want the following:

$$U\omega\,|x> = |x>$$

Put another way, we are trying to identify the particular eigenstate $|\omega>$ that $U\omega$ acts on in a manner different from the other eigenstates. This operator, U_ω, is often referred to as a quantum oracle. It is some unitary operator that operates on two qubits. That defines the U_ω operator, but there is a second operator, the U_s, where the s is a superposition of possible states. The operator is as follows:

$$Us = 1\,|s> <s|{-}I$$

The first step is to initialize the system to a state. That state will be a superposition of states, often denoted as follows:

$$|s \geq \frac{1}{\sqrt{N}} \sum_{x=0}^{N-1} |x>$$

We are simply stating that the state $|s>$ is a superposition of all possible states $|x>$. The next step is called the Grover iteration, r, and is executed N times. This step r is simply to apply the operator U_ω and apply the operator U_s. The third step is to perform the measurement of the observable Ω. This measurement will provide some eigenvalue λ_ω. As we iterate through the process, we eventually get to the proper answer. This review should help refresh your memory of Grover's algorithm. In the next section, we look at code that implements a simple version of Grover's algorithm.

17.4.2   The Code for Grover's Algorithm

The following is the complete code for Grover's algorithm in QASM:

```
version 1.0
qubits 3
# Grover's algorithm for
# searching the decimal number
# 6 in a database of size 2^3

.init
H q[0:2]

.grover(2)
# This is the quantum oracle discussed
{X q[0] | H q[2] }
Toffoli q[0], q[1], q[2]
{H q[2] | X q[0]}

# diffusion
{H q[0] | H q[1] | H q[2]}
{X q[1] | X q[0] | X q[2] }
H q[2]
Toffoli q[0], q[1], q[2]
H q[2]
{X q[1] | X q[0] | X q[2] }
{H q[0] | H q[1] | H q[2]}
```

If you consider the preceding code, it is not quite as daunting as it might seem at first glance. Consider the first code you see:

```
H q[0:2]
```

This initializes a Hadamard gate. The next sections simply use different gates: the Hadamard gate, Pauli-X gate, and Toffoli gate.

When shown in the editor, it looks like what you see in Figure 17.9.

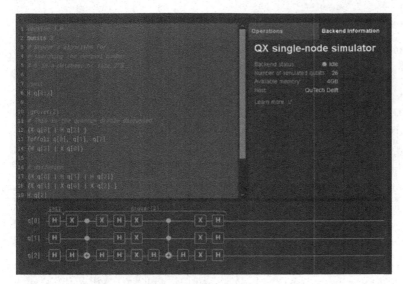

FIGURE 17.9 Grover's algorithm

The results are shown in Figure 17.10.

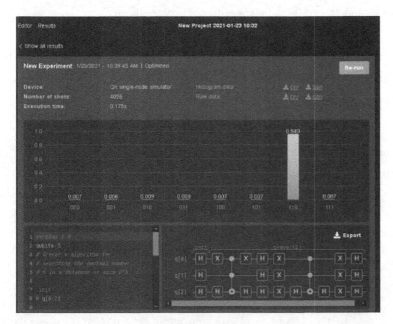

FIGURE 17.10 Grover's algorithm results

This screen allows you to visualize a histogram of the output. Also notice that at the top you see the number of shots, the execution time, and other data. You can export your results as well. The online editor for QASM is quite easy to use and convenient.

17.5   Deutsch-Jozsa Algorithm

This is another algorithm from Chapter 10. We will briefly review it here and then work through code that implements this algorithm.

17.5.1   Deutsch-Jozsa Algorithm Reviewed

Recall from Chapter 10 that Deutsch-Jozsa is a modification of the Deutsch algorithm. The issue is actually rather straightforward. The Deutsch algorithm looks at functions of one variable. The Deutsch-Jozsa algorithm generalizes this to functions of n variables. Recall this problem involves a black-box quantum computer that implements some function that takes in n-digit binary values and produces either a 0 or 1 for the output of each such value. The output will either be balanced (an equal number of 1s and 0s) or constant (either all 1s or all 0s). The goal of the algorithm is to determine if the function is constant or balanced.

The actual algorithm begins with the first n bits in state $|0>$, and the final bit is in the state $|1>$. Then a Hadamard transform is applied to each bit. Now we have a function, which we will call f(x), that maps the state $|x>|y|$ to $|x>|y \otimes f(x)>$. In this case, the symbol $\otimes$ denotes addition modulo 2. As the values of x are put through the oracle f(x), either a 1 or 0 is produced. The output will be 0 if f(x) is balanced and 1 if f(x) is constant. For n bits input, the final output will be n 0s if f(x) is constant. Any other output (any combination of 0s and 1s, or all 1s) indicates that f(x) is balanced.

17.5.2   The Code for the Deutsch-Jozsa Algorithm

We begin with the namespace opening and the open statements for other namespaces, as shown here:

```
version 1.0

qubits 2
# The Deutsch-Jozsa algorithm an oracle is used to
# determine if a given binary function f(x) is constant or
# balanced.
# Constant f(x)=fc1=0 OR f(x)=fc2=1
# Balanced f(x)=fb3=x OR f(x)=fb4=NOT(x)
# The algorithm requires only a single query of that
# function f(x).


# Initialize qubits in |+> and |-> statew
.initialize
prep_z q[0:1]
X q[1]
{H q[0]|H q[1]}
```

```
.oracle_fc1
# do nothing or I q[0:1]


#.oracle_fc2
# X q[1]


#.oracle_fb3
# CNOT q[0],q[1]


#.oracle_fb4
# CNOT q[0],q[1]
# X q[1]


.measurement
H q[0]
measure q[0]
```

Figure 17.11 shows what this looks like in the editor.

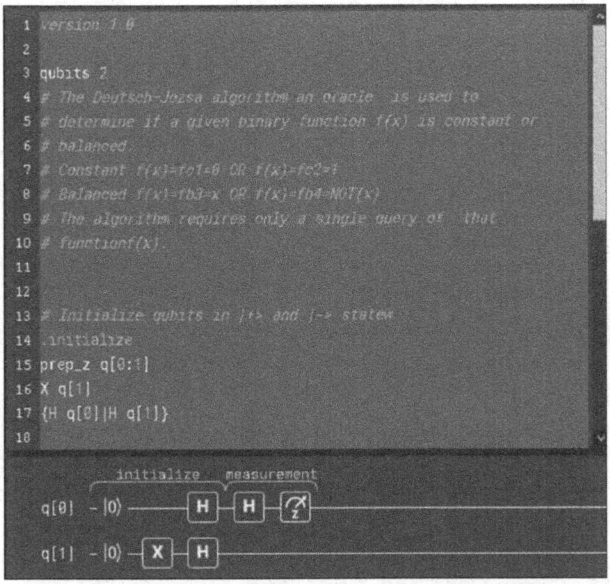

```
 1  version 1.0
 2
 3  qubits 2
 4  # The Deutsch-Jozsa algorithm an oracle  is used to
 5  # determine if a given binary function f(x) is constant or
 6  # balanced.
 7  # Constant f(x)=fc1=0 OR f(x)=fc2=1
 8  # Balanced f(x)=fb3=x OR f(x)=fb4=NOT(x)
 9  # The algorithm requires only a single query of  that
10  # functionf(x).
11
12
13  # Initialize qubits in |+> and |-> states
14  .initialize
15  prep_z q[0:1]
16  X q[1]
17  {H q[0]|H q[1]}
18
```

FIGURE 17.11   Deutsch-Jozsa algorithm

As with the code we saw previously in this chapter, this is primarily just a collection of gates operating on qubits—and that is what a great deal of quantum programming is.

The Deutsch-Jozsa algorithm is relatively easy to implement in QASM. The visualization of the gates and operations shown at the bottom of the editor is quite helpful in understanding quantum algorithms.

17.6 Summary

In this chapter, you were introduced to QASM. Using the online tool at https://www.quantum-inspire.com, you can access both simulators and actual quantum processors. That makes QASM a very valuable tool for learning quantum programming. It is best if you work through at least the algorithms presented in this chapter. For more advanced readers, you may wish to attempt to implement an algorithm that was not actually coded in this chapter. Combining the information in Chapter 16 with this chapter, you should have a comfortable working knowledge of quantum programming.

Test Your Skills

REVIEW QUESTIONS

1. The syntax `T q[0]` will do what?

    a. Execute the Toffoli gate in the first qubit

    b. Execute the Toffoli gate on all qubits

    c. Execute the T gate on the first qubit

    d. Execute the T gate on all qubits

2. In QASM, what does the command `measure_all` do?

    a. Measure the qubit in the x-, y-, and z-bases.

    b. Measure all the qubits in the z-basis.

    c. Measure all the qubits in the x-, y-, and z-bases.

    d. Nothing. This is an error.

3. What does the following symbol represent in the QASM display?

    a. CNOT gate

    b. Hadamard gate

    c. Measurement

    d. Error correction

4. What is the purpose of the `error_model depolarizing_channel`?

    a. To trap depolarizing errors

    b. To trap any quantum error

    c. To cause a random error between each operation on a qubit

    d. To set up error trapping

Appendix

Answers to Test Your Skills Questions

Chapter 1

1. c. Ring

2. a. $\begin{bmatrix} 6 \\ 3 \\ 9 \end{bmatrix}$

3. b. 10

4. d. 5

5. a. 11

6. b. 17

7. a. 4.12

8. d. $\begin{bmatrix} 15 & 25 \\ 15 & 30 \end{bmatrix}$

9. a. Yes

10. $\begin{bmatrix} 1 & 0 & 0 \\ 0 & 1 & 0 \\ 0 & 0 & 1 \end{bmatrix}$

Chapter 2

1. 5 + 5i

2. 4 + 12i

3. −10 + 2i

4. 5/2 − i/2, or in decimal form 2.5 − 0.5i

5. = $\sqrt{5}$, or in decimal form 2.2361

6. a

7. −1. All Pauli matrices have a determinant of −1.

8. There is no difference.

9. c

10. All Pauli matrices have the eigenvalues +1 and −1.

Chapter 3

1. d. It is both a particle and a wave.

2. a. Particles have specific energy states rather than a continuum of states.

3. b. No two fermions can occupy the same state within a quantum system at the same time.

4. d. There can be up to six electrons, in pairs, and each pair has an opposite spin.

5. a. A sequence that converges to an element in the vector space

6. c. Fourier transforms

7. d. It is an eigenvector corresponding to an operation.

8. a. The ket side of the notation

9. a. Planck's black body radiation

Chapter 4

1. c. Anywhere

2. a. In a sequential fashion

3. a. Omega

4. c. Theta

5. a. Bubble sort

6. a. NAND

7. b. OR

8. d. NAND

9. c. They can be used to create any Boolean function.

10. d. Instruction Set Architecture

Chapter 5

1. b. .1

2. a. .55

3. c. .475

4. b. $4 \notin A$

5. b. The intersection of A and B

6. b. The sending computer

7. c. Noisy channel theorem

8. a. Adding the two entropies

9. a. Joint entropy

10. d. A density matrix

Chapter 6

1. b. 2π is 360 degrees in radians.

2. c. The wave function

3. a. Born's rule

4. d. The superposition of possible eigenstates collapses to a single eigenstate based on interaction with the environment.

5. b. 1

6. c. The wave function

7. c. Wigner function

8. d. Klein-Gordon

9. a. A 4×4 matrix with complex components

Chapter 7

1. b. It demonstrated that hidden variables are not responsible for entanglement.

2. Calculate the tensor product of these two vectors:

3. a. 4

4. c. E91

5. b. decoherent histories interpretation

6. d. John Bell

7. d. Copenhagen interpretation

Chapter 8

1. b. Phase shift gates

2. a. Unit length and d. Orthonormal

3. d. Born's rule

4. b. Gottesman–Knill Theorem

5. c. Quantum

6. b. Measurement

Chapter 9

1. c. To facilitate storing qubits in photons

2. a. State |0>

3. b. The motion of the ion in the saddle point

4. a. 4

5. b. Measurement plan

6. c. A degree or more kelvin above absolute zero

7. b. solid state

Chapter 10

1. c. Deutsch's algorithm

2. b. Grover's algorithm

3. c. Three

4. b. The period-finding portion

Chapter 11

1. b. log(N)

2. d. y2 = x3 + Ax + B

3. A discrete logarithm is some integer k that solves the equation xk=y, where both x and y are elements of a finite group.

4. The system has two parameters called p and g. Parameter p is a prime number, and parameter g (usually called a generator) is an integer less than p, with the following property: for every number n between 1 and $p-1$ inclusive, there is a power k of g such that n = g^k mod p. One public key is g^a and the other is g^b.

5. C = M^e % n

6. Let n = pq and let m = (p–1)(q–1). Choose a small number, e, that's co-prime to m (note: two numbers are co-prime if they have no common factors). Find d, such that de % m = 1. Publish e and n as the public key and keep d and n as the secret key.

Chapter 12

1. c. It will need larger key sizes.

2. b. It will need to be replaced.

3. a, b, and c

4. b. Minimal

5. d. They are not predicated on specific mathematical problems that a quantum computer can solve.

Chapter 13

1. a. If G is a group under some operation, and H is a subset of G that also forms a group under that operation, then H is a subgroup of G.

2. a and b

3. d. cyclic, shift

4. c. Shortest Integer Problem

5. b. NTRU

6. a. Ajtai

7. a. Ajtai

Chapter 14

1. d. A set, an identity element for each operation, two operations, and their respective inverse operations

2. a. Matsumoto-Imai

3. b. Hidden Field Equations

4. d. MQDSS

5. b. Hidden Field Equations

Chapter 15

1. a. Merkle-Damgaard construction

2. d. McEliece

3. d. McEliece

4. a. Niederreiter

5. a. torsion group

6. b. isometric

Chapter 16

1. c. Result

2. a. iteration

3. b. Encapsulation

4. a. `Microsoft.Quantum.Intrinsic`

5. d. Rotate about a given Pauli axis.

Chapter 17

1. c. Execute the T gate on the first qubit

2. b. Measure all the qubits in the z-basis.

3. a. CNOT gate

4. c. To cause a random error between each operation on a qubit

Index

Register Your Product at pearsonITcertification.com/register

Access additional benefits and **save 35%** on your next purchase

- Automatically receive a coupon for 35% off your next purchase, valid for 30 days. Look for your code in your Pearson IT Certification cart or the Manage Codes section of your account page.

- Download available product updates.

- Access bonus material if available.*

- Check the box to hear from us and receive exclusive offers on new editions and related products.

Registration benefits vary by product. Benefits will be listed on your account page under Registered Products.

Learning Solutions for Self-Paced Study, Enterprise, and the Classroom

Pearson IT Certification delivers training materials that address the learning, preparation, and practice needs of a new generation of certification candidates, including the official publishing programs of Adobe Press, Cisco Press, and Microsoft Press. At pearsonITcertification.com, you can:

- Shop our books, eBooks, practice tests, software, and video courses
- Sign up to receive special offers
- Access thousands of free chapters and video lessons

Visit **pearsonITcertification.com/community** to connect with Pearson IT Certification